THE FIRST RUSSIAN REVOLUTION
1825

THE DECEMBRIST MOVEMENT

THE ASSASSINATION OF GENERAL MILORADOVICH BY KAKHOVSKY.

THE FIRST
RUSSIAN REVOLUTION
1825

THE DECEMBRIST MOVEMENT
Its Origins, Development, and Significance

BY

ANATOLE G. MAZOUR, Ph.D.

STANFORD UNIVERSITY PRESS
STANFORD, CALIFORNIA

Stanford University Press
Stanford, California

Library of Congress Catalog Card Number: 61-11048

Printed in the United States of America

First published 1937 by the University
of California Press. Reissued in 1961
by Stanford University Press; second
printing 1963

PREFACE

TO THE SECOND PRINTING

THE REISSUE of this work, which has been out of print for the last fifteen years, has been prompted by repeated requests from libraries and students. The interest of Stanford University Press, and the kindness of the University of California in relinquishing its copyright, have now made such a reissue possible.

The text appears in its original form. The only change is in the addition of a bibliographical supplement (pp. 319-20), which lists the most important writings to have appeared since the book was first published.

For technical reasons the reproduction of the plates is not quite so good as in the first printing, since the original illustrations are no longer available. For the same reason the map from Pestel's *Russian Justice (Russkaia Pravda)* is omitted.

A. G. M.

Stanford, California
March 1961

CONTENTS

[ix]

LIST OF PLATES

MAPS

LIST OF ABBREVIATIONS

THE FIRST RUSSIAN REVOLUTION
1825

THE DECEMBRIST MOVEMENT

Chapter I

THE BACKGROUND OF THE DECEMBRIST MOVEMENT

1. THE ECONOMIC PROBLEM

O N MARCH 12, 1801, Alexander I came to the Russian throne. The Empire which he was to rule represented, "officially, a harmonious and grandiose structure; but on closer sight, in detail, it was chaotic and disorganized, a picture with prolix and careless touches, intended for a distant observer."[1] On more than one occasion Alexander showed great unwillingness to attempt the ruling of such an empire; he preferred to renounce "the unattractive position," settle down on the banks of the Rhine, and find happiness in the study of nature.[2] It was the lamentable situation of his country, which he hoped to alleviate by granting to his people a liberal constitution, that compelled the young Emperor to resist the temptation.[3]

There were valid reasons for Alexander's apprehensions. He had inherited from his father an administration beset with extraordinarily difficult problems of all kinds. Serfdom, which had reached its peak in the last decades of the eighteenth century, was one of the most perplexing problems. Financial affairs were in a precarious state. There was a considerable national deficit, an accumulated debt amounting to more than two hundred million rubles,[4] and a complicated bureaucratic machinery further to handicap the administration. The army was in a pitiful condition and, like all the other instruments of government, in need of immediate attention.[5] This was particularly important, since international complications threatened to involve Russian intervention in European affairs. Public sentiment in favor of liberal reforms was steadily increasing, a fact definitely indicated by the joy and excessive hopefulness displayed by Russian society during the early period

[1] Kliuchevsky, *Ocherki i riechi*, 385.

[2] Shilder, *Imperator Aleksandr I*, I, 277.

[3] *Ibid.*, I, 280–282; Czartoryski, *Memoirs*, I, 257.

[4] *Z.M.N.P.*, III (1906), 177.

[5] *Russkaia Starina*, III (1895), 150–152; (1895), 197–201.

of Alexander's reign. The coming of Alexander I to the throne, it was believed, signified a new era of political reform.

SERFDOM

The cry for nation-wide reform was the result of conditions general, as well, to many other countries, namely, the decline of a medieval society and the rise of a modern, urban capitalistic state. The decline of the feudal order found expression in a strong political movement such as in France culminated in the events of 1789; in England, in an economic liberalism that was best expressed by Adam Smith, and in Germany and Italy, in an intensive nationalism. The crumbling of the medieval structure of society in Western Europe was of world significance and Russia could not escape its effects; the pillars of Old Russia—autocracy, orthodoxy, and the institution of serfdom—were slowly weakened by these social undercurrents. Because of the peculiar national conditions, political liberalism and popular discontent fused in Russia, forming what is known as the Decembrist movement.

Earlier policy of Alexander I.—The question of serfdom occupied the mind of Alexander I from the very beginning of his reign, and measures for curbing the "rights" of the landlord were discussed by the Emperor's intimate circle, known as the "unofficial committee," in their earliest secret meetings. The sympathetic interest of the young Emperor in the peasant question was keen, as can be seen from his early view concerning state peasants.[6] He realized full well that "the ugly structure of the government of the Empire" badly needed to be remodeled.[7]

Shortly after his accession Alexander presented through his attorney-general a memorandum to the State Council in which the Emperor urged the abolition in all Russia of the selling of peasants without land.[8] Unfortunately, the State Council after much debate considered the matter premature. Alexander but feebly resisted the decision of the Council and the situation remained virtually unaltered.[9] The only action that Alexander dared to take was to order the President of the Academy of Sciences not to publish in

---

[6] *P.S.Z.*, Nos. 20217, 20576, 20964; *Russkaia Starina*, XII (1877), 665.

[7] Bogdanovich, *Istoriia tsarstvovaniia imp. Aleksandra I*, Appendix to Vol. I, 38.

[8] A law to this effect had been issued previously, but it was limited to the Ukraine only. See *P.S.Z.*, Nos. 18706, 19892, 25107.

[9] Semevsky, *Krestiansky vopros v Rossii*, I, 241.

the *St. Petersburg News* advertisements which announced the sale of serfs.[10] However, this order was easily circumvented: the landlord who wished to sell his serfs merely announced that certain peasants were available for service, and prospective buyers knew the meaning of such a notice.

The bill proposing that obligations of the peasants to the landlord be more definitely specified by law met a similar fate.[11] Besides the self-interest of the landowning classes, the stubbornness of the conservatives in the State Council in respect to this matter shows also a lack of any intimate knowledge of Russian conditions. In those days most of the dignitaries knew more about European conditions than they knew about conditions in Russia, and the French language better than their own.[12] "No laws," some of them argued, "will make the poor independent of the rich; the poor peasant, if he does not depend upon the landlord, will become dependent upon his richer neighbor." Even some of the liberals, among them Count Nicholas Mordvinov, were unable to size up the situation properly. Mordvinov constantly advised reforms but warned against any changes in respect of serfdom. "In a sparsely inhabited country," he argued, "where financial capital is scarce, where urban industry is little developed and where there is an insufficient labor supply, freedom and unrestricted mobility of the peasants are bound to result in various complications."[13] Others feared that the slightest reform of serfdom would have disastrous results—perhaps even a general peasant revolt. In justice to some of the nobility, it must be said that a few viewed the issue more soberly. For example, Count Paul Stroganov ardently recommended reforms and opposed the idea that emancipation must necessarily lead to peasant unrest.[14]

But among the nobility there were few like Stroganov. The French Revolution was still fresh in the minds of all noblemen, and everyone instantly associated emancipation of the peasant with some sort of Russian Jacquerie.[15] This feeling was strengthened by M. Laharpe, a Swiss and former tutor of Alexander, who after

---

[10] *Russkaia Starina,* IX (1877), 34.

[11] Ikonnikov, *Graf N. S. Mordvinov,* 31–35.

[12] Schiemann, *Geschichte Rußlands,* I, 396–397.

[13] Liakhov, *Osnovnye cherty sotsial'nykh i ekonomicheskikh otnoshenii v Rossii v epokhu Aleksandra I* (M., 1912), 125.

[14] Semevsky, *op. cit.,* I, 243–244.

[15] *Russkaia Starina,* IV (1895), 192–194; *Arkhiv kn. Vorontsova,* XI, 148.

his return from Western Europe had become more conservative. Disheartened by bitter experience, he strongly recommended wise autocratic government and extremely careful handling of the peasant problem. He even insisted that any reforms should be called "peasant improvements" rather than "peasant emancipation."[16]

As the discussion of serfdom continued in the committee and the Council, Alexander, on December 12, 1801, issued an Ordinance permitting merchants, townsmen, and state peasants to acquire land property.[17] But the suggestion that the same right be granted to serfs was defeated. At the same time grants of land with peasants virtually ceased, and another attempt was made to check the "tyranny and cruelty" of the landlord.[18]

"The Free Farmers."—Officially, emancipation seemed to be doomed by the opposition of the conservative State Council and by want of more determined action by the young Emperor. But a new ray of hope came, this time inspired by a nobleman who was himself a product of Western liberal culture. In November, 1802, Count Rumiantsev in a memorandum to Alexander suggested the gradual abolition of serfdom, following it soon after with a carefully detailed project.[19] Rumiantsev's plan became the basis of the law of February 20, 1803, which provided for the creation of a new class of peasants, the so-called "free farmers."[20] In this project the following measures were suggested: landlords were to be permitted to emancipate their peasants collectively, that is, by whole communities; such action was to be by mutual agreement between the landlord and the freed peasant community; each peasant was to be equipped with a strip of land the size of which was left to be determined by the landlord; the communities could redeem themselves immediately by paying the required amount to the landlord in cash, in installments, or in kind; they could redeem their freedom completely or in part. If the individual peasant or the community failed to act in the spirit of the contract, the peasant's status was to be restored; that is, he was once more to become a serf. In short, Count Rumiantsev attempted to shift the entire burden from the state to the individual landlords, leaving the

---

[16] *Z.M.N.P.*, CLIII, 202–204; Shilder, *op. cit.*, II, 48–52.

[17] *P.S.Z.*, No. 20075.

[18] *Russkaia Starina*, VI (1872), 281–284; *P.S.Z.*, No. 20217; *Arkhiv kn. Vorontsova*, XII, 405, No. 38.

[19] *Russky Arkhiv*, 1869, 1953.

[20] *P.S.Z.*, Nos. 20620, 20625.

whole matter to the discretion of the landlords. Events soon showed that he had relied too much upon the good will and wisdom of the landlords. In Alexander's entire reign there were only one hundred and sixty-one redemptions, affecting 47,153 male serfs—less than one per cent of the entire serf population. Of these, seventeen provided for freedom without remuneration, of which one redemption was by the bequest of a landlord of the Vilna district, whose act affected 7,000 serfs. The other sixteen redemptions included altogether 415 serfs, of whom 199 had formerly belonged to Count Rumiantsev, author of the project.[21]

Alexander fails to end serfdom.—It was not until 1808 that a law was promulgated which prohibited the sale of serfs in open markets, a scene that had offended many natives and amazed foreign visitors.[22] Another restriction placed upon the landlord was the loss of his right to exile his serfs to hard labor, a privilege taken from him on January 23, 1802.[23] In reality, however, this restriction meant little, for if the landlord wished to punish his serfs, he could always find means to do so.[24] Though land grants including peasants virtually ceased and a few bills were passed which tended to restrict serfdom, yet in some respects serfdom was even expanded, as the Law of 1804 and the Manifesto of 1810 indicate. The Law of October 18, 1804, permitted merchants to buy serfs, though with land only.[25] The Manifesto of May 27, 1810, granted first-guild merchants and foreign investors the right to buy land with peasants living on it, though from the state only.[26]

If some laws tended to alleviate the lot of the peasants, others tended to make it heavier. The expense of judicial procedure prevented the peasant from seeking justice. Numerous exactions of landlord or state, such as road construction or repair, one of the most annoying obligations, or service in the military colonies, to be described more fully elsewhere, made the lot of the peasant intolerable.[27] "The entire burden of taxation and obligations, the ruinous extravagance of the nobility, all falls upon that respectable but unfortunate class," states the Decembrist, Yakubovich,

---

[21] Semevsky, *op. cit.*, I, 267.

[22] *P.S.Z.*, No. 23157; *Russky Arkhiv*, XII (1878), 492.

[23] *P.S.Z.*, Nos. 20119, 23530.

[24] *Ibid.*, No. 29507.

[25] *Ibid.*, No. 21481.

[26] *Ibid.*, No. 24244, paragraphs 7–8.

[27] *Iz pisem i pokazanii dekabristov*, 6, 9–10, 60, 77–78.

in a letter to Nicholas in 1825, referring to the peasants.[28] Many
of the landlords were absentees and therefore had no idea of the
wretched condition of both their serfs and their estates. "The
largest and best part of the nobility," writes A. Bestuzhev, "is
in the army or resides in the capital, demands luxury, entrusts
the estates to stewards, who, in turn, rob the peasants and deceive
their employers, and as a result nine-tenths of the estates in Russia are ruined or mortgaged."[29]

Alexander I had cherished for a long time the hope of liberating the peasants. When visiting Mme de Staël's salon in Paris in
1814, he made a statement to the effect that with God's aid serfdom under his reign would cease to exist.[30] But surrounded chiefly
by conservative leaders, especially in the later years of his reign,
Alexander hesitated. Notwithstanding his noble aspirations, therefore, and his long-felt hope of achieving liberal legislation, the
peasant issue by 1825 was at a standstill; the landlord was holding
tenaciously to that outworn institution, and the serf was dreaming as never before of regaining his freedom and his land. "When
I think how little has been done within the state, the thought
presses my heart like a heavy weight and wearies me," Alexander
declared shortly before his death.[31]

The Decembrists and serfdom.—Such was the atmosphere in
which the generation of the Decembrists was reared; they reached
maturity at a time when national reforms, and particularly the
crucial question of serfdom, were under serious consideration and
frequent attack. In this respect two generations of two centuries,
the eighteenth and the nineteenth, are closely linked, united by an
effort which made progress as time went on. Novikov, Radishchev,
Krechetov, Pnin and Turgenev, Pestel, Ryleev—all these writers
and thinkers are links in the chain of developments, representatives of two generations and of two centuries but of one idea,
namely, national reform, including especially the emancipation
of the peasants. In the publications of Novikov in the reign of
Catherine II, distinct signs of this movement began to appear, but
in no literary work was it voiced with such pronounced vigor and
protest as in the *Journey from St. Petersburg to Moscow*, by A. N.

---

[28] *Ibid.*, 77.

[29] *Ibid.*, 39; *Viestnik Evropy*, VIII (1900), 688ff.

[30] Varnhagen von Ense, *Denkwürdigkeiten des eignen Lebens*, III Theil (2
Auflage, 1843), 216.

[31] Presniakov, *Aleksandr I*, 175.

Radishchev. Here is the first literary production in which the author declared openly his disgust with the existing state of affairs.

Tendencies in favor of emancipating the serfs were also revealed in the various studies of the younger men of that time. Whether it was the "dissertatio inauguralis" of Kaisarov, the thesis of Dzhunkovsky, which received the award of the Free Economic Society, or the writings of contemporary economists like Storch or Kunitsyn, all alike concluded that serf labor was in conflict with national prosperity; that progress could be achieved only if the economic structure was based upon free labor and private ownership instead of upon an enslaved and landless peasantry. "Freedom for the peasants," remarks a contemporary in his diary, "will not be slow to prosper that class of people which feeds and enriches the whole of Russia—the class that contributes the largest number of defenders of the fatherland and therefore deserves respect."[32]

If earlier writings, such as Novikov's magazines, based their arguments on pure sentimentality and on moral and religious principles, the writers of the early nineteenth century presented arguments of sounder economic value. The abolition in 1807 of serfdom in Poland and in 1816–19 in the Baltic Provinces gave increased impetus to the trend which sought to embrace the entire Russian Empire, not merely parts of it, and this sentiment was particularly reflected in the Decembrist movement. Nearly every member of the Decembrist Society opposed serfdom; some, among them Trubetskoi, saw in that institution a menace to the state; others, including Fonvizin, felt that serfdom was a handicap, a retarding economic factor; still others, like A. Bestuzhev, Steingel, and Turgenev, felt that it was unethical and historically unjustified.[33] Whatever the basis for resistance, the fact is undeniable that the Decembrists unanimously opposed serfdom.

The interest of the Decembrists in the agrarian problem was not merely academic. Being, many of them, of the land nobility, they quite naturally became concerned with the land problem. Furthermore, in a country like Russia, where agriculture was the dominant factor in the economic life of the nation, the land and serfdom were so closely related that the latter became, perforce, the cardinal issue of any social or political movement. Through direct contact with the peasants, and by feeling personally the hardships of the

---

[32] "A. A. Tuchkov i ego dnevnik." *Viestnik Evropy*, VIII (1900), 695–696.

[33] Dovnar-Zapolsky, *Idealy dekabristov*, 157, 164, 172.

agrarian crisis, by familiarizing themselves with similar problems
in Western Europe, and by studying current economic theories,
the Decembrists acquired their views upon the various issues involved. Thus Pavel Pestel and Nikita Muraviev became keen
students of constitutional government, and Nicholas Turgenev devoted his whole life to the study of taxation and especially serfdom. Financial difficulties confronting the government, as well
as the indebtedness and widespread bankruptcies among the landlords, convinced Turgenev that serfdom had outlived its useful-
ness and must give way to an emancipated society. The growing
urban population and the interrelationship of the rural and the
urban groups, together with the increasing dependence of the nation upon foreign trade and export, were additional indications
of the necessities of the time. How serfdom was to be abolished,
whether it should be followed by breaking up the large estates or
by landless or partial emancipation, whether it should be made
compulsory by the state or made effective through widespread
propaganda and individual decision were questions upon which
there was no united opinion. One thing is important to notice,
namely, that the chief factor in forming a common ôpinion and
in uniting the younger generation into a political group was the
unanimous agreement of the Decembrists concerning the institution of serfdom: it must vanish. As one of the participants declared, the knot must be untied by the government, otherwise it
would be untied by force and there would be disastrous consequences. The Pugachev rebellion still lingered in the memory of
many and especially of those who could draw lessons from the
past.[35]

In his testimony, Pestel, the leading figure of the Decembrist
movement, stated:[36]

The desirability of granting freedom to the serfs was considered from the
very beginning; for that purpose a majority of the nobility was to be invited
in order to petition the Emperor about it. This was later thought of on many
occasions, but we soon came to realize that the nobility could not be persuaded.
And as time went on we became even more convinced, when the Ukrainian nobility absolutely rejected a similar project of their military governor.

It is evident that the original idea of the Decembrists was to
achieve the emancipation of the peasants through peaceful measures, and the persuasion of serf-owners, in the hope that emancipa-

[34] *Viestnik Evropy*, I (1909), 166ff.; *Ostafievsky Arkhiv*, I, 544–546.
[35] Trubetskoi, *Zapiski*, 80.   [36] *Materialy*, IV, 101.

ALEXANDER RADISHCHEV.

tion might come as a grace from the throne rather than by force from below. For a long while increasing rumors to this effect gave encouragement to many. Yakushkin wrote:[37]

During the visit of the Emperor in Moscow there were rumors that he wished to emancipate the peasants, which was believable, since he had freed the peasants of three Baltic gubernias; true, on such conditions that their predicament was worse than before.

As time went on, however, hope for peasant emancipation by legal means had to be abandoned. "Constitutional ideas," as Pestel states, or, in other words, revolutionary plans, began to appear. The origin of these "constitutional ideas" becomes clearer when attention is turned to other issues which challenged Russia at this time.

INDUSTRY

Industry in Russia during the eighteenth century developed along lines different from those of industry in Western Europe.[38] The reason is to be found in the deep-rooted attachment of the Russian peasant to the soil. In Western Europe industry drew its labor supply chiefly from the free landless peasants. In Russia industry had to depend, for the most part, on serf labor, that is, peasants who were attached to the soil, or on proscribed industrial labor drawn from among social outcasts. These sources produced unfavorable conditions for the development of the skilled industrial proletariat that is requisite for any industrial society. The difference in this respect between Western Europe and Russia was striking. In Europe the dawn of capitalism signified the emancipation of the peasant, his detachment from the soil, and the urbanization of large masses of a landless agricultural proletariat.

Industry in Russia, instead of following along capitalistic paths and discarding the medieval order, endeavored to adjust itself to the old institutions; thus it attempted to transfer from agriculture the institution of serfdom and to adapt it to its own purposes. And so Russian industry developed distorted types of factories of a semifeudal character, which proved totally inadequate for the needs of the modern state.[39] This resulted in the formation of a

[37] Yakushkin, I., *Zapiski*, 27.

[38] Cf. Kulisher, "La grande industrie aux XVII° et XVIII° siècles: France, Allemagne, Russie." *Annales d'Histoire Économique et Sociale*, January, 1931, 39–46.

[39] On the various types of industrial enterprises inherited from the eighteenth century see Mavor, J., *An Economic History of Russia* (London, 1925), I, Book 3.

class composed of laborers who might be called industrial serfs as distinguished from agricultural serfs—a class unknown in Western Europe.

During the first quarter of the nineteenth century the general European situation aided in stimulating industrial expansion, but under the political conditions existing in Russia it served only to intensify the national crisis. An expanding industry was a challenge not only to the old economic and social order but to the political order as well. A modern industrial society demanded a new social relationship, larger contingents of free workers, a free and more prosperous peasantry with a purchasing power to absorb industrial produce, and last, but not least, political readjustment. Among the Decembrists Pestel realized this fact more than any other member except perhaps Nicholas Turgenev. But political developments in the first quarter of the nineteenth century failed to keep pace with economic demands; whatever industry developed, therefore, was soon retarded in its growth by the ruling feudal class.

Industrial expansion and serfdom.—The rapid economic progress of early nineteenth-century Russia can be explained by the situation prevailing in Western Europe and by the frequent wars. Industrial expansion during this period was artificial, economically unsound, and forced soon to cease as the peculiar conditions changed. Its first combat with France having ended in the shameful treaty of Tilsit, Russia was forced to break off relations with England and to join the continental blockade.[40] However, the treaty of Tilsit had its positive as well as its negative side, for it resulted in the elimination of one of the most serious competitors in the Russian market, namely, the English, and stimulated, though artificially, the home industry upon which Russia was compelled to depend.[41] But it nearly wrecked the agrarian class by prohibiting the exportation of grain and raw materials to England, which had been the chief customer of Russia for these goods.[42] Furthermore,

[40] On the continental blockade and its influence upon Russian economic life see Predtechensky, "K voprosu o vliianii kontinental'noi blokady na sostoianie torgovli i promyshlennosti v Rossii." *Izvestiia Akademii Nauk*, Seriia VII, No. 8 (1931), 910–920. See *P.S.Z.*, Nos. 22653, 22664; *S.I.R.I.O.*, LXXXIII, 281–283; Martens, *Recueil des traités et conventions*, XI, No. 409.

[41] Tugan-Baranovsky, "Voina 1812 goda i promyshlennoe razvitie Rossii." *Otechestvennaia Voina i Russkoe Obshchestvo* (M., 1912), VII, 108–110; *Russky Arkhiv*, VIII (1907), 529–531.

[42] *Arkhiv grafov Mordvinovykh*, III, 471–473; IV, 479–486.

the industrial expansion increased the demand for social reform, which was strongly opposed by the die-hard agrarian nobility who ruled the state.

From another angle, industrial expansion under the conditions existing at that time in Russia signified a paradoxical situation. As industry increased, it needed wider markets. Yet in the world market Russia could hardly compete with countries more advanced economically and politically than itself, for the latter were able to produce better commodities at a lower cost. Russian industry was therefore forced to depend mainly upon the home market, and the home market was unable to absorb the increasing volume of production. It had potentialities, but as long as serfdom existed they could not be properly realized. Serfs with medieval obligations to state and landlord could not constitute a great purchasing power. Besides, the peasant masses were satisfied with the products of the small home industries, and the wealthy few preferred foreign goods. Furthermore, modern capitalistic society rests upon the principle of the continuous utilization of financial capital, not its hoarding. Yet as long as serfdom existed capital could not be exploited. A large amount of the laborers' wages was spent in the form of quit rent to the landlord, whence it seldom returned to the industrialist. Neither did industry profit by capital which the peasant succeeded in saving from his meager income, for he hoarded every penny he could, and his standard of living was very low. Such a state of affairs tended to confine industry within the limits set by a medieval Russia rather than to expand it greatly. That the Decembrists were fully aware of this situation and sympathized with the manufacturer is seen from the various sources. They recognized the discriminatory policy of the agrarian ruling class and its retarding effects upon industry, and they sincerely wished to remove them. The Decembrists came out, therefore, as the defenders of a free middle class, which in a modern capitalistic society constitutes the backbone of a nation. "The middle class," writes one Decembrist, "is respected and is important in all other countries; in our country this class is miserable, poor, burdened with obligations, deprived of means of a livelihood."[43] Another, in defense of the commercial class, writes :[44]

In the first two ranks of the commercial class there are many educated men, capable, and possessing character, who bear the mark of Russian nationalism,

---

[43] *Iz pisem i pokazanii dekabristov*, 37–38. [44] *Ibid.*, 79.

sufficiently resourceful, but without encouragement from the government, who remain within a limited scope of activity. Lacking capital to organize corporations, they surrendered all advantages of foreign trade to aliens, being satisfied with unimportant enterprises.

Here, in other words, the Decembrists prove that they were beginning to break with the traditions of their class and to take a broader outlook upon national affairs. They realized that the greatly scorned "city shopkeeper" had a place in the state and that not only must he be tolerated but also even encouraged, allowed to enjoy government protection, and given assistance and political recognition. In this respect the Decembrists were far ahead of some of the nobles who constituted the Legislative Assembly in 1767 and who resisted any measure in this direction.

From what has been said it might be concluded that the agrarian class, at least, was content with the situation. But this is not true. Several conditions produced by the general state of affairs caused dissatisfaction among the land nobility. In 1825 the state of agriculture was far from enviable. If the continental blockade aided industry, it nearly ruined agriculture. Not until 1816 did the Russian grain export trade begin to recover, as the following figures show.[45]

Date	Export of wheat in tons
1801–1805	174,558
1806–1810	29,000
1811–1815	83,000
1816–1820	283,000

This table is self-explanatory. It is not to be wondered at that the nobility became alarmed, turned anti-French, opposed the continental blockade, and thereby determined the events that followed Russia's intervention against Napoleon. The postwar recovery period, however, did not last long, being checked by the prevailing European crisis. But before we consider this subject a few words must be said in respect to the disastrous financial situation in which Russia found itself at this time and which contributed to the discontent in the country.

Financial crisis.—Closely related to agricultural and industrial conditions was the problem of Russian finances, which, during the first quarter of the nineteenth century, were in a pitiful state. The reign of Catherine II had ended not only with a deficit, but

[45] Pokrovsky, V., *Sbornik svedenii po istorii i statistike vneshnei torgovli Rossii* (St. Petersburg, 1902), 3.

also with the nation in debt to foreign countries. The partition of
Poland was followed by the taking over of that country's financial
obligations, thus increasing Russia's indebtedness still more. The
wars that followed in the reign of Paul and later that of Alexander
I completely shattered the finances of the country. From his prison
cell the Decembrist Kakhovsky, endeavoring to explain the causes
of the revolt of 1825, wrote :[46]

> From 1810 to 1822 the national income increased four times, and therefore
> it could be imagined how taxation had increased; yet the national debt not only
> did not decrease but went up exceedingly. The value of our money dropped and
> the ruble became worth twenty-five kopecks.

The following figures describe the situation better than any words
could do.[47]

Date	National deficit in rubles
1801	7,064,799
1804	18,457,817
1807	26,228,198
1808	124,017,535
1809	143,361,514
1822	351,244,048

By 1825 foreign and domestic indebtedness reached its peak. At
the end of Alexander's reign the foreign debt of Russia had reached
the stupendous figure of one hundred and six million rubles.[48] This
was more than a crisis: it was total bankruptcy. This was the
price that Russia was to pay for her archaic order and for the liberation of Europe from Napoleon. Postwar agriculture and industry could grant little aid to the government, and an impoverished,
half-enslaved peasantry could not be taxed further, for it was
already in need of relief from heavy assessments. So great were
the accumulated tax arrears that in 1826 the government was
forced to cancel taxes amounting to eighty million rubles. Yet
even this drastic measure did not relieve the situation, for in 1829
the arrears had again reached the sum of one hundred and seventy-
eight million rubles.[49]

Tariff policy.—The printing press, to which the government resorted so extravagantly, did its share in devaluating the paper

[46] *Iz pisem i pokazanii dekabristov*, 28.

[47] Migulin, *Russky gosudarstvennyi kredit*, I (1899), 38, 79; Lokot', P.,
Biudzhetnaia i podatnaia politika Rossii (M., 1908), 160.

[48] Guriev, A., *Ocherki razvitiia gosudarstvennogo dolga v Rossii* (St. Petersburg, 1903), 23.

[49] Lokot', *op. cit.*, 113.

ruble, which in 1801 was worth 66 kopecks, ten years later dropped
to 23½, and in 1821 was worth only 25⅔, and in 1824, 26½ kopecks.[50] Another measure to which the government resorted was
the tariff, used indiscriminately, regardless of national needs, and
motivated exclusively by political rather than economic reasons.
During the reign of Alexander the tariff policy shows a distinct
lack of consistency, rapidly shifting from protectionism to free
trade, and vice versa. Thus between 1803 and 1807 tariff rates show
a tendency toward free trade; between 1810 and 1815 the government followed on the whole a purely protectionist policy, which
resulted in 1812 in the second war with France. Between 1816 and
1819 Russia followed a middle course, characterized by the tariff
conventions with Austria and Prussia. These were entirely against
Russian interests and seriously damaged national industry. The
tariff agreements of 1818–19 with Austria and Prussia were the
most liberal to which Russia had consented, and they were met
with popular grumbling as being ruinous to domestic and foreign
trade. To remedy the developing crisis the government turned
again to a strictly protectionist policy, and in March, 1821, an
official announcement declared that the tariff agreements of 1818–
19 were abrogated. But it was too late. Writes the Decembrist
Steingel:[51]

> Suddenly the tariff [of 1810] was altered in 1816 in favor of Austria, Poland,
> and Prussia. . . . Many merchants went bankrupt and the people on account of
> it were deprived of a means of livelihood and the ability to pay taxes. The
> blunder was soon realized, and was corrected by the tariff of 1822, but the
> damage done was irreparable. A large amount of silver and gold left the
> country . . . and never came back.

After the unsuccessful revolt, another Decembrist, A. Bestuzhev,
wrote to Nicholas I on the same subject:[52]

> The instability of the tariff resulted in the impoverishment of many manu-
> facturers and aided in discouraging others; it destroyed confidence in the gov-
> ernment among its own as well as foreign merchants. Consequently, a still
> sharper drop of our money and general complaints against the lack of cash in
> the country.

The history of the Russian tariff in this period is a good example
of the wavering policy of the government and of the lack of eco-

[50] Lodyzhensky, *Istoriia russkogo tamozhennogo tarifa*, 163; Migulin, *op.
cit.*, I, 81.
[51] *Iz pisem i pokazanii dekabristov*, 58. Cf. Tugan-Baranovsky, *op. cit.*, 112.
[52] *Iz pisem i pokazanii dekabristov*, 38.

nomic stability characteristic of the latter part of the reign of
Alexander I.

Postwar crisis.—"We need not be afraid of foreign enemies,"
wrote Kakhovsky to Nicholas I from prison, "but we have domestic
enemies which harass the country : the absence of laws, of justice,
the decline of commerce, heavy taxation and widespread poverty."[53]
The statement sufficiently summarizes the postwar crisis that came
on the heels of the victories over Napoleon. For a while Russian
agriculture began to recover, even to enjoy an unprecedented period of prosperity. What aided the situation was the fortunate
coincidence of rapidly rising prices of agricultural commodities
during the years 1816–19. But with the beginning of 1819 prosperity began to decline as rapidly as it had risen, and a crisis was
imminent. "In the markets for agricultural produce," states a contemporary writer, "there was at the commencement of 1819, a
tendency to dullness and decline of prices."[54] Wounds inflicted
upon most of the European nations by the Napoleonic wars began
to heal slowly and economic life began to recover. Many people,
former soldiers employed on the battlefield, returned to their
everyday life. This fact tended to decrease Russian sales abroad.
Also, during the continental blockade England, being isolated from
her granary, Russia, had been forced to seek other means of feed-
ing her population. Considerable new English capital was therefore invested in agriculture and agricultural machinery and the
resulting increase in grain production in England aided her to
become more nearly independent; the corn laws tended to decrease
the importation of grain still further, as the following table shows.[55]

IMPORTS INTO THE UNITED KINGDOM

Year	Wheat 000's of quarters	Barley 000's of quarters	Oats 000's of quarters
1815	192	2	120
1816	210	15	75
1817	1,064	134	484
1818	1,594	694	987
1819	472	373	586
1820	585	29	682
1821	130	14	101
1822	43	19	56
1823	16	...	28

---

[53] *Ibid.*, 30.
[54] Tooke, T., *A. History of Prices* (London, 1838), II, 79–80.
[55] Page, H. (ed.), *Commerce and Industry* (London, 1919), II, 140.

The decline in prices of agricultural commodities and the recovery of the countries involved in the recent wars caused a general crisis in agriculture as well as in industry.[56] It is needless to describe in detail what this meant, particularly to Russia with its predominantly agricultural population and its infant industry.[57] The conservative element at the helm of the state saw the way out of this crisis by a still further strengthening of the monarchical régime. All it strove for was the preservation of serfdom and autocracy and the eradication of "free thinking." It refused to appreciate the seriousness of the crisis or to understand the demands of the time but sought rather the protection of its class interests regardless of the economic abyss into which the Empire was being driven.[58] With this background, it was only to be expected that attempts at political reform would meet with dismal failure, as subsequent pages will show.

2. THE POLITICAL PROBLEM

Political reorganization within the government was urgently indicated in the early nineteenth century by the rapid changes to be witnessed in Western Europe, together with those that took place at home. Liberals and conservatives seem to have agreed that administrative reorganization was exigent, and the assassination of Paul was the best proof that even the patience of ardent legitimists could be exhausted. As to how far such reorganization should be carried out and what classes were to enjoy the advantages thereof, opinions differed.

Karazin's letter.—Shortly after Alexander became Emperor he received a letter, the author of which assumed the name of Marquis Posa.[59] In glowing terms the letter expressed the hope that the reign of Alexander would mark in Russia a new era, namely, that of a limited constitutional monarchy.[60] After a long description of conditions in the country and of the expected reforms, the author ended his letter with a political dictum expanded.

[56] Gulishambarov, *Vsemirnaia torgovlia v XIX vieke i uchastie v nei Rossii*, 42.

[57] *Iz pisem i pokazanii dekabristov*, 9–10, 38–39, 58.

[58] Shebunin, "Iz istorii dvorianskikh nastroenii 20-kh godov XIX vieka." *Bor'ba Klassov*, I–II (1924), 50ff.

[59] Marquis Posa is the hero of Schiller's famous drama, *Don Carlos*.

[60] *Russkaia Starina*, IV (1871), 68–80; Shilder, *Imperator Aleksandr I*, II, 32–34.

Nations will always be what governments desire them to be. Tsar Ivan Vasilevich [the Terrible] wished irresponsible slaves, to have with him mean and cruel people, and he had them. Peter wished to see us imitators of foreigners; unfortunately, we became excessively so. The wise Catherine began to educate the Russians, and Alexander will complete this great work.... Genius-benefactor of my dear Fatherland!

Reading the letter with great interest, Alexander immediately ordered that the author be found, and the next day Vasilii Karazin was presented to the Emperor and left face to face with him.

"Did you write me this letter?" asked Alexander.

"I am guilty, Sovereign," replied Karazin.

"Then let me embrace and thank you for it," said Alexander. "I should like to have more subjects like you. Always continue to talk to me openly, always continue to tell me the truth!"[61]

The incident seems trivial, but it is characteristic of the time, and there is no valid reason to doubt the sincerity either of "Marquis Posa" or of Alexander. From the beginning of his reign and at times to the point of naïveté, the Emperor evinced a desire to carry out his ambitions. His enthusiasm, as well as that of his immediate associates, provoked the sardonic remark of Count Semion Vorontsov that "the present condition of the country is nothing more than a temporary termination of tyranny; our fellow-countrymen are like Roman slaves during the Saturnalia festivals, after which they relapse into slavery."[62] A cruel statement, but justified, alas, by future developments.

"A Charter for the Russian People."—Alexander was young, sincere, but inexperienced, and he immediately fell under the influence of two court groups: those representing the Old Guard— the Senatorial group, as they were called, who idealized the reign of Catherine, sought mild political improvements, and advised leaving serfdom alone; and a second group, composed chiefly of the younger generation, who favored wider national reform. The first group was headed by men like Derzhavin, the Counts A. and S. Vorontsov, and Admiral Mordvinov; the second included such men as P. Stroganov, Czartoryski, Novosiltsov, and others, who constituted the Emperor's "unofficial committee."

[61] *Istoricheskie dokumenty iz vremeni tsarstvovaniia Aleksandra I* (ed. 8), 98–99.

[62] *Arkhiv kn. Vorontsova*, XVII, 6. Vigel, a close observer and contemporary, remarks in his *Memoirs:* "Young Russia impetuously fell in love with young Alexander. And when is love not blind?"—Vigel, *Zapiski*, II, 13.

As soon as Alexander had formed his "unofficial committee," that is, the close circle of friend-advisers, he proposed that it begin to work on various projects for political and administrative reforms, commencing with the Senate.[63] The "unofficial committee" at the same time also set to work to compose a "Charter for the Russian People," which they believed would be proclaimed on coronation day.[64] The projected charter included several important provisions, for example, a guaranty of individual liberty, freedom of speech and of press, and religious tolerance. It provided for the establishment of a judicial system independent of the other departments of the administration.[65] Alexander was crowned, but the Charter for the Russian People remained on paper only, buried among other archival material, and serving merely as a reminder of the first of a series of futile attempts by the new administration to introduce constitutional reforms.

The Senate and constitutional reforms.—One of the first attempts of Alexander I to introduce reforms concerned the Senate, a body created by Peter the Great on February 22, 1711.[66] Though the original purpose had been to concentrate in this body the national judicial and administrative functions, in reality, because of the attitude of the sovereigns following Peter I, the Senate had fallen into obscurity and had become mainly a judicial body. The policy of Emperor Paul in particular had diminished its prestige to a minimum.[67] Alexander now planned to restore to the Senate its former status and perhaps to transform it gradually into a legislative institution.

On June 5, 1801, Alexander issued an order to the Senate in which he demanded a report concerning its rights and duties.[68] At the same time the Emperor expressed his regret that the Senate had fallen into such a "humiliating condition" and his hope that its former prestige might be restored. The order produced a favor-

---

[63] *Proceedings of the Unoffical Committee. In* Bogdanovich, *Istoriia tsarstvovaniia Aleksandra I*, I, Appendix, 39.

[64] The Charter may be found in Semennikov, *Radishchev. Ocherki i Issledovaniia*, 180–195. A thorough examination and authentic text of the "Charter," as well as an account of the tragic fate of Radishchev, may be found in a very recent publication: *Literaturnyi Arkhiv. A. N. Radishchev. Materialy i Issledovaniia* (M., 1936).

[65] Shilder, *Imperator Aleksandr I*, II, 75–78.

[66] *P.S.Z.*, No. 2321.

[67] Gradovsky, A., *Nachala russkogo gosudarstvennogo prava* (St. Petersburg, 1881), II, 258.

[68] *P.S.Z.*, No. 19908.

able impression upon all those who had long hoped for reforms, for they were inclined to consider it as the first important step in the direction of a limited monarchy.[68]

After long debates in the Senate and among other statesmen concerning what were or should be the powers of that body, a report was made to the Emperor in compliance with his order of June 5, 1801. The debates together with the recommendations compose an interesting document, for they demonstrate a complete lack of agreement in respect to the matter. There were those who suggested that the Senate be made a purely judicial institution independent of the office of the attorney-general; others felt that it should be a legislative body, or a purely administrative body, or exclusively a repository and guardian of the laws of the Empire (*dépôt de lois*). One man recommended that it should be some sort of Upper Chamber, though he failed to provide for a Lower Chamber.[70]

Such were, briefly, the more important suggestions made to Alexander in reply to his request. Greatly disappointed was the Emperor with these fruitless discussions and conflicting opinions, which promised no fulfillment of his dreams of liberal government. This was the last chance given the Senate to become a politically important factor in the Empire, yet it failed to take advantage of the opportunity. On September 8, 1802, the Emperor issued an Edict defining the rights and duties of the Senate.[71] Certain writers seem to consider the Edict an act limiting the monarchy, but this is grossly erroneous. That it accomplished nothing may be seen from the fact that soon after the death of Alexander the new administration once more raised the problem of reorganizing the Senate.[72] Despite all the opportunities given to the Senate, autocracy remained unshaken : the Senate remained the same impotent body that Alexander had found upon his accession to the throne.[73] The mountain which had labored to bring forth an elephant brought forth only a mouse !

Among other measures for the reorganization of the national

[68] Storch, *Rußland unter Alexander I*, I, 20–23.

[70] Bogdanovich, *op. cit.*, I, Appendix, 45, 56–57; Derzhavin, G., *Sochineniia* (St. Petersburg, 1878), VII, 363–370; Ikonnikov, *Graf N. S. Mordvinov*, 58–59; *Istoriia Pravitelstvuiushchego Senata*, III, 28ff.

[71] *P.S.Z.*, No. 20405.

[72] *S.I.R.I.O.*, LXXIV, 50–207, *passim;* XC, 125–145.

[73] Czartoryski, *Memoirs*, I, 292–294; Miliukov, P., *Russia and its Crisis* (Chicago, 1905), 173–174, footnote.

administration was the Edict of September 8, 1802, which provided
for the creation of a Ministry. The chief advantage in abandoning
the old principle of college administration, copied by Peter I from
Sweden, lay in the acceptance of the more modern principle of
individual responsibility. "The measure which we so often discussed is in full action," wrote Alexander to Laharpe in November,
1802, "the Ministry is formed and has functioned well for more
than a month. Affairs have, as a result, acquired more clarity, are
more orderly, and I know immediately whom to call for when something does not run the way it should."

The Ministry, however, was in no way an indication of a step
toward a limited monarchy, for, as can be inferred from the foregoing quotation, it was responsible to the Crown exclusively. Aside
from solidifying the growing bureaucracy, it availed little toward
liberal government; it even consolidated still further the power of
the Crown, for it deprived the Senate of some rights which that
body might have exercised, and transferred them to the Ministry.
The Minister was a servant of the Crown, and supreme within his
Department. Small wonder that some of the "Old Guard," representing the Senatorial group, opposed the Ministry and were inclined to consider it, as an institution which usurped the powers
of the Senate, a "legalized evil."[74]

Speransky's project.—Among the statesmen and advisers of
Alexander I who were concerned with constitutional projects,
Count Mikhail Speransky occupies the most distinguished place.
In 1803 Speransky was instructed to work out a plan for the political reconstruction of the Empire, with emphasis upon the relationship between executive and legislative powers. Speransky was
an able student of eighteenth-century political philosophy, a subject in which he had been deeply interested ever since his early
schooldays.[75] He immediately set to work and was soon able to present the required plan to the Emperor, but the approaching struggle with Napoleon completely obscured domestic political reform,
and, like other similar projects, Speransky's plan was cast aside.

After the unsuccessful war with Napoleon and the signing of the

---

[74] Vigel, *op. cit.*, II, 8–9; III, 108–110; *Byloe*, I (1906), 30; *Iz pisem i
pokazanii dekabristov*, 29; *Russky Arkhiv*, II (1881), 155–161; *S.I.R.I.O.*, III,
34 ff. The best account of the view held by the "Senatorial Group" may be
found in the Memorandum of S. P. Vorontsov to Count V. P. Kochubei of
1803. See *Arkhiv gr. Vorontsova*, XV, 443–452.

[75] *Russkaia Starina*, II (1902), 285–287.

COUNT M. M. SPERANSKY.

treaty of Tilsit, Alexander again turned his attention to internal reforms, which, because of the general postwar dissatisfaction, had become imperative. In 1808 he appointed Speransky assistant minister of justice and instructed him to supervise the work of the legislative commission, then occupied with the codification of the Russian civil laws. Also, in the same year the Emperor commanded him to present a general plan for political reforms. Beginning the task with intense ardor, at the end of 1809 he presented his plan, one of the most elaborate and systematic projects ever submitted to Alexander.

Speransky's project was entitled "An Introduction to the Code of State Laws." It is a document of considerable length, divided into two main parts: the first, a treatise on the general condition of national affairs, and the second, specific constitutional reforms recommended by the author. In his treatise Speransky says:[76]

When wisdom begins to discern the value of liberty, it sweeps aside with scorn all the toys with which it amused itself during childhood.... All complain about the complexity and confusion in our civil laws. But how can they be corrected without the establishment of firm state laws?... Of what good are civil laws when their tablets can be smashed every day upon the first rock of autocracy? People complain of the confused finances. But how can finances be organized in a state which lacks public confidence, where there are no national laws or order which could protect them? Of what use is education? Only to enable the public to observe more clearly its miserable condition,... In the legal chaos there are laws not only vague and insufficient, but contradictory to each other.... I do not mention here subjects of a more important character, namely, the relation of the peasants to their owners, that is, the relation between millions of people, composing the most useful part of the population, and a handful of parasites, who acquired, God knows why and how, all rights and privileges.

In such language one of the most prominent statesmen of nineteenth-century Russia presented in harsh but real colors the picture of his country. Speransky foresaw the development of capitalism, and that it would be in conflict with the existing form of government. He recommended an administrative reorganization whereby political rights were to be given to a larger proportion of the population though still only to the "better classes." Though he believed that serfdom was destined to come to an end, he still feared to tamper with it, referring to the issue as premature and therefore dissociating it from political reforms. Briefly, the essence of Speransky's plan might be diagramed as shown overleaf.

[76] Miliukov, *op. cit.*, 174–175.

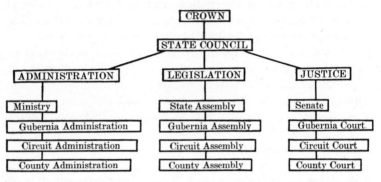

The government was to be organized in the form of a pyramid, its base touching the largest number of citizens. The higher the branches of the government ramified, the smaller became the respective numbers of the personnel, the more rigid their individual qualifications, and the more selective the process. Thus, at the bottom Speransky placed the County, Circuit, and Gubernia Administrations, Assemblies, and Courts, representing respectively the executive, legislative, and judicial branches. In the center, above these, he placed the State Assembly, which was the National Legislative body; the Ministry together with an Executive Senate represented the executive power of the State; and the Judicial Senate was to be the highest institution in its domain. Above these, in the center, the author placed the State Council and, finally, above all, the Crown.

The striking feature of the scheme is that Speransky did not permit the three branches of government to function independently, but coördinated them by means of the State Council. The Ministry was to be responsible to the Crown alone, and, because of a long process of careful sifting, the membership of the Senate could by no means be called a truly representative national body; yet the plan represented a long step toward constitutional government. True, the scheme was far from perfect, but Speransky did not claim infallibility for it, indicating that "perfection could not be achieved by a single stroke." The plan came, however, at a time when Alexander had become less disposed to listen to political projects, regardless of their merits.

Fall of Speransky.—Speransky's project was examined by Alexander I, but as time went on and promulgation of the plan was indefinitely postponed, hope dwindled. A large number of the no-

bility, led by men like Rostopchin, disliked Speransky, considering him a Russian Jacobin, and a campaign was begun to oust him.
With the approaching Franco-Russian struggle and the resulting
political tension, the general opposition to all reforms increased,
and with it mounted the antagonism toward Speransky. Before
such obstruction, progressive legislation was forced to halt. Not
only was Speransky's project rejected, but also, through the influence of the angered nobility, its author was suddenly ordered
to leave the capital.[77] "I do not know," remarks a contemporary,
"whether the death of a ferocious tyrant would have created such
general elation" as did the fall of Speransky.[78] Of all the measures
recommended, only one timid step was taken in the direction of
fulfillment of his plan, namely, the reorganization of the Ministry
and the creation of the State Council.[79] This was an improvement
on the old procedure of passing hasty and often arbitrary legislative measures, but, since the monarchy remained unaltered, this
body in reality was forced to play the rôle of consultant rather than
to enjoy any legislative power. Hence its influence was negligible.

The "Political Pattern" of Jeremy Bentham.—In connection
with the various constitutional projects offered at this time, a certain curious incident reveals a phase of thought then prevailing.
In 1814 Jeremy Bentham, the well-known English political writer,
addressed a personal letter to Alexander offering his services in
reorganizing the government along "a pattern of her own." Promising fruitful results from the "political pattern" which he had
conceived, Bentham declared that, were it accepted, it would add
laurels to Alexander's crown as well as to his own. Said he: "In
this happily compounded character, addressing them through my
pen, Your Majesty would still shew himself."[80] Bentham was probably ignorant of the fact that greater "patterns" than his had been
cast aside by Alexander. But the incident shows that there were
political thinkers who still hoped that reforms might come through
the generosity of the governing class rather than through participation of the citizens.

Other projects.—Of the other projects offered to Alexander,
there must be mentioned one by Admiral Mordvinov and another

---

[77] Grech, *Zapiski o moei zhizni*, 349–351.
[78] Vigel, *op. cit.*, IV, 33.
[79] *P.S.Z.*, No. 24064.
[80] *Iz Dalëkogo i Blizkogo Proshlogo. Sbornik v chest' N. I. Kareeva* (Petrograd, 1923), 249–251.

by Count Novosiltsov. Mordvinov suggested a representative form of government but with such property qualifications that, had his plan been carried out, it would have established a plutocratic government *par excellence.*[81] According to the plan drawn up by Novosiltsov, the greater number of the people were so far removed from the national government that the whole project, to use the expression of one historian, was nothing but "political hypocrisy." The only striking feature of this document was the outline it provided for a federal form of government, a point which later became of vital moment and constituted one of the important disagreements between Muraviev and Pestel, respectively the northern and the southern leaders of the Decembrist organizations. Novosiltsov's project was presented to Alexander in such a form that there remained nothing to do but to sign it. But time passed, and, like the other projects, it remained in the archives. Novosiltsov's was the last constitutional plan written at the order of Alexander I. It marked the end of the period of liberalism and the beginning of what one writer called "reactionary bacchanalia."

Failure of proposed reforms.—What were the chief reasons for the failure of the liberal ambitions of Alexander I? First, Alexander's determination was insufficient to prevail against the influence of the court nobility, which was powerful enough to rid itself of the most profound statesman of that time, Count Speransky.[82] Second, the failure of constitutional government in Poland, although ascribable in large measure to the nationalistic aspirations of the Poles, brought a general disappointment which led to a reactionary policy in Poland and which had, as well, political repercussions in Russia proper.[83] Third, external events had much to do with the domestic policy of the government. Occupied much of his time with matters in Western Europe and concerned more with continental affairs than with those purely national, Alexander entrusted the Empire to men like Arakcheev, who represented the extreme reactionaries, and the government, according to the Decembrist, A. Bestuzhev, "continued to slumber carelessly on a volcano."[84] The reaction gradually began to extend to all phases

[81] *Arkhiv gr. Mordvinovykh,* IV, pp. iii-iv; *Byloe,* I (1906), 41–44.

[82] Metternich characterized Alexander I as a man who "showed a peculiar mixture of masculine virtues and feminine weaknesses."—*Memoirs of Prince Metternich,* I, 315; Grech, *op. cit.,* 193–194.

[83] *XIX Viek,* I, 492–493; *Russky Arkhiv,* II (1908), 287–290.

[84] *Iz pisem i pokazanii dekabristov,* 40.

of life, affecting everyday affairs and suppressing every form of liberal expression. But "mind is like gun powder—dangerous when pressed."[85] How this "pressure" took form and the consequences it bore will now be considered.

3. GENERAL REACTION

THE CRUSADE AGAINST LIBERALISM

The shadow of Metternich, which hovered over Europe for more than thirty years, encompassed also the vast Russian Empire. In Russia, as in Western Europe, the reactionary spirit dominated the economic and political life of the country and every sphere of social activity. Alarmed by the growth of liberal ideas among the younger people, the older generation began to fight tooth and nail the tide of "dangerous ideas" coming from the west: they were determined to uphold the three pillars of Old Russia—Orthodoxy, Autocracy, and Nationalism. The war of 1812–14, which took on a broadly national character, and especially the burning of Moscow, greatly stimulated the chauvinistic sentiment. It was a call to die-hard conservatives to raise their banner, entrench themselves, and declare open warfare against the western "Jacobin spirit." Though this reaction was general throughout Europe, nowhere did it bring such disastrous retardation as in Russia. In Western Europe it was opposed by a strongly organized liberal-revolutionary movement; two great social forces met face to face, and a crusade against a "red menace" was conceivable. But in Russia such a crusade did not seem justifiable, for here the liberal movement was barely incipient. Nevertheless, the Russian government approached it from the European angle and enormously magnified its danger. Fighting political windmills everywhere, the authorities saw revolution in the most timorous opposition and were in constant fear lest the nation become infected with French ideas. The government was suspicious of every appearance of political, social, or religious activity; it considered all societies potential *Carbonari* and forbade them entirely, except those sponsored by itself. Hence the crusade against revolution in Russia turned into a petty persecution of various developments of national life, destroying thus the finest elements within the state.

Karamzin's Memorandum.—Symptoms of this reaction are best to be noted in the writings of the time. Of these none was more

---

[85] *Ibid.*, 36.

illuminating than the Memorandum which the celebrated historian, Nicholas Karamzin, presented in 1812 to Alexander I under the title, *Old and New Russia.*[86] The document can justly be considered the landmark of an epoch; it expressed the mood of those conservatives who for several generations controlled the destinies of the Empire. Though the thought is logical, the arguments are questionable, and Karamzin, as a historian, might have been expected to show keener foresight.

Status quo was the keynote of the whole document, and its essence is well compressed in one of Karamzin's own sentences: "The strength of the state is to be found in the strength of the sentiment of obedience displayed by the people."[87] His faith in men being greater than his faith in institutions, Karamzin believed that a strong ruler and a stable government were all a nation could desire. No Senate nor State Council, nor any other political body should gain power in the state, because for this to happen would be equivalent to placing "two fierce lions in one cage." The only remedy for all evils in the state was a strong monarchical government and the revival of a nationalistic spirit. According to Karamzin, the greatest fault of Peter I was that he disturbed the natural course of development in Russian history and imposed upon his people an alien social order. "We became citizens of the world, but ceased in some respects to be citizens of Russia," states Karamzin. For Russia, therefore, the wisest course was to withdraw from continental affairs and to follow her own national destiny. The document sardonically criticized the suggested reforms of Speransky, which Karamzin considered a dangerous attempt to imitate the Napoleonic Code.[88] In short, the salvation of Russia lay in looking backward instead of forward, in returning to the glorious days of Moscow when the nation, undefiled by alien influence, was ruled by strong, wise monarchs. The nature of the Memorandum can be summarized by the epigram which Pushkin dedicated to Karamzin's *History of the Russian State:*

> In his *History* beauty and simplicity
> Prove without bias
> The necessity of autocracy
> And the charm of the whip.

---

[86] The Memorandum is cited in full in Pypin, *Obshchestvennoe dvizhenie v Rossii,* Appendix.

[87] Masaryk, *The Spirit of Russia,* I, 91.

[88] Korf, M. A., *Zhizn' grafa Speranskogo,* I, 161–165.

Shishkov and Rostopchin.—Among the contemporaries of Karamzin, who also reflected the reactionary age, was Admiral Shishkov, who advocated in the literary field what Karamzin advocated in politics; namely, to purge from Russian literature every sign of foreign influence and to restore patriarchal Russia and the old church Slavonic language.[89] The servility of the literati to the state needs no better example than Admiral Shishkov. Along with Shishkov stands Count Rostopchin, the shrewd and famous demagogue, governor of Moscow in 1812, and author of numerous proclamations and leaflets against the French. Though his writings presented the French as the vilest creatures on earth, his views did not prevent him from settling in Paris immediately after the war of 1812–14. Shishkov and Rostopchin were two limbs of one tree, rooted in the soil of Old Russia.

Religious fervor.—Another indication of the state of affairs during the second half of the reign of Alexander I was the religious-mystical fervor which accompanied the political reaction. In this respect the Holy Synod headed by Prince A. Golitsyn demonstrated the darkest aspects of the period. Convinced that "Satan ages and feels the approach of the end of his reign on earth and therefore uses his last and most cunning efforts" to pervert man, Golitsyn undertook a campaign against every appearance of what he thought was "the policy of Satan." As head of the Holy Synod and later of the Ministry of Education, Golitsyn did much damage to national education. The postwar period is characterized by the rise of various religious creeds, by extensive activities of the Jesuit Order, and by the growing movement of obscurant pietism. The increasing influence of the Jesuits led to interference on the part of the government: on January 1, 1816, an order was issued expelling all Jesuits from the capital.[90] Finally on March 13, 1820, the Jesuit Order was entirely banned and its members compelled to leave the country.[91]

Numerous sects and circles, such as the one which assembled in the drawing room of Mme Tatarinova, reveal the impotence and spiritual bankruptcy of the postwar generation. Disappointed with official Orthodox religion, disillusioned in their hope of reform, and crushed by the recent political storm, these individuals attempted to seize upon some philosophy in order to find a pur-

[89] *Russkaia Starina*, CVI (1901), 383–384.
[90] *P.S.Z.*, No. 28198, p. 115, col. 1.   [91] *Ibid.*, No. 28198.

pose in life. Lacking faith in a new social order—the thing that
they most needed—they lost their balance and their hold on reality.
The result was a renunciation of reality and a constant search for
a "true religion" or "pure Christianity." It was this general attitude that made it possible for Mme Krüdener to become the heroine
of the day and spiritual adviser to Alexander, and stifled every
attempt toward enlightenment. A further illustration is afforded
by the experience of the Russian Bible Society, the original purposes of which were made a plaything in the hands of reactionaries
and actually turned into a weapon against liberal expression. In
its beginning the Bible Society attracted many liberal members of
sincere purpose, some of whom, for example, General Mikhail Orlov, were among the founders of the Decembrist movement.[92] But
the Society soon changed into a militant reactionary body, which,
instead of pursuing its original aim of disseminating education
and promoting literacy, occupied itself with the eradication of the
"fruits of Satan."

Education and censorship.—The most destructive effect of the
reactionary policy—a direct outcome of the Holy Alliance and
the famous Carlsbad decrees—was in the field of education. Two
names notorious for their association with the darkest days of
the Russian universities are those of Mikhail L. Magnitsky and
Dmitry Runich. In March of 1819 Magnitsky was appointed
member of the National School Board and sent to inspect the University of Kazan. After a few days he made a very unfavorable
report : Latin was not sufficiently studied; religion was not offered
at all; the administration through its mismanagement squandered
money ; professors were propagating dangerous ideas.[93] In an attempt to present evidence of heresy on the part of the professors,
Magnitsky reported excerpts from their lectures to the Ministry
of Education. For example, from the lectures of Professor Soln-
tsev, an eminent scholar in political theory, Magnitsky cited the
following: "A citizen has all rights concerning his life and activities as long as these are not directed for evil purposes and are not
detrimental to his fellow-citizens nor to the state." On this Magnitsky commented abruptly, "Justification of suicide." Another
quotation from the same lectures reads: "War is a condition of

[92] *S.I.R.I.O.*, LXXVIII, 526–528; *Ostafievsky Arkhiv*, I, Nos. 216, 218, 221,
239, 240.

[93] *Z.M.N.P.*, XI, 1903, 41–42.

MIKHAIL L. MAGNITSKY.

continuous violence." This brought the criticism: "That is a definition of brigandage, not of war."[94] Upon such evidence as this Magnitsky recommended nothing less than the complete closing of the University. This Alexander refused to do, but he decided to send someone as a reliable administrator. It is easy to imagine the fate of the University of Kazan when on June 8, 1819, none other than Magnitsky was sent as Rector of the University with full powers, granted by the Emperor, to reorganize that institution. In less than a month eleven professors were expelled, and the police régime which Magnitsky introduced into the University amounted to its virtual closing.[95]

The University of Kazan was not the only victim of the reactionary onslaught. What Magnitsky had done in Kazan was repeated by Runich in the University of St. Petersburg. In 1822 a number of professors, among them outstanding men in their respective fields, were dismissed. The chief accusation against them was their alleged inclinations toward atheism and their mildly expressed sympathies with the constitutional form of government.[96] Upon the least protest students were immediately regarded as rebels and threatened with and on some occasions actually punished by exile, conscription, or imprisonment. In the universities of Dorpat and Vilna professors were expelled for teaching rationalistic philosophy.[97] In July, 1822, the government prohibited the University of Dorpat from enrolling students who had formerly attended foreign universities because those students "brought with them and propagated customs of disobedience from the universities abroad." In February, 1823, Russian students were forbidden to attend certain German universities on the ground that these were seats of antireligious and immoral ideas. A similar policy was enforced in many other universities, causing deep indignation among many

---

[94] Skabichevsky, *Ocherki istorii russkoi tsenzury*, 138; Feoktistov, *Magnitsky*, 81–82.

[95] The best account of the administration of Magnitsky may be found in the study by E. M. Feoktistov, *Magnitsky, materialy dlia istorii prosveshcheniia v Rossii;* see pp. 66–68, 100. See also Zagoskin, N., *Istoriia kazanskogo universiteta za pervye sto let ego sushchestvovaniia* (Kazan, 1904), particularly III, 340–348; Dovnar-Zapolsky, *Obzor noveishei russkoi istorii*, 251–297. Cf. Morozov, P., "Moë znakomstvo s M. L. Magnitskim." *Russky Arkhiv*, X (1875), 241–250.

[96] *Russkaia Starina*, II (1876), 279–280; CVI (1901), 385–386; V (1901), 363–367; *Ostafievsky Arkhiv*, I, 579–580.

[97] *Istorichesky Viestnik*, XXIX (1887), 612–619.

young men of liberal ideas, some of whom were members of the Decembrist Society.[98]

Another expression of the "reactionary bacchanalia," which aroused the opposition of many of the younger generation and of certain poets, including Pushkin, was the rigid censorship that held the press in its claws and often displayed unbelievable intolerance.[99] The early part of Alexander's reign had marked a breathing spell for the press, and a number of laws had been promulgated abolishing in certain cities and ports the office of censorship. These laws had facilitated the importation of foreign books, which had virtually ceased in the reign of Paul I.[100] But even in the earlier days of Alexander, when liberty seemed at the doorstep of Russia, numerous books had been confiscated and certain subjects were outlawed in the press. Serfdom was one of the forbidden subjects; its discussion involved a heavy penalty. On certain occasions books were ordered destroyed and authors received strong reprimands from the Emperor.[101] If such incidents could occur during the administrative honeymoon of the liberal Emperor, what was to be expected when the reactionary forces were in full power?

About 1812 the department of censorship became exceedingly arbitrary. Numerous rules muzzled the press, dictated the nature of topics to be discussed, and completely subjected authors to the caprices of intolerant censors. Such subjects as constitutional and political problems were excluded from the press, and it was almost impossible to write on questions of immediate importance. On a few occasions editors succeeded in including delicate topics, such as comments on the French or the United States constitutions, but for the most part writing was under the strictest governmenal surveillance. The manner in which political comments were made palatable to official taste can be judged from the following incident. After 1815, when the war had ended, the government ruled that "journalists who wrote in 1812 must now, in 1815, write differently, adjusting [statements] little by little with the intentions of the government and assisting in promoting peaceful relations."[102]

[98] *Iz pisem i pokazanii dekabristov*, 36, 64–69.

[99] *Ibid.*, 36, 67–68; Dovnar-Zapolsky, *Memuary dekabristov*, 129–133; *Materialy*, II, 71, 166–167; *Obshchestvennye dvizheniia v Rossii*, I, 488. See also Pushkin's poem, "Poslanie k tsenzoru" (An Epistle to the Censor).

[100] *P.S.Z.*, Nos. 20139, 20375, 20376, 20460, 20537.

[101] Semevsky, *op. cit.*, I, 282–291; Skabichevsky, *op. cit.*, 89.

[102] Skabichevsky, *op. cit.*, 114.

Not only political writings suffered under the heavy blows of rigid censorship, but purely artistic productions as well. The celebrated poet, Zhukovsky, who, it might be mentioned, was very conservative, had a difficult time in publishing his translation of the ballad by Walter Scott, *The Eve of Saint John,* because the censor considered it immoral. Likewise the censor regarded as immoral Schiller's *Jeanne d'Arc* and Goethe's *Egmont.*

A few amusing incidents illustrate the tremendous difficulties that the writer of that time had to overcome and the petty attacks that he was likely to meet. A certain poem which included the word "maid" was presented for approval to the notoriously autocratic censor, Krasovsky.[103] On the margin the censor wrote, "What kind of maid?" Another poem contained a line reading: "Silently my glance would rest upon you," to which Krasovsky added, "Here is some sort of double meaning." A second line, "Oh, that I might give my whole life to you," aroused the censor's question, "What will there be left for God?" Finally, when the censor came to the line, "And to rest my head upon your bosom!" he passed the final verdict, "The verse is an extremely sensual one."[104]

In those days it was indeed easier for a camel to pass through the eye of a needle than for a writer to pass through the gate of the censor. "Sensuality" and "double meaning" were seen everywhere. But these were not the only faults that might prevent a poem from being published. If the author had the misfortune to be inspired during Lent to write poetry in honor of love or a woman, it was considered sacrilegious. It is needless to describe further the stupid attacks of the censors in this period, though pages might be filled with citations which would seem to have been written by a hand from the darkest past. How ironical that this should have been the epoch of Alexander I, the pupil of the Republican Laharpe!

MILITARY COLONIES

Economic and financial difficulties forced the administration of Alexander I to seek means of avoiding utter disaster. One of the measures evolved was the creation of military colonies, an idea conceived by Alexander, the origin and enforcement of which com-

---

[103] An able sketch of Krasovsky by his former secretary may be found in *Russkaia Starina,* IX (1874), 107–125. See also *ibid.,* IV (1871), 440–442; VI (1872), 582–588.

[104] Dovnar-Zapolsky, *Idealy dekabristov,* 76–77; Skabichevsky, *op. cit.,* 177–179.

prise in Russian history a page both curious and tragic. As early as the time of Catherine II military expenditures of Russia had reached an enormous proportion, amounting to about 50 per cent, of the entire national budget.[105] The reign of Alexander marked a still further increase, and immediate measures for relief were imperative. The only logical solution was to reduce the army to its minimum, a measure which certain military experts actually recommended to the Emperor. But Alexander refused to take such a step at a time when Europe was still in turmoil and the army was necessary "pour soutenir prépondérance politique."[106]

Their origin.—It was in the search for means of reducing army expenditures that the idea of military colonies came into being. Such a plan, it was thought, would achieve a threefold purpose: it would relieve the peasant population from frequent recruiting, which imposed upon them unbearable hardships; it would free a large part of the army for agriculture; and, finally, the army would become self-sufficient and thereby lessen the burden of taxation. It may also be added that the government, by creating a permanent military class, would free itself from dependence upon the grace of the nobility, which contributed its peasants for military service. This idea, however, aroused apprehensions both among many members of that class and particularly among the Decembrists. If some of the older nobility feared that this might result in an independent hereditary military class, the Decembrists predicted that the colonists "would form in the state a special caste, which, having nothing in common with the people, would become a tool for oppression."[107] Whatever the economic advantages of the colonies might have been, their unpopularity from the very beginning is beyond doubt.

The exact origin of the idea of military colonies was long a subject of dispute, and there were various theories to explain how it occurred to Alexander. Some insisted that the whole plan evolved under the influence of General Scharnhorst's policy in Prussia; others maintained that General Servan's book convinced Alexander of the wisdom of the project.[108] But with the appearance of Evstaf'ev's study, the latest and most reliable, it has been definitely

---

[105] *Z.M.N.P.*, III (1906), 92–93.

[106] "Rasskazy A. P. Ermolova." *C.I.O.I.D.R.*, IV (1863), 232.

[107] Trubetskoi, *op. cit.*, 15.

[108] *Graf Arakcheev i voennye poseleniia*, 89; Shilder, *op. cit.*, IV, 23.

COUNT A. A. ARAKCHEEV.

established that the whole plan, especially as enforced in 1816, was copied from the Austrian military colonies along the Turkish border.[109]

Earlier plans, 1810.—On November 9, 1810, an order was given to Count Arakcheev to establish a military colony in the Mogilev Gubernia, and the territory designated for this purpose was handed over to the Ministry of War.[110] The natives were compelled to leave their land, and were transferred to the south, and military units were brought in to replace them. Married soldiers received homes and the unmarried were distributed among the families as agricultural laborers. From the first the plan was destined to entail enormous difficulties and great human suffering. Of the peasants sent south by government orders, few reached their destination, perishing from hunger, cold, and drunkenness, heartbroken by the miserable lot which had befallen them.[111] In any circumstances the wisdom of the whole plan might be doubted, but, managed by Russian bureaucracy and headed by a man like Arakcheev, who had neither imagination nor sense of humor, such an enterprise was most dangerous. Novosiltsov once made a statement to the effect that the first generation of the military colonies would be miserable and the succeeding ones would make the whole of Russia miserable.[112]

Arakcheev's appointment and its significance.—To appreciate fully the fate of the colonists it is sufficient to describe the man to whom the management of the military colonies was entrusted, Count Arakcheev. In the history of the nineteenth century the name of Arakcheev stands as a symbol of darkest reaction and cruelest oppression. Arakcheev's epoch coincided with that of Metternich in Western Europe, but Arakcheev and Metternich were quite unlike though their period is commonly characterized by the same term, reaction. Metternich was a product of Western Europe: cultivated, suave, keen, and well versed in European diplomacy. This could not be said of Arakcheev, a product of Russian soil. Lacking refinement, he used to pride himself on being a "true Russian uneducated nobleman."[113] Tactless, bigoted, and unsympa-

---

[109] Evstaf'ev, *Vosstanie novgorodskikh voennykh poselian*, 40–41.
[110] *P.S.Z.*, No. 24413a.
[111] *Russky Arkhiv*, I (1875), 49–50.
[112] Bernhardi, *Geschichte Rußlands*, III, 173.
[113] Korf, *op. cit.*, II, 159–160; Kizevetter, *Istoricheskie ocherki*, 289; *Russkaia Starina*, X (1873), 458.

thetic with suffering, he was hated by more people than was any other statesman of his time. As an army officer during the reign of Paul I, Arakcheev practiced the most bestial tortures on the soldiers; on one occasion, when in a rage, he bit off a soldier's ear.[114] Says one contemporary: Arakcheev was active as an ant and poisonous as a tarantula. To him every man was a thief with but one ambition: to get rich.[115] Though brutal, he was at times sentimental. He was exceedingly fond, for example, of the trills of the nightingale, and the welfare of that bird concerned him so greatly that in 1817 he ordered all the cats in his village to be hanged.[116]

As some of his papers indicate, Arakcheev was a typical bureaucrat. In one of his reports to the Emperor, giving the cost of a building for the home of two families in the colonies, he estimated it at 4,865 rubles and 71¾ kopecks![117] He was meticulous at home as well as in all the enterprises entrusted to him. "Every woman on my estate," writes Arakcheev, "must give birth every year, preferably a son to a daughter. If some one gives birth to a daughter, I exact a fine; if a dead child is born, or a miscarriage—a fine also; and if there is a year that the woman does not deliver a child, then she is to present ten arshin[118] of linen."[119] Arakcheev was loyal and patriotic; he loved Russia, but the Russia of which he conceived was a country run on a schedule elaborated by him, a nation marching in a goose step, not the Russia of the millions who constituted it. Nothing alarmed him more than the prospect of peasants becoming rich. According to Arakcheev, once the peasant were rich, he would begin to think of freedom and of leaving the soil.[120]

If a monument were to be erected to old bureaucratic Russia, the figure to top it should unquestionably be that of Arakcheev. And it was to this man that authority was given to enforce the plan of military colonies! In justice to Arakcheev, it must be added that originally he opposed the plan; it was Speransky who favored military colonies.[121] But the determination of Alexander to carry out

[114] *Russky Arkhiv*, VIII (1893), 541; Grech, *op. cit.*, 552.

[115] *Russkaia Starina*, X (1873), 447–448, 452–455.

[116] Dovnar-Zapolsky, *Idealy dekabristov*, 13.

[117] Bogdanovich, *op. cit.*, V, 352.

[118] An *arshin* is about 28 inches.

[119] Dovnar-Zapolsky, *Obzor noveishei russkoi istorii*, 313.

[120] *Russkaia Starina*, X (1873), 458.

[121] See *Russky Viestnik*, IV (1890), 108–116. For a general characteristic of Arakcheev see Mazour, A. G., "Le comte Aleksej Andreevič Arakčeev." *Le Monde Slave*, June, 1936, 365–390.

the plan "even at the price of paving the road from St. Petersburg to the colonies with human bodies" compelled Arakcheev to accept the appointment.[122]

Revival of the plan, 1816.—The coming of war in 1812 forced the authorities temporarily to abandon the establishing of military colonies, but in 1816 the idea was taken up with vigor. On August 5, 1816, an order was given to transform one of the counties in the Novgorod Gubernia into a military colony.[123] In the following year similar colonies were established in the South.[124] The original plan was somewhat altered: instead of bringing in new settler-soldiers, it was decided to turn the peasants of the designated zones into soldiers and, in addition, to bring in soldiers of the regular army. "Old people became known as invalids, children as 'cantonists,' adults as soldiers."[125] The soldiers' wives were ordered to join their husbands. By reason of illness or attachment to children, many wives refused to comply with the order, but Arakcheev, who had pitifully failed in his own family life and to whom the family institution meant nothing more than a means for breeding, rejected these as insufficient reasons. The sick could recover, he argued, and the right of husbands to have with them their wives was so sacred as to be above all maternal instincts.

In accordance with the new scheme every village was transformed into a military camp. All peasants under the age of fifty had to shave off their beards and crop their hair, and all under the age of forty-five were forced to wear military uniforms. Children over seven were taken to the so-called "cantonist" settlements, where they were kept till the age of eighteen. Here they received special military training, were taught elementary subjects and a trade, and after the age of eighteen were enrolled in reserve battalions. Girls were married by order of the military authorities.[126]

The antagonism aroused by this system is beyond description. In the fall of 1817 a group of peasants approached the Grand Duke Nicholas, begging him to prevent the enforcement of military colonies. They appealed to him as follows:[127]

---

[122] Lykoshin, "Poseleniia voennye." *Entsiklopedichesky Slovar*, XXIV (48), 664.

[123] *P.S.Z.*, Nos. 26389, 26390, 26803, 27107.

[124] *Ibid.*, No. 26772.

[125] Grech, *op. cit.*, 555.

[126] *Istorichesky Viestnik*, XXV (1886), 353–356; LV (1894), 741–742.

[127] *Russky Arkhiv*, VIII (1893), 535; *Russkaia Starina*, IV (1904), 14.

Increase our taxes, conscript for military service a son from every house, take from us everything and send us into the steppes; we should more gladly consent to this. We have arms, we will work and be happy there; but do not take our effects, the customs of our fathers, and do not turn us all into soldiers.

But the plea was of no avail, and the government continued to enforce the plan. Revolt being the one recourse, the population in the military settlements waited only for an opportune moment to rid itself of the heavy burdens imposed by the system. Everywhere, but particularly in the South, there was strong opposition, expressed in numerous petitions and riots. In 1817, 1818, and 1819 serious outbreaks occurred in the northern and southern colonies. The rebellion in the South, especially that of Chuguev in the summer of 1819, reached such dimensions that Arakcheev was called with an army force. After many days of bitter struggle the rebels were forced to surrender. They paid a high price for their resistance; three hundred and thirteen persons were sentenced to corporal punishment, of whom twenty-five died shortly afterwards. The rebellion was crushed, and Arakcheev could report to Alexander that peace and justice were restored.[128]

Failure of the colonies.—From start to finish the military colonies proved a failure. Their outward appearance gave a favorable impression: newly built houses, paved streets, neat uniforms. Everything ran on schedule like clockwork, but underneath was the grumbling of the peasants, ready to revolt at any moment. Even the higher officers complained of the terrible régime and the depressing atmosphere.[129] Yet those who visited the colonies for inspection were successfully deceived. During the Emperor's visits a roasted sucking pig or a goose would be carried from one home into another; wherever the Emperor entered the same dish would be displayed to convince Alexander that the colonists were prosperous and well fed. Black backs covered with sores from frequent beatings were concealed under neat military uniforms, and Alexander usually left well pleased with the condition of the colonies.[130] Even such men as Speransky fell into the deception.

Except a few in the South, the colonies never became self-sufficient, as had been hoped, but had to be supported by the govern-

---

[128] Bogdanovich, *op. cit.*, V, 358–368; V, Appendix, 86–89; Turgenev, *La Russie et les Russes*, II, 456–459.

[129] *Russkaia Starina*, IV (1871), 644–645.

[130] *Russkaia Starina*, I (1875), 88, 90–91; Lee, *The Last Days of Alexander and the First Days of Nicholas*, 85–86.

ment.[131] From a military point of view the experiment was equally
a failure. Conditions in the colonies can be judged by the fact that
the death rate greatly exceeded the birth rate.[132] Soldiers who had
spent most of their lives in the army were unable to return to the
soil, and peasants who had spent their lives in the fields could not
be turned into successful soldiers. The rigid military discipline
prevented any initiative, and constant interference, often by men
wholly ignorant of agriculture, resulted in crop failures and mismanagement. The threat of corporal punishment for the slightest
offense was always over the heads of the colonists. Bribery became
widespread in the administration, though Arakcheev tried hard to
stamp it out.[133]

However, by 1825 military colonies were established in the following gubernias: Petersburg, Novgorod, Mogilev, Ekaterinoslav,
and Kherson. The total population of the colonies and "cantonist" settlements was 748,519, not counting girls under age.[134] In
spite of the evident military and economic failure of the colonies
they continued to exist until 1857, though from the first many
members of Russian society opposed them. Among the numerous
evils against which the Decembrists raised their voice, the military
colonies and serfdom occupied the foreground. The rebellious spirit
of the colonists gave hope to many of the Decembrists, for if the
revolution were crushed in the capital, they thought, they might
retreat to the colonies, where accumulated discontent would support their cause.[135] This assumption was well founded but the course
of events developed most unexpectedly, surprising the leaders,
and therefore the plan to exploit a favorable situation failed to
materialize.

[131] *Velikaia Reforma*, II, 99.

[132] Lykoshin, *op. cit.*, XXIV (48), 668.

[133] *Russky Viestnik*, III (1890), 108–109.

[134] Semevsky, *Politicheskie i obshchestvennye idei dekabristov*, 171.

[135] *Materialy*, I, 376; III, 52; IV, 12; *Russkaia Starina*, IV (1904), 14–15;
Zavalishin, *Zapiski dekabrista*, 185, 207; *Stoletie Voennogo Ministerstva,
1802–1902*, VII, part 1, 596.

Chapter II

THE LIBERAL IDEA

1. MASONRY

RUSSIA AS DESCRIBED in the preceding pages was the country of the older generation. There are numerous proofs that the younger generation, becoming ever more discontented with the situation, had its own conception of the Fatherland. Patriotic in the truest sense of the word, enthusiastic, as youth generally is, idealistic, and unselfish, the young people gradually voiced their protest and commenced to plan for the fulfillment of *their* country, Young Russia.

In its early stages opposition to the government grew without plan, organization, or strong leadership, expressing itself usually in two forms, palace revolutions, led by small cliques at court, or mass uprisings like that of Stenka Razin or of Pugachev. The last quarter of the eighteenth century, however, marks a growing popular and intellectual movement which contributed to the formation of social ideals and of a better organized opposition. Though the eighteenth century was seemingly of a colorless political character, it transmitted to the succeeding century certain traditions and a pattern for organization which a new generation readily appropriated to its own ends.

One form of the liberal tradition inherited from the eighteenth century was reminiscent of the once popular Masonic lodges. Masonry in Russia had first appeared in the middle of the eighteenth century. It had progressed rapidly until the nineties, when it was checked by government interference. Not only had Masonic lodges been the earliest groups to provide an opportunity for men interested in reform to come into closer contact, but they had also contributed gradually to the development of more unified social organizations. However, Freemasonry was not universally concerned with political problems; its philosophy was chiefly moral.[1] Stressing individual self-perfection rather than politics, it embraced within its organizations mystics and pietists, philan-

---

[1] Anderson, *The Constitutions of Free-Masons*, 53–56; Pypin, *Russkoe Masonstvo*, 381–282; *Russkaia Starina*, XVIII (1877), 466.

thropists, extreme reactionaries, and liberals.[2] Each member interpreted the principles of Masonry according to his individual point of view. Some men saw a moral purpose in Masonry; some believed it was of civic value in the training of loyal citizens; others were attracted to Masonry out of mere curiosity.[3] The well-known Elagin Grand Lodge, for example, emphasized moral perfection. It was believed that, once the individual reached perfection, his social status did not matter, for freedom of spirit meant more than political freedom. Another lodge, "La Grande Loge Astrée," of the nineteenth century, was even more conservative. Its constitution specifically provided that

> . . . . a Mason must be an obedient and loyal subject to his sovereign and fatherland; he must obey the civil laws and carry them out accurately; he must not participate in any secret or open societies which would be harmful to his country or sovereign; and he must not by speech or by writing assist in disapproving of the sovereign or his laws.[4]

Liberal Masonry.—But not all the lodges nor all the members were conservative. Certain Masons, though religious, were liberal Christians and they openly opposed the official church, as some writings show. "In the early days of Christianity," writes one Mason, "the vessels were wooden but the priests were golden; nowadays the vessels are golden and the priests are wooden."[5] Small wonder that the clergy opposed the Masons and constantly sought the support of the government against them. There were lodges which even advocated what were for those days radical ideas. The organization of the Masons was on a purely democratic principle; etiquette and social rank were forgotten during the meetings.[6] Their social ideas were well expressed in their hymns, one of which reads:[7]

> Abandon pride and wealth,
> Abandon showiness and rank;
> They will only serve as obstacles,
> To them our temple gates are closed.

---

[2] *Russky Arkhiv*, I (1884), 16–18; VI (1901), 302–303; Pypin, *Religioznye dvizheniia*, 137.

[3] Longinov, *Novikov i moskovskie martinisty*, 0123–0126.

[4] Semevsky, *Politicheskie i obshchestvennye idei dekabristov*, 323; *Russkaia Starina*, CXXXII (1907), 87; Vernadsky, *Russkoe Masonstvo*, 195–197.

[5] Sokolovskaia, *Russkoe Masonstvo*, 178.

[6] *Russkaia Starina*, XI (1874), 466–67; Vernadsky, *op. cit.*, 189–197.

[7] Eshevsky, *Sochineniia*, III, 439.

Some of the French lodges were even more radical, and young officers initiated abroad were especially imbued with republican ideas.[8]

Philanthropy was another interest of the Masonic organizations, which, incidentally, became so noteworthy in the reign of Catherine II that the Empress became apprehensive, and the result was the suppression of the Masonic lodges and the confinement of one of their most active leaders, Novikov, in the Schlüsselburg fortress. Some of the Masonic societies were strong advocates of social justice, and though they tolerated serfdom, they insisted upon humane treatment of the serfs.[9]

The liberal tendency of the Masons during the earlier period, 1810–1820, had attracted many Decembrists. Nicholas Turgenev, for example, had at one time greatly hoped that Masonry might become an important factor in the emancipation of the serfs.[10] Many Masons were cosmopolites and strongly favored international conciliation. In general, Masonry sought the eradication of religious prejudices, class, racial, and national discrimination, and the establishment of international coöperation.[11] In his satires Novikov opposed monastic orders, and referred to the necessity for the emancipation of the peasants, free speech, and universal education.[12] The Moscow Masons were instrumental in connection with a constitutional project presented on one occasion to Grand Duke Paul by his tutor Panin.[13] Like the Illuminati, the liberal Masons did not believe in immediate radical reforms, but in gradual reform through the long and persistent education of the individual in society.

Nineteenth-century Masonry.—The Masons and the Illuminati have been associated, often without justification, with the revolutionary movement all over Europe, and they were suppressed wherever conservative government was in the saddle. The persecutions in Western Europe in the eighties of the eighteenth century resulted in the suppression of all secret societies in Russia. But the beginning of the nineteenth century witnessed a rapid re-

---

[8] *Russkaia Starina*, CXVII (1904), 28.

[9] *Velikaia Reforma*, II, 175; Semevsky, *op. cit.*, 335.

[10] Turgenev, *La Russie et les Russes*, II, 374–382.

[11] *Russky Arkhiv*, III (1890), 403–404; Sipovsky, "Novikov, Schwarz i moskovskoe Masonstvo," in his book, *N. M. Karamzin*, 3.

[12] Nezelenov, *N. I. Novikov*, 155–157, 183, 198.

[13] Tikhonravov, N., *Sochineniia* (M., 1898), III, part 1, 273.

vival of Masonic activities, a restoration of former lodges, and a noticeable indifference, if not a favorable attitude, on the part of the authorities.[14] "The Dying Sphinx" was the first Masonic lodge to resume its functions, on January 15, 1800. On June 10, 1802, the lodge "Les Amis Réunis" opened in St. Petersburg, and a year later the "Neptune" was opened in Moscow. On October 11, 1805, the lodge "Alexander zur Mildtätigheit des gekrönten Pelikans" began to meet in the capital. On March 4, 1810, the lodge "Palestine" was founded. The first Masonic magazine, *The Friend of Youth,* was issued in Moscow on January 1, 1807.[15]

The influence of the Masons upon the administration can be seen from the fact that in 1803 Börber, the Grand Master of the "Grand Directorial Lodge of Vladimir," succeeded in arranging an audience with the Emperor. In the brief conversation Börber convinced Alexander of the idealism and the genuine patriotism of the Masons. The Emperor, it is said, was so impressed by Börber's arguments that he not only promised to lift the ban on the Masonic organizations but even inquired about the possibility of himself joining the order.[16]

As the years advanced the Masons were met with increasing tolerance. As late as 1816 Alexander, when asked by the governor of Moscow for permission to open a lodge in that city, replied : "I give no open permission but I shall look through my fingers at the matter; experience proves that there is nothing harmful in them; therefore you may do as you please."[17] Among many distinguished statesmen who joined the Masonic lodges were Grand Duke Constantine, General Benckendorff, General Langeron, and Count Potocki.[18] There were persistent though unauthenticated rumors that Alexander himself was a Mason.[19] In 1810 Speransky was enrolled by I. Fessler, at that time the most influential Mason in Russia.[20] The Fessler lodge was known not only for the idealistic Christianity that it preached but also for its "political heresies."[21]

[14] *Russky Arkhiv,* I (1908), 103–104.

[15] Pypin, *op. cit.,* 522–523 ; *Russkaia Starina,* CXXXII (1907), 84.

[16] *Masonstvo v ego proshlom i nastoiashchem,* II, 167–168 ; Pypin, *Obshchestvennoe dvizhenie v Rossii,* 297–298.

[17] *Iz pisem i pokazanii dekabristov,* 67 ; *Russky Arkhiv,* II (1895), 171.

[18] Bogdanovich, *Istoriia tsarstvovaniia imp. Aleksandra I,* VI, 405.

[19] *Russky Arkhiv,* V (1886), 198.

[20] Korf, M. A., *Zhizn grafa Speranskogo,* I, 256–261.

[21] *Masonstvo . . . , op. cit.,* II, 176, 179.

In 1810 Masonic activities became so widespread that the government began to fear the continued influence of the organization, and an order was given to police authorities of the capital to investigate all the lodges. After the investigation the Masons were permitted to continue their work, provided they presented a monthly report indicating the nature of their activities.[22]

With the end of the war of 1812–1814, there was a special increase in the numbers in Masonry. There are no exact data on the number of lodges existing in the capitals of Russia, Moscow and St. Petersburg; but there are some figures showing the rapid increase of lodges in Russian Poland, from which it may be safely assumed that a similar tendency prevailed in Russia proper.[23] These figures are as follows:[24]

Year	Number of lodges
1815	13
1817	20
1821	32

It is an interesting fact that, whereas in the eighteenth century Masonic organizations included members mostly of the highest nobility, the Masons of the nineteenth century were far from being so exclusive. The later Masonic societies enrolled many members from the middle class—merchants, the intelligentsia, and men of various vocations. Gradually the number of such members became so impressive that lodges were formed in accordance with vocational interests, thus adding to the Masonic organization a guild character.[25] The popularity of the lodges evidently attracted many undesirable members, some of whom sought more than moral philosophy, a fact which aroused apprehension among the more conservative Masons, including the famous Mason-mystic, Alexander Labzin.[26] Rampant reaction in the country and the secret report of some of the conservative Masons, who pictured the lodges as revolutionary hotbeds, caused the government to act more decisively.[27] On August 1, 1822, all secret societies, including the Ma-

---

[22] *Russkaia Starina*, I (1883), 42; *Masonstvo ...*, *op. cit.*, II, 177–178.

[23] Korobka, "Polskie obshchestva 20-kh godov i dekabristy," *O Minuvshem* (1909), 189ff.

[24] *Masonstvo ...*, *op. cit.*, II, 238.

[25] *Ibid.*, II, 162–163.

[26] *Russkaia Starina*, XII (1894), 101.

[27] *Russkaia Starina*, III (1877), 456.

sonic lodges, were entirely forbidden.[28] However, by this time there was established the "Union of Welfare," the secret Decembrist society, which, by providing a ready organization, gave opportunity to those who wished it, to carry out their social and political ideals.

Masonry and the Decembrists.—A great many of the Decembrists at one time or another were Masons, and many of them had been initiated when they were in Paris.[29] Pestel and Alexander N. Muraviev were members of the Masonic lodge "Trois Vertus"; the latter had been enrolled in France.[30] Ryleev was an active Mason for a short time, from 1820 to 1821, in the lodge "Zum flammenden Stern."[31] Küchelbecker was a member of "La Grande Loge Astrée" until it was outlawed.[32] Many of the ideas held by Masons and Illuminati were absorbed by the Decembrists and later used for their purposes. The mysticism characteristic of Masonic lodges seldom appealed to the Decembrists, nor were they sympathetic with the political idealism and the somewhat naïve method by which it was advocated. Some Decembrists more determined in their views, among them Yakushkin, one of the most radical members, opposed Masonry from its beginning. To Yakushkin, the ardent positivist and atheist, the mysterious rites seemed laughable.[33] To others, like Baron Steingel, who was profoundly religious, Masonry was offensive.[34] Yet a large number of the Decembrists joined the lodges, some of them participating actively for a long time.

What, then, could have attracted the Decembrists to the Masonic lodges? In the stifling Arakcheev atmosphere, writes a former Mason, the lodges served as neutral territory, oases in the desert of bureaucracy.[35] Some men were attracted merely through curiosity, or they sought only social pastime;[36] with others political aims were the chief interest.[37] Alexander N. Muraviev considered the Masonic lodges as a kind of screen behind which the secret political society

---

[28] *Ibid.*, CXXX (1907), 270; *P.S.Z.*, No. 29151.

[29] Pypin, *Obshchestvennoe dvizhenie*, 327–328; *Russky Arkhiv* (1868), 1350; *Russkaia Starina*, CIII (1900), 638–641.

[30] *Materialy*, IV, 45–46; *Russky Arkhiv*, X (1908), 218–230; III (1885), 27.

[31] *Russkoe Bogatstvo*, VII (1905), 44.

[32] *Materialy*, II, 145.

[33] *Materialy*, III, 48; Pavlov-Silvansky, N., *Sochineniia*, II, 257, 282.

[34] *Obshchestvennye dvizheniia v Rossii*, I, 15.

[35] *Russkaia Starina*, XI (1874), 466.

[36] *Ibid.*, I (1870), 155; CIII (1900), 642–643.

[37] *Russky Arkhiv*, II (1895), 171.

would be enabled to work more safely.[38] There were other men who thought that political groups could be organized within the lodges. An attempt was made in the lodge "Trois Vertus" to form a liberal group with political aims, but it met with little success.[39] Mikhail Novikov thought the lodges could render great service to the secret societies by becoming a source from which reliable men could be drawn. Some Decembrists actually joined the Masons for this purpose, but finding no responsive group, soon left them.[40] By 1822, that is, on the eve of the complete abolition of the Masonic organizations, most of the Decembrists had left the lodges, a move which was only natural since Masonry had proved too narrow a field for politically ambitious young men who sooner or later had felt the necessity of organizing societies of their own.[41] At the time the lodges were closed the Decembrists had developed considerable activity independent of the Masonic societies, and in the South a still more interesting evolution had taken place. Here the southern secret political society "Les Slaves Réunis" was a direct offshoot of the southern Masonic lodge of the same title.[42]

The affiliation of the Decembrists with the Masons, though temporary, left an indelible imprint upon the later secret political organizations. The general principles of secret organization, the nature of the oath, the initiation rites, even the symbols, and, as with the aforementioned southern society, even the name, were closely copied from the Masons. When General Orlov, one of the founders of the Decembrist organization, suggested to Turgenev that a secret political society be founded, he presented it as a lodge and explained its organization in terms of Masonic "higher degrees."[43] Turgenev, sympathetic with the ideas of Weishaupt and continually dreaming of freeing the serfs, accepted the invitation. Orlov and Turgenev then evolved a plan for combining the duties of higher-degree Masons with political aims, for example, the emancipation of the peasants. Chiefly because of Orlov's departure from the capital, the project was abandoned. But the plan is illuminating, for it shows the relationship of Masonry to the earlier

---

[38] *Materialy*, III, 20.

[39] *Ibid.*, I, 23–24, 25.

[40] *Russky Arkhiv*, IV (1897), 583.

[41] *Minuvshie Gody*, III (1908), 309–311.

[42] *Russkaia Starina*, XXI (1878), 187–189; Volkonsky, *Zapiski*, 402–403; Pypin, *Obshchestvennoe dvizhenie*, 361–364.

[43] *Materialy*, IV, 154, 168, 181–82; *Krasnyi Arkhiv*, XIII, 76–77.

liberal movement: the Masonic lodges served as a pattern for secret political societies and brought together many of the men who later led the revolt against Russian autocracy.

2. LIBERAL THOUGHT

There were factors other than the Masonic lodges which aided the spread of liberalism. According to one writer, the second half of the eighteenth century places a line of demarcation between Asiatic provincialism and European cosmopolitanism. European ideas began to reach farther east, shattering the medieval structure of society by injecting into it the liberal thought of the age of enlightenment. The roots of nineteenth-century liberalism lay in the preceding century, in which was made the first significant breach in the wall that separated lethargic Russia from the long-awakened western European countries.

The liberal tradition seems to have been well established at the beginning of the nineteenth century. There was yet no organized movement, as in Western Europe, but the idea was present. Though embryonic, it needed only time to evolve into effective opposition against the government. The Napoleonic wars, Russian participation in European affairs, and increasing contact with the West so stimulated the growth of these ideas that, when the whole of Europe, including Russia, was in the throes of postwar reaction, there was a minority in Russia to display a certain degree of open resistance. That minority refused to bend its neck to Arakcheev, the powerful favorite of Alexander, and under the shadow of the Holy Alliance and of Metternich succeeded in forming a secret political organization to oppose the onslaught of the reaction.

Contacts with Western Europe.—Direct contacts with Western Europe came through the travel of individuals and through European writings. When Peter I began to send young men to the West to be trained, they returned with something more than technical skill: they brought political and social ideas as well as a knowledge of shipbuilding and military science. The works of such writers as Grotius, Hobbes, Locke, Pufendorf, Mably, and later of Rousseau, Diderot, Montesquieu, and Voltaire were well known to many Russians. Prince M. Shcherbatov, the famous leader of the nobility during the reign of Catherine II, in his debates in the Legislative Assembly and later in his writings, displayed a profound knowledge of the political writings of Western Europe. Most of the De-

cembrists were pupils of the Encyclopedists, they were deeply
influenced by the revolutionary movement in France and other
countries, and they cherished the ideas of their predecessors,
Krechetov, Radishchev, or Pnin, the earlier liberals to suffer for
their ideals. Even such a Francophobe as Rostopchin was swayed
markedly by French literature.

Nearly all the Decembrists showed that they had acquired their
ideas of liberal political institutions through their acquaintance
with foreign literature and with the revolutionary movement in
Western Europe.[44] Many became familiar with the writings, either
in the original or in translation, of such men as Adam Smith,
De Lolme, Condorcet, Bignon, Benjamin Constant, Beccaria, Benjamin Franklin, Say, Tracy, Jeremy Bentham, Scott, Byron, Filangieri, and others.[45] In economics Adam Smith quite conquered
the minds of all thinking people. The author of *The Wealth of
Nations* was hailed as the "famous writer of our times for explaining the true origin of state economy" and as the "great man who
perceived great truths."[46]

In the early nineteenth century increasing intercourse with
Western Europe deprived Russia of her political isolation. Travel
and study abroad, particularly in Germany, became fairly common; a large number of Russian students went to the universities
of Leipzig, Heidelberg, Göttingen, Strassburg, Berlin, and Königs-
berg to be educated. Developments during the years 1812–1814
hastened the disintegration of Old Russia, brought the Russian
Empire into the family of western nations, and revealed more
clearly the striking political, social, and economic contrasts between Western Europe and backward Russia. During those tense
years many were forced into closer contact with the political order
in Russia and were repelled by its antiquated and inefficient institutions. These years disturbed the provincial existence of many
of the country people, forcing from their estates into the army
local Russian noblemen, many of whom found themselves in the
European arena where world issues were to be determined.

Return of the army from abroad.—It is scarcely to be expected
that the Russian soldier, after participating in events of such mag-

[44] *Materialy*, I, 156, 178, 226, 306–307, 343, 430, 481–482; IV, 90, 91–92;
Krasnyi Arkhiv, XIII, 164.

[45] *Vospominaniia i rasskazy deiatelei tainykh obshchestv 1820-kh godov*, I,
55. (Hereafter cited as *Vospominaniia i rasskazy*.)

[46] Tugan-Baranovsky, *Russkaia fabrika*, 72, 205.

nitude, could bring home the same views that he had held before the war. The first glimpses of the Russian veterans when they returned to their own land were depressing. Yakushkin, a prominent member of the Decembrists, describes them as follows :[47]

> From France we returned to Russia by sea. The First Division of the Guard landed at Oranienbaum and listened to the *Te Deum* performed by the Archpriest Derzhavin. During the prayer the police were mercilessly beating the people who attempted to draw nearer to the lined-up troops. This made upon us the first unfavorable impression when we returned to our homeland. . . . Finally the Emperor appeared, accompanied by the Guard, on a fine sorrel horse, with an unsheathed sword, which he was ready to lower before the Empress. We looked with delight at him. But at that very moment, almost under his horse, a peasant crossed the street. The Emperor spurred his horse and rushed with the unsheathed sword toward the running peasant. The police attacked him with their clubs. We did not believe our own eyes and turned away, ashamed for our beloved Tsar. That was my first disappointment in him; involuntarily I recalled a cat transformed into a Beauty, who, however, was unable to see a mouse without leaping upon it.

Numerous army officers, returning from France, were revolted by the administrative chaos, official abuse, and widespread bribery in their country.[48] Mikhail Fonvizin, one of the Decembrists, wrote :[49]

> During the campaigns through Germany and France our young men became acquainted with European civilization, which produced upon them the strongest impression. They were able to compare all that they had seen abroad with what confronted them at every step at home: slavery of the majority of Russians, cruel treatment of subordinates by superiors, all sorts of government abuses, and general tyranny. All this stirred intelligent Russians and provoked patriotic sentiment.

But these were only the first disappointments the returned veterans were to experience. Gradually they began to discover that they had come back to an alien country. Strange must have sounded the language of the quasi patriots, for example, Rostopchin or Shishkin, to the heroes of Borodino, Leipzig, and Paris. How laughable must have seemed the propaganda leaflets picturing the French as devils from hell; how childish the wrath of writers such as Batiushkov, who appealed to his countrymen to take vengeance on the French, "those Barbarians, Vandals, the nation of monsters who dared to talk about liberty, philosophy and love of human-

---

[47] Yakushkin, *Zapiski*, 12–13.

[48] *Russkaia Starina*, CXVI (1903), 481–499.

[49] *Obshchestvennye Dvizheniia v Rossii*, I, 183.

ity !"[50] How naïve must have seemed the national attire of those who labored to express patriotic sentiments! How disgusting the fanaticism of Prince Golitsyn, the Minister of Spiritual Affairs and Public Instruction, the blind loyalty and stupid reaction of Count Arakcheev, the venality of Magnitsky and Runich, and the ignorance of the censor Krasovsky! Says Yakushkin :[51]

In 1814 life for youth in Petersburg was tiresome. During the two years events had passed before our eyes which had determined the fate of nations and to some degree we had been participants of them. Now it was unbearable to look at the empty life in Petersburg and listen to the babbling of the old men who praised the past and reproached every progressive move. We were away from them a hundred years.

The masses who had been told that they were fighting "Napoleonic despotism" came back to find at home a régime more despotic than Napoleon's had been. After being brought into closer touch with western movements, meeting revolutionary leaders in the West, and becoming familiar with conditions in France, men could not readily submit to the old state of servitude or even passively witness it. How could the institution of serfdom be maintained, soldiers be treated like chattels, and arbitrary rule be continued undisturbed? This situation, characterized by that ultraconservative historian, Bogdanovich, as "in some respects unsatisfactory," naturally aroused indignation and deep patriotic resentment.[52] "I was at that time," recalls a contemporary, "an avowed liberal, being absorbed by this spirit during my sojourn in France. And who of the young men in those days was on the side of reaction? All were singing a constitutional song in which the leader of the choir was Emperor Alexander Pavlovich."[53]

Nationalistic influences.—To stress too greatly the influences of Western Europe upon the liberal trend in Russia would be erroneous. In many respects the movement was purely national. Numerous circles read, in addition to the literature from abroad, the writings of their countrymen : the stirring *Journey* of Radishchev, the inspiring poetry of Griboedov, the patriotic poems of Ryleev, and the delightful verses of Pushkin, so often directed against the government. All these moved men not only to think but also to act.

---

[50] *Russkaia Starina*, V (1883), 349.

[51] Yakushkin, *Zapiski*, 13.

[52] Bogdanovich, *op. cit.*, VI, 413; Volkonsky, *op. cit.*, 387.

[53] *Russkaia Starina*, IV (1871), 491.

Nor were the constitutional projects of the Decembrists blindly copied from western patterns. The Decembrists never intended, as one of the survivors has stated, "to transplant France into Russia."[54] True, the revolutionary movement in the West served as a stimulus for action, but that action was necessitated by national conditions. The policy of the secret societies as well as their political plans had to be adjusted to the peculiar national environment. Kliuchevsky fittingly remarks that, whereas the fathers of the Decembrists "had been educated to become Frenchmen, the fathers' sons were French-educated men longing to become Russian." Despite the ugly forms of patriotism which arose during the war, there were also indications of a healthy national renaissance after 1815. Writers like Pushkin, Griboedov, Lermontov, Ryleev, the pride of Russian literature, can be truly considered children of that national revival. Among the Decembrists were men, who, though admitting that Russia had much to learn from Western Europe, insisted that it should also value its national traditions and individual character.[55]

About this time various circles in which political affairs were discussed came into being, and many people began to study social science and economics.[56] Certain private homes became centers of coteries to consider current topics.[57] Here political views were crystallized and gradually formulated into definite theories or beliefs. Domestic and foreign problems were debated and the *status quo* was severely criticized. Russia's rôle in the suppression of the liberal movement in the West and the national aspirations of the Greeks was branded as treason, and Alexander's submission to Metternich's schemes was felt to be unpatriotic.[58] There was a popular demand that Alexander should cease to be a European monarch and become once more the Russian Emperor; that he should cease to be a constitutional monarch on the Vistula and an autocrat on the Neva and that he should introduce reforms to alleviate the terrible burden on the people.

The government paid little attention to these well-justified de-

---

[54] *Russky Arkhiv* (1870), 1636–1637.

[55] Fonvizin, M., "O podrazhanii russkikh inostrannym." *Biblioteka Dekabristov*, Series IV, 104–108.

[56] Yakushkin, *op. cit.*, 13–14.

[57] Lorer, *Zapiski dekabrista*, 66–67; *Literaturnye salony i kruzhki*, 43–92 *passim*.

[58] *Vospominaniia i rasskazy*, I, 76; Basargin, *Zapiski*, 10.

mands, fearing any concession to the liberals lest it result, as
Rostopchin warned, in a "Russia broken into pieces, crushed under
a foreign yoke." This attitude only stimulated the transformation
of the coteries into secret political societies, which eventually gave
rise to the Decembrist movement. Before considering this movement, however, it is necessary to relate one more incident, the revolt of the Semenovsky regiment, which helped to intensify the
unrest in the country.

3. THE FIRST SIGNAL: THE SEMENOVSKY INCIDENT

Military service for a private during the first half of the nineteenth century was nothing less than a calamity. Aside from the
extreme length of the term, twenty-five years, army life was intolerable. Corporal punishment for the least offense, emphasis upon
triviality, accuracy of step and uniform, were matters of stringent
importance. Even the most disciplined units grumbled against the
unnecessary cruelty.[59] The revolt of the Semenovsky regiment lifts
the curtain only slightly on those sorrowful conditions. If in this
regiment, the pride of the Emperor, violence against the terrible
conditions could finally break out, one can imagine the plight of
other regiments.[60]

The Semenovsky regiment.—The Semenovsky regiment was the
most favored and beloved of Alexander I.[61] The Emperor used to
say: "The Preobrazhensky regiment is a royal regiment, but the
Semenovsky regiment is mine."[62] Its officers were all of the higher
nobility and many of the educated liberals among them were participants in the Decembrist movement. Relations between privates
and officers were cordial and the shameful corporal punishment
had been abolished. Notwithstanding these apparent leniencies,
discipline was maintained, and the regiment, during the entire
period of the Napoleonic wars, endured all the hardships of the
campaigns without a sign of insubordination. In 1815 it returned

[59] Muraviev-Apostol, M. I., *Vospominaniia i pisma*, 43; *Dekabristy. Sbornik
otryvkov iz istochnikov*, 60–63 (hereafter cited as *Dekabristy*); *Materialy*, V,
42–43, 406–407; *Russky Arkhiv* (1866), 1255–1257, 1432–1433.

[60] *Russky Arkhiv*, I (1875), 349.

[61] Shortly after the uprising Alexander wrote from Troppau: "Personne n'a
pu en être plus profondément peiné que moi. L'attachement personnel que j'ai
toujours porté à ce régiment, pour y avoir servi moi-même, l'honneur de l'uni-
forme russe, la gloire de l'armée, tout s'est trouvé atteint, heurté, par cette
scandaleuse sédition."—*Russky Arkhiv*, I (1875), 349.

[62] *Russkaia Starina*, IV (1883), 83.

to St. Petersburg from abroad, with a record of which any military unit might be proud.[63]

To the conservatives who were unable to conceive of military discipline without corporal punishment and other cruelty, the spirit prevailing in the Semenovsky regiment did not seem right. Grand Duke Nicholas, later Emperor, who was in command of the first and second brigades of the bodyguard, thought this spirit seemed "loose and extremely corrupted." "Subordination disappeared," he complained, "and was preserved only at the front; respect for officers completely vanished, and military appearance was only on paper." The Grand Duke could not realize that soldiers who had returned from western fronts, visited European countries, and witnessed the significant political life of France could no longer be treated as chattels.[64]

In 1815, the same year in which the Semenovsky regiment returned from abroad, a certain subscription was sponsored by Arakcheev. Either because it was backed by Arakcheev or for some other reason, not a single officer of the Semenovsky regiment contributed to it. Arakcheev did not wait long to demonstrate his displeasure.[65]

Schwarz and his discipline.—In 1820 Arakcheev and the Grand Duke Mikhail Pavlovich succeeded in dismissing General Potëmkin, an excellent and highly respected officer of the Semenovsky regiment, and appointed in his place Colonel Schwarz.[66] The soldiers were sorely displeased, for Colonel Schwarz, according to one of his contemporaries, was an officer who "though not a great fighter, had the gift of arousing greater hatred among the soldiers than the cruelest tormentor."[67] Immediately after taking over his duties, Schwarz restored corporal punishment and introduced brutal and humiliating penalties.[68] On October 16, 1820, a number of soldiers with brilliant records from their former service, whose chests were decorated with the highest honor, the cross of St. George, were flogged. This action violated an old tradition, for the members of the order of St. George were usually exempt from such a penalty.

---

[63] *Russky Arkhiv*, XI (1902), 410–411.

[64] Presniakov, *Apogei samoderzhaviia*, 21; Semevsky, *op. cit.*, 128–130.

[65] Muraviev-Apostol, *op. cit.*, 42.

[66] *Russkaia Starina*, III (1883), 687–688.

[67] *Russky Arkhiv*, XI (1902), 417–419. Cf. *ibid.*, II (1903), 279–283.

[68] *Russkaia Starina*, V (1873), 636; IV (1871), 534; IV (1883), 85–86; Lorer, *op. cit.*, 58–59.

Mutiny.—The breach proved too much for the old veterans, heroes of the recent campaigns. Next evening, during the hour assigned for muster roll, the First Company asked their sergeant-major to file a complaint and demanded that the chief of the company be called. When he appeared, the soldiers declared that they could no longer endure the existing conditions and that he must accept the complaint against Colonel Schwarz.[69] The chief, Captain Kashkarev, was embarrassed, knowing that such a complaint would only complicate matters. He therefore attempted to persuade the soldiers to recall the complaint, but they refused to listen to his advice and declared that they were expressing the opinion of the entire regiment. The next day the First Company was placed under arrest in the fortress, but the remaining eleven companies immediately went out, demanding either the release of their comrades and the dismissal of "that German" [Colonel Schwarz] or that they be allowed to join their imprisoned comrades. The authorities sent the whole regiment to the fortress and later dispersed it among various military units.[70]

Results of the Semenovsky incident.—Many soldiers of the disbanded Semenovsky regiment were sent at first to Finland and later to the Caucasus. In spite of the clemency which was generally expected, some were sentenced to be flogged and sent to Siberia, to Orenburg, or to Omsk; others later found themselves in various regiments located in the South.[71] A large number were sent to the Third Corps, in which the southern Decembrists had placed so much hope.[72] The strangest thing about the affair was that Colonel Schwarz was found guilty by the trial commission of cruelty and negligence, but Alexander, in consideration of his excellent record, only dismissed him from his post. In 1828, however, Colonel Schwarz entered the army again, and, when some twenty-two years later a court martial found him guilty of torturing soldiers, he was dismissed for life and forbidden to reside in the capital. Thirty years were required to obtain justice![73]

Certain consequences derived from the Semenovsky incident. Some of the officers of the dispersed regiment never abandoned relations with their old veteran-friends; among these was Muraviev-

[69] *Russky Arkhiv*, II (1875), 126; *Dekabristy. Sbornik materialov*, 142–145.
[70] *Russky Arkhiv*, II (1875), 419–431, 437.
[71] *Ibid.*, III (1875), 420; *Russkaia Starina*, IV (1883), 78–82.
[72] *Materialy*, IV, 385.
[73] Semevsky, *op. cit.*, 163.

Apostol, one of the leading southern Decembrists. He met with the soldiers secretly, having friendly discourse with them on political questions, disseminating discontent, hoping that when the hour of revolt should come, these faithful veterans would support the uprising; and a great number of them did participate in the southern revolution of 1825.[74] Instead of preventing or at least localizing the spirit of rebellion, the measures taken by the government only spread it over a wider area. The Semenovsky incident was the prologue of the December drama of 1825.

The uprising had also its political effect. The news of the affair reached Alexander while he was in Troppau, where the European diplomats had assembled to solve important continental problems, and made a painful impression upon the Emperor and his suite.[75] In despair he drew still closer to Metternich's schemes for maintaining peace in Europe. Two days after the news was delivered to him, Alexander wrote to Arakcheev that he suspected the cause of the rebellion was not Schwarz's cruel treatment of the soldiers. Both Alexander and Grand Duke Constantine believed that the real cause of the revolt lay in the activities of the Masonic lodges and other secret societies opposed to the work of coöperation with Austria at Troppau as well as to the "general mental infection" that had caused the unrest.[76]

The belief that the revolt was caused by underground societies increased when there was scattered among the soldiers in the capital a secret leaflet, the contents of which, revolutionary in nature, appealed to them to rise against the régime in power. Proclaiming Emperor and nobility guilty of responsibility for the condition of the country, the pamphlet called for the overthrow of the "tyrant" and the establishment of a representative government elected by the . . . army![77] The author of this leaflet was never discovered. At first Karazin was suspected, arrested, kept in prison for six months, and afterwards exiled to his estate.[78] This man was the same Karazin whom Alexander had once requested to talk openly and always

---

[74] On the propaganda among the soldiers of the disbanded Semenovsky regiment, see *Materialy*, IV, *passim*. On the actual participation of the former soldiers of the Semenovsky regiment in the later southern revolution, see *Materialy*, IV, 371–384, 390, and VI, *passim*, which is of particular importance.

[75] *S.I.R.I.O.*, LXXIII, 22–24; *Russkaia Starina*, IV (1871), 255.

[76] *C.I.O.I.D.R.*, IV (1864), 188–192; *Russkaia Starina*, I (1870), 63–64; IV (1883), 87–88; Schilder, *op. cit.*, IV, 185–186.

[77] *Dekabristy*, 37–40; *Byloe*, II (1907), 83–86.

[78] *Istorichesky Viestnik*, LXXIX (1900), 1047–1053.

to tell the Emperor the truth. For some time Muraviev-Apostol, the later Decembrist, was believed to be implicated in the affair, but he was not molested. The incident remains to this day a mystery, but the matter seriously alarmed Alexander, who from then on wholeheartedly adhered to Metternich's political doctrines and agreed to all his plans.[79] Metternich could claim a great victory, for his opportunity, which required Alexander's coöperation, had come in time to show that Russia was not immune to the revolutionary disease which, since 1815, the Austrian statesman had endeavored to cure.

Discontent in the army was not confined to the uprising in the Semenovsky regiment: it ran deeper than this single and more dramatic occurrence. General unrest among the soldiers, whose lot was unbearable, increased so greatly that in 1821 a special police was established for the army.[80] Ten days after the Semenovsky revolt a contemporary closely associated with the affair, in writing to Count Vorontsov about the incident, made the following interesting statement:[81]

Carbonari appear only when a people is led to a state of despair, and we have the elements for its appearance, beginning with the defenders of the state themselves. The military men are the only ones who are esteemed in our country, and at the same time they are the most unfortunate people. The despair of the Semenovsky regiment proves it more than anything else.

Army life with its stupid discipline and its trampling of the least expression of individual self-respect produced at last sufficient explosive material, for the many had nothing to lose and everything to gain in a revolution. The authorities feared that the Semenovsky incident might be followed by outbreaks in other regiments, and there was reason for such fear.[82] Among the documents now available are records of the strong propaganda that was being disseminated in the army by members of the Decembrist society. "Pray," asks one of these members, who endeavored to persuade his comrade to join the society, "in whom do you have hope?" The reply was: "My hope is God." Then follows an argument which deserves quotation.[83]

[79] *Memoirs of Prince Metternich*, III, 402.

[80] Zablotsky-Desiatovsky, *Graf P. D. Kiselev i ego vremia*, I, 156–157.

[81] *Arkhiv kn. Vorontsova*, XXIII, 420; *Istorichesky Viestnik*, IX (1882), 665–666.

[82] *Russky Arkhiv*, II (1875), 329.

[83] *Materialy*, IV, 307–308; *Russky Arkhiv*, VI (1902), 294.

But your hope is unsound. . . . We advise you to listen to us. You do not know our intentions yet. . . . You could do some good deed by convincing the lower ranks and filling their hearts with the belief that as long as the Romanov family existed there will be no good. If we get together we will destroy the burdens of the people and the army, who are oppressed by unnecessary and useless misery. . . . All will be corrected when we coöperate together. Then we will have a constitution, the peasants will be freed, you will be free and will receive reward for your unwarranted penalty.

These were the aims of many men: a constitution and compensation for "unwarranted penalty." The hope of obtaining improved conditions through legal channels had faded; no other recourse remained to the younger generation than to resort to revolutionary action. Forced upon them, this idea was gaining ground, creating a wider cleavage between the ruling class and the generation seeking the introduction of constitutional government. Not Arakcheev with his iron military rule, nor the rigorous censorship of Krasovsky, nor the religious bigotry of Golitsyn and his policy of "Christian education" could check the growing opposition. "Oh, Sovereign," Steingel endeavored to explain from prison, "to eradicate free thinking there is no other means than to destroy a whole generation of men, born and educated during the last reign!"[84] Not until many years later did the government discover this truth, when in the Crimea, under the thundering guns of the more advanced European nations, Russia met shameful defeat.

From 1820 on, various political groups began to organize secret societies with revolutionary aims, similar to those of Western Europe.[85] These developments opened the way directly to the catastrophe of December 14, 1825.

---

[84] *Iz pisem i pokazanii dekabristov*, 70.

[85] *Materialy*, I, 482 (No. 4, paragraph 2); IV, 102–103, 104; Turgenev, *op. cit.*, I, 94–95.

Chapter III

THE RISE OF THE DECEMBRIST SOCIETY

EARLIER IDEAS OF SECRET SOCIETIES

MANY MEN accepted the idea of secret political organization in the first quarter of the nineteenth century. This was the time of secret Masonic lodges, the German *Tugendbund*, Italian and Spanish *Carbonari*, and Greek *Hetairia Philike*. In Russia the idea was conceived simultaneously by several men who later became prominent in the Decembrist movement. General Mikhail Orlov, Nicholas Turgenev, and Nikita Muraviev all had vague ideas of secret organization as a means of achieving certain political reforms. In 1811, Nicholas Muraviev, founder of the military school in St. Petersburg, under the influence of Rousseau's *Social Contract* attempted to organize a secret society which he thought would lead to the establishment of a new social order. This could be accomplished, he believed, only on some distant island, presumably Sakhalin, where a virgin soil would be favorable to the new society.[1] But the war of 1812 destroyed the amusing dream of this youth. Another attempt was made, in Poltava Gubernia in southern Russia by Peter Borisov, a cadet, who founded a group or "Pythagorean Sect" called the Society of Friends of Nature. This organization, which was the forerunner of the Society of United Slavs, about which more will be said elsewhere, aimed to establish a republic like that of Plato.[2] Plans like these were usually vague, impractical, and sentimental, but they indicate the general mood of the younger people who were seeking social improvement and who realized the shortcomings of the contemporary régime.

The rise of the idea of secret organization simultaneously in various parts of Russia is attributable to several factors: contacts

[1] Semevsky, *Politicheskie i obshchestvennye idei dekabristov*, 379–380. Somewhat similar idealistic plans were later developed by the Decembrist, D. Zavalishin. See *Pamiati Dekabristov; Sbornik materialov*, III, 127; also *Gosudarstvennye prestupleniia v Rossii v XIX vieke*, I, 57; *Russkaia Starina*, XXX (1881), 491–492.

[2] Nechkina, *Obshchestvo Soedinënnykh Slavian*, 20–23; Semevsky, *op. cit.*, 310–311.

in the army, where the young men met and found common interests, opposition to the policy of the government after the war, and acquaintance with similar situations and conspiratory societies in Western Europe. The awakening social consciousness was trying to find some outlet; instead, it met government suppression. For example, when the officers of the Semenovsky regiment organized a sort of club where they dined together, read, and discussed various political and social problems, Alexander expressed his disapproval.[3] Denial of freedom of speech and of the press and of the right to assemble even for the most innocent purposes compelled the more ambitious youths to pursue their ideas secretly.

In 1814, while abroad, General Mikhail Orlov became acquainted with the German *Tugendbund,* a patriotic organization which had sprung up at the time of Napoleon's invasion of Prussia. Its chief aim was to educate the masses and stimulate patriotic sentiment.[4] The constitution of this society seems to have impressed General Orlov favorably. Inspired by the *Tugendbund* and by Alexander's declaration in Paris, "Our external enemies are defeated, let us now fight the internal enemies," Orlov returned to Russia, retired from the army, and occupied himself with administrative work in order "to eradicate the internal Napoleons."

Orlov revealed his plans to Count Dmitriev-Mamonov, a liberal nobleman who had become famous for his generosity during the campaign of 1812.[5] Count Dmitriev-Mamonov, being a practical man, warned Orlov that the "internal Napoleons" were much stronger than the external Napoleon had been, and that he doubted whether they could be so easily overcome. Not discouraged by the difficulties the two men agreed to coöperate and to do everything possible to achieve what European countries in the West had accomplished. Another reason for Orlov's ambition to act speedily was his concern over Alexander's policy toward Poland, which he considered dangerous. His personal appeal to the Emperor to change this policy being disregarded, Orlov decided that there remained but one recourse—a conspiratory society.[6] If fulfillment of the patriotic mission required this step, Orlov was willing to go that far, for the country was in distress, he thought, and the need

---

[3] Yakushkin, I., *Zapiski,* 14.

[4] Lehmann, *Der Tugendbund,* 152, paragraphs 2–3.

[5] *Russkaia Starina,* IV (1890), 175–184; *Russky Arkhiv* (1868), 95–98.

[6] *Krasnyi Arkhiv,* XIII, 160; Turgenev, *Rossiia i russkie,* I, 63; *Russkaia Starina,* XII (1877), 661–662.

for reforms was paramount. After all, "one can belong to a secret society and at the same time remain a noble character," Orlov endeavored to explain to Nicholas I after the abortive revolt.[7]

In 1816 Orlov and Dmitriev-Mamonov agreed upon general principles and began work on a plan for the foundation of a secret organization. They invited Nicholas Turgenev to join them, but he rejected the offer, considering the project impracticable. The name of the proposed society, the "Order of Russian Knights," was characteristic of the time. According to the program it was to be a semi-Masonic, militantly nationalistic society, aiming at a limited aristocratic monarchy. The plan was a total failure, but it is interesting as one of the earliest of the modest attempts to form a conspiratory political society.[8]

1. THE UNION OF SALVATION

The first organization to lay a basis for the Decembrist Society was established in St. Petersburg on February 9, 1816, under the name of *Union of Salvation* or *Society of True and Faithful Sons of the Fatherland*.[9] The founders included a few close friends: Alexander Muraviev, Nikita Muraviev, Prince Sergei Trubetskoi, Ivan Yakushkin, Matvei and Sergei Muraviev-Apostol, all officers of the Guard and members of the high nobility.[10] The establishment of the Society came about very simply. The officers mentioned gathered in St. Petersburg, at the home of Muraviev-Apostol, where Nikita Muraviev suggested the organization of a secret political group. After a short discussion the six men wholeheartedly agreed that in the interests of Russia such an organization was desirable.[11] They also agreed that a constitution should be drawn up and that upon unanimous approval new members should be enrolled. It is interesting to note that of these six, four were officers of the Semenovsky regiment and participants in the activities of the club mentioned above. This handful of young men formed the nucleus of the later Decembrist movement. Soon they enrolled a few new

---

[7] *Krasnyi Arkhiv*, XIII, 161.

[8] *Iz pisem i pokazanii dekabristov*, 145–157. The failure may also be ascribed to the fact that in 1817 Count Dmitriev-Mamonov became insane. See *Istorichesky Viestnik*, II (1887), 357–363; *Russkaia Starina*, CXVII, 491–493; *Dakabrist N. I. Turgenev. Pis'ma k bratu S. I. Turgenevu* (M., 1936), *passim*.

[9] *Materialy*, I, 9.

[10] *Ibid.*, I, 9, 298; II, 198, 203, 204; III, 6, 42, 55; IV, 100, 256, 273–274.

[11] Yakushkin, *op. cit.*, 15–16.

members, among them Pavel Pestel, who was to play the most prominent rôle in the events that were to follow, Mikhail Fonvizin, and, somewhat later, Mikhail Orlov.[12] The enrollment of Pestel was of special significance; he was the ablest leader in the entire group.

Pavel Pestel.—The appearance of Pestel, that typical Russian Jacobin, marks a new epoch in the history of the Society. Pavel Ivanovich Pestel, whose father was governor-general of Siberia and notorious for his corrupt administration, was born on July 24, 1793. At the age of twelve he was sent to Germany to be educated and he returned four years later to graduate with special honors from the St. Petersburg Military Academy.[13] In the war of 1812–1814, Pestel took part in the famous battle of Borodino, where he was seriously wounded. After the war he was appointed aide-de-camp to General Witgenstein, and in 1821, when twenty-seven, he was promoted to the rank of colonel and given the command of the Viatsky regiment.[14]

Until Pestel came into the Union of Salvation there was some uncertainty, but with him a definite course was begun. Pestel was a born leader and conspirator. He had a broad education, clear vision, and possessed an iron will;[15] he was well versed in political theory and international affairs; his erudition impressed many of his acquaintances: after a conversation with Pestel, Pushkin wrote the following in his diary for April 9, 1821 :[16]

Morning spent with Pestel. A wise man in the complete sense of the word.... We have had a conversation on metaphysics, politics, morality, etc. One of the most original minds I know.

Through his devotion of heart and soul to the cause of the Society Pestel won the leadership of the movement and the admiration of many members of the organization. Writes Yakushkin :[17]

Pestel always talked wisely and stubbornly defended his opinion, in the truth of which he always believed as is usually believed of a mathematical truth. He was never misled by unattainable political ideals. Perhaps this was the reason why, among all of us, during the ten years, he alone did not weaken for a moment but worked ardently in the interests of the secret society.

---

[12] *Materialy*, I, 136–137; III, 72, 98; IV, 100; *Krasnyi Arkhiv*, XIII, 160–162.

[13] Pavlov-Silvansky, *Dekabrist Pestel*, 6–8.

[14] *Materialy*, VIII, 375.

[15] Basargin, *Zapiski*, 4, 8.

[16] Pushkin, *Sochineniia* (St. Petersburg, 1903), V, 347.

[17] Yakushkin, *op. cit.*, 30; *Krasnyi Arkhiv*, XIII, 161; cf. *ibid.*, XIII, 94.

Returning from Western Europe filled with revolutionary spirit, Pestel plunged immediately into political activities, and until the end of his life was occupied with one purpose: to introduce the republican form of government into Russia.

Aims of the Union.—From the beginning the aims of the Union of Salvation seem to have been vague.[18] Later testimony of the Decembrists shows that the program of this society comprised the emancipation of the peasants and the introduction of a constitutional monarchy.[19] Other Decembrists, among them Yakushkin, maintained that the Union sought to rid the country of foreigners and of alien influence in general.[20] The Union of Salvation, according to the same authorities, limited its activities to moral propaganda alone. Pestel, however, testified that the Society "was a revolutionary organization from the very foundation and during its entire existence did not cease to be such." Furthermore, Yakushkin stated that the objectives of the Society, known only to the members of the highest degree, were representative government and the refusal to take the oath of allegiance to the new sovereign unless he agreed to a limited monarchy.[21] These aims are important to bear in mind, for they appear to set the precedent for the fatal uprising of December 14, 1825.

According to Alexander Muraviev, the aim of the Society was to prepare Russia for constitutional government, which the Society sought to achieve through education and the enrollment of new members.[22] Among the papers seized belonging to one of the members, an illuminating *Instruction* was found, designed for members of the Decembrist Society. It advised each member to protest against Arakcheev's reign, the military colonies, serfdom, and corporal punishment. Each member was pledged to oppose the idleness of the nobility, blind confidence in authorities, and cruelty and negligence of the police and of the courts, and to demand public trial.[23] Judging from the various testimonies and memoirs, one may safely conclude that originally the aim of the Society was social reform tinged with a strongly nationalistic sentiment and the establishment of a moderate constitutional government.

---

[18] *Materialy*, I, 17; III, 18, 42; IV, 256.

[19] *Ibid.*, III, 122; IV, 154.

[20] *Ibid.*, III, 49.

[21] *Ibid.*, III, 49; IV, 154, 177.

[22] *Ibid.*, III, 6; I, 258–259.   [23] *Dekabristy*, 69.

Division of opinion.—Though originally a small circle, the Society soon began to show definite political cleavages.[24] A majority of the members were willing to accept a mild political program, but they opposed revolutionary plans, favoring a somewhat flexible party organization and the employment of legal methods. A minority showed an inclination toward revolutionary action and even, if necessary, regicide. The Union of Salvation was too small an organization to withstand a split within its ranks and too weak to endure such diverse views. For a short time, therefore, it underwent a critical test of existence, nearly coming to an end in 1817. This fact provoked Pestel's sardonic remark that Russia must first produce an *Encyclopédie* before it could think of a revolution.[25]

But the Society was not destined to disappear so easily. In an effort to organize it on a firmer basis, a special committee was elected and authorized to draft a constitution and provide for a reorganization. The committee, which consisted of four members, included Pestel.[26] Pestel immediately became the center of this committee, for, of all the members, he alone had definite plans for the Society, the program it should adopt, and the tactics it should follow.[27] To Pestel mere theory was senseless. He therefore began to urge the committee to espouse a definite goal, including a constitutional monarchy, the emancipation of the peasants, and various political reforms. He also insisted that the Society remain a strictly secret organization and elect a member to act as president, with dictatorial powers and the responsibility of executing the program. From the beginning Pestel's ambition was practical and explicit. He demanded that every member of the Society pledge himself not to retire from any civil or military position that he might happen to hold, so that in the event of revolution the important positions in the state would be in the hands of members of the secret Society.[28] Should Alexander I fail to grant reforms in his lifetime, his successor was to be refused the oath unless he pledged himself to a limited monarchy.

Constitution of the Union.—In February, 1817, the committee completed the constitution for the Society, a document which clearly showed the influence of the Masonic lodges and other nine-

---

[24] *Obshchestvennye Dvizheniia*, I, 187.
[25] *Materialy*, IV, 179.
[26] *Materialy*, IV, 113.
[27] Dovnar-Zapolsky, *Memuary dekabristov*, 46.
[28] Yakushkin, *op. cit.*, 19.

teenth-century secret organizations.[29] In accordance with this constitution the members were divided into four groups of "degrees,"
each having its own elaborate initiation and pledge of loyalty.[30]
These degrees were as follows: Boyars, Elders (*Muzhia*), Brethren, and Friends. The Boyars were the original founders of the
Society, who elected from among themselves the Supreme Council.
The second group, the Elders, were the initiated members, who,
though they had joined later, were informed of the real aims of the
Society.[31] The Brethren were only on probation; they were pledged
to strive for the aims of the Society, though they knew little either
of the organization or its real purpose. The fourth group, the
Friends, were merely the sympathizers from among whom the
Society sought its prospective candidates.[32]

Opposing the constitution arose particularly Yakushkin, supported by Fonvizin, who considered the whole organization too
rigid. He demanded democratization of the Society, and for this
purpose about the middle of 1817 he went to St. Petersburg where,
along with Trubetskoi, he insisted upon a moderate policy and the
"gradual influencing of public opinion" rather than revolutionary
action. Pestel opposed this policy and urged more decisive action,
endeavoring to show how France had prospered under the Committee of Public Safety and to convince the members of the Union
of Salvation that radical measures were sometimes imperative.
This, writes Prince Trubetskoi, made an unfavorable impression
and left among the conservative members a lasting distrust of
Pestel.[33] Among such diverse opinions, progress seemed very difficult. For a time activities were chiefly concerned with propaganda,
though attention was also given to the enrollment of new members.
Each member was instructed to lead a virtuous life, resist all evil
in the state, proclaim abuses of the authorities, find new reliable
members, and watch the conduct of his fellow-members.

Reorganization of the Union.—Notwithstanding the elaborate
organization and ambitious political aims, the Union of Salvation
shortly came to a standstill, the more conservative element suggest-

---

[29] *Materialy*, IV, 154, 168, 181–182.

[30] *Ibid.*, I, 305.

[31] *Ibid.*, IV, 47, Answer 2.

[32] *Ibid.*, I, 17, 24–25; III, 18, 49; IV, 111.

[33] Trubetskoi, *Zapiski*, 12–13. Orlov in his Memorandum to Nicholas I also
remarks about the "general lack of confidence" in Pestel. See *Krasnyi Arkhiv*,
XIII, 161; *Materialy*, I, 305–306; IV, 214, 223.

ing that it be dissolved completely. But a handful of leaders remained firm, loyally continuing to carry on the principles which the Society had laid down at its foundation and determined to redouble their efforts to establish a better social order. In 1817 the entire Court, accompanied by the Guard, went to Moscow to commemorate the war of 1812 by founding the Church of Christ the Savior, and remained there nearly ten months. Since virtually all members of the Union of Salvation were in the Guard, they found themselves together and arranged a conference at which it was decided to undertake a radical reorganization of the Society. The assembled members decided to dissolve the old, cumbersome organization and to set up a temporary one, called the Military Society, under the leadership of two members.[34] At the same time a committee, consisting of four members, was named to draft a new constitution.[35]

The conference proceeded under the influence of certain news which had produced considerable tension. It was at the time when military colonies were being mercilessly enforced by Arakcheev,[36] the Polish constitution had just been granted, and Alexander's speech at the opening of the Diet had been delivered at Warsaw. To add to the excitement, shortly before the arrival of the Emperor, a letter came from Trubetskoi in St. Petersburg, reporting persistent rumors that Alexander favored an autonomous Poland and was considering the removal of the capital to Warsaw and the annexation to Poland of some of the bordering Russian provinces.[37] This news was communicated to the convened members, and, though sheer nonsense, it produced such indignation that the assassination of Alexander was seriously proposed. A number of men, among them Lunin, Yakushkin, Alexander Muraviev, showed their readiness to carry out the terroristic act.[38] It was only after a discussion lasting through the day and night that the plan was abandoned. Yakushkin was so disappointed that he withdrew and for three years remained aloof. Not till 1821, because "he knew too much" of the Society's affairs, was he persuaded to join again.

While the members of the Union were in conference they received the text of the *Tugendbund* constitution, which a colleague had obtained in Germany. The committee which was to draft the

[34] *Materialy*, III, 36.

[35] *Ibid.*, III, 18.   [37] *Ibid.*, I, 49, 51–52, 139; III, 6, 10.

[36] *Ibid.*, IV, 112.   [38] *Ibid.*, I, 277, 306; III, 53, 73, 122; IV, 256.

new constitution made a study of the document, modified it, and
after four months' labor produced what they called the *Green Book*
or *A Code of the Union of Welfare.* This became the constitution
of the society known as the Union of Welfare.[39] This Union was
destined to maintain itself for a much longer period than had the
Union of Salvation, to expand its activities, and to play a greater
rôle in the Decembrist movement than that of the earlier Union.

2. THE UNION OF WELFARE

The Green Book.—With the completion of the new constitution,
the constitution of the Union of Salvation was discarded, and the
new society, the Union of Welfare, came into being. The temporary
Military Society which had succeeded the Union of Salvation was
dissolved, and its former members joined the new organization.[40]
The constitution of the Union of Welfare, known as the Green
Book, was closely copied from the constitution of the German
Tugendbund.[41] A few changes were made in order to adjust the
document to the needs of the Union, and they throw a significant
sidelight upon its nature. From a political point of view the Green
Book proved more liberal than the constitution of the *Tugendbund;* from an economic standpoint, however, it was more conservative. For example, certain articles were omitted; namely, the
clauses whereby each member of the *Tugendbund* pledged loyalty
to the Sovereign, swore to protect the dynasty from "the onslaught
of the immoral spirit of the time," and to spy on members and report all treason.[42] However, the Green Book also lacked the provision of the original constitution which obligated every person who
joined the *Tugendbund* to pledge the emancipation of his serfs.[43]

The preface of the Green Book stated that it was the hope of the
Union of Welfare that the government would consider the society
favorably. This hope was justified by a reference to Catherine's
well-known *Instruction,* where similar doctrines, such as the necessity of public education, had been advocated.[44] Membership in the
society, the introduction states further, was open to all Russian

---

[39] *Materialy,* I, 305.

[40] *Ibid.,* I, 307; Yakushkin, *op. cit.,* 31–32; *Obshchestvennye Dvizheniia v
Rossii,* I, 22–23.

[41] *Materialy,* I, 329; *Krasnyi Arkhiv,* XIII, 77.

[42] Lehmann, *Der Tugendbund,* 152, Art. 8; 184, Art. 184ff.

[43] *Ibid.,* 156, Art. 21–22.

[44] The Constitution of the Union of Welfare, Book I, Art. 4.

male citizens eighteen years of age, irrespective of class, provided they were Christians. Every member was expected to lead a socially virtuous life and to assist his fellow-members whenever necessary.[45]

Organization of the Union of Welfare.—According to the Green Book the organization of the Union of Welfare was to be as follows. The members who accepted the constitution were to elect six persons to form the Supreme Council (*Korennoi Soviet*). The whole society was divided into "administrations" (*upravy*), each administration being headed by a chairman to oversee the activities of the members of the group entrusted to him, and every member had to belong to an "administration." The chairman of each group was obliged to make regular reports to the Supreme Council concerning the activities of his respective administration.[46] The Union of Welfare eliminated all former elaborate initiation ceremonies, against which many complaints had been launched. New members were accepted through the general agreement of the members of the administration. The initiates were merely pledged to maintain secrecy and to obey all society rules.[47]

Four fields of activity.—Analyzing the new constitution more closely, one finds that political activities seem to be entirely excluded. All problems relating to political life were expected to be solved by time—in the distant future.[48] Meanwhile, the Union of Welfare offered to its members four different fields of activity: philanthropy, education, justice, and national economy. By philanthropic activity the society meant taking charge of hospitals or orphanages, seeking prison reforms, establishing unemployment agencies and homes for the aged and invalid, or advocating among landlords the humane treatment of the serfs.[49] In the field of education each member was expected to assist in the building of schools, to train children to love their country and revere their national culture more than foreign culture, to participate in scientific and literary societies, and to fight various forms of corruption in the state and the abuse of soldiers in the army.[50] In the

[45] *Ibid.*, Book II, Art. 2.
[46] *Ibid.*, Book III, Art. 1–15; *Materialy*, I, 106–107, 230.
[47] *Materialy*, I, 17–18, 26, 250–251.
[48] *Ibid.*, I, 230, 258–259; *Dekabristy*, 84–102; *Obshchestvennye dvizheniia v Rossii*, I, 207.
[49] The Constitution of the Union of Welfare, Book IV, Art. 9–22.
[50] *Ibid.*, IV, Art. 23–55.

field of justice members were urged to accept various legal and political appointments and in such capacities to oppose bribery and other evils, to report all noticed violations of the law, and to prevent the sale of serfs and other persons into the army.[51] Finally, under the national economy, the society recommended that its members strive for agricultural, industrial, and commercial development, and for the establishment of insurance companies and other agencies which would stimulate national prosperity.[52]

It may be stated at the beginning that in all these fields very little was achieved. In the first place, it is to be noted that the entire problem of serfdom was limited to the modest advice to members to advocate the humane treatment of serfs. The question of emancipation was left to individual discretion. Such a policy suggests that the Union hesitated to express a definitely negative view upon the most vital of the national issues. A number of members attempted to free their serfs, but they met with little success. The failure is explained chiefly by the fact that individual action could solve nothing in a problem of such magnitude as serfdom. Also, the government placed all kinds of difficulties in the way of emancipation, discouraging both peasants and landlords from beginning the complicated legal process.[53] There were similar failures in other fields. Some of the members organized Lancasterian schools; a number of them introduced various improvements in their regiments, and others joined various circles, such as the literary organization known as the Society of the Green Lamp.[54] But all these attempts were suppressed by the heavy hand of the authorities before they could achieve any real significance.

Conservatism of the Green Book.—The Green Book impressed even contemporary readers as a moderate, if not entirely conservative, social document. That it was innocent of revolutionary ideas may be inferred from the fact that originally a number of members suggested that it be submitted to the Emperor for official approval, as was done in a similar situation in 1808 in Prussia. But to do so was considered unwise; it was thought better that the organization should remain strictly secret.[55] When General Orlov

---

[51] *Ibid.*, IV., Art. 56–67.

[52] *Ibid.*, IV, Art. 68–77.

[53] *Krasnyi Arkhiv*, XIII, 250–257.

[54] *Pamiati Dekabristov*, II, 178–179; *Obshchestvennye Dvizheniia v Rossii*, I, 187–188.

[55] *Materialy*, I, 26, 230, 307; IV, 101; Semevsky, *op. cit.*, 424–425.

first read the Green Book, he concluded that its authors were "more German ideologists than French Jacobins."[56] Turgenev relates that many members often asked, "But where is stated the aim of the Society ?", upon which the reply was usually given: "To endeavor to spread political enlightenment and increase the number of members."[57] The Green Book was known to Alexander. It is said that, after he became familiar with it, he concluded that "the majority of secret societies at the beginning nearly always have only a philanthropic aim, but afterwards change it, turning into a plot against the government."

Certain writers are inclined to think that the reason for the conservative character of the Green Book is to be found in the fact that Pestel was not a member of the committee that prepared it. It so happened that he was in Mitava at the time of its preparation and was unable to exert any influence. Pestel did indeed accept the constitution very reluctantly, recognizing it only after much opposition.[58] Another explanation, and one probably more nearly true, is that the Green Book presented only a small part of a greater project. The Union of Welfare planned to write a second part in which the political aims of the Union would be expounded. This part has never been found, and it is doubtful that it was ever written except in a rough draft.[59] Later, unforeseen developments prevented its completion.

Though the constitution of the Union of Welfare included no provisions of a political nature, it is assumed from the later testimony of different members that its main purpose was to curb monarchical power, to emancipate the peasants, and to introduce various reforms.[60] The Green Book was really written for the layman, and he was told that the purpose of the society was chiefly cultural and educational activity. It is not surprising, therefore, that many members wondered why the society should be conspiratory or the constitution not presented for approval to the Emperor and to certain distinguished statesmen.

The tacit political aims.—Notwithstanding the conservative

[56] *Krasnyi Arkhiv,* XIII, 160; Dovnar-Zapolsky, *op. cit.,* 4.

[57] *Krasnyi Arkhiv,* XIII, 122.

[58] *Materialy,* I, 209, 307; IV, 203; *Russkoe Proshloe,* I (1923), 20.

[59] Bogdanovich, *Istoriia tsarstvovaniia imp. Aleksandra I,* IV, 419, footnote; *Krasnyi Arkhiv,* XIII, 77; *Materialy,* III, 24–25; *Russkaia Starina,* CXVIII (1904), 242–243.

[60] *Materialy,* I, 139; Dovnar-Zapolsky, *Tainoe obshchestvo dekabristov,* 33–34.

character of the Green Book, according to Alexander Muraviev, one of the responsible leaders, the Society definitely sought the destruction of serfdom, equality before the law, public trial, abolition of state monopoly on alcohol, abolition of military colonies, shorter terms of military service, and other reforms.[61]

Pestel has given a very precise description of the political aspects of the Union of Welfare. "The contents of the Green Book," stated Pestel, "constituted a mere evasion of the real aim, if the Union should be discovered, or for the initiates."[62] Members of the Union, relates Pestel elsewhere, unanimously agreed upon the necessity of introducing a new order in Russia. They believed that this could be accomplished through the increase of the Union's membership. But no agreement existed with respect to details and, particularly, with respect to the means of enforcing the new social order. Pestel explained that many projects were suggested, but no one of them was definitely accepted, probably because the Union "was not ripe for it." To eliminate further fruitless discussion and to increase confidence in the organization, it was determined that the members should be told that the leaders had already worked out plans for the enforcement of their program, which was to remain known to them only.[63]

The Green Book in the South.—In the North the majority of the members readily accepted the provisions of the Green Book, but in the South the situation was entirely different. In 1818 Pestel was transferred to the South as aide-de-camp of the newly appointed commander-in-chief of the Second Army, Witgenstein, whose headquarters were in Tulchin. Here Pestel immediately undertook to organize a branch of the Union of Welfare. Though he opposed the Green Book because of its conservative character, he still considered it useful as a means of protection in an emergency. Should the authorities discover the Union, he thought, it would serve to prove the innocence of the organization. Pestel had little faith in moral education alone. He believed it necessary to overthrow the political and social structure of the state, and he constantly insisted that, unless the Union should set a definite program, it would be weakened by continuous intrigues and division of opinion.[64] In founding the southern branch of the Union of Wel-

---

[61] *Materialy*, III, 17–18; *Vospominaniia i rasskazy*, I, 120.

[62] *Russkaia Starina*, CXVIII (1904), 252.

[63] *Materialy*, IV, 84.   [64] *Ibid.*, IV, 87.

fare, Pestel therefore injected into it a spirit different from that
of the northern branch. Though he met opposition from his close
associate, Ivan Burtsev, a man of more moderate views who had
helped him organize the branch, Pestel succeeded in making notable progress.[65]

The more impotent the Union became in the North, the more
active the southern branch grew. Slowly and persistently Pestel
worked, forcing his view upon the other members. He sought the
adoption by the Union of his republican program and exploited
every occasion for that end. He even went so far as to suggest that
a dictatorship be set up within the Union, assuming, of course,
that he would be the dictator. But this proposal aroused the determined opposition of other members, who considered such a step
too important to be decided by the southern branch alone.[66]

Slow progress in the North.—In the North the organization was
confronted by serious difficulties. The important Moscow branch
was slowly dying because it lacked leadership. Matvei Muraviev,
Yakushkin, and Fonvizin had to leave; the former active leader
of the Moscow group, Alexander Muraviev, abandoned the Union
entirely, and Prince Sergei Trubetskoi went abroad.[67] These were
heavy losses to the group, and the remaining members were unable to make any progress at all. Similar conditions existed in other
cities, for example, Nizhny-Novgorod, Tambov, Smolensk, and
Poltava, where attempts to establish branches of the Union of
Welfare had been made.

Pestel was well aware of the situation, and, as a practical leader,
he realized that it was intolerable. He clearly foresaw that if a
revolution were to occur, St. Petersburg, the national capital and
the center of all political institutions, must be the guiding spirit
of the events. By entrenching its members in the local government,
Pestel thought, the Union of Welfare would be enabled to para-
lyze all resistance from the government. The army, if won, could
be of great assistance in the North. In such circumstances no cleavage between the North and South could be permitted; to be successful, the Union would be compelled to seek the perfect coördination
of its two main branches.[68] With this purpose in mind, in Novem-

---

[65] Yakushkin, *op. cit.*, 45.
[66] *Materialy*, I, 10. Cf. IV, 161–162.
[67] *Ibid.*, I, 139.
[68] *Materialy*, IV, 87, 102–103; Pavlov-Silvansky, *Dekabrist Pestel*, 67–71.

ber, 1819, Pestel arrived in St. Petersburg, where he spent nearly six months, attempting to establish a closer relationship between the two groups.

Pestel's attempt to revolutionize the North.—Pestel also came to the capital with another mission: to force the Union of Welfare to adopt a more liberal platform. This he finally succeeded in doing, when at one of the meetings of the Supreme Council he brought up the question whether the monarchical or the republican form of government was more desirable for Russia. Pestel came out as the staunch supporter of a republican form of government; his opponent, Feodor Glinka, defended the monarchical idea. At first glance the whole question might seem academic, but when it is remembered that the decision of the Supreme Council meant law for the Union, it is easily understood why Pestel pressed the issue.

Adoption of a republican platform.—Glinka attempted to show that a republican form of government would prove ruinous to Russia because of the peculiar geographic and ethnographic features of the country. Pestel attempted to show that this was not true, citing the United States, which in both respects resembled Russia, yet, in spite of its republican form of government, had made great progress. He further argued that a constitutional monarch could not be relied upon, for it was in the nature of monarchs in general to oppose liberal legislation and to believe that constitutions "could be changed like tariffs" whenever the rulers deemed it necessary.[69] Pestel, thanks to his gifted ability in clarifying his views and his genius in presenting complex problems simply, succeeded in swaying the majority to his side. When a vote was taken, all except one, Glinka, gave their consent to the republican form of government. Even that very moderate gentleman, Nicholas Turgenev, when asked his opinion, replied: "Un président sans phrases."[70]

After receiving the Council's favorable vote, Pestel forced the issue further. He now asked what means should be used to introduce the republican form of government into Russia. Pestel suggested that regicide would perhaps be necessary for this purpose. Nikita Muraviev agreed with Pestel, but this time the majority rose against such a radical policy, fearing that an act so drastic would lead Russia to anarchy, though Pestel tried to prove that a provisional government with dictatorial powers could prevent

[69] Dovnar-Zapolsky, *Tainoe obshchestvo dekabristov*, 68.
[70] *Materialy*, IV, 102. Cf. Turgenev, *Rossiia i Russkie*, I, 174–183; *Russkaia Starina*, CVII (1901), 623–631.

chaos in the country.[71] After a heated discussion the matter was dropped, but the incident clearly illustrates Pestel's political ideas and the revolutionary aims which he pursued in the South to his last day.

Pestel's interpretation of his victory.—Though the Supreme Council rejected his other ideas, yet the victory which Pestel gained when that body approved his republican plans was of great significance. Pestel interpreted the act as a formal adoption of a republican program toward which the Union should at once begin to work. Returning to Tulchin in May, 1820, he brought the news to the southern branch of the Union of Welfare that the Supreme Council had approved the republican platform. All the southern members, except Burtsev, who doubted whether a republican government would be fitting for Russia, accepted the program.[72] For Pestel a wide field was opened; the decision of the Supreme Council had apparently legalized his plans and given recognition to the southern branch. Under his guidance the southern organization became the radical wing of the Decembrist movement, and the northern group, only half-heartedly acceding to the republican idea, represented the more conservative element.[73] Thus the gap between the northern and southern branches began to appear rather early; it gradually widened and became one of the causes of the failure of the whole movement.

Decadence of the Northern Society.—The northern group, lacking the able leadership of Pestel, his political convictions and determination, lagged with its work.[74] Not only was this group conservative, but also it was comprised of members not especially suited to conspiratory work. Furthermore, rumors that the government had learned of the existence of the organization intimidated many members. Their fears were perhaps not groundless, for after the uprising of the Semenovsky regiment, the police had increased their vigilance, and on January 4, 1821, Alexander I confirmed a project providing for the establishment of a secret military police.[75] There were suspicions that the indiscriminate enrollment of members had brought unreliable persons into the

---

[71] *Materialy,* I, 312.

[72] *Materialy,* IV, 156–157; Pavlov-Silvansky, *op. cit.,* 9, 10.

[73] *Materialy,* I, 323.

[74] *Ibid.,* I, 15, 179, 299.

[75] Zablotsky-Desiatovsky, *Graf P. D. Kiselev i ego vremia,* I, 157–158; Schilder, *Imperator Aleksandr I,* IV, 548–550.

Union.[76] These doubts were justified much later when it was discovered that Mikhail Gribovsky, a member of the Union and the
Supreme Council, had proved a traitór, secretly reporting to the
government the plans of the organization.[77]

Fearing difficulties, some of the members recommended the dissolution of the organization. There were a few, however, who
wished to continue their efforts, but they also wanted to rid themselves of those who were fearful of further activities. These were
willing that the Union should have fewer members, for they wished
to consolidate the conspiratory organization and place the work
upon a firmer basis. They criticized the Union for not acting en-
ergetically enough and demanded that it pursue a more determined
course.[78] Constant protests by the more radical members prepared
the way for the Moscow conference of 1821, where various representatives met to decide the future of the Union of Welfare.[79]

The Moscow conference.—Two factors compelled the Union of
Welfare to seek a general conference: internal dissension and the
increased watchfulness of the government. It became imperative
to summon representatives and decide what course to pursue:
whether to continue the Union in spite of all obstacles and how
to eliminate the unfit element in the organization. The initiative
came from the Moscow group, though the idea had ripened among
many members elsewhere. The initiating group designed a plan
whereby representatives of the main branches, St. Petersburg and
Tulchin, would meet in January, 1821, to decide the urgent
problems.

For this purpose Fonvizin was sent north and Yakushkin south
to discuss with the leaders the holding of a conference.[80] In the
North the idea was met favorably.[81] In the South, Pestel also
seemed glad to accept the invitation and was even eager to represent the branch himself. But apprehension that the government
might become suspicious of his departure persuaded him not to

---

[76] *Russkaia Starina,* IV (1872), 601; *Materialy,* III, 122.

[77] *Dekabristy,* 109–116; *Russky Arkhiv,* III (1875), 423–430; Schilder, *op. cit.,* IV, 204–215; Chernov, "K istorii politicheskikh stolknovenii na Moskovskom s'ezde." *Zapiski Saratovskogo Universiteta,* IV (1925), 132–133.

[78] Yakushkin, *op. cit.,* 44; *Russkaia Starina,* VI (1872), 600–601.

[79] A detailed study of the conditions which led to the Moscow conference of
1821 may be found in the admirable monograph of Chernov, "Neskol'ko spravok o 'Soiuze Blagodenstviia' pered Moskovskim S'ezdom 1821 goda." *Zapiski
Saratovskogo Universiteta,* II (1924), 34ff.

[80] *Materialy,* IV, 155.   [81] Cf. *Krasnyi Arkhiv,* XIII, 82–83.

do so. The mission was given to two other members, Komarov and Burtsev, both conservative men. The appointment of these men proved significant, as later developments will show. From Tulchin, Yakushkin went farther south, to Kishenev, to the headquarters of General Orlov, and extending to him a similar invitation, and Orlov consented to participate in the projected conference.[82]

Early in January, 1821, various delegates arrived in Moscow. The northern society sent Turgenev and Glinka. From the South there came, in addition to Komarov and Burtsev, General Orlov as the outstanding leader of his group and the *persona grata* of the Union of Welfare.[83] The Supreme Council was invited and other members, who had the right to participate in the discussions but not to vote. The members gathered at the home of Fonvizin.[84]

Orlov's proposal and withdrawal.—From the beginning the assembled delegates reflected the kaleidoscopic political body which was the Union of Welfare. At the first meeting General Orlov came out with a plan which created a furor among the delegates, and, according to Yakushkin, "could even seem criminal." Orlov proposed that the Union should become more active and establish a secret printing shop where antigovernment literature could be published and disseminated over the entire country. He also suggested that the Union begin to counterfeit money; to do this, he said, would enable the organization to expand its activities and at the same time to undermine the credit of the government. The plan surprised the delegates, to say the least. But when Orlov saw that the members rejected his proposal, he announced his withdrawal and appeared no more at the meetings.[85]

The question arises as to whether Orlov was sincere when he offered this extreme plan or whether it was merely a pretense which he thought would enable him to make a graceful departure. In an article written much later, Orlov's son denied the whole incident and declared it an invention of the "only Decembrist who returned from his exile with a feeling of profound bitterness."[86] But the arguments of Nicholas Orlov, in this attempt to apologize for his father, are not very convincing; they were based on "orally related episodes" of many years before, and were ably refuted by Yakushkin's son.[87] Yakushkin, the Decembrist and participant in

[82] Yakushkin, *op. cit.*, 44–46, 47, 55. Cf. *Krasnyi Arkhiv*, XIII, 162.

[83] *Materialy*, IV, 108.   [85] Yakushkin, *op. cit.*, 54.

[84] *Ibid.*, III, 64, 73.   [86] *Russkaia Starina*, IV (1872), 780.

the conference, explained that the reason for Orlov's radical proposal was the fact that, influenced by his betrothed, he wished to terminate his relations with the Union.

The real motives of Orlov are difficult to prove. Later, in his *Memorandum* to Nicholas I, he cleverly avoided mentioning the Moscow conference and in general gave little important information, thereby arousing the fury of the Emperor.[88] There is little evidence concerning the whole incident except Yakushkin's *Memoirs*.[89] Whether Orlov was sincere or was only seeking a means of breaking off his relations with the Union cannot be definitely determined. Yakushkin's explanation of the act as due to matrimonial motives is doubtful: the previous career of General Orlov supports the view that his conduct was motivated by larger ideals. Returning after the war of 1812 as the hero of Paris, he displayed great interest in political affairs.[90] Dynamic and responsive to the sad conditions of the masses, he appealed to Alexander to emancipate the peasants and hoped to achieve social reforms through different organizations. As a member of the literary society "Arzamas," as one of the active members of the Russian Bible Society, and as organizer of Lancasterian schools, he had always one aim in mind—to lead Russia out of her medieval condition.[91] And all three projects equally failed. The granting of a constitution to Poland aroused Orlov's indignation, but his effort to prevent it proved futile. Later he undertook the organization of the Order of Russian Knights, a semipolitical, semi-Masonic society which never developed beyond plans on paper. His propaganda among the soldiers of his division made him believe that men would follow him wherever he ordered them.[92] In 1820 Orlov formally joined the Union of Welfare and as a member was able to observe the slow progress the society was making.[93] All these disappointments, together with his belief in the possible support of his soldiers, may have impelled Orlov to insist upon more revolutionary action.[94]

[87] *Ibid.*, VI (1872), 597–602.

[88] *Krasnyi Arkhiv*, VI, 231–232; Dovnar-Zapolsky, *Memuary dekabristov*, 15–22.

[89] *Krasnyi Arkhiv*, XIII, 84. Cf. Yakushkin, *op. cit.*, 54–55; *Materialy*, I, 41, footnote.

[90] *Russkaia Starina*, XII (1877), 633ff.

[91] Zablotsky-Desiatovsky, *op. cit.*, I, 223–224; *Ostafievsky Arkhiv*, I, 102, 260–307 *passim*, 339, 456, 483.

[92] Zablotsky-Desiatovsky, *op. cit.*, I, 157–158.

[93] Gershenzon, *Istoriia molodoi Rossii*, 29.

[94] *Zapiski Saratovskogo Universiteta*, IV (1925), 117–120.

Following Orlov's withdrawal came that of Komarov. Komarov, who represented the southern branch and who sought an occasion for his own departure, found the incident timely. After Orlov had finished his speech, Komarov declared that he could not associate with a conspiratory organization and, advising the members to dissolve the society, he withdrew his own membership.[95] It seems strange indeed that this same Komarov should have represented the southern branch of the Union.

Fictitious dissolution of the Union.—The government was not unaware of the conference. Thanks to the traitor, Mikhail Gribovsky, the authorities were well informed of the proceedings and the actions of some of the members.[96] The conference was warned from St. Petersburg by some friends that the government was aware of the gathering. Therefore, at the following meeting, under the chairmanship of Turgenev, the matter of the tactics to pursue under the existing conditions was discussed.[97] Since the least careless act might lead to disaster, it was thought wiser that the conference should fictitiously dissolve the Union. This would achieve a double purpose: it would mislead the government and at the same time help to rid the Union of those members that had become a burden to it. This plan was accepted and evidently did produce the desired effect: news that the society had come to an end soon reached the government.[98] Tacitly, however, the leaders resolved that the Green Book should be amended and that four chief branches should be established, in St. Petersburg, Moscow, Smolensk, and Tulchin under the leadership of Turgenev, Fonvizin, Yakushkin, and Burtsev respectively.

Further details of this plan are confusing and obscure. But there is good reason to suspect that the northern group, which was unsympathetic with Pestel's ideas and disliked his domineering character, wished to overthrow his leadership and to restore the prestige of the North. That this supposition is well founded can be seen from the fact that Burtsev, not Pestel, was selected as leader of the Tulchin group. Pestel's strong disapproval of the dissolution of the Union indicates that he was among the members

---

[95] *Obshchestvennye Dvizheniia v Rossii*, I, 30–31.

[96] *Materialy*, III, 74, p. ii; *Dekabristy*, 109–116; *Russkaia Starina*, VI (1872), 601–602.

[97] *Krasnyi Arkhiv*, XIII, 84–85.

[98] *Istoriia Rossii v XIX vieke* (Izd. Granat), I, 77.

who were misinformed of the actual decision of the conference.[99] Burtsev, as a rival of Pestel, faithfully carried out the promise which he made in Moscow, namely, that upon his return to the South he would declare the Union dissolved, then commence to organize a new society, enrolling all former members except those who had been Pestel's adherents.[100] That he had done this, Burtsev later confessed to Basargin, another member of the southern organization.[101]

When Turgenev returned to St. Petersburg, he announced to the members that the conference had decided to dissolve the Union of Welfare. Only to a few of the members did he relate the actual state of affairs. Muraviev agreed with the decision of the conference, though he made little headway in carrying out his promise to continue the work, and the situation was similar in the other centers where the conference had planned to establish its branches. But in Tulchin, thanks to Pestel, the Union did not die.[102]

Pestel rejects the decision.—When Komarov and Burtsev returned to Tulchin, they immediately reported the dissolution of the Union. Some of the members approved this action, but the greater number were against it. Pestel was deeply disappointed with the decision and thought the conference had gone beyond its powers. He felt that it had no right to dissolve the Union, its powers being limited to the adopting of new regulations or the amending of the old constitution. He therefore determined to ignore the decision and continue upon his own initiative to work as before. The organization which he sponsored became officially known as the "Southern Society." Those elected to the Directory, "Boyars," as they were called, were Pestel, Yushnevsky, and Nikita Muraviev.[103] Muraviev was elected in his absence, the members hoping that he would agree with the attitude that they had taken and accept the nomination. The aims of the Southern Society were proclaimed in a more precise fashion than those of the Union of Welfare. They were: " . . . by decisive revolutionary means to overthrow the throne and in extreme necessity kill all persons who might represent invincible obstacles," and to establish a republi-

[99] *Zapiski Saratovskogo Universiteta*, IV (1925), 136–139.
[100] Yakushkin, *op. cit.*, 57.
[101] Basargin, *op. cit.*, 11; Presniakov, *14 dekabria 1825*, 30–32.
[102] *Materialy*, III, 50.
[103] *Ibid.*, IV, 101, 108–109, 110.
[104] *Ibid.*, IV, 115, 157–58.

can form of government.[104] The chairman of the Directory, Pestel, was given wide dictatorial powers, but it was understood that on the eve of the projected revolt the Boyars must be called and the final decision made by them. Thus the Southern Society became entirely independent, though Pestel constantly maintained that the northern group must continue and that both societies must be regarded as inseparable parts of a national organization.[105] The nomination of Muraviev as a third member of the Directory was evidence of that idea. Events thus made the Southern Society the guiding spirit of the entire movement; it carried on the ideas and traditions of the Union of Welfare and forced the North to take revolutionary action.

[105] *Ibid.*, IV, 156, 157.

Chapter IV

THE RISE OF THE NORTHERN AND SOUTHERN SOCIETIES

1. THE NORTHERN SOCIETY

THE NORTHERN CONSTITUTION

W HEN TURGENEV RETURNED to St. Petersburg, he conveyed the news to the northern members that, in accordance with the decision of the Moscow conference, the Union of Welfare had been dissolved. Only to a few of his most reliable colleagues did he reveal the truth of the matter, that the Union was to be reorganized with fewer and more trustworthy members. Among those invited by Turgenev to organize the society on the new basis were Prince Evgeny Obolensky, Colonel Mikhail Naryshkin, Councilor Alexis Semënov, and a few others.[1] No progress was made at first. During the year 1821 the Guard Corps, which included the most active members, left the capital for the western part of Russia; any further organization was therefore impossible and for the time being had to be abandoned. Only a few individuals attempted to continue the work, among whom was Nikita Muraviev, who, with the assistance of Prince Sergei Trubetskoi, soon founded the northern council.[2] Nikita Muraviev himself undertook the task of drawing up a constitution for the future Russia. The North, in spite of the republican platform adopted in 1820, remained the stronghold of the conservative liberals, opposing the radical South led by Pestel.\

Nikita Muraviev.—The author of the northern constitution, Nikita Muraviev, was captain of the Guard. Hardly seventeen, he had joined the army in 1813, participated in many battles in the fateful years of 1813–14, and had been among the troops which entered Paris. His former French tutor, an admirer of Robespierre, his visit to Paris, the heart of revolutionary Europe, where he met many outstanding men who were participants in events which stirred the whole continent—all this, according to one of his con-

---

[1] *Gosudarstvennye prestupleniia v Rossii v XIX vieke*, I, 39; *Materialy*, III, 196.

[2] *Ibid.*, I, 323.

temporaries, "deeply affected the cultured, though not yet ripened and experienced mind of Muraviev and he became a hot-headed liberal."[3] Upon his return to Russia he joined the Decembrist movement, being one of the founders of the first organization, the Union of Salvation. In 1817 he became a member of the then well-known literary society, "Arzamas," and showed great interest in Russian writings. When Karamzin's famous history was published, in spite of the fact that it was popularly praised, Muraviev severely criticized it, commenting, in conclusion, that "History belongs to the people and not to the Tsars." In 1820 Muraviev was one of the northern members who supported Pestel's republican program, including the possible necessity of regicide, and in 1822 he was elected leader of the Northern Society.[4] His political convictions, he relates, were acquired during and after the war. Two things impressed him especially: the promise by the Allies to Prussia of representative government for her participation in the war and Alexander's speech in Warsaw, in which he expressed his hope for constitutional government in Russia.[5] For a time Pestel had great faith in Muraviev as the political leader of the North and sent him extracts from his projected constitution. Later, however, when Muraviev began to write his own constitution and revealed his conservative tendencies, Pestel began to lose faith in him and even demanded that he be replaced as leader.

Muraviev's political views.—By conviction Nikita Muraviev remained a republican, and the constitution he produced for the Northern Society was only an expedient.[6] He considered the constitution as a screen behind which it would be safer to act.[7] Feeling that his republican ideas were too advanced for the majority of the members, he wrote the constitution in accordance with the popular demand. It was also thought to counterbalance Pestel's constitutional project, with which Muraviev had familiarized himself when visiting Tulchin. Later, when he received a rough draft f Pestel's *Russian Justice*, he examined and then immediately destroyed it, finding the document contradictory to the principles of the Northern Society.[8] Since there was no alternative except to

[3] Vigel, *Zapiski*, IV, 140; V, 50; Grech, *Zapiski o moei zhizni*, 489.

[4] *Materialy*, I, 230.

[5] *Ibid.*, I, 294–295.

[6] *Ibid.*, I, 175.

[7] "... Comme un rideau derrière lequel nous formerons nos colonnes."—*Materialy*, IV, 162; Dovnar-Zapolsky, *Memuary dekabristov*, 54.

[8] *Materialy*, I, 323.

draft a constitution more according to their views, the Northern Society had chosen Muraviev for this purpose.

The political program drawn by Muraviev for the Northern Society was, in many respects, vitally different from Pestel's program. According to this program Russia was to become a constitutional monarchy and not a republic, as Pestel wished. However, Muraviev's view was not shared by all the members: a few of them, like Arbuzov, Peter Beliaev, Dimitry Zavalishin, Kakhovsky, and Ryleev, were believers in a republican form of government.[9] Ryleev, who was the most liberal member in the North, opposed Muraviev's project, chiefly because of its system of property classification and the inadequate supply of land provided for liberated peasants.[10] There were those, however, who considered even Muraviev's conservative constitution as nothing less than a "utopia."[11] Most of those who believed in a republic, it might be added, did not wish to enforce their ideas immediately, but preferred that the issue be decided later by a National Assembly.[12] Other members displayed a liberal-bourgeois sentiment, favoring a limited monarchy and the extension of membership to other classes as well as the nobility and the military men. This, they hoped, would attract worthy urban citizens, though some members considered the participation of these impossible, since all merchants were "boors."[13]

The constitution of Muraviev.—The northern constitution is preserved in two different editions, the second being more nearly complete than the first. There is also a third draft, drawn from memory by Muraviev while he was under arrest in 1826 and intended for the investigation committee. All three documents supplement one another and are essentially alike.[14] The constitution begins with a preamble which reads in part as follows:[15]

The experience of all nations and of all times has proved that autocratic government is equally fatal to rulers and to society; that it is not in accordance either with the rules of our sacred religion or with the principles of

[9] *Ibid.*, I, 178; IV, 89, 95; *Russkaia Starina*, XXX (1881), 492; *Byloe*, I (1906), 139ff.; Shchegolev, *Dekabristy*, 165–166.

[10] *Materialy*, I, 211, 218; *XIX Viek*, I, 360–361.

[11] *Materialy*, III, 198; Dovnar-Zapolsky, *op. cit.*, 166–167, 172–174.

[12] *Materialy*, I, 174.

[13] *Ibid.*, I, 179.

[14] Yakushkin, V. E., *Gosudarstvennaia vlast' i proekty gosudarstvennoi reformy v Rossii*, 131ff.; *Dekabristy*, 236–249; *Materialy*, I, 107; Dovnar-Zapolsky, *op. cit.*, 96ff.

[15] The second edition does not have a preamble.

NIKITA MURAVIEV.

common sense; it is not permissible to let the basis of government be the despotism of one person; it is impossible to agree that all rights shall be on one side and all duties on the other. Blind obedience can only be based on fear and is unworthy of either a wise ruler or a wise subject. . . . All the European nations are attaining constitutions and freedom. The Russian nation, more than any of them, deserves one as well as the other.[16]

The constitution contains ten chapters. The first chapter declares the Russian people "free and independent" and the sovereignty of the state to reside within the people alone; chapters two and three define the status of the citizen and his rights. Serfdom and slavery were to be abolished: "A slave who touches the soil of Russia becomes free." All social distinction was forbidden "as contrary to Faith . . . for all were born for the good, and all are simply people: weak and imperfect."[17] Freedom of speech and of press, religious tolerance, and trial by jury were to be assured. The land was to remain in the hands of the landlords, but the personal property, gardens, tools, and chattels, belonging to and used by the peasants were to be respected as theirs.[18]

According to Muraviev's plan, Russia was to be divided into thirteen States and two Provinces, each State into Districts, and each District into Counties. The legislative power was to be in the hands of a National Assembly (*Narodnoe Vieche*), a bicameral body consisting of a Supreme Council (*Verkhovnaia Duma*), and a House of Representatives. The Supreme Council consisted of forty-two members, three from each State, two from the Moscow and one from the Don Provinces. The powers of the Supreme Council included the right to impeach ministers, judges, and other responsible statesmen, and the right to ratify treaties and appointments made by the Executive. The House of Representatives was to consist of approximately four hundred and fifty members, one for every fifty thousand inhabitants. This body was to initiate all laws, levy taxes, and appoint State Executives, but it had no right to modify the constitution, a power belonging to a National Assembly elected for that particular purpose.

The executive powers were to be in the hands of a hereditary Emperor, or, as the constitution named him, the "Supreme Functionary of the Russian Government." The Emperor was to have the power of veto, to be commander-in-chief of the national army

[16] *Materialy*, I, 209; *Dekabristy*, 236.
[17] Chapter III, Article 13.
[18] Chapter III, Articles 23–24.

and navy, to conduct negotiations with foreign nations, conclude treaties, and make appointments, the exercise of the latter two powers being subject to the consent of the Supreme Council. At every session of the legislative body the Emperor was to present an account of the condition of the country and to recommend laws which he considered necessary. It is interesting to note that, because of Alexander's frequent absences from Russia and the detested ascendency of Metternich over the Emperor, Muraviev included a clause which forbade the Executive to leave the territory of Russia; violation of this provision was to mean his abdication.

The reader's first impression of the constitution is one of a democratic document providing for the establishment of a parliamentary system already generally familiar in Western Europe. But a closer study of Muraviev's project reveals an entirely different picture. If, on the one hand, his constitution abolished serfdom and all class distinctions, it left, on the other hand, the free peasant, with his beggarly land allotment, in such a state that he virtually remained at the mercy of the landlord. It would seem, from the provision concerning serfdom and the political rights of the masses, that Muraviev had constantly kept in mind the advice of Mably, namely, "Admit to the government of the state only men possessed of heritable property, for they alone possess a mother country."[19]

According to the first edition of Muraviev's constitution, all citizens were to be divided into two groups: active and inactive. The former were divided into four groups, according to their property status. Moreover, as the table below indicates, a definite distinction was drawn between the various classes of property holders.

Group	Personal Property	or	Real Property
I	60,000 silver rubles		30,000 silver rubles
II	30,000 silver rubles		15,000 silver rubles
III	4,000 silver rubles		2,000 silver rubles
IV	1,000 silver rubles		500 silver rubles

In a predominantly agricultural state, as Russia was especially in the early nineteenth century, such a scheme was most favorable to the landlord: in order to be elected to any political office he had to own property valued at only half the valuation required of the urban capitalist. This distinction becomes clearer when the polit-

---

[19] Aulard, *The French Revolution*, I, 122.

ical rights are examined. Citizens of the first group might hold any office in the state; citizens of the second group might be elected members of the Upper Chamber of the State Legislatures; those belonging to the third group were unable to rise above the membership of the Lower Chamber of State Legislatures; finally, citizens of the fourth group enjoyed only the right to be elected to minor offices in the local government or to act on the jury. Such a discrimination, based on property ownership, virtually placed the entire peasantry and the city middle classes beyond the pale. The whole scheme was so inequitable that even the Northern Society criticized it severely and the author was compelled to modify certain provisions. In the second edition Muraviev changed the property qualification for all offices except for membership in the National Assembly.

In spite of its inadequacy, the constitution of Muraviev has a democratic aspect and shows a distinct similarity to the constitution of the United States. The author frequently revealed his sympathy with that form of government and closely copied it, particularly the executive and legislative branches.[20] It was also from the United States constitution that Muraviev borrowed the idea of the federal principle. In the preamble of the document he stated:[21]

Vast territory and a large army represent an obstacle to certain nations to be free; those who do not have such handicaps suffer weakness. Only a *federal* or *allied form of government* can solve this problem, satisfy all conditions and combine the *greatness of a nation with liberty* for its citizens.

Muraviev therefore wished Russia to become a federation of nationalities, a principle vehemently opposed by Pestel as a dangerous political doctrine.[22] The entire country, according to Muraviev, was to be divided into thirteen States and two Provinces, each one enjoying considerable autonomous privileges. As the national capital Muraviev assigned Moscow, though in another edition of the constitution he selected Nizhny Novgorod for that purpose.

Defects of the constitution.—The constitution which Muraviev had written, as previously stated, accorded for the most part with the demand of the northern leaders. In the South it was rejected

---

[20] *Materialy*, I, 175, 178; *Russky Arkhiv*, 1870, 1839–1840.

[21] Yakushkin, *op. cit.*, 131–132; *Materialy*, I, 109.

[22] Pestel, P., *Russkaia Pravda*, 22–23; *Minuvshie Gody*, I (1908), 10–14.

as a plan which "legalized aristocracy," Pestel reading and returning the written copy to Muraviev with the opinion "unsatisfactory." Pestel had two main objections : the federal principle, which
he considered dangerous for Russia on the ground that it would
weaken the state and make it an easy prey for foreign powers,
and the predominance of a "terrible aristocracy of wealth," which
the constitution, if enforced, would have established.[23]

Pestel's first argument was unsound; practice has shown that in
this respect Muraviev the "moderate" showed greater foresight
than did Pestel the "radical." In his second argument, Pestel was
right. The weakest point in Muraviev's political scheme was undoubtedly his "legalized aristocracy," and, above all, the unsatisfactory solution of the peasant problem. Time and again it has
been proved that the peasant preferred serfdom to landless emancipation. When Yakushkin suggested emancipation to his peasants,
the first question they asked was whether the land which they tilled
would be given to them. The answer was that they would be entitled to rent it. "Then," they replied unanimously, "let things
remain as they are : we are yours and the land is ours."[24] In the
first edition of his constitution Muraviev proclaimed the liberation of the peasants, but provided no land at all for them after
they were liberated. Later, in the second edition, he admitted that
the "peasants' houses and their gardens are recognized as their
property," and in his final draft, written in prison, he granted
about five acres for each peasant family and provided that the
village commune be preserved. But even these measures can be
considered the equivalent to landless emancipation; the social and
political disasters which followed much later were caused in large
part by an inadequate emancipation similar to that which Muraviev had recommended as a solution of Russia's gravest problem—serfdom.[25]

"A Curious Conversation."—Besides the constitution, Nikita
Muraviev wrote another interesting document under the title, *A
Curious Conversation.*[26] This was intended to be used as a means
of propaganda among the masses. It was later followed as a guide
by Sergei Muraviev-Apostol in his endeavor to win the support

[23] *Materialy*, I, 302.

[24] Yakushkin, I., *Zapiski*, 35–36 ; *Krasnyi Arkhiv*, III, 250–257.

[25] *Krestiansky Stroi*, I, 219–223.

[26] *Materialy*, I, 321–322.

of the army in the South. The *Curious Conversation* is interesting
as a type of propaganda which the leaders of the Decembrist
movement had planned eventually to use. Ryleev regretted that
Muraviev had not completed it, remarking: "Such literature is
most convenient for influencing public opinion."[27] The document
presents a dialogue, Question and Answer, and reads in part as
follows:

Q.: How did liberty originate?
A.: Every blessing is from God. Creating man according to His own image
and establishing Good as an eternal gift and Evil as eternal torment, He
granted man Liberty! ...
Q.: Are all men free?
A.: No. A small number of men enslaved a large number.
Q.: Is it necessary to acquire freedom?
A.: It is.
Q.: How?
A.: It is necessary to establish rules or *Laws* as it used to be in Old Russia.
Q.: How was it in Old Russia?
A.: There were no Autocrats.
Q.: What is an Autocrat?
A.: An Autocrat or Despot is one who alone holds the land, recognizes no power
of reason, nor the laws of God nor Man; he alone, without excuse, rules by
his own caprice.
Q.: Did not the Lord create Autocracy?
A.: The Lord never created any evil.
Q.: What kind of government was there in Russia without Autocracy?
A.: There was always the People's Assembly.
Q.: Why did not this evil end with the rule of the Tartars?
A.: ... The people who tolerated the yoke of Batu and Sortan have tolerated
in the same manner the power of the Moscow Princes, who imitated in
everything these [Tartar] tyrants.

The *Curious Conversation* was read by Nicholas I along with
other papers relating to the Decembrists. "Quelle infamie!!" he
remarked on the margin of the document.[28]

Provisional government under consideration.—The Northern
Society had to consider what course it would follow if the Emperor refused to accept the constitution, should it be presented
to him as some of the leaders planned to do. What if the constitution were rejected and revolution should occur and the leaders
suddenly find themselves at the helm of state?

Pestel suggested the dictatorship of a Provisional Government,
but the North rejected his plan, probably fearing the "Southern

---

[27] *Ibid.*, I, 176.   [28] *Ibid.*, I, 322, footnote 1.

Napoleon," as some called him. Many members believed that, as the first step toward the establishment of a firm government, the Senate should be compelled to issue a Manifesto summoning a National Assembly. At the same time the Senate should also be forced to issue a Declaration drawn up by the Society expounding the aims of the revolution. Such a Declaration, composed by Baron Steingel, a member of the Northern Society, was actually in readiness on the eve of the uprising. In this Declaration, the Society on behalf of the Senate proclaimed the overthrow of the old régime, the establishment of a Provisional Government, and the promise that a new government would be established by the National Assembly. The people were asked to maintain peace and order and to respect private property.

Until the National Assembly met, it was planned that the Senate should appoint a Directory which would act as a provisional government. Since the appointment of members of the Society might arouse antagonism between societies as well as among some members within each society, it was thought advisable to elect reliable outside men. Two candidates for the Directory were seriously considered, namely, Mordvinov and Speransky. Other candidates proposed for this post were Turgenev and Pestel.[29] The latter was opposed by the conservatives; the others were equally distasteful to the more liberal members, including Ryleev, who mockingly suggested that they were "Asiatics who needed medals and gray hair."[30] The candidacy of Mordvinov, the typical representative of the aristocracy, who "wished to combine a constitution with serfdom," met particular criticism.[31]

Lack of final agreement.—The constitution drawn by Muraviev for the Northern Society, though fairly elaborate, did not represent the final word of the organization. In his testimony Pestel emphatically stated:[32]

Of all the constitutions which were written or suggested, and which were discussed, none of them was completed. Some were only half finished, others

---

[29] *Materialy*, I, 45, 104, 158–159, 176, IV, 167–168, 355; *Russkaia Starina*, XI (1898), 348; *Russky Arkhiv*, III (1875), 435; Schilder, *Imperator Nikolai I*, I, 320, 520, footnote 366; *Arkhiv gr. Mordvinovykh*, VIII, 697–698; Aldanov, M., "Speransky i dekabristy." *Sovremennye Zapiski* (Paris), XXVI (1925), 224–240.

[30] Semevsky, *op. cit.*, 492.

[31] *Materialy*, I, 292–293, 365.

[32] *Ibid.*, IV, 86; *Russky Arkhiv* (1870), 1639.

entirely fragmentary. There was nothing complete and not a single one was unanimously accepted; so that it might be truly said that the Society had no definite constitution in mind nor had made any final decision.

But the constitution of Muraviev reflected the sentiment of the liberal northern upper class.[33] The two constitutions, the northern and the southern, also reveal the serious disagreements which gradually developed between the two societies. These differences are revealed more clearly when the constitution written by Pestel is examined. Here it may be stated that one of the chief motives which seemed to unite the two societies was the common desire to avoid a revolution involving the masses. Possible civil war, anarchy, and general chaos seriously worried Muraviev as well as Pestel, who hoped to prevent it by a strong, dictatorial provisional government.[34] Both societies hoped that the revolution could be carried out by a small military group, as had been the Spanish revolution of 1820 under the leadership of Riego and Quiroga.[35] The newly initiated members in the North were told that the death of Alexander would be the signal for action, but the older members were informed that action might be taken in his lifetime, and the Emperor be forced to sign Muraviev's constitution. The Society recommended recourse to violence—the expulsion of the royal family or regicide—only if the Emperor should refuse to sign the constitution or if his consent under pressure should result, as happened in Spain, in unsatisfactory government.[36] Muraviev conceded the establishment of a republican form of government should regicide become inevitable. By adhering to these plans, the Northern Society believed that Russia might be spared the bloodshed and social upheaval which France had suffered in the eighteenth century.

The problem of an accord between the two societies on the day following the revolution, should it be successful, does not seem especially to have troubled the Decembrists. Ryleev thought that the chief aim of both societies should be the overthrow of the existing government. The societies must not concern themselves with

---

[33] Dovnar-Zapolsky, *Idealy dekabristov*, 412–418.

[34] *Materialy*, IV, 92, 155.

[35] On the enthusiasm that the Spanish revolution of 1820 aroused among the Decembrists, see *Russkaia Starina*, XXX (1881), 488; *Iz pisem i pokazanii dekabristov*, 12–13; Gorbachevsky, *Zapiski i pisma*, 73; Petrov, *Rossiia i Nikolai I v stikhotvoreniiakh Espronsedy i Rossetti*, 47ff.

[36] *Materialy*, I, 177, 364, 433.

the future political and social structure of the state; they were only to present their different constitutional projects to the National Assembly, which alone should have the right to pass the final word in this respect.[37] Had the two opposing groups been victorious in overthrowing the old régime, it is incomprehensible how they could have established a stable government, once the social storm was aroused.[38]

2. THE SOUTHERN SOCIETY

"Muraviev seeks interpreters of Bentham, but we do not act with pens."—ALEXANDER POGGIO[39]

THE SOUTHERN CONSTITUTION

The activities of the Northern Society were only remotely radical in nature. Here and there a reference to violence appears, but it is immediately overshadowed by the predominant program of attaining by peaceful means the cherished political ideal. Even the ideal was dimly conceived by most of the members of the Northern Society as an event of the distant future. A study of the Southern Society reveals a different concept. As mentioned previously, the organization in the South arose as a result of the refusal to accept the resolution of the Moscow conference and then dissolve. When the southern delegate, Burtsev, reported the decision to Pestel, Burtsev secretly hoped to be rid of his colleague, whose radical ideas he disliked. The result of Burtsev's news was entirely unexpected. There came into being a truly conspiratory society with clearly formulated plans and practical aims, which in its short existence developed remarkable activity and achieved surprising results.

When the news of the dissolution of the Union of Welfare was conveyed to the southern members, they held a meeting at the home of Pestel and showed a resolute determination to continue the organization. Yushnevsky, wishing to retain in the society only those who feared no consequences and who really desired to work, warned the members of the serious responsibility that they were taking upon themselves. Thereupon Colonel Avramov, a member of the Union of Welfare, declared that, even if he alone were left, he would consider himself as the organization. This bold statement

[37] *Ibid.*, I, 175, 177–178; Kotliarevsky, *Ryleev*, 144ff.

[38] Zavalishin, *Zapiski dekabrista*, 142.

[39] Dovnar-Zapolsky, *Memuary dekabristov*, 201.

inspired most of the members to vote in favor of continuing to pursue the aims originally set.[40]

Once the decision was made, the meeting proceeded to discuss the future organization and program. The greater number was in favor of revolutionary action and the establishment of a republican form of government. Later, Pestel justly stated that the program was really one which had been adopted by the Union of Welfare in 1820, though it had been more readily accepted in the South. It was decided to entrust the executive functions of the Southern Society to a Directory under the chairmanship of Pestel, with headquarters at Tulchin, the center of the organization. In addition, two important branches of the Society were established, one at Kamenka under the leadership of Prince Sergei Volkonsky, the other under Sergei Muraviev-Apostol and Mikhail Bestuzhev-Riumin. The headquarters of the Society remained at Tulchin, whence Pestel directed its activities.

The Southern Society adopted precisely the form of organization and program for which Pestel had labored so long and so zealously. As chairman of the Directory, he enjoyed wide powers, and the aim of the Society was set to his heart's content, namely, the introduction of a republic through revolution. The enforcement of the plan after the overthrow of the existing régime was to be entrusted to a dictatorial government which would resolutely work toward the final goal, a task which might require eight or ten years. This ultimate conclusion Pestel undertook to set forth in his elaborate treatise called *Russian Justice,* a title borrowed from certain ancient Russian laws. A study of this document is necessary before proceeding further, for it embodies the ideals of the Southern Society.

"Russian Justice."—As stated in the preceding chapter, Nikita Muraviev turned from left to right, from his position as a republican to that of a very moderate constitutionalist, because he felt his views had been "too advanced." Pestel, on the contrary, gradually turned from right to left and became an ardent republican protagonist.[41] Pestel's political views are best expounded in his *Russian Justice, or The Instruction to the Supreme Provisional Government,* written between 1821 and 1825. This work, although incomplete, sufficiently indicates his main political beliefs.

[40] *Materialy,* IV, 108–109.
[41] *Krasnyi Arkhiv,* XIII, 178, 189, 195; *Materialy,* IV, 89–90.

The author originally planned to write a book of ten chapters on the political philosophy of the Society, but only five chapters were actually written, three in full, the other two roughly sketched. The more elaborate parts were read to the Society, were generally discussed, and the view of the members taken into consideration. The work might therefore be regarded as a collective study, expressing the opinion of the entire Society.[42] "It contains," Pestel wrote, "the obligations to be imposed upon the Provisional Government and serves as a guaranty that this government would act in the interests of the welfare of its fatherland only." The absence of such a program or charter, Pestel thought, was the cause of great social disasters and political upheavals in other countries; only clearly stated aims could assure peace after the overthrow of the old régime.[43]

The arrest and execution of the author cut short this treatise. On the eve of Pestel's arrest, December 13, 1825, the document was buried near Tulchin, but later one of the Decembrists, Zaikin, was sent from St. Petersburg, in fetters and accompanied by a special guard, to indicate the place where the *Russian Justice* was hidden. After working a whole night, the officials found the document, sealed it and, with the utmost secrecy, delivered it to the capital.[44] More than three-quarters of a century elapsed before the public was given its first opportunity to read the contents.[45]

Unified nature of the state.—*Russian Justice* embodied an outline of Pestel's political program, over which he had worked for several years. The whole thesis was a product of the rationalistic school, which dominated the minds of that time. The "old feudal order" and "aristocracy" Pestel pronounced dead, and on their ruins there was to rise a new state based on the political principle, "welfare for all, not for a few but for the majority." As an ardent Jacobin, Pestel could not tolerate any idea which would conflict

---

[42] *Materialy*, IV, 204, 222, 275, 349.

[43] *Ibid.*, IV, 90–91; Pestel, P., *Russkaia Pravda*, 10–11.

[44] *Materialy*, IV, 127–134; see also Chernov, S. N., "Poiski 'Russkoi Pravdy' P. I. Pestelia." *Izvestiia Akademii Nauk, Otdel Obshchestvennykh Nauk*, Series VII, No. 7 (1935).

[45] Pestel's *Russian Justice* was first published by P. E. Shchegolev in 1906. It is a careless edition and contains numerous errors which often mislead the reader. See *Byloe*, V (1906), 278–283. It remains to this day desirable that a more accurate edition be available for students of the period; it is regrettable that the publication of *Russian Justice*, as promised by the Soviet State Publishing House, "Tsentrarkhiv," has not yet been completed.

Русская Правда

или

Заповѣдная Государственная Грамота

Великаго Народа Россійскаго

служащая

Завѣтомъ для Усовершенствованія

Государственнаго Устройства Россіи

и Содержащая

Вѣрный Наказъ какъ для Народа

такъ и для

Временнаго Верховнаго Правленія.

TITLE PAGE OF PESTEL'S "RUSSIAN JUSTICE."

with his concept of a unified political system. The nation he considered as an enormous solid rock; no cultural or political autonomy was conceded: one nation, one government, one language, one political and economic order for the entire country. Therefore, any idea of federalism, such as Muraviev had developed, Pestel decisively placed aside as dangerous and likely to lead Russia to disruption and the restoration of the old appanage system.[46] According to Pestel, the federal basis of government would lead to the "love of one's province" more than of the state as a whole, resulting in different laws, different administrations, and the rise of "small separate states" within the state. Each autonomous unit would claim that it had a better administration than that of the national government, thus creating seeds for future strife and further division within the state. Such disintegration Pestel sought to prevent by insisting upon a "single, indivisible state."[47]

The national-minority problem.—It is well known that Russia is a conglomeration of nationalities, each having its own language, its own ethnographic peculiarities, and its own cultural and political ambitions. This fact Pestel ignored; only those nationalities which in the past had enjoyed national independence were to be entitled to it. Pestel therefore suggested that the Polish people alone be granted autonomy; all others were to remain within Russia and abandon their "useless hope" of nationhood.[48] Even Polish independence Pestel granted none too easily; it was to be conditioned by two important requirements. The first was that Poland and Russia must conclude a permanent alliance: Russia was to guarantee Polish integrity, and in return Poland would pledge to Russia the use of her army, should the latter find itself at war with some other power. The second requirement was that Poland should adopt the same republican form of government that Russia was to have.[49] Pestel urged the incorporation with Russia of all the bordering nationalities which had not yet been absorbed by the Russian state but were unable to maintain their national independence or which were necessary to Russia to assure its national safety. For example, according to his program, the Caucasus, a troublesome

---

[46] *Russkaia Pravda,* 22–23.

[47] *Ibid.,* 23–24. Cf. Destutt-de-Tracy, *Kritischer Commentar über Montesquieu's "Geist der Gesetze,"* I, 192–200.

[48] *Russkaia Pravda,* 14, 18.

[49] *Ibid.,* 18–19, 20.

spot, and Mongolia, which was only under the nominal sovereignty
of China, were to be annexed to Russia.[50] Even Finland with her
highly developed national spirit Pestel ignored, advising that it
be amalgamated with the Russian nation.[51]

The question might arise, What was to become of all the nationalities in the highly centralized state which Pestel had conceived? His
answer was simple: they must all become assimilated, adopt the
Russian culture and language—in a word, they must become Russian in every sense.[52] Every nationality, no matter what its past or
what degree of civilization it had reached, must forget its history,
its very selfhood. Moldavians in the south, Baltic Germans, Lithu-
anians, Esthonians, and Latvians in the west, Finns in the north,
Tartars, Kirghiz, Kalmuks, and other people in the east—all were
to be put into the Russian melting pot, where the future homogene-
ous nation was to take shape.[53] The Gypsies were given two alterna-
tives: they were either to become Orthodox Christians and settle
down on the land or they were to leave the country altogether.[54]
With respect to the Jews, those who proved to be unassimilable
Pestel planned to deport, with the assistance of the government,
from Russia to Asia Minor, where they were to establish their own
independent state.[55]

The astonishing arbitrariness with which Pestel handled the
delicate national-minority problem in Russia justly provoked the
statement of one writer that "to Pestel tribes, peoples, finally the
entire mass of 'citizens' were imagined as a deck of cards which he
shuffled and laid out according to his own judgment."[56] In justice
to Pestel it should be added that scarcely any previous writer had
stressed so much the necessity that the state should give attention
to the economic development of the different peoples, particularly
those of the borderland countries.

Having established the states as one indivisible national unit,
Pestel went on to expound the social status of the citizen. All social

[50] *Ibid.*, 15, 16–17.
[51] *Ibid.*, 15, 41–42.
[52] *Ibid.*, 55.
[53] *Ibid.*, 15–18, 40–50, 53–56.
[54] *Ibid.*, 46.
[55] *Ibid.*, 50–53. Anti-Semitic sentiments were not alien to many Decembrists,
including Pestel. See Perets, V. N. and L. N., *Dekabrist G. A. Perets* (Leningrad, 1926), 25–27.
[56] Syromiatnikov, "Politicheskaia doktrina 'Nakaza' P. I. Pestelia." *Sbornik
statei, posviashchennykh V. O. Kliuchevskomu* (M., 1909), 694.

ranks, castes, and other distinctions were to be abolished; there was to be but one class—citizens of Russia.[57] All discriminations based on birth or property were considered to be remnants of the old feudal society and were not to be tolerated in the modern state. Every citizen was allowed to follow whatever vocation he chose.

The agrarian problem.—Pestel's solution of the agrarian problem was a logical sequence of his political creed: namely, that since all men were born equal, all the land must be held as common property.[58] He loathed the accumulation of wealth in the hands of the few and maintained that every person, as a citizen of the state, was entitled to his share of land.[59] This doctrine was a revolutionary step which far outran the other projects of the Decembrists with their modest five-acre allotments. Serfdom was to be resolutely stamped out and the nobility once and for all deprived of the right to own serfs. However, should there be some "outcast who would think by word or deed of resisting or criticizing this, the Supreme Provisional Government is immediately obliged to place such a villain under arrest and punish him most severely as the enemy of his country and traitor against the first fundamental civil right."[60]

Pestel reached his own conclusion about the complicated land problem. There were two points of view, the first of which was as follows:

... the land is common property of the human race and not of private persons, and therefore cannot be divided among a few men. As soon as there exists even a single person who does not possess any land, the will of God and the laws of nature are totally violated and the natural rights eliminated by force and tyrannical government.

The other point of view was that all land must be put into use as private property, otherwise agriculture would be in danger of becoming stagnant. Pestel accepted neither point of view and developed his own philosophy, a fact which shows that he had seriously considered the agrarian problem.[61]

According to Pestel, all the lands, private, state, church, and monastic, were to be taken over by the state and placed in two categories.[62] The land in the first category was to be designated for

---

[57] *Russkaia Pravda*, 59, 60.

[58] *Ibid.*, 202–204.

[59] Cf. Hall, Charles, *The Effects of Civilization on the People in European States* (London, 1849), 78–81.

[60] *Russkaia Pravda*, 66.   [61] *Ibid.*, 203.   [62] *Ibid.*, 85–86, 87.

equal distribution among peasants or others who wished to practice agriculture. Every citizen in the country was entitled to a strip of land which he might till himself, though the citizens in greater need were to be considered first. Under the jurisdiction of the county the land was to be divided into lots, each sufficient for a family of five people.[63] Land granted by the state to the individual citizen could not be sold, exchanged, or mortgaged by the person who tilled it but was to remain the property of the state for the benefit of all the citizens, to whom it would assure a livelihood. This measure, according to Pestel, would eliminate pauperism in the country, for every citizen in time of extreme need would turn to agriculture. "Every Russian," says Pestel, "no matter where he may happen to be, or where he may seek his fortune, can always remember that if success betrays his efforts there will always be in his county, that political family of his, a haven and bread for him."[64]

The common land in the second category was designated for quite different purposes, this part being intended to produce a surplus. It belonged to the state, which could rent or sell it when necessary or when economically expedient. Income derived from this land was to constitute a national fund to be used for the development and scientific improvement of farming methods, and also to assist individual peasants who were ambitious to acquire land. Pestel advised the granting to worthy peasants of loans and the opportunity to acquire land. To such peasants the government could sell land belonging to the state, and this land, once sold, could not under any circumstances be taken away from the peasants. Land given them by the state from the first category could be reclaimed, in the event of any violation of law. Pestel was evidently inclined to believe that the basis of Russian prosperity lay in agriculture and that the backbone of the national welfare was a strong, rich peasantry, or at least one that was sufficiently equipped with land.

In the land reforms which Pestel recommended he seems to have been influenced by Abbé Antoine de Cournand, author of the socialist pamphlet published in 1791 under the title, *Of Prosperity; or, The Cause of the Poor pleaded before the Tribunal of Reason, Justice and Truth*. Cournand suggested that the French government take under its control one-third of the entire arable land. Of

---

[63] *Ibid.*, 204–206.   [64] *Ibid.*, 207.

this land the government was to assign to each citizen at birth a lot sufficient to supply his needs, and after his death the lot was to return to the state. For the use of the land the citizen was to pay rent, and this would constitute the main source of national revenue. The remaining two-thirds of the land was to be apportioned without charge among all tillers of the soil. Lots might be rented by the individual holders, but could not be sold or bequeathed.[65] Pestel, who was well versed in the revolutionary literature of France, was probably familiar with the agrarian plans proposed in 1791, among them those of Cournand.[66] But Pestel's plan, though similar to that of Cournand, shows distinct differences—for example, the absence of rent to the government or the right of the individual tillers to acquire land.

In the field of industry and commerce as well as in agriculture, Pestel held the view of the physiocrats, namely, *laissez faire, laissez passer*. He was a firm believer in individual initiative and urged that no handicaps be imposed on those engaged in any of the fields mentioned. "It is known," he writes, "that the best means of causing national prosperity to flourish is granting liberty . . . liberty is the main necessity for national industry."[67] For this reason he strongly emphasized the importance of eliminating all obstacles to free trade, such as excessive taxes, tariffs, and other regulations, thus granting to industrialists a free hand.

Political program.—The Provisional Government which Pestel felt it necessary to establish immediately after the revolution was to serve for at least eight or ten years as a link between the old régime and the newly established order. During this period it was pledged to maintain individual liberty, religious tolerance, and the freedom of the press. It is interesting to note that all societies, whether open or secret, were to be banned from the country, for the first were useless and the second harmful.[68]

The political structure of Russia Pestel planned as follows: the whole country was to be divided into fifty districts, called Circuits, and three Appanages.[69] The fifty Circuits composed ten Provinces. The national capital was to be Nizhny Novgorod, which was to be renamed Vladimir.[70] As the basis of the national government Pestel took the smallest political unit, the County Precinct. The County

[65] Aulard, A., *The French Revolution,* I, 229–230.
[66] Semevsky, *op. cit.,* 536.
[67] *Russkaia Pravda,* 71, 72, 195–196, 240.
[68] *Ibid.,* 237.
[69] *Ibid.,* 24.
[70] *Ibid.,* 26–27.

Precinct meeting elected representatives for its own locality, the County, and the Circuit Assembly. To the Circuit Assembly, besides the election of its administration, was assigned another function, the election of representatives to the Provincial Assembly, which in turn would elect representatives to the National Assembly.[71] The five executives who composed the State Duma were elected by the National Assembly, which comprised fifty members or Boyars, elected for life by the people. The functions of the Supreme Assembly were to ratify all legislation and to see that no laws were passed that would conflict with the law of the land.[72] The whole structure is obviously too inadequate to be regarded as Pestel's final aim, and is evidently only a rough sketch. Had he been able to develop it, Pestel would undoubtedly have revised and improved the plan.

Many important details remain obscure, such as the exact function of the executive branch and its relations to the legislative branch. The judicial branch is also inadequately described. From the fragmentary notes, it might be assumed that the author held decidedly advanced views for his time, for example, those with respect to crime and punishment. Says Pestel:[73]

Punishment is not vengeance, but a means for restraining other people from similar crimes; correct, if possible, the criminal himself and place him in a position whereby he will be unable to violate the peace and welfare of society and its private citizens .... capital punishment must never be used. ... Praised be the Russian government which will conceive such great truth!

Though in the domain of economics Pestel was a staunch believer in a *laissez faire* policy, in politics he evidently had less faith in the citizen, who, he insisted, must be watched by a special secret political police in order to prevent any possible subversive activity. Alongside the civil liberties which Pestel was willing to grant, the prospect of a secret police spying upon the free individual citizen seems a little illogical. But Pestel assures the citizen that for such a task the state would have to select only wise and honest men, men of irreproachable character. However, as one critic justly remarks, Pestel overlooked the fact that people of such admirable quality are not usually inclined to engage in such an occupation.[74] But in order

[71] *Ibid.*, 214–218.

[72] Bogdanovich, *Istoriia tsarstvovaniia imp. Aleksandra I*, VI, 483–484.

[73] *Russkaia Pravda*, 100–101.

[74] Kulczycki, L., *Istoriia russkogo revoliutsionnogo dvizheniia*, 101; *Russkaia Pravda*, 112.

to secure an orderly state, Pestel was willing at times, even at the expense of consistency, to throw overboard a part of the valuable Bill of Rights.

Russian Justice portrays the political ideal to which Pestel gave his best years and for which he finally gave his life. When under arrest, he declared to Prince Volkonsky: "Do not worry, I shall not confess even if I am torn to pieces; only save *Russian Justice*."[75] Of his earlier writings, the most interesting work, only recently published, was a short exposition entitled *Practical Beginning of Political Economy*, written about 1820. This exposition seems to have been written under the strong influence of Adam Smith, though some commentators seem to believe it was rather the influence of the Swiss economist, Simonde de Sismondi.[76] The document is significant, for it shows the political progress which Pestel made during the few years between 1820, when he considered emancipation only gradually to be achieved, and the period of his writing *Russian Justice*, 1821-1825, in which he began to believe in a republican government.

Pestel's place in the liberal movement of Russia.—The writings of Pestel and his whole political philosophy were affected by a number of distinguished thinkers of his time. Among them were Holbach, Helvétius, Filangieri, Bentham, Say, Adam Smith, and particularly Destutt-de-Tracy, the well-known commentator on Montesquieu.[77] Wrote Pestel:

> From my ideas of a constitutional monarchy to that of a republic I was swayed chiefly by the following subjects and logic. The works of Destutt-de-Tracy in French impressed me immensely. He proves that every form of government where the state is headed by one person, particularly if that person enjoys hereditary rights to it, will inevitably end with despotism. All newspapers and political writings have so much glorified the growth of prosperity in the United States, ascribing the cause to its form of government, and this seemed to me a proof of the superiority of a republic.

But this influence should not be overemphasized. Though it is true that Pestel was swayed by many of the economists and writers named, yet he cannot be accused of blindly copying these men, as is assumed by some students. Possessing a keenly analytical mind

---

[75] *Materialy*, IV, 205, 209.

[76] Simonde de Sismondi, Jean C. L., *Nouveau Principes d'Économie Politique* (Paris, 1819). See *Zapiski Russkogo Istoricheskogo Obshchestva v Prage*, II (1930), 126, 137. Cf. *Krasnyi Arkhiv*, XIII, 174–175.

[77] Destutt-de-Tracy, *Commentaire sur "l'Esprit de lois" de Montesquieu. Materialy*, IV, 91; *Minuvshie Gody*, I (1908), 4–5.

and a sound economic philosophy, he also displayed an undoubted capacity for original thought. Pestel has often been accused of pursuing a course that would lead to the fulfillment of a personal ambition. He was blamed for scheming to transform the state into a uniform police institution (*Zwangsanstalt*), in which every citi- ˙zen would be subject to a "net of rules which determine not only outward conduct, but his way of thinking."[78] This is a gross mis-interpretation, for the critic totally disregarded the fact that the system of which Pestel approved was really an "Instruction" to a Provisional Government, as the title indicates, and not a plan for a permanent form of government. Not one of the northern or southern members showed greater zeal in assuring individual free-dom and prosperity than did Pestel. As an admirer of Napoleon he considered it the duty of the state to provide means for the at-tainment of that condition, but with the assistance of all citizens, through their participation, civil discipline, hard work, devotion to the common cause, and readiness for self-sacrifice.[79] This could in no way be interpreted as a "police institution for the control of outward conduct and even of thinking." The sacrifice that Pestel demanded from the citizens was to be imposed not on a certain group within society, but was to be a duty expected of every citi-zen of the state,[80] an idea which the Northern Society, with its definitely aristocratic political views, could not so easily accept as the more democratic Southern Society.

If on one hand Pestel was accused of autocratic tendencies and of striving to become a "Russian Napoleon,"[81] on the other, he was hailed as the father of Russian indigenous socialism.[82] Herzen called Pestel "the socialist before socialism,"[83] and one of his commenta-tors went so far as to interpret *Russian Justice* as the first attempt to expound communism.[84] All these views seem far-fetched. Pestel

---

[78] *Sbornik statei, posviaschchennykh Kliuchevskomu*, 718.

[79] *Russkaia Pravda*, 3, paragraph iv.

[80] *Ibid.*, 60.

[81] *Sbornik statei, posviashchennykh Kliuchevskomu*, 716–717.

[82] Pazhitnov, *Razvitie sotsialisticheskikh idei v Rossii*, I, 32, 35–36, 38; Ivanov-Razumnik, *Istoriia russkoi obshchestvennoi mysli* (ed. 2; St. P., 1911), I, 125.

[83] Herzen, A., *Du développement des idées révolutionnaires en Russie*, 74; Herzen, *Sochineniia* (Petrograd, 1919), VI, 352.

[84] *Minuvshie Gody*, I (1908), 13. An admirable survey of the various interpre-tations of the Decembrist movement and Pestel's *Russian Justice* may be found in Paradizov, *Ocherki po istoriografii dekabristov* (M., 1929).

PAVEL PESTEL.

detested aristocracy and every political and social feature associated with it, and he sought a rational basis for political society.[85] For this purpose he was willing to use even religion as a means for the enforcement of his political ideal. He definitely stated:[86]

The clergy must be recognized as a part of the government and a most respected part. It must be a branch of the state administration . . . and clergymen are both state employees and Russian citizens, such as are generally all state employees occupying positions in the government administration.

In demanding the equal distribution of land, Pestel seems to have intended to disarm the aristocracy, which he hated above everything else, particularly the aristocracy of wealth, as he called it. He wrote:[87]

The distinctive characteristic of the present century is the evident struggle between the people and the feudal aristocracy. During this struggle there begins to arise an aristocracy of wealth, which is far more harmful than feudal aristocracy . . . for it brings the entire people into subjection.

Fearing an aristocracy of wealth more than an aristocracy of birth, he demanded that it be mercilessly destroyed by the government, though how Pestel, with his doctrine of *laissez faire,* would have prevented the growth of such a class it is difficult to see. Although he realized the importance of industry, Pestel placed greater faith in agriculture, in which he saw a firmer economic foundation, and his picture of the future Russia was more like a country of prosperous peasants than one of industrial magnates.[88] Finally, it might be added that Pestel, unlike the United Slavs, placed little faith in the masses as a political factor. On the very eve of the uprising, it is said, he made the following statement: "The mass is a nonentity; it is nothing but what the individual wishes it to be."[89] At times the immensity of the task of stirring the inert masses to action and the colossal difficulties disheartened even Pestel. One evening in November, 1825, in a conversation with Lorer, member of the Southern Society, Pestel suddenly said:[90]

Nikolai Ivanovich, everything I shall tell you here, let it be a secret between us. I have not slept nights, thinking over constantly an important step upon which to decide. . . . Receiving oftener and oftener unfavorable information from the branches, becoming convinced that the members of our Society are cooling off more and more toward *notre bonne cause,* that no one is doing any-

---

[85] *Minuvshie Gody,* XII (1908), 171–172.

[86] *Russkaia Pravda,* 62, 194.

[87] *Ibid.,* 59.

[88] *Ibid.,* 209–210.

[89] *Ivanov-Rasumnik,* op. cit., 1, 103.

[90] Lorer, *Zapiski dekabrista,* 79.

thing for its success, that the Emperor is even informed about the existence of
our Society and only waits for a plausible pretext to seize us all, I have determined to wait till 1826, go down to Taganrog, and appeal to the Emperor
to listen to the urgent necessity of granting Russia all reforms and thereby
destroy the Society and prevent further development.

Lorer tried to convince Pestel of the absurdity and the risk of such
an undertaking, which indeed he seemed sufficiently to appreciate.
It was evidently one of those depressing moments too well known
to all under-cover workers.

Pestel can be considered neither a Bonapartist nor a socialist.
Though he placed complete faith in individual leadership, there is
little evidence that he had any schemes for becoming a Russian
Napoleon. On the contrary, he desired to follow the example of
that great American rebel and statesman whose political sincerity
and total absence of personal ambition impressed many men at
that time. To Poggio, member of the Southern Society, Pestel once
declared that, after the revolution, he intended to imitate President Washington, abandon politics and retire—not to a Mount
Vernon—but to a monastery.[91] Nor could Pestel have been a socialist, for his political program definitely indicates that he never
advocated complete nationalization or socialization of the land, but
emphatically recommended small private landownership, an un-
healthy element for any socialist program. His future Russia, as
he pictured it in *Russian Justice*, would be predominantly of such
a class. Pestel's program was directed against the large landowners; had the whole scheme been put into effect, part of their
land would probably have become nationalized and the rest would
have fallen into the hands of a middle-class peasantry. But would
the "aristocracy of wealth" which Pestel dreaded so much have
been completely wiped out by this process? Of course not, for his
plan gave full freedom to the individual to accumulate wealth, including land, and even to buy land from the state. "There will
always be the wealthy, and that is a good thing," he states, evidently
referring to the more prosperous. But nothing in Pestel's program
could prevent the individual citizen from attaining the wealth
which Pestel feared. Is that the ideal of the socialist?

Pestel strove to assure a minimum income for the great masses,
and if in this process some were to exceed that minimum so much
the better. He feared not so much a rich peasantry as he did the

---

[91] *Materialy,* IV, 160, 182. Cf. Herzen, *Sochineniia,* VI, 352.

concentration of financial capital in the hands of a few who would be able to control the state as well as to make the people dependent upon them; that is what Pestel had in mind when he referred to an aristocracy of wealth. He dreaded a strong "Wall Street" in the state. Universal suffrage, he believed, would prevent that social evil. In this respect he went far beyond his time, and vastly farther than his contemporary, Nikita Muraviev, the strong exponent of property qualification as a basis of suffrage.

Pestel was no socialist, nor communist, nor, in a strict sense, a materialist; to Pushkin he once remarked: "Mon cœur est matérialiste, mais ma raison s'y réfuse." Pestel was a true product of his time: in religious views he was a deist; in economic, a physiocrat, and in political, a bourgeois liberal. But in the application of his liberal views to Russian conditions he went far ahead of his generation, as is particularly demonstrated by his agrarian program. No one before him or during his time had formulated the idea of political democracy in Russia in terms so precise, with such conviction, and in so true a spirit of prophecy as did Pestel. To quote his own words:

It seemed to me that the essence of the present century consisted in the struggle between the masses and the aristocracy of various kinds, the aristocracy of wealth as well as the hereditary. I judged that these aristocracies would finally become more powerful than the Monarch, as in England, and that they were essentially the main obstacle to national welfare and could be eliminated only under a republican form of government.

Disregarding his rank and completely breaking his class affiliation with the detested aristocracy, Pestel frankly came out with a program for a new social and political order and undertook to carry it out by a revolution. With the mass as a political "nonentity" he hoped to achieve this painful operation by a swift *coup d'état,* as happened in Spain, which would aid in maintaining order and preventing bloodshed. But in order to avoid the grave error of Riego, Pestel determined to go a step farther, and by destroying the royal family in Russia deprive the legitimists of any claimant to the throne and eliminate any possibility of the Sovereign's gradually defeating the revolutionary gains; hence his idea of the necessity of regicide and the special terroristic group, "garde perdue," as he called it. To choose such a course in Russia was no small deed: it required considerable political courage and faith in the undertaking. This alone is sufficient to place Pestel among the notable revolutionaries of his country. His fate, which ended his young life on the gallows, only confirms this view. During his brief lifetime he had already enjoyed wide popularity and admiration among most of the people who knew him. At a dinner given to the Emperor at Tulchin on one occasion, a contemporary relates: "An officer demanded of another sitting by him, who was the individual who had the greatest influence here? He replied, the Emperor. No, said the other, it is that little man, whom you see there, pointing to Pestel."[92] As for later generations, Pestel will always be remembered as one of the martyrs for freedom in Russia and as the author of the unique political document of Alexander's reign, a treatise that expressed ideas far in advance of all the Decembrists and their time.

---

[92] Lee, *The Last Days of Alexander*, 101.

Chapter V

DEVELOPMENTS IN THE NORTH

AFTER THE MOSCOW CONFERENCE, the Northern Society continued a flabby existence, and its members naïvely thought the fault was with its organization. In October, 1823, the Society decided to form a triumvirate in order to assist the leader, Nikita Muraviev, and to awaken interest among the members. Evgeny Obolensky and Sergei Trubetskoi were chosen. Of these Trubetskoi deserves a moment of attention, since he soon became not only the leader but the elected "dictator" in the fateful days of December 13–14, 1825, and therefore carried the heavy responsibility for the final developments as well as final failure of the Society.

The rôle of Trubetskoi in the uprising will be discussed elsewhere; here must be mentioned a few characteristic details of his personality so far as it has any immediate relation to the subject under consideration, the Society during 1823–24. Trubetskoi consented to accept the leadership because of his conviction that Russia faced a political upheaval unless something radical was undertaken. As he endeavored later to explain to the Committee for Investigation, the frequent peasant uprisings, the general opposition to the military colonies, and the cry against widespread corruption convinced him that the state demanded urgent attention. Timely reform, thought Trubetskoi, would prevent revolution and could be carried out by means which would not involve violence nor destroy the old foundation of the nation. Fundamentally, Trubetskoi and Muraviev held the same views: a constitutional monarchy, political and social emancipation on a basis very similar to that outlined in the constitution of Muraviev, and, above all, an immediate summoning of a National Assembly to adopt officially the future form of government and thus prevent any possible social unrest and the undermining of the prestige of the state. So much did Trubetskoi fear revolution, which would involve the masses, that he even naïvely cherished the hope of obtaining the consent of the Emperor to introduce a limited monarchy and to call for an Assembly to officiate that act. Therefore the introduction of the triumvirate brought nothing new as far as the political program of the Northern Society was concerned, and the two societies, Northern and Southern, remained as far apart as before.

Attempts at united action.—The broad revolutionary plans which Pestel outlined in his *Russian Justice* demanded an organization on a national scale.[1] St. Petersburg was to give the signal for revolutionary action; the capital, where the government apparatus was concentrated and where the Guard and the fleet, which were expected to support the uprising, were located, would be the most strategic point at which to begin. Playing a subordinate part, the rest of the army and the local administration were to support the movement in the center. This was Pestel's view, and the importance of maintaining close contact with the North was never for a moment overlooked, as his persistent efforts to establish an accord between the two societies indicate.[2] At the Kiev conference of 1822 the Southern Society emphasized the restoration of close relations with the northern members.[3] It was with this purpose that Pestel began in 1823 the frequent dispatch of delegates to the capital, and came himself to St. Petersburg in 1824.[4]

During the year 1823 Pestel persistently continued to send men to negotiate with the northern leaders for a closer alliance between the two societies. In February he dispatched Colonel Davydov with a personal message to Nikita Muraviev, in which Pestel set forth his views and urged united action.[5] His second emissary was Prince Bariatinsky, who arrived in the capital in June, 1823, with instructions to find out whether the South could expect assistance from the Northern Society, should the former revolt.[6] On the heels of Prince Bariatinsky followed Matvei Muraviev-Apostol with even greater designs: he established himself in the capital as the representative of Pestel, seeking the enrollment of new members, and secretly endeavoring to take over the leadership from Nikita Muraviev and to convince Trubetskoi of the wisdom of amalgamating with the South. "You are spending time here on conversations and disputes," he would argue. "You are not in agreement and you never will be. You only sophisticate, and the Southern Society is organized. I have been telling you for a long time: hasten and ally with it; a new form of government has already been drawn up and accepted;

[1] *Materialy*, IV, 157–158, 185, 187.

[2] *Ibid.*, IV, 101–105, 115; *Iz pisem i pokazanii dekabristov*, 112.

[3] *Materialy*, IV, 275.   [5] *Ibid.*, IV, 162.

[4] *Ibid.*, I, 87–88; IV, 276.   [6] *Ibid.*, IV, 162, 188, 352.

the South has a large army—this the Colonel [i.e., Pestel] will confirm, and here you have neither one nor the other."

After Muraviev-Apostol there came Volkonsky and again Davydov, who sought an understanding in respect to the political program of future Russia.[7] But all these missions and arguments achieved little: Nikita Muraviev remained adamant and, in spite of much persuasion, did not commit himself to any pledge. To the southern emissaries he gave only vague replies that he would do whatever was possible to develop revolutionary activities and complained of the political shallowness of the officers of the Guard, who "thought only of how to enjoy themselves at balls" rather than of becoming members of political organizations.

However, the frequent missions of the southern members were not entirely without results: individual members, for example, Prince Obolensky and Ryleev, were swayed to the cause of the South and favored a closer union.[8] Particularly conspicuous among these was that fiery northern member with the temperament of his Italian ancestors, Alexander Poggio, who ceaselessly hammered for the adoption of Pestel's program.[9] Nevertheless, the prosouthern group in the North remained in a minority, and the two societies continued aloof until their end. The views of the individual leaders, of course, do not explain the political gap between the two groups; the chief reason lies much deeper, namely, in the different social and economic undercurrents that distinguished the two societies, "the Decembrist Gironde and Montagne," which made their divergent views unavoidable.[10] The Northern Society counted among its members a considerable number of large landowners of the more eminent noble families and officers of the Guard, who were disinclined to the rash action and republican ideas preached by the southern members. In the South any similar element was virtually absent: most of the men belonged to a class which enjoyed neither great economic wealth nor political power. Here the social stratum was chiefly made up of poorer army officers, many of whom were landless and held their bourgeois-democratic ideas by virtue of their economic status. This was especially demonstrated by the Society of the United Slavs, which constituted the most radical wing of the Decembrist movement.

---

[7] Volkonsky, *Zapiski dekabrista,* 413, 420.
[8] See Zavalishin, *Zapiski dekabrista,* 335.
[9] Dovnar-Zapolsky, *Memuary dekabristov,* 194–195.
[10] *Bunt Dekabristov,* 47.

Pestel's arrival in St. Petersburg.—Dissatisfied with the meager results of his emissaries to the capital as well as with the achievements of the Northern Society, Pestel determined to intervene personally to remedy the situation. From his sympathizers in the North he had received information to the effect that the Society was not unanimous, that some members were not in agreement with Nikita Muraviev. Poggio came south and insisted that Muraviev be ousted and that Pestel begin to exert greater influence in the capital through his representative, Matvei Muraviev-Apostol. The southern members thought it wise to send Pestel himself in an endeavor to coördinate the activities of the two organizations, though they hesitated, fearing that if this effort failed, the last hope for an agreement would be lost. Moreover, the appearance of Pestel in person, some members thought, might have only a negative effect and intensify the already strained feelings of the leaders of the two factions. In spite of these fears the step was taken for the one reason which outweighed all other arguments: the strategic importance of the national capital, where the most serious blow could be inflicted upon the old régime. Control of the capital would almost certainly signify victory, a fact which Pestel had kept constantly in mind, insisting continually that without northern support the South must not start an uprising.[11] In March, 1824, he appeared in St. Petersburg in a last attempt to end, as he stated it, "the wandering in the mist," to coördinate and to stimulate activities, and to seek the adoption of a single revolutionary program.[12]

Pestel came to St. Petersburg accompanied by two other members, this action being calculated to weaken the opposition, which constantly tried to present him as a dictator. Pestel's task was not an easy one. He knew that the vital issue would be the program set forth in *Russian Justice,* which he was prepared to defend to the last, considering it the will of the whole Southern Society, not merely his personal view.[13] There were other difficulties to overcome, among them the Polish question. The Southern Society had pledged the Poles national independence; the Northern Society vehemently rejected this policy on the ground that no organization had the right to decide a matter involving the integrity of national territory. A nation which for centuries had become accustomed only to expansion would never tolerate territorial losses, argued

---

[11] *Materialy,* IV, 169.
[12] *Ibid.,* IV, 115.   [13] *Ibid.,* IV, 353, 354.

the northern leaders.[14] Besides, it would be unwise to grant independence to a state that was considered a potential enemy of Russia.[15] Even Ryleev rebelled against this policy, denying that the Society had any right to settle the Polish question. Other problems, less important but equally difficult, included the questions as to what government should be established immediately after the overthrow of the old one or what was to be done with the royal family. All these demanded a settlement to be arrived at with utmost caution and perfect understanding if victory was to be achieved.

Preliminary negotiations.—Upon his arrival in the capital Pestel began first to confer with individuals, apparently seeking to prepare the way for collective negotiations later. First he interviewed Prince Trubetskoi, to whom he complained that nothing had been done in the North, that no one wished to do anything, and that Muraviev was not replying to his letters. He praised the Southern Society, recommended to Trubetskoi that a similar organization, based on rigorous discipline, be founded in the North and that the societies be united under one administration.[16] Trubetskoi, characteristically, expressed no definite opinion, promising neither support nor opposition; one moment he favored a republican form of government, the next moment he questioned it.[17] He opposed regicide, believing that it would discredit the Society in the eyes of the public, to which objection Pestel replied that the act would be carried out by persons not associated with the Society, but Trubetskoi remained doubtful about it.[18] A compromise between the two leaders was utterly impossible, for they seemed to speak in different languages.

With Prince Obolensky Pestel accomplished much more. After Pestel had explained his mission in the capital and had emphasized the importance of common action, Obolensky promised that he would exert his influence in favor of the unification of the two organizations and the adoption of the Southern constitution.[19] Reassured by Obolensky, Pestel next had a long conference with Ryleev, who at that time had already become one of the most influential members of the Northern Society. Later, in his testimony, Ryleev gave a detailed account of this conference, which throws a flood of light upon the cautiously planned policy of Pestel.[20] At

[14] *Ibid.*, I, 300.
[15] *Ibid.*, I, 96, 180.
[16] *Ibid.*, I, 15–16.
[17] *Ibid.*, IV, 162.
[18] *Ibid.*, I, 27–28, 87, 96, 101, 140; IV, 198–200.
[19] *Ibid.*, I, 255–257.
[20] *Ibid.*, I, 154.

first Pestel, wishing merely to ascertain Ryleev's opinion, politely inquired what he would regard as the best form of government for Russia, he himself pretending to be undetermined, or, as Ryleev later stated, "within two hours he was an admirer of the United States, a defender of the English Constitution, and a follower of the Spanish." Ryleev explained that he considered the best form to be a federal republic, like the United States, but with an Emperor who would be granted powers similar to those of the President of that Republic. Pestel only remarked that such a plan was indeed a "happy thought" which deserved serious consideration.[21]

Conference with the Council.—Following his interviews with individuals, Pestel went a step farther and took up the task of conferring with the Society on a collective basis. When the Council assembled, Pestel joined the gathering and the real negotiation began. Nikita Muraviev was unable to attend the first meeting because of the illness of his wife. His absence made Pestel's task of overcoming the opposition much easier; Pestel eloquently described to the Council the existing situation and the necessity for the two societies to find a common ground, and apparently he made a profound impression. "It was difficult to resist so charming a personality as that of Pavel Ivanovich Pestel," writes Obolensky in his *Memoirs.*[22] But the champion of the opposition, Nikita Muraviev, had not yet been faced, and the final decision therefore remained undetermined.

At last, a few days later, Pestel and Nikita Muraviev met. The two leaders began to discuss their plans, and immediately serious differences of opinion appeared. Muraviev wished less secrecy; Pestel insisted upon a strictly conspiratory organization, in which, in order to eliminate all political feuds and to maintain perfect unity, not even all the members were to be informed of its real aims. Muraviev disliked any idea of terror; Pestel developed his idea of the "garde perdue" which would rid the country of the royal family. Muraviev hoped to introduce his constitution without serious political disturbance; Pestel also hoped to avoid social upheaval, but he maintained that the new order would not come at once, that it would take a long time, perhaps a decade, for its enforcement. He recommended that during the transitional period a provisional government with dictatorial powers be set up; also,

[21] *Ibid.,* I, 178–179.
[22] *Obshchestvennye Dvizheniia v Rossii,* I, 238.

KONDRATY RYLEEV.

that the Senate and the Synod be forced to proclaim this government lawful. "The entire plan," recollects Muraviev, "appeared to me as unfeasible and impossible, barbarian and morally repellent." The views of both leaders were so far apart that further conversation seemed useless, and an agreement was out of the question.[23]

Pestel's failure.—At the next meeting of the Council, Pestel was again present. This time the opposition was reënforced not only by Nikita Muraviev but also by Pestel's bitterest enemy, Turgenev, who later in his *Memoirs,* in order to protect himself, disgracefully denied his participation in the discussion.[24] Turgenev was respected in the North for his erudition and regarded as a profound authority on the land problem in Russia. He considered Pestel's agrarian program chimerical, questioning its economic soundness and endeavoring to show the retarding effects that it would produce upon the development of national industry. His arguments against Pestel's agrarian plans deeply impressed the assembled members.[25] Muraviev attacked the political program, declaring that he would never accept a plan like that of Pestel and that he considered himself justified in rejecting the opinion of a majority if it did not meet the approval of his conscience.[26] Thus neither the economic nor the political program was accepted, the first being rejected by Turgenev, the second by Muraviev. In such a situation further efforts to draw the two societies together were futile. Neither side was willing to yield on the vital issues of its program, each remaining convinced that its course was the right one.[27] Both sides fearing total rupture, the two parties therefore agreed on minor issues: that neither one would start a revolt without notifying the other and that they would exchange plans of their activities. Such a decision was really in favor of the northern group, for it meant that the Northern Society would be informed of any action by the Southern Society, which was seriously considering revolution. All that Pestel achieved, therefore, on the mission in which he had placed so much hope, was the faint promise of Obolensky to work in favor of his plan. Muraviev remained as much opposed as ever.[28] On the

---

[23] *Materialy,* I, 323–324, 325–326.

[24] Turgenev, *Rossiia i russkie,* I, 230–232. Cf. Volkonsky, *op. cit.,* 418, 421–422.

[25] Dovnar-Zapolsky, *Tainoe obshchestvo dekabristov,* 246; *Materialy,* IV, 162.

[26] *Materialy,* I, 308–309.

[27] *Ibid.,* I, 174–175.   [28] *Ibid.,* IV, 163.

eve of his departure Pestel made a last effort to achieve his goal by endeavoring to weaken the northern organization from within, by withdrawing members and offering them responsible membership in the Southern Council. Such an offer he made to Trubetskoi, who refused it.[29] Pestel returned home, deeply disappointed with his visit to the capital and with the cold reception with which his plans were met by the leaders in the North. Moreover, Pestel's stubbornness aroused a bitter feeling against him among the opposition, who accused him of an attempt "to foist written hypotheses in the tone of an apostle, of which only God knows whether they are applicable or not."[30]

Ryleev as leader of the North.—The two societies remained apart, yet Pestel's constant pressure upon the northern members had accomplished more than he suspected. It aided in spreading his revolutionary ideas, and, though it failed to unite the two societies, it tended to galvanize the phlegmatic element; it proved the necessity for better organization in order to resist the enroachment of Pestel, especially his establishment of a permanent representative in the capital who sought to enroll new members for the Southern Society; finally, it inspired some of the leaders, such as Ryleev, the noted romantic poet and idealist.

Early in 1825 Nikita Muraviev, because of certain family affairs, had to retire from the Council, and Trubetskoi was commissioned to Kiev. In the absence of the two important members, Ryleev virtually became the sole leader of the Society, and in this interval he developed feverish activity and got some surprising results. Ryleev was of a temperament very different from that of his predecessor.[31] Muraviev was practical and never allowed his conviction to conflict with reality. A republican in political matters and a deist in his religious views, he did not hesitate to place these convictions aside when he set to work on a practical program for the Society. He therefore adopted a constitutional, or limited, monarchy on the ground, however, that autocracy was not "in accord with the rules of our sacred faith." Ryleev was more dynamic, but less able to attain a balance between idealism and reality, and therefore, perhaps, ended more tragically. He was an agnostic, a forerunner of Thomas Hardy, believing in an "It," but this belief

---

[29] Pavlov-Silvansky, *Sochineniia*, II, 232.

[30] *Materialy*, IV, 353; Dovnar-Zapolsky, *Memuary dekabristov*, 274–275.

[31] *Materialy*, I, 57.

failed to establish any relationship between himself the agnostic and practical everyday life. Small wonder, when the whole under-taking failed, that Ryleev was crushed and immediately turned to the other extreme, advising his wife to pray for his soul and to complain "neither to Him nor to the Sovereign," because to do so would be senseless and sinful.[32] Ryleev endeavored to convince Nicholas that he had made peace with the Creator and retracted his erring political views. Between his earlier revolutionary poems and the last letters to Nicholas, there is a vast distance indeed. But if the former were dictated by his poetic enthusiasm and genuine sense of civil responsibility, the latter came as a result of a pathetic moral annihilation and a pathological mental state following seven months of imprisonment, torture, and expectation of execution.

Muraviev was conservative, well balanced, and rational—an academician type. Ryleev was a liberal, less determined in his views, adhering to his political ideas in large measure because of a poetic intuition. Muraviev came to his political creed through cold logic, Ryleev through ecstatic feeling; if the former came into the Society attracted by a certain goal, Ryleev was drawn into it like a moth drawn by the flickering flame in the night. This he seemed to have sensed prophetically when he wrote in his well-known poem, *Nalivaiko :*[33]

> My coming doom I feel and know
> And bless the stroke which lays me low,
> And, father, now with joy I meet
> My death; to me such end is sweet.

Ryleev was too emotional to elaborate political doctrines, conceiv-ing them rather as a poet conceives ideas of some beautiful form.[34] If Muraviev was the brains of the Society, Ryleev was its soul. Like Pestel, Ryleev was religiously devoted to the aims of the secret society and leaned toward the southern views, though, unlike Pes-tel, he pursued his course without specific plans. His revolutionary program might be formulated in his own words: "Circumstances will show what it is necessary to do."[35] Standing between the North and the South, hesitant between the constitutional monarchy of

---

[32] Ryleev, *Sochineniia* (M., 1934), 517, 518.

[33] From K. F. Ryleev, *Nalivaiko.* Tr. by T. Hart-Davies (Calcutta, 1879).

[34] *Materialy*, I, 144.

[35] Kotliarevsky, *op. cit.*, 159.

Muraviev and the Jacobin republic of Pestel, he dimly imagined future Russia as a republic with "certain monarchical features" and an Emperor with powers like those of the President of the United States.[36] However, even that was merely a personal supposition not to be foisted upon Russia but only to be presented to the future National Assembly.[37]

It was this constant vacillation that led Ryleev to his physical defeat and moral breakdown. Liberal toward other oppressed nationalities, for example, the Ukrainians, as shown in his poem "Voinarovsky," he displayed surprising intolerance toward the Poles. His patriotic sentiments are well revealed in his "Meditations," which convinced his literary critics that "there is blood in the author's veins;"[38] and in discussing the Polish question with Pestel, Ryleev's patriotism was tinged with a strong chauvinistic flavor. He refused to recognize any possible agreement with the Polish Secret Patriotic Society whereby future territorial concessions might be involved, and was hesitant even to grant national independence to Poland, a potentially hostile state.[39] These inconsistencies alone are sufficient to show the vagueness of his political conceptions. He lacked the reserved nature of Pestel and Nikita Muraviev, a trait so important for conspiratory work, and had not the Council passed a rule forbidding excessive enrollment of members, Ryleev would probably have brought in many more people than he actually did.

If upon his visit to the South in 1824 Trubetskoi was impressed by the dominant influence of Pestel, he was equally impressed in the North when he returned a year later to find the Society very much alive and "greatly enlarged."[40] Through N. Bestuzhev and Arbuzov, Ryleev established contact with the Marine Guard, which, in his opinion, was to play a prominent part in capturing the capital as well as in transporting the royal family abroad after the overthrow of the old government.[41] He succeeded in enrolling new members, equally enthusiastic and visionary, some of whom were to play a prominent part in the approaching events. Among them were the four Bestuzhev brothers, the poet, Odoevsky, and Küchelbecker, the navy men, Torson and Zavalishin, the economist, Steingel, the excellent administrator, Batenkov, and Kakhovsky, the

---

[36] *Materialy*, I, 175.

[37] *Ibid.*, I, 174.

[38] *Ostafievsky Arkhiv*, II, 270.

[39] Kotliarevsky, *op. cit.* 146–147.

[40] *Materialy*, I, 10.

[41] *Ibid.*, I, 182–183; Zavalishin, *op. cit.*, 339.

Russian Karl Sand—men who were, in the words of Pokrovsky, "the intelligentsia of the nobility who became revolutionaries not by virtue of their noble rank, but because of being intelligentsia in spite of their noble origin."[42] These new men gave a different character to the Society in the North: most of them were small landowners and hardly any of them owned serfs.[43] Ryleev was the son of a small bankrupt landlord whose property in Kiev the government had sequestered, a fact which aroused the passionate protest of the twenty-year-old son and future Decembrist, who indignantly wrote: "Ye powerful and wealthy! Are your hearts not human? Had you no feeling at all when you took away the last farthing from the suffering?"[44]

Moreover, a distinct change was noticeable with the appearance in the Society of such men as Ryleev, Wilhelm Küchelbecker, Batenkov, and Steingel, who were not army men: Ryleev was associated with the Russian-American Company; Küchelbecker was a lecturer and writer; Batenkov was associated with the military colonies, and Steingel was a retired government clerk and director of a private school for boys in Moscow.[45] The appearance of civil members indicated that the small circle which originally began with military men had expanded and begun to embrace members of other social classes. Ryleev favored the extension of membership to representatives of the merchant class, though others seemed to have little opinion of them; but the fact that such a proposal was made is significant.[46] These newly initiated members, of different social ranks, were naturally bound to break away from the conservative program of the previous leaders, like Muraviev, and to adopt a broader program, based on national rather than class principles. Had time allowed, the course of development would perhaps have taken a turn similar to that in the South, where the younger generation, with economic and political traditions less rooted in the past, constituted a dominant majority. But the brief existence of the Northern Society checked such a development and the poten-

---

[42] Pokrovsky, *Dekabristy. Sbornik statei*, 78–79.

[43] *Krasnyi Arkhiv*, XV, 170–198 *passim*.

[44] Letter of Ryleev to his mother, March 6, 1815.—*Sochineniia*, 435.

[45] Ryleev retired from military service in 1818. He came to the conclusion that his character did not permit him to be a soldier, "for," he wrote to his parents, "military service under present circumstances requires only scoundrels, and I, fortunately, cannot be one . . . ."—*Sochineniia*, 446.

[46] *Materialy*, I, 179.

tialities of the Society in the North had it functioned under the leadership of such men as Ryleev, Batenkov, Kakhovsky, or Bestuzhev, remain to be guessed.

The funeral of Chernov.—As a writer of high merit, Ryleev awakened many people. His inspiring poetry praising liberty and passionately condemning the rule of Arakcheev, his "verses not smooth but delightful because of their bitterness and audacity," as Grech said, were read by many people in Russia and circulated in handwritten form, since they often failed to pass the censor. Written in collaboration with A. Bestuzhev, his popular verses, "Oh, how nauseating even in my own land," or "Where are those islands?" were set to music and sung in virtually all circles, in conservative circles like that in the home of Bulgarin as well as in those where participants openly advocated the necessity of "d'en finir avec ce gouvernement."[47] The government used every means to eradicate the songs and destroyed them whenever found. But, written in the form of folksongs in which the sad conditions of the masses were well reflected, they passed from mouth to mouth and no power could have stamped them out.[48]

Ryleev exploited every opportunity for the benefit of the Society, even the funeral of his cousin and close friend, Constantine Chernov, an army officer and member of the Northern Society, who, while fighting a duel to clear the honor of his sister, was killed by another officer, Novosiltsov. This inspired Ryleev to write the fiery poem "On the Death of Chernov" and gave him the opportunity to transform the funeral into a political event, an imposing demonstration in which all the Society members and sympathizers and all those in revolt against the existing conditions were brought together.[49] Both men were killed, but popular sympathy was on the side of Chernov. Novosiltsov was a descendant of the powerful, wealthy noble family of the Orlovs; Chernov, though belonging to the nobility, came from a humble, obscure family, and this social distinction was used by the Society in protest against the aristocracy, or, as one contemporary writes, "to express in a silent procession the sympathy with the one who represented the idea of the protection of the weak against the strong, the virtuous against the

---

[47] Ryleev, *Sochineniia*, 269, 271; Grech, *Zapiski o moei Zhizni*, 517; *Literaturnye Salony i Kruzhki*, 142–143.

[48] *Vospominaniia Bestuzhevykh*, 79.

[49] *XIX Viek*, I, 317–319, 333–337; *Obshchestvennye Dvizheniia v Rossii*, I, 233–237, 410.

vile.''[50] ''Ryleev,'' writes another contemporary, ''the sworn foe of
the aristocracy, began to fan the fire and ended with the challenge
of Chernov to Novosiltsov.''[51] The first was true; as for the second,
that Ryleev was responsible for the duel, it is doubtful, for Chernov
voluntarily chose to die in order to destroy his enemy so that he
could serve ''as an example to the base snobs that gold and noble
birth could not disdain innocence and gentility of the soul.''[52]

The Terror. ''Une Garde Perdue.''—The Decembrists were an
offspring of the romantic-revolutionary movement in which the
Diegos and the Sands were the heroes of the day, hailed openly by
many writers. Intensive reading in ancient history brought popularity and reverence to heroes of the past who had sacrificed their
lives for the common welfare. In the ancient world, in the writings
of Cicero, Tacitus, Plutarch, Titus, and Polybius, the Decembrists
found the heroes whom they endeavored to imitate. The romantic
twenties of the nineteenth century brought a revival of interest
in ancient history, particularly that of Greece, and the idealiza-
tion of men like Brutus. Yakushkin, who was first at the Moscow
conference to offer to assassinate Alexander, kept on his table,
among other books, the letters of Brutus to Cicero, which he greatly
treasured and read to his friends.[53] The ''steel-white dagger'' as the
''iron-hearted friend'' and symbol of freedom as well as weapon
against tyranny was glorified by Ryleev, Pushkin, and Lermontov.
Warned once by Batenkov that revolutions usually lead to the ''despotism of a single ambitious man,'' Ryleev replied that ''there always existed a freeman's dagger against such an ambitious one.''[54]
Ryleev, as leader of the Northern Society, though himself unable
to play the part of Brutus because of his too kindly nature,
earnestly hoped that such a man would come to relieve Russia from
despotism. The appearance in St. Petersburg of Yakubovich and
Kakhovsky was opportune for the romantic mood of Ryleev, who
had had in mind for some time some sort of ''garde perdue,'' such
as Pestel was planning; they were necessary, for when the hour
struck, the Society could ''unleash'' them for the necessary terroristic act.[55]

---

[50] *XIX Viek*, I, 319; *Russky Arkhiv*, VI (1890), 169–170.
[51] *Russky Arkhiv*, III (1880), 321.
[52] *XIX Viek*, I, 334.
[53] Yakushkin, I, *Zapiski*, 26.
[54] *Russkie Propilei*, II, 104.
[55] *Materialy*, I, 88, 105, 180, 193–194, 363–364, 435.

Yakubovich.—Alexander Yakubovich was a brilliant officer who had returned to the capital in 1825 as the hero of many daring campaigns against the natives in the Caucasus. Seriously wounded in the head, he had undergone a dangerous operation and terrific suffering, and he now contemplated suicide. However, the lamentable condition of the country, caused as he thought by Alexander, led him to decide that before his death he would deliver Russia from the Emperor. He had also a personal grudge against Alexander. Being once punished for participating in a duel, Yakubovich had been sent south, where he had spent six years in continuous and daring fighting, yet the Emperor had never ordered his former status or privileges to be restored to him.[56] An embittered feeling of hopelessness and revenge brought him to the capital to fulfill his plan of assassinating the Emperor. With that done, he suggested sarcastically to Ryleev, the Society might call a Great Assembly where the members could talk to their hearts' content.[57] Yakubovich was a true child of his time, so well presented by Lermontov in the character of Pechorin in his novel *A Hero of Our Time;* "a romantic storm in a glass of water," one writer describes Yakubovich. At that time Ryleev and other members, considering the assassination of Alexander as premature and possibly ruinous to the plans of the Society, implored Yakubovich to postpone his decision, and he complied, but his ardent ambition was remembered for possible future use.[58]

Kakhovsky.—Peter Kakhovsky, though in spirit kindred to Yakubovich, was intellectually far superior. Like Yakubovich, Kakhovsky earnestly desired to carry out the assassination of the Emperor, but he motivated his ambition not by any personal sentiment, but by the sole conviction that ridding the nation of a tyrant was a moral act and not a crime. "What can be sweeter than death after feeling that one has contributed something to one's country?" he wrote from his prison cell. "A person carried away by a pure idea, sacrifices himself not in order to receive glory or a line in history, but to perform the good for the sake of good, without reward." The psychology of Kakhovsky, his sincere desire to offer his life in order to liberate his country, derived not from any personal grudge, as with Yakubovich, nor from his extreme loneliness,

---

[56] *Ibid.*, II, 285–286, 290; Volkonsky, *op. cit.*, 415–416.

[57] *Materialy*, I, 181; II, 292.

[58] *Ibid.*, I, 19, 35–36, 68, 181–182, 269, 434.

PETER KAKHOVSKY.

personal obscurity, or material want, nor his ambition to demonstrate by his "boundless generous soul" the nobility of his character.[59] These alone would not be sufficient to explain Kakhovsky's conduct, as Professor Shchegolev has so admirably proved. Kakhovsky spent much of his time in the study of political history and he was keenly observant of the revolutionary developments in Western Europe, as his prison letters distinctly show. His faith in the Russian people and in the idea of terror as a weapon of the people against tyranny came to him on his long journey across the country from St. Petersburg to the Caucasus, whither he went for a cure, from his brief visit to his estate in the Gubernia of Smolensk, and finally from his travel abroad. "Journeying from the north to the south of Russia," writes Kakhovsky, "I endeavored to investigate the condition of the various classes of people; from everywhere I heard protests against the government and the rulers appointed by it."[60] In Europe he observed that "the prisons of Piedmont, Sardinia, Naples and in general of the whole of Italy and Germany were filled with chained citizens. The lot of the people became so oppressive that they began to regret the past and bless the memory of Napoleon the conqueror! These are the incidents which enlightened their minds and made them realize that it was impossible to make agreements with sovereigns."[61] The sincerity of Kakhovsky was not denied even by Nicholas I, who remarks in his *Memoirs:*[62]

Kakhovsky talked boldly, harshly, positively and frankly. . . . Yet he was young, filled with love for his Fatherland, though in the most criminal fashion.

In 1825 Kakhovsky returned from Western Europe to St. Petersburg with the intention of proceeding to Greece, where he was to follow the example of Byron and join the struggle for Greek independence. In St. Petersburg he met his old acquaintance, Ryleev, who immediately realized that Kakhovsky was just the man the Society needed.[63] Regicide, Ryleev considered as a possibly necessary measure to assure victory, though, later in his testimony, he wondered how such a thought could ever have entered his mind. At any rate, the idea of having the future Russian Sand in the capital to "unleash" when the moment arrived, was evidently the chief motive for persuading Kakhovsky to remain in the North. But disagreements between the two soon began to crop out, and

[59] Shchegolev, *Dekabristy*, 157, 179–180.

[60] *Iz pisem i pokazanii dekabristov*, 19. [62] *Mezhdutsarstvie*, 33.

[61] *Ibid.*, 13. [63] *Obshchestvennye Dvizheniia v Rossii*, I, 243.

often led to sharp encounters. Kakhovsky was impatient, Ryleev hesitant; the first was ignorant of the plans as well as of the exact nature of the Society and its program; the second deliberately kept him in ignorance and demanded only one thing of him, that Kakhovsky obey the orders of the "Council." To Kakhovsky, Ryleev described the "Council" as a powerful body backed by an equally powerful organization, and Kakhovsky naturally wondered what was the obstacle to action. His desire to enroll as a member of the Society conflicted with the designs of Ryleev, who believed that the assassination of the Emperor should not be carried out by anyone associated with the Society, thus casting a shadow upon it. This attitude often irritated Kakhovsky and made him suspicious of Ryleev, a feeling which increased as time went on and made him believe that he was kept merely as a tool for some future exploit. "If he [Ryleev] considers me a dagger," remarked Kakhovsky once to Alexander Bestuzhev, "then please tell him to watch not to hurt himself. I have noticed for some time that Ryleev wishes to persuade me, but he will be deceived. I am ready to sacrifice myself for the Fatherland, but I shall not lie down before him or anyone else merely as a stepping stone to any elevation."

At times Kakhovsky was almost ready to depart from the capital because of financial difficulties, but Ryleev generously extended him the necessary amount in order to detain him at a place where he was easily available. In offering him financial aid, Ryleev insisted that he either join the army and remain in St. Petersburg or seek an appointment in the military colonies, where reliable members were necessary in order to prepare the inhabitants for rebellion; he even offered to pay for his military uniform.[64]

Kakhovsky often found himself in great want, even in desperation. "Do me a favor, Kondraty Feodorovich, save me!" writes Kakhovsky to Ryleev on November 6, 1825. "I have no more strength to endure all the misfortunes which I meet daily. Disregarding loneliness and unpleasantness, I am even unable to appease hunger: since Tuesday I have not eaten anything."[65] The request was evidently complied with, for Kakhovsky remained in the capital and soon found himself in the midst of unexpected developments. From all accounts, it is clear that, whatever the plans of the Decembrists were in the North, the earliest that the uprising could be hoped for

[64] *Materialy,* I, 372–373; *Obshchestvennye Dvizheniia v Rossii,* I, 243.
[65] *Russkaia Starina,* XII (1888), 600.

was sometime in 1826.[66] No one, even in view of the unfolding revolutionary activity, could have predicted that events would move so rapidly toward their tragic end, in which Kakhovsky was to play no small part.

Unexpected developments.—Early in November, 1825, Prince Trubetskoi returned to the capital from the South and brought with him first-hand information about the Society there. He reported to Ryleev and Obolensky that revolution might occur at any time, thanks to the presence of the soldiers of the former Semenovsky regiment and the consolidation of the Society by its alliance with the Poles and its amalgamation with the United Slavs. The Society, he said, had at its disposal about 70,000 soldiers who would obey their orders, and its leaders were planning to rise in 1826, regardless of whether or not the North would support them. Trubetskoi therefore inquired what plans were being considered in the capital. Ryleev was skeptical. Notwithstanding the desirability of extending assistance, he stated, they were not yet fully prepared to do so.[67] On the heels of Trubetskoi there came to the capital a special delegate, Kornilovich, sent by Sergei Muraviev-Apostol to inform the northern members of the plans of the Southern Society, in accordance with the agreement reached in 1824 by Pestel.[68]

But suddenly all plans and negotiations became superfluous: an avalanche of events forced the leaders to take rapid measures to meet the unexpected situation. News reached St. Petersburg that the Emperor had died in Taganrog.[69] The death of Alexander I and the question of his successor had been considered as a pretext for a *coup d'état* on more than one occasion, but no one had expected it so soon. Against their own wishes, therefore, the leaders were forced hurriedly to undertake the plot, which was doomed from the very beginning because of its lack of preparation, unity, and faith.[70] The year 1825, according to Obolensky, had been met "with a smile of happiness and hope," but it ended with great personal and general social catastrophes.[71] However, before proceeding with the narration of the unsuccessful uprising of December 14, 1825, it is necessary to relate what had been taking place in the South in the period that we have just reviewed in the North.

---

[66] *Materialy*, I, 140, 373; IV, 103–104, 169.
[67] *Ibid.*, I, 10, 94, 95–96, 100, 179–180, 270–271.
[68] *Ibid.*, I, 21, 94, 268; IV, 200.
[69] *Materialy*, I, 458.
[70] *Ibid.*, I, 10, 435–436.   [71] *Obshchestvennye Dvizheniia v Rossii*, I, 242.

Chapter VI

DEVELOPMENTS IN THE SOUTH

FROM THE FIRST the Southern Society progressed more rapidly than the Northern. As indicated earlier (see p. 84), affairs in the South were guided by a Directory, though in reality they were in the hands of Pestel, with the center of activities at Tulchin, a southern town in which the headquarters of the Second Army were located. The Society had two important branches: one at Vasilkov, headed by Sergei Muraviev-Apostol and Mikhail Bestuzhev-Riumin, the other at Kamenka under the leadership of Prince Sergei Volkonsky and Vasily Davydov. Because of the energy of the young leader, Bestuzhev-Riumin, the Vasilkov branch very shortly became the active center, expanding soon to such a degree that it had a larger membership than the main organization at Tulchin. Two of the most striking achievements of the Vasilkov branch were the connection it established with the Polish Secret Patriotic Society and the amalgamation with it of another revolutionary organization known as the Society of the United Slavs.

Alliance with the Polish Society.—Negotiations between the Southern Society and the Polish Society did not begin until 1823, though each party was vaguely aware of the other's existence much earlier. Many Poles had been in touch with Russian army officers during the latter's stay in Poland and had observed the liberal movement among them. For the time being, the Poles had refrained from linking their cause with any Russian organization, as many still hoped that Alexander would gradually grant Poland constitutional government and autonomy. But the increasing reaction destroyed their hopes, and the Polish Patriotic Society became more active, looking for any alliance which would aid its cause and undermine the chief foe. The Southern Society, for its part, could not afford to overlook possible assistance from the Polish Patriots. The viceroy of Poland was the Grand Duke Constantine, who in the event of the death of Alexander would succeed to the throne; furthermore, a large part of the Russian army, for example, the Lithuanian Corps, was on Polish territory. To neutral-ize that potential force, which autocracy might use against the revolutionaries to crush the uprising, became the aim of the Southern Society. An understanding between the two societies, therefore, seemed mutually beneficial, and steps toward it were undertaken.

Who made the first move is not clear; it is assumed, and not without justification, that the initiative was taken by the Poles, since they were constantly on the lookout for allies abroad.[1] The first contacts must have been established in the latter part of 1822, for at the annual conference of the Southern Society, held at Kiev early in 1823, Bestuzhev-Riumin announced that he had discovered the existence of a secret Polish organization. The assembled members became interested and immediately authorized him, together with Sergei Muraviev-Apostol, to open negotiations for the establishment of coördinated action.[2] Communication was soon established through Count Chodkiewicz, who, though he did not belong to the Society, was acquainted with the Polish leaders.

The Polish Secret Society.—The Polish Secret Patriotic Society was an offspring of Polish Masonry (*Wolnomularstwo Narodowe*) and of a former political organization, "True Poles" (*Prawdziwych Polaków*) that had sprung up in 1814. It was founded in 1821 under the leadership of Lukasinsky, with headquarters in Warsaw and with one sole aim—to gain national independence for Poland.[3] To win this end the Society was willing to use any possible aid from outside, including Russia, and, as some evidence indicates, its plea was not without success elsewhere, particularly in England.[4] Rumors were spread among the Polish members, and through them reached the ears of the Decembrists, that Lord Canning was in favor of an independent Poland. Whether the English statesman was sincere in this matter is not known, but rumors were sufficient to stimulate the growing patriotic movement in Poland. For diplomatic reasons the Russian government was careful not to commit itself to any statements concerning the issues, and the whole matter remains obscure. There is some evidence that many Polish secret societies, Masonic and political, maintained relations with England, France, and Sweden, and hoped, in the event of revolt, to obtain from them financial and moral aid.[5] To gain an ally in

---

[1] Korobka, "Polskie obshchestva 20-kh godov i dekabristy." *O Minuvshem,* 220; *Russkaia Starina,* XII (1895), 160.

[2] *Materialy,* IV, 106, 116.   [4] *Materialy,* IV, 108, 289–290.

[3] Askenazy, *Tsarstvo Polskoe,* 73–74.   [5] Korobka, *op. cit.,* 220–221.

Russia would have been especially desirable, since that country occupied the largest part of Poland and was probably the strongest obstacle to its national aspirations.

In southern Russia the Poles might have expected to find a sympathetic attitude toward their cause among army men who were seeking liberal government in their own country and among the Ukrainian nationalists. There is some suspicion, and with reason, that the early Masonic lodge, *Les Slaves Réunis,* had been in large part sponsored by the Poles as a means by which Poles and Ukrainians might meet. Also, there is the belief that the participation of Julian Lublinsky in the Society of United Slavs was not without forethought. Though plausible, these suppositions remain unproved by any evidence at present available.

The preliminary negotiations, which began in 1823 between Sergei Muraviev-Apostol and Bestuzhev-Riumin on one hand and Count Chodkiewicz on the other, led to the more official conference of the members of the two societies at Kiev, in the spring of 1824.[6] Fearing possible betrayal, both sides were extremely cautious, limiting their negotiations at first to general, noncommittal statements.[7] Bestuzhev-Riumin insisted that Poland and Russia must forget their former animosity and ally themselves against their common foe—the present government, equally oppressive to both countries. He admitted that his Society recognized the fact that Poland must become independent, though the delicate boundary question was not mentioned. Muraviev-Apostol, who spoke very little at the meeting, also made a plea for friendly relations and evidently broke the ice when he stated:[8]

Sentiments of national hatred born in the time of barbarism must vanish in the age of enlightenment, when it is known that the interests of all nations are identical. For this reason the Russian Society offers Poland the restoration of her former independence and is ready by all means to assist in the eradication of the mutual antipathy between the two peoples.

After three conferences the members reached an agreement whereby the Southern Society promised to recognize the independence of the future Poland and consented to the cession of Russian Polish provinces to that state.[9] The boundary between independent Poland and Russia was not settled, but, according to the map drawn

---

[6] *Gosudarstvennye prestupleniia,* I, 150–151.

[7] *Ibid.,* I, 151; Askenazy, *op. cit.,* 78.

[8] *Materialy,* IV, 107, 283.   [9] Cf. *Materialy,* IV, 116, 282–283.

by Pestel and found among his papers, the former was to receive the gubernias of Minsk, Volhynia, Vilna, and Grodno.[10] Later, Pestel, in testifying before the Committee of Investigation, reported the negotiations somewhat differently. He stated:[11]

The whole conversation with the Poles lasted not more than an hour and was mere talk. The subjects of negotiations were: (1) Independence of Poland, vaguely mentioned. But not a word was said about the Litovsk, Belostok, Podolsk, or Volynsk gubernias. (2) Mutual assistance in case of foreign war. (3) Similar form of government. (4) The Poles were to treat the Tsarevich Constantine the same as we were to treat the other Grand Dukes. (5) They were to keep us informed about their societies in Europe and to impose no obligations upon themselves toward anyone without our preliminary consent.

Each organization pledged itself to refrain from interfering with the functions of the other, the only obligation of either being to give assistance in the event of revolution. The Polish Society agreed to begin a revolt simultaneously with the Decembrists, provided they were informed two weeks ahead. It agreed to detain Constantine, Viceroy of Poland, in Warsaw when revolution broke out, and to disarm the Lithuanian Corps, which might become a decisive force against the revolution.[12]

In January, 1825, Pestel and Volkonsky, representing the Southern Society, met with the Polish delegates, Jablonowsky and Grodecki, at Kiev. Pestel assured the Polish representatives that "not only the entire people, but the army as well, wish to throw off the yoke of despotism." Since the Southern Society had not received any definite statement concerning the matter, Pestel asked for the opinion of the Polish Society, concluding as follows:[13]

There is no middle course; you must announce whether you are with us or against us. We will, without your assistance, win freedom by force for ourselves. But you, if you miss this opportune occasion, will have to abandon forever your hope of becoming an independent nation.

Pestel therefore requested information from the Poles concerning their organization and their political program, promising in return to give the same information in respect to the Southern Society. Prince Jablonowsky gave his opinion, but only as a personal one, that Poland could not have a republican form of government, though the decision lay entirely with the Polish people. Jablonow-

---

[10] See Appendix.
[11] *Materialy*, IV, 207. Cf. Pestel's map.
[12] *Gosudarstvennye prestupleniia*, I, 153–161 *passim; Materialy*, IV, 370–371.
[13] *Gosudarstvennye prestupleniia*, I, 158.

sky hinted that Poland must be restored within the boundaries of the second partition, but Pestel only confirmed the agreement of the Society to recognize Polish independence; the boundary question was to remain open for future negotiations. In the event of revolution, Polish representatives consented to prevent the departure of Grand Duke Constantine from Poland, so as to deprive the monarchists of a claimant to the throne: he was to be arrested, and the Polish revolutionaries were to do with Constantine whatever the Russian revolutionaries should decide to do with Alexander I. In other words, should it be decided to execute Alexander, as the southern members seriously contemplated, Constantine would share the same fate. The leading part in the revolt was to be taken by the Russian Society; the Polish Society was to aid in establishing communication with similar secret societies in Western Europe. To these measures the Poles seem tacitly to have agreed, and to have agreed as well to refuse to enroll Russians in their Society; the Southern Society promised the same in respect to Poles.[14] But the long-accumulated national animosity between the two sister states was a hindrance to a fullhearted agreement even between the two revolutionary parties. Little aware of the approaching end, the conference decided to meet again in 1826. Unexpected events, as will be seen later, destroyed further plans, crushed the Decembrist movement, and retarded the Polish national cause for a long time to come.

The Society of United Slavs.—Another organization with which the Southern Society came into relationship was that of the United Slavs. The origin of the Society of United Slavs can be traced to the year 1817, when the two brothers, Peter and Andrei Borisov, both army officers, admirers of Pythagoras and true "middle-class Voltaireans," organized a small group, at first under the name of *Primeval Concord,* later *Friends of Nature.* Very little is known of these short-lived "Pythagorean Sects," except that their few members attempted to apply semi-Masonic, semi-utopian ideas to grim Russian reality, striving toward "moral perfection and the purification of religion from prejudices."[15] The romantic, sentimental idealism expressed in its slogan, "La Gloire, l'Amour et l'Amitié," faded very soon, to be succeeded by a more serious or-

---

[14] *Materialy,* V, 203–204, 215; *Gosudarstvennye prestupleniia,* I, 161; Askenazy, *op. cit.,* 80–82.

[15] *Materialy,* VI, pp. xxxv-xxxvi, footnote 2.

ganization with a definitely political character.[16] "Cruel treatment
of the soldiers by their commanders and oppression of the peasants
by their landlords" sobered the founders of these societies, and they
began to look toward more practical ideas. Peter Borisov later related the following to the Committee of Investigation :[17]

After the Society of the *Friends of Nature* came to an end, I often discussed with my brother how it could be revived. Different grievances made my
brother dissatisfied with the government; from childhood I had been fascinated by democracy; while still at home I very often quarreled over my
Greeks and Romans with my brother, who did not agree with my political
opinions—he was an enemy of democracy. But in 1823 our opinions became
more nearly alike and we determined to organize a society, which, when it
should become considerably increased, would demand from the Sovereign
fundamental laws for which he himself would be responsible. A moderate
monarchy occupied the thoughts of my brother, and I, to avoid quarrels, as
formerly, often agreed with him, though against my sentiments.

In 1823 the two Borisovs met Julian Lublinsky, the Polish nobleman, deist, and ardent revolutionary, who, in the same year, on
the charge of being a member of a conspiratory society, had been
arrested in Warsaw and sent in chains to his home town, Novograd-
Volynsk.[18] They asked Lublinsky to help them in improving the
organization which they had endeavored to establish with so much
ardor and such meager results. Lublinsky consented to assist "the
young philosophers" in working out a "Catechism" or a new program, and their efforts gave rise to the Society of United Slavs—
an organization strikingly different from the original conception
of it and far more democratic than the Southern Society.[19]

The democratic nature of the Society of United Slavs might be
explained by the social status of the greater part of its membership.
Nearly all the members represented the poorest of the nobility, the
class soon to constitute in a great measure the "classless intelligentsia" (*raznochintsy*). Most of them were army officers of low
rank, with a small salary upon which they and often their families
had to depend. Many of their parents were noble only in name,
with little land, to say nothing of serfs. Virtually they were middle-
class noblemen "who had not yet tasted the poison of power" and
who, according to one writer, constituted the dough out of which

---

[16] *Ibid.*, V, 39, 52, 82.

[17] *Ibid.*, V, 53, 56.

[18] *Katorga i Ssylka*, VI (1926), 58. Cf. *Materialy*, V, 414.

[19] *Ibid.*, V, 29, 53, 412, 419; *Katorga i Ssylka*, V (1926), 59–63.

CENTER OF ACTIVITIES OF THE UNITED SLAVS.

the government baked its bureaucracy.[20] Some were on charity, like the mother of Bechasnov; a number were government clerks, among whom were men of doubtful rank, such as Ivanov, the secretary of the Society; and one, Timofei Duntsov, was of peasant stock, who, by means of a false passport and title, under the assumed name of "Paul Wigodoski," succeeded in procuring a government position.[21] Naturally, such members could not look toward the future of Russia in the same way as did Nikita Muraviev or Sergei Trubetskoi. Emanating from an obscure southern town of the Poltava Province and conceived by Russian "democratic Pythagoreans," their political program could be expected to differ widely from the one elaborated by the "heavy epaulets" in the capital.

Program of the United Slavs.—Three factors, the United Slavs believed, constituted the basis of human welfare in the state which they had designed. These were industrial, moral, and intellectual. The first, they held, eliminated poverty by developing industry; the second, by awakening man's conscience stimulated humanitarianism and diminished human passions; the third, by establishing a social philosophy was of assistance against evil.[22] Of equal importance was the elimination of all forms of prejudices, class distinctions, lavishness, idleness, and religious intolerance, against which every member was obligated to fight.

Far more striking was the political program of the United Slavs. Here the Society was the first of its kind to rise above purely national sentiments and to outline plans for a larger social order based on cultural rather than national kinship. Most illuminating are the first lines of the oath which each initiated member was required to take. They read:[23]

Entering the United Slavs for the liberation of myself from tyranny and for the restoration of freedom, which is so precious to the human race, I solemnly pledge on these arms brotherly love, which is to me divine and from which I expect the fulfillment of all my desires.

Believing that "Time and Genius" would draw the details, the United Slavs never developed their program so fully as did the Northern and Southern societies.[24] They had only a rough design, but this is sufficient to illustrate the general nature of their organi-

---

[20] Gorbachevsky, *Zapiski i pisma*, 91; *Materialy*, V, 38, 118.

[21] Nechkina, *Obshchestvo Soedinënnykh Slavian*, 32.

[22] Gorbachevsky, *op. cit.*, 57.

[23] *Materialy*, V, 17. See Appendix.   [24] *Ibid.*, V, 30.

zation. Briefly, the aims were as follows: the establishment of a republic in Russia, the abolition of serfdom and of all class distinction, and the introduction of a "pure democratic" government. This program, however, was not to be limited to Russia alone. The United Slavs strove for the liberation from autocracy of all Slavdom and aimed at means of eliminating antagonism by uniting these peoples into a federal state similar to that of the ancient Greeks, though much improved.[25] Unification of all the Slav peoples was one of the vital issues and no one was to shrink before any sacrifice that the fulfillment of this task might demand. The territory of each people within that federal state was to be well defined, each was to be assured of democratic government and the enjoyment of a broad cultural, political, and economic autonomy. The emblem of the United Slavs was an octagonal insignia symbolizing the eight Slavic peoples: Russian, Polish, Bohemian, Serbian, Bulgarian, Croatian, Moravian, and Hungarian(!). Upon the emblem were four anchors representing the four seas, Baltic, White, Black, and Mediterranean, which signified the glory, wealth, and naval power of Slavdom.[26]

The execution of such an extensive plan was not an easy matter, and the United Slavs seemed to have realized the tremendous difficulties that they would be forced to overcome while striving for an improved social order. The leaders were convinced that a mere *coup d'état* by a small number of army officers was insufficient: the program demanded the participation of the masses, and without their assistance all efforts were destined to failure. "Military revolutions," states one of the prominent members of the United Slavs, "though they achieve their aims more quickly, are more dangerous because of that fact; they are not the cradle, but the coffin of liberty, in whose name they are executed."[27] But the participation of the masses required their long preparation, for while serfdom existed no one could expect the enslaved peasants to represent a creative force. This fact the United Slavs realized full well, but their proffered remedy was of doubtful value. Nevertheless, the plan aroused the admiration of the leaders of the Slavs,

---

[25] *Ibid.*, V, 18, 19, 53. On the Pan-Slav idea among the Decembrists, see Georgievsky, "Slaviansky vopros v mirovozzrenii dekabristov." *Uchenye Zapiski Ist.-Fil. Fakulteta . . . Dalnevostochnogo Universiteta* (Vladivostock), II, 2 (1921), 103.

[26] *Materialy*, V, 207, 278.   [27] Gorbachevsky, *op. cit.*, 58.

because it displayed a genuine devotion to the ideal of freeing Russia and Slavdom as a whole.[28]

The United Slavs suggested that all those who joined the organization should promise to allow their serfs to redeem themselves. Members who had no serfs were to sacrifice one-tenth of their meager income for the creation of a special fund set aside for the redemption of all serfs.[29] In addition, public schools were to be built and education made possible for the emancipated peasantry, as only through enlightenment would political liberty be feasible. Though ready to defend this program to the last, the United Slavs were prepared for the long, hard struggle before them. "Liberty," stated Gorbachevsky, "is bought neither with tears nor with gold, but with blood," and once "the sword is drawn against the Sovereign, the sheath must be thrown aside so far as possible."[30]

Amalgamation of the Southern and Slav societies.—The center of the United Slavs was a small town in the south of Leshchin, near Vasilkov, where, also, the headquarters of one of the branches of the Southern Society was located. For a long time the United Slavs had been apprehensive of the army officers of the former Semenovsky regiment, suspecting them of having a secret society of their own.[31] Their suspicions were soon confirmed by one of their members, Tiutchev, himself a former officer of the Semenovsky regiment, who after the disbandment had been sent south.[32] Tiutchev was acquainted with Muraviev-Apostol and, apprehending that the latter was engaged in some secret political activity, mentioned it on one occasion to Peter Borisov. In order to obtain some light on the nature of the suspected secret society, what were its aims and who were its members, the leaders of the United Slavs authorized Tiutchev to continue his intercourse with Muraviev-Apostol, to reveal nothing concerning the United Slavs, but to gather all possible information and report it at once to the Society.[33]

Shortly afterward Tiutchev informed Borisov that he had discovered a secret society and had even been asked to join it; that this society had one aim, namely, a political revolution, that it had worked out a definite program and had even drawn a constitution

---

[28] An excellent idea of the genuineness of the leader of the United Slavs, Peter Borisov, is given by Yakushkin and Alexander Muraviev. See Yakushkin, I., *Zapiski*, 133–134; *Vospominaniia i rasskazy*, I, 140–141.

[29] *Materialy*, V, 53, 267.

[30] Gorbachevsky, *op. cit.*, 59.

[31] *Ibid.*, 44–45.   [32] *Materialy*, V, 31.   [33] *Ibid.*, V, 455.

for future Russia, which Muraviev-Apostol and Bestuzhev-Riumin had shown to him; and that the uprising was definitely set for the year 1826.[34] Overwhelmed by the news, the Slavs immediately began to force the issue further. On August 30, 1825, representatives of both societies met in order to discuss the possibility of some agreement between the two organizations. To their amazement, the representatives of the United Slavs discovered that Tiutchev had already informed the Southern leaders of the existence of his Society, thereby violating his instructions.[35]

When the members of the Society of United Slavs were told of the newly discovered organization and the projected unification, a number of them opposed such a plan. Indignant because the existence of their Society had been revealed, some insisted that negotiations with the Southern Society should be terminated at once, others that all the promises and projects that had been previously unfolded by Muraviev-Apostol and Bestuzhev-Riumin should now be supported by more substantial proof. A few who were violently opposed to any relations with the Southern group went so far as to demand the death of Tiutchev for disclosing the existence of the United Slavs, arguing that this harsh punishment would prevent similar violations in the future. Those in favor of amalgamation gradually gained ground, persuading the opposition that both societies were striving toward practically the same goal, and that the Slavs would never be able to achieve their aim alone. After a long and heated discussion, it was determined to continue the negotiations and to find a basis for agreement.[36]

From the start it became evident that both groups were eager to increase their membership and wished to consolidate every available force for the execution of their ambitious plan, though neither side wished to reveal its intentions. There were visible differences between the two organizations, most of them arising from the fact that the predominant and more numerous group in each society was of a different social status, and this situation created a gap not easily to be bridged. On more than one occasion disagreements with respect to the sort of members to be enrolled, the right of initiation, of selection, or of recommendation, caused friction. For some unknown reason Muraviev-Apostol and Bestuzhev-Riumin were prejudiced against the officers of the Chernigovsky regiment,

---

[34] *Ibid.*, V, 111.

[35] *Ibid.*, V, 432, 454, 455–456.   [36] Gorbachevsky, *op. cit.*, 48.

but the Slavs favored their enrollment. This caused a violent dispute between the two sides and a threat on the part of the Slavs, voiced by a certain member, Kuzmin, who frankly told the Southern representatives that the Slavs never intended to beg them for permission to be patriots, that they could cause the regiment in question to rebel any day, and that the Slavs could always find the road to Moscow and St. Petersburg without any need of their guidance.[37] The incident threatened to create a serious feud, but this fact was quickly realized and Muraviev-Apostol withdrew his opposition.

Though relations were on a delicate basis, yet the courtly manner and eloquence of Muraviev-Apostol and Bestuzhev-Riumin favorably impressed those negotiating for the Slavs. The Southern members pictured their organization in such colors that anyone ignorant of the actual state of affairs could have been deceived, especially the Slavs who were impatiently longing for action and constantly inquiring about the date set for the uprising. Muraviev-Apostol advised them to join the Southern Society if they wished to succeed; without the assistance of the Southern and the Polish societies, he told them, the Slavs would never win in combating autocracy. As a matter of fact, Bestuzhev-Riumin told them, the Southern Society was so strong that it neither wished nor needed the additional enrollment of members; the chief and only task for them now was to prepare the army. Such announcements, of course, increased the agitation of the Slavs. During negotiations the Southern leaders were apparently determined to act swiftly and indiscriminately. They told the Slavs all sorts of fabulous tales about the strength of the Southern Society. In glowing terms they told of the readiness of Moscow and St. Petersburg to begin a revolution, and—what was far from being true—of the preparedness of the Guard, as well as the rest of the army, to come to their assistance. All over the Empire and even abroad, in Posen, Galicia, and in Warsaw, they said, the Society had established its branches— statements which were entirely untrue. The constitution drawn for future Russia, they said further, was unanimously approved by many eminent men of France, Holland, Germany, and England, as well as in the North. They cited to the Slavs an impressive list of names, saying that these were the men who had consented to support the revolution; among them were Generals Orlov, Kiselev,

---

[37] *Ibid.*, 76–77.

Raevsky, and other well-known military men. The first, it may be recalled, withdrew from the Society at the Moscow conference and never came back, and it is doubtful whether the others were even aware of its existence.[38] In a word, the Slavs were urged to hasten if they wished to join the victorious march of the revolution. Is there any wonder that a good many of them urged immediate amalgamation? No word was spoken concerning the serious disagreements with the Northern Society and the only too-recent failure to bring into accord Tulchin and St. Petersburg. Impressed by these representations, the Slavs were caught and gradually drawn into the Southern Society.

Results of the amalgamation.—One objection of the leaders of the United Slavs to amalgamation was the fact that they had originally sworn to fight for an All-Slav Republic and that they were therefore bound not to desert the idea. Bestuzhev-Riumin argued that the unification of the two societies would only further such a plan and that a free Russia would also mean freedom for all other Slavs.[39] Furthermore, Russia must think of her own problems first and only afterwards of those of other peoples.[40] Through the inspiring speeches of the Southern exponents the United Slavs were won to the idea of first liberating Russia, then their Slav brethren. They determined to unite with the Southern Society, thus unwittingly merging their interests to share, a few months later, the tragedy of the Decembrists. At the request of Bestuzhev-Riumin, the United Slavs handed over all the papers concerning their society, all the names of its members, and became a mere branch of the Southern Society.[41] Everything seemed to have been happily arranged, but as one of the participants described this moment :[42]

> Amidst the general ecstasy the penetrating look of an observer could have noticed that not all the Slavs sincerely rejoiced over the union of their Society with the Southern one; he would have noticed a sad note, just as an experienced traveller, present at a noisy and cheerful celebration of savages at the funeral of one of their members, could detect in the eyes of the father or wife the lonely feeling of separation and a tear for the deceased one, unobserved by the crowd.

The unification of the two societies had both positive and negative results. It consolidated two revolutionary groups into one stronger organization with a common program to introduce liberal

---

[38] *Materialy*, V, 34; Gorbachevsky, *op. cit.*, 49, 51.

[39] Gorbachevsky, *op. cit.*, 53.

[40] *Materialy*, V, 31.   [41] *Ibid.*, V, 41.   [42] Gorbachevsky, *op. cit.*, 80.

government and to bring about social reforms. But the optimistic pictures of Bestuzhev-Riumin had impressed some of the more radical members of the United Slavs with the notion that, once the two societies were joined, they were strong enough to begin a revolution at almost any time. "When do we begin?" was the question often heard among these men. This misconception led to folly and on some occasions barely escaped disaster. It frightened the leaders of the Southern Society, and Muraviev-Apostol made every effort to dampen such revolutionary ardor.

Another wedge between the members of the two groups was their various political views: the Southern members were not at all inclined to cherish the same ideas of a social revolution that the Slavs held. "Our revolution," stated Bestuzhev-Riumin to Borisov in an instructive manner, "will be similar to the Spanish revolution of 1820; it will not cost a single drop of blood, for it will be executed by the army alone, without the assistance of the people."[43] When Borisov questioned him concerning the measures which the Provisional Government would take to assure the enforcement of the constitution and who would rule Russia while the constitution was in process of its enforcement, Bestuzhev-Riumin's reply was the one recommended by Pestel, namely, that the Provisional Government would have to stay in power perhaps for a decade in order to establish the new political order. But who was to appoint the government to establish this order? Borisov continued persistently to inquire. Only military men? By what right, he wondered, would they rule the country for a decade and what would prevent them from turning into a permanent dictatorship? Bestuzhev-Riumin became indignant. "How can you ask me such a thing? We, who will assassinate the legitimate Sovereign, would not tolerate the government of usurpers! Never! Never!" To which Borisov calmly replied: "All that is true, but Julius Caesar was assassinated in the midst of Rome, defeated by his grandeur and glory, while over the assassins, the fiery patriots, triumphed the pusillanimous eighteen-year-old youth, Octavius."[44] It was evident that, in spite of the amalgamation of the two societies, necessitated by tactical reasons, they were not allied in heart. Deep down there was the contradiction of two social classes: one, the liberal aristocracy represented by such men as Prince Volkonsky, Muraviev-Apostol, and

---

[43] *Materialy,* V, 31; Gorbachevsky, *op. cit.,* 73.

[44] *Materialy,* V, 63; Gorbachevsky, *op. cit.,* 73–74.

Bestuzhev-Riumin; the other, the more radical, pauperized aristocracy, virtually middle-class, represented by men like Gorbachevsky, Borisov, or Kuzmin.[45]

The difference between the leaders of the Southern Society and
those of the United Slavs was most evident in their attitude toward
the question of how far the army was to be involved in the revolution. Certain officers insisted that with cudgels they could force
their soldiers to rebel; others maintained that a few kegs of vodka
and a little money would be sufficient.[46] Muraviev-Apostol, who
often had a tendency to use religion as a weapon against his opponents, regarded the soldiers as mere tools, to whom the ideas of the
revolutionaries would be a mystery; the soldiers, he felt, could be
aroused only through religious motives, by the reading of the Bible,
in which antiautocratic ideas were expressed. Later, as will be seen,
he used that policy, attempting to make the soldiers rebel by having
a priest read his Catechism to them.[47]

These views the former members of the United Slavs deter-
minedly rejected; it could not have been otherwise, for such ideas
were characteristically aristocratic and therefore alien to the
Slavs. Gorbachevsky, for example, insisted that, although the
soldiers were unable to analyze all the complicated political and
economic problems, still it would be better to explain these to them
and to declare openly the cause of the revolution. "Cunning
Machiavellianism" he considered much worse than a frank discussion of the subject with the army.[48] The greater number of the
Slavs hoped for a revolution in which the masses were not to remain mere onlookers but would be active participants; in which
not only the peasant class, but also the laborers in the cities could
join in the struggle for the establishment of a future democratic
society. The Slavs endeavored to get in touch with the workers in
Kiev, and for this purpose dispatched one of their members,
Andreevich, to that city to discover any conditions particularly
favorable to an uprising; for example, at such places as the arsenal.
The seizure of the arsenal by the workers, they realized full well,
would be of great strategic importance. As he talked things over
with the workers, Andreevich assured them that there were men
who were aware of their wretched state and who sincerely wished

---

[45] Gorbachevsky, *op. cit.*, 88–92.   [47] *Materialy*, V, 130, 177, 228.
[46] *Ibid.*, 90, footnote.   [48] Gorbachevsky, *op. cit.*, 83–85.

to relieve them.[49] This step has been completely overlooked by many students of this period. It showed the true revolutionary spirit of the Slavs, and indicates a whole political philosophy far beyond that of the Southern Society: faith in the people themselves rather than in a small military-revolutionary group, and a vision of the future encounter between autocracy and democracy as a struggle between the masses on one side and the privileged wealthy class on the other.[50]

In this respect the United Slavs were the true forerunners of the twentieth-century Russian revolutionaries. Though violence was distasteful to them, in the event of necessity the Slavs did not shrink from it. They were even prepared to go much farther than the Southern Society was willing to go, as is evidenced by their attitude toward regicide.[51] Many former members offered their services in order to "free Russia from the tyrant at one stroke."[52] Pleased, Bestuzhev-Riumin hastened to inform Pestel that he had been able to find men for the projected "garde perdue" to assassinate the Emperor. Thus, the most revolutionary act, the assassination of Alexander, though planned by the Southern Society, would probably have been executed by the Slavs had not events interfered. The amalgamation of the two societies brought within the ranks a true revolutionary element which impatiently waited only for the occasion to strike. This opportunity was to come sooner than had been expected.[53]

---

[49] *Materialy*, V, 477.

[50] *Ibid.*, V, 386–388, 389.

[51] *Ibid.*, V, 35–36, 63, 333–334.

[52] *Ibid.*, V, 47–49; Gorbachevsky, *op. cit.*, 86–87.

[53] See Nechkina, "Krizis Iuzhnogo Obshchestva Dekabristov." *Istorik Marksist*, VII (1935), 30.

Chapter VII

THE REVOLT IN THE NORTH

I foresee that there will be no success, but an upheaval is necessary, for it will awaken Russia, and we with our failure will teach others.—K. RYLEEV.

THE DECEMBRISTS had fully accepted the idea of overthrowing the government by force and establishing a new political order. Their opinions varied with respect to the lengths to which such a revolution should be carried: there were the "pronunciamento" of Trubetskoi, the "garde perdue" and temporary dictatorship recommended by Pestel, and the social revolution of the United Slavs. Whatever the differences, however, the fact that the Decembrists had agreed upon violence to enforce their program remains undeniable. In this respect three projects are of particular interest, all of them sponsored by the Southern Society.

Plans of the Southern Society.—First was the plan presented by the Vasilkov branch in 1823, providing that the revolutionaries should seize the Emperor on his visit to the Bobruisk fortress.[1] Following this act, the Eighth and Ninth infantry divisions were to march toward Moscow, and the Second Army was to capture the chief military staff in the South; simultaneously, the Northern Society was to take possession of the government in the capital.[2]

The second plan, suggested in 1824 by Sergei Muraviev-Apostol and Bestuzhev-Riumin and supported mainly by the Kamenka branch, was somewhat as follows. At the time of the southern maneuvers, which were to take place near Belaia Tserkov and to be attended by Alexander, the Emperor was to be assassinated in his bedroom at night and the entire military staff arrested. The army was then to move toward Kiev, capture it, and proceed north to Moscow. As commander of the Chernigovsky regiment, Bestuzhev-Riumin was to remain in the south to maintain order, and Muraviev-Apostol was to go north to organize the revolt in the capital. But Alexander did not attend the maneuvers at Belaia Tserkov, and so the whole plan fell through.[3]

---

[1] Bobruisk was a fortress near Minsk in western Russia.

[2] *Materialy*, IV, 104, 188, 194, 275, 392; Gorbachevsky, *Zapiski i pisma*, 198–201.

[3] *Materialy*, IV, 137–138, 165–166, 169, 171.

The third plan, offered by Pestel, shifted the center of activities from the South to the North; the revolution was to begin in the capital, and the southern members were to seize the government in their territory. All the details of this plan—forcing the Senate to proclaim the revolutionary government as the only authority in the state, deporting or, if necessary, assassinating the royal family, and establishing a dictatorship[4]—have been sufficiently described in the foregoing chapters.

In 1825 the Southern Society seriously contemplated a revolt when the Corps should gather for maneuvers near Leshchin. The plan was evolved as a protest against the removal from his regiment of Colonel Shveikovsky, a member of the Society, to which the loss of a regiment was a heavy blow. Because of its unpreparedness, the Society decided to postpone the uprising for about a year.[5] Up to the last day no plan had been definitely accepted, for time alone could have determined its details and the manner of its enforcement. All the Society could do was to adopt very general principles and to set the approximate date for action upon them in the summer of 1826. The chief sponsor of an uprising in 1826 was the Vasilkov branch, where the impatient United Slavs had been constantly occupied with preparations for early revolt.[6] The Northern Society, under the leadership of Ryleev, had only tacitly agreed to support the enterprise, though both societies hoped revolution would be possible in the summer of 1826.[7] But unforeseen events brought about a new situation and swept aside all previous schemes.

Death of Alexander.—On November 19, 1825, Alexander I died at Taganrog in southern Russia. Since the deceased Emperor had no children, he should have been succeeded by his oldest brother, Constantine, at that time governor-general in Warsaw.[8] But Constantine, on January 14, 1823, had formally renounced his right to the throne, thus placing his younger brother, Nicholas, next in the line of succession.[9] The whole matter had been prearranged by a small circle of the royal family as if such an important act was a purely family matter and of no concern to the state. The renun-

---

[4] *Ibid.*, IV, 102–103, 104.

[5] *Ibid.*, IV, 169, 221, 258–259.

[6] Gorbachevsky, *op. cit.*, 95–96.

[7] *Krasnyi Arkhiv*, XIII, 11; *Materialy*, IV, 278–279.

[8] *P.S.Z.*, No. 17910.

[9] Korf, M. A., *Vosshestvie na prestol imp. Nikolaia I*, 30.

ciation of Constantine was embodied in a special Manifesto, signed by Alexander on August 16, 1823, sealed copies of which were deposited by the Emperor in the Uspensky Cathedral in Moscow and in the Senate and State Council in St. Petersburg, with the endorsement "Not to be opened until after my death." Through Arakcheev, the Metropolitan was informed that the document was to be kept secret, though Alexander himself indirectly mentioned its contents to a number of his associates, including Karamzin, Arakcheev, and some foreign members of royalty, for example, Wilhelm, Prince of Prussia. The choice of Nicholas as successor to the Russian throne was known to fewer men than was the abdication of Constantine. Did Nicholas know of it or did he merely feign ignorance? It is not clear and opinions vary, nor is it relevant to the subject of our immediate concern. The fact of the matter is that Alexander, for reasons known to himself only, showed great unwillingness to discuss the question with those who had the right to be informed about it.[10] Several sources indicate that Alexander hinted to Nicholas that some day he might have to take upon himself the responsibility of the state.[11]

Interregnum.—On November 27, 1825, the day that the news of Alexander's death reached St. Petersburg, the Guard, including Nicholas, and officers of state institutions, took the oath of allegiance to Constantine, and three days later in Moscow similar action was taken. Being unaware of the Manifesto, the authorities felt that the state should not suffer a long interregnum.[12] The following day many windows had on display pictures of the new Sovereign, "Constantine I, Emperor and Autocrat of All-Russias."[13] Constantine, however, reiterated, most emphatically, his renunciation of his right to the throne, and declared his loyalty to Nicholas.[14] For nearly three weeks correspondence on the subject passed between St. Petersburg and Warsaw, while the empire remained without a sovereign, or, as the London *Times* neatly summarized it, "in the strange predicament of having two self-denying Emperors, and no active ruler."[15] This extraordinary situation aroused public re-

---

[10] Korf, *op. cit.*, 17–18.

[11] Shilder, *Imp. Nikolai I*, I, 207; *Russkaia Starina*, XXX (1881), 494.

[12] *Istorichesky Viestnik*, LXV (1896), 435.

[13] *Obshchestvennye Dvizheniia v Rossii*, I, 435.

[14] *The Morning Herald* (London), January 31, 1826, p. 4, col. 4; Schiemann, T., *Geschichte Rußlands*, II, 22–23. Cf. *Katorga i Ssylka*, VIII (1925), 65ff.

[15] *The Times* (London), January 7, 1826, p. 2, col. 3.

sentment, expressed in the popular sarcastic question : "When will
the sheep finally be sold ?"[16] When on December 12 it became clear
that Constantine was determined not to return to the capital,
Nicholas, having learned, also, of the possible political complications threatened by the secret society, resolved "day after tomor-
row to become Emperor or devoid of breath." He called in the
commander of the Guard, Voinov, "the honorable and courageous
man, though with limited capacities," as Nicholas characterizes
him, informing the old General of his decision and the necessity of
summoning the State Council in order to confirm the act. December 14 was set as the date for the Senate and the Guard to take the
oath of allegiance.

The Society during the interregnum.—The death of Alexander
had always been considered by the Decembrists as the occasion for
action. When the general confusion concerning the succession began, and the army, having taken the oath to Constantine, was requested to take it again to Nicholas, the Decembrists decided to
take up arms without delay. Ryleev was pessimistic about a successful outcome ; nevertheless, he insisted on action, "for it would
awaken Russia" and the failure would be a lesson to later generations.[17]

The Northern Society, thanks to influential members who were
daily in touch with responsible statesmen, was well informed of
the confusion at court. The Society watched developments with
keen interest, but it is doubtful whether the leaders at first knew
just what to do. The earlier conference, hastily summoned, demonstrated that the organization was still too weak numerically to
begin a revolt, and there was not time enough to come to any agreements with the South.[18] Yet Ryleev and Nicholas Bestuzhev were
convinced that, should the present opportunity escape, they would
not have another for a long time.[19]

Ryleev, and Nicholas and Alexander Bestuzhev, in discussing
the situation, at first thought of issuing a leaflet and spreading it
secretly among the soldiers. After writing about half of it, they
changed their minds and decided to visit personally as many
military headquarters as possible, spreading rumors and noting
the general feeling among the soldiers. They wandered everywhere,

---

[16] Trubetskoi, *Zapiski*, 33.

[17] *Vospominaniia Bestuzhevykh*, 82 ; Rozen, *Zapiski dekabrista*, 63.

[18] *Materialy*, I, 184, 435–436, 458.   [19] *Ibid.*, I, 18–19.

talking to every soldier they met, telling the men how the army had been deceived, that the actual will of Alexander I was deliberately hidden, and reminding them that the emancipation of the peasants and the shorter terms of military service promised by Alexander had been denied.[20] Ryleev and the Bestuzhevs spent two sleepless nights on these "promenades."[21] The soldiers willingly lent their attention to the propaganda about their hard lot and how they had been deceived, but no one knew what to do nor what to suggest. So the idea of propaganda among the soldiers was abandoned and attention turned to the consolidation of the Society in readiness for approaching developments. Gatherings became more frequent, and the home of Ryleev became the pulse of all activities.

Nicholas and Constantine.—When the question of taking the oath to Nicholas arose, the Society maintained that, once loyalty had been pledged to Constantine, it must remain sacred unless he appeared in person and declared his renunciation. The sincerity of this attitude is very doubtful, for the Decembrists were not interested in placing either Nicholas or Constantine on the Russian throne. That they opposed the candidacy of Nicholas is without question, but neither were they much in favor of Constantine. Logically, they had to oppose both candidates. The prospect of having Nicholas as Emperor of Russia was not a happy one. Nicholas had received his entire training in the army, chiefly in the field of engineering, and he had fully adopted his father's military conceptions.[22] From his youth he had displayed a despotic character and had tolerated no innovations; moreover, he was prone to consider every leniency a "lack of proper discipline." "Strict subordination," writes Masaryk, and "unquestioning obedience, were Nicholas' system. In his psychology men were mere machines, or at most animated slaves."[23] Having been absorbed with military affairs, Nicholas lacked diplomatic and political training, and he possessed none of the qualities, such as tolerance, tact, and vision, that are the attributes of any real statesman.[24]

If to political circles Nicholas was unacceptable, to military men the prospect of his possible reign seemed most unpleasant.[25] While

---

[20] *Ibid.*, I, 160–161.

[21] *Vospominaniia Bestuzhevykh*, 81.

[22] Shilder, *op. cit.*, I, 36–37, 111, 343.

[23] Masaryk, *The Spirit of Russia*, I, 105.

[24] Tatishchev, *Imp. Nikolai i inostrannye dvory*, 49.

[25] Shilder, *op. cit.*, I, 204; *Vospominaniia i rasskazy*, I, 123.

in the army Nicholas had succeeded in arousing both the displeasure of higher officers and the hatred of privates.[26] The officers keenly remembered their former disagreements with him. His ascendancy, they knew, would signify the restoration of the dark days of Colonel Schwarz, who had encouraged brutality as a means of dissuading the soldiers from liberal ideas. The army, therefore, was definitely against Nicholas.[27] His accession could only be favored by the Empress Dowager, who did not wish to see Constantine on the throne, with his Polish morganatic wife as Empress, and by the conservative element at court, which insisted upon a policy of *status quo.*[28] The candidacy of Constantine was scarcely more agreeable to the military men than that of Nicholas.[29] Constantine had been commander of the Guard during the years 1813–14, and in 1814 he had been appointed commander-in-chief of the army in Poland. This force counted approximately 80,000 men, a considerable number, which the Southern Society, not without reason, had always feared as a potential counterrevolutionary factor unless they could get rid of its commander. Thanks to the efforts of Constantine, however, military life had become less burdensome : the long twenty-five-year term, practiced in Russia, had been reduced in Poland to only ten years ; army men had been better paid and more satisfactorily equipped.[30] These changes were undoubtedly known to many men in the Russian army, and some were inclined to associate the name of Constantine with liberal reforms.[31] Colonel Bulatov testified that many had hoped Constantine would abolish the military colonies, and though some feared he would be under the influence of Polish councilors, still these were preferable to the reactionary German element which had been predominant at court and would be still more so with the accession of Nicholas.

Constantine's reputation as a liberal, unfortunately, was quite unwarranted by actual conditions. Very few persons were aware of the conflict between the Polish people and Constantine. Even his

[26] *Iz pisem i pokazanii dekabristov*, 43–44 ; Schiemann, *Die Ermordung Pauls und die Thronbesteigung Nicolaus I*, 124.

[27] Polievktov, *Nikolai I*, 32–33 ; Vigel, *Zapiski*, V, 70–71 ; Semevsky, *Politicheskie i obshchestvennye idei dekabristov*, 81–82.

[28] Grand Duke Constantine was married the second time to a Polish Countess, Joan Grudzinska, later Princess Lowicz. *Russkaia Starina*, XX (1877), 379–380.

[29] *Obshchestvennye Dvizheniia v Rossii*, I, 246 ; *Krasnyi Arkhiv*, XVII, 156ff.

[30] Askenazy, *Tsarstvo Polskoe*, 46–48.

[31] Presniakov, *14 Dekabria 1825*, 53–54 ; *Krasnyi Arkhiv*, XII, 28, footnote 2.

military reforms, which seemed to have alleviated the hardships of soldiers in Poland, were not so ideal as some writers were inclined to describe them. As a commander Constantine overemphasized trivial exactness.[32] In some respects he resembled General George B. McClellan, of the United States army during the Civil War, though he lacked McClellan's military skill.[33] Like McClellan, Constantine placed organization above everything else, but he had no idea what to do with it. To Constantine an army was largely for parade purposes; war "only spoiled soldiers," and campaigns, he believed, ruined military discipline.

If as a general Constantine was mediocre, as a statesman he was even less distinguished, for he had spent, as had Nicholas, most of his life in the army. Yet he was fond of meddling in religious as well as political affairs. Constantine had a dislike of the Catholic clergy, which, in his opinion, was striving to create a special caste, a *status in statu* in Poland.[34] Detesting constitutions, he never tried to conceal his feeling, though he was administering what was nominally a constitutional government. "I will show you a constitution," he would threaten Polish officers; and openly demonstrate his lack of respect for the institution he was theoretically supposed to defend.[35] As Governor-General of Warsaw and Commander-in-Chief of the army in Poland, he often interfered with the political administration, disregarding fundamental principles of the Polish Constitution and thereby antagonizing even the moderate parties. Unable to control his temper, which often became a fury, as reactionary and despotic in nature as his father, Constantine, by his rule in Poland, provoked an opposition which in 1830 burst into open revolt.[36] His political creed is well expressed in his letters to his brother Nicholas. "Change nothing of what was done by our dear, excellent and adorable, deceased brother, neither in most important affairs nor in trivial ones," he wrote to him on December 8 (20), 1825.[37] Small wonder that Prince Metternich favored Constantine's accession to the throne of Russia rather than

---

[32] *Russkaia Starina*, CII (1900), 356–358; Potocka (Tyszkiewiez), *Memoirs*, 246–247.

[33] Morse, John T., *Abraham Lincoln*, I, 313, 366; Michie, P. S., *General McClellan*, 459ff.; Campbell, J. H., *McClellan* (New York, 1916), 33–36.

[34] *Russkaia Starina*, I (1878), 5.

[35] *Ibid.*, XX (1877), 88, 96; Semevsky, *op. cit.*, 73.

[36] *Russkaia Starina*, XX (1877), 99–100; *The Cambridge Modern History*, X, 448.

[37] *S.I.R.I.O.*, CXXXI, 3.

that of Nicholas, because of his anticonstitutional views and especially since Constantine "hated the English, scorned the French,
and Prussia he considered as infected with revolutionary spirit."
Such being his state of mind, he could be counted upon to maintain
friendly relations with conservative Austria.[38] The experienced
Austrian diplomat partly sensed the truth, for La Ferronnays,
the French Ambassador to St. Petersburg, reporting on December
15 (27), 1825, his first impression of the young Emperor, adds:
"I have now reason to think that he loves Prussia, hates Austria,
fears England, envies France and has no faith in the stability of
our government."[39]

As far as the liberal party was concerned, there was little choice
between the two candidates, Constantine and Nicholas; both were
hated, the only difference being that the latter was more hated than
the former.[40] The slogan of the December revolt, "Constantine and
Constitution," was more of a catchword than a seriously intended
program. To the Decembrists, at least the conscientious ones, either
candidate could serve only as a cat's-paw for their political plan.
As the outlined Manifesto by Trubetskoi shows, this plan was
roughly as follows: a National Assembly was to be called to decide
the future of the country; in the meantime civil rights were to be
granted to all classes, though the word "freedom," Trubetskoi explained, must be avoided lest the peasants rebel. The same Manifesto contained several other liberal provisions, to which neither
Nicholas nor Constantine would ever have consented, nor did the
Decembrists expect them to do so.[41]

Preparations for revolt.—On December 9 the Northern Society
began to consider more seriously a means of resisting any attempt
on the part of Nicholas to force them to take the oath of allegiance
to him.[42] The next day it became definitely known in the capital
that Constantine had refused to accept the crown, and the Society
was placed in a dilemma: should it consent to accept Nicholas or
revolt? The one course meant an end of the Society, the other was
equally dangerous. Sergei Trubetskoi, as a member of the Council,
frankly stated that, once Constantine had renounced his right of

---

[38] Tatishchev, *loc. cit.* 49.

[39] *Russky Viestnik*, III (1893), 167. See also *Lettres et Papiers du Chancelier
de Nesselrode*, VI, 269.

[40] Zavalishin, *Zapiski dekabrista*, I, 197.

[41] *Materialy*, I, 65–66, 244–245.

[42] *Ibid.*, I, 248.

succession, the Society must begin to act without delay.[43] Ryleev supported him, stating that circumstances themselves called the Society to action and that it would be unforgivable pusillanimity, even a crime, if the Society were to miss such an opportune moment.[44] Realizing that they were facing a situation which might decide the future of the nation, the members selected Trubetskoi as "dictator," and gave him full power to act at his own discretion.[45] Their selection for this important task was most unfortunate, for Trubetskoi was motivated by social prestige rather than revolutionary genius.

Prince Sergei Trubetskoi was a member of a very old and noble family, whose ancestors could be traced to the well-known Lithuanian Gedymin royal family. Among the Trubetskois were many distinguished men who had played prominent rôles in the history of Russia.[46] It is not surprising, therefore, that Nicholas was shocked when he found Trubetskoi named among the rebels. When the "dictator" was brought before him, the young Emperor came up, and, pointing a finger at Trubetskoi's forehead, said: "What was in that head when you, with your name and family, entered into such an affair? Colonel of the Guard, Prince Trubetskoi! Are you not ashamed to be affiliated with such a rabble!"[47] But the name of Trubetskoi saved his life. If anyone deserved to mount the gallows along with the five other martyrs, unquestionably it was Trubetskoi. As the leader of the Decembrist movement from its very origin, he was as much morally responsible in the North as Pestel was in the South.[48] As someone remarked bitterly, Trubetskoi could not be hanged because his epaulets were too heavy; it was inconvenient for the government to proclaim publicly that the "rabble" had been led by a member of the oldest and most eminent Russian noble family.[49]

But to return to the events immediately preceding December 14. Shortly before the fatal day the Northern Society was in virtually continuous session at the home of Obolensky and, more frequently, of Ryleev, who had taken cold during the preceding sleepless

---

[43] Trubetskoi, *op. cit.*, 34–36; *Materialy*, I, 245–246.

[44] *Materialy*, I, 185, 215.

[45] *Ibid.*, I, 64, 160.

[46] *Skazanie o rode Kniazei Trubetskikh*, 5.

[47] Trubetskoi, *op. cit.*, 41.

[48] Borovkov, Z., "Zapiski." *Russkaia Starina*, XI (1898), 352.

[49] *Materialy*, I, p. ix; *Russky Arkhiv*, II (1885), 20, 24; *S.I.R.I.O.*, LXXVIII, 393.

nights, while wandering with the Bestuzhevs; the cold developed
into angina and made it difficult for Ryleev to talk. The frequent
gatherings could not escape the attention of the government.
Lately the Society had become less discriminating than it had ever
been in inviting new members and sympathizers. Among the latter
was the army officer, Yakov Rostovtsev, who, after attending the
first meeting, determined "to save the Sovereign, Fatherland," and
along with them the people who were only "blind tools." Rostovtsev
immediately presented a report to Nicholas I, warning him of the
plans of the Society and advising him, "for the sake of his own
glory," not to accept the crown until Constantine came to the capital.[50] Rostovtsev naïvely presented a copy of this report to Obolensky, thus "placing a candle to the Lord and to Satan." When the
Society learned the news confirming the suspicion of the members
that Nicholas knew about the conspiracy, there was only one alternative: either to abandon all plans and dissolve immediately, or
gallantly to rise. The Society chose the latter course, deciding that
it was "better to be seized on the street than in bed," as one of the
members stated.[51] It may be added that from later evidence it is
clear that the Northern Society overestimated the betrayal of Rostovtsev. The latter in his report to Nicholas mentioned no names,
as the Society had greatly feared, though Nicholas cunningly tried
to learn who were the members.[52] The plotters suspected Rostovtsev,
being unaware that more complete information had reached the
capital through the traitors, Maiboroda, Sherwood, and Boshniak,
who will be referred to later in connection with the uprising in the
South. On the same day that Nicholas received information about
the Society in the North, he also received news in much greater
detail concerning the Southern Society. This news was of far more
importance, for the report included many names of members of
both societies and would undoubtedly have involved eventually all
the members in the capital, even had they remained inactive.[53]

On December 13 the Northern Society met for the last time in
order to make the final decision, for the next day the army was to
take the oath of allegiance to Nicholas. Everyone at this memorable
gathering was in a state of romantic delirium. "But how beautiful

---

[50] *Vospominaniia Bestuzhevykh*, 82–83; Shilder, *op. cit.*, I, 256–258.

[51] *Vospominaniia Bestuzhevykh*, 83.

[52] *Russky Arkhiv*, I (1873), 467–469, 470.

[53] Shilder, *op. cit.*, I, 232–243.

Ryleev was that evening," recollects M. Bestuzhev in his *Memoirs.*[54] Ryleev talked with difficulty, but inspiringly, particularly when he appealed to the members to fulfill the patriotic duties of the citizen toward his country. "We are destined to die," he exclaimed, though he continued to urge the members to join the rebellion. His beautiful sparkling eyes, inflamed cheeks, and genuine sincerity galvanized the listeners, and they agreed to follow his advice. The fact of the next day's uprising was definitely accepted; there was nothing else to do, for the Society "had gone too far."[55] Later, in describing the memorable evening, Alexander Bestuzhev stated: "Departing, we were so firmly determined either to succeed or die, that we did not come to the least agreement in event of failure," and Prince Alexander Odoevsky enthusiastically exclaimed: "We shall die, oh, how gloriously we shall die!"[56] A curious example of civil heroism strongly colored with Oriental fatalism!

First disappointments.—In the beginning the Society had hoped for the assistance of the Grenadiers and the Marine Guards, among whom active "cells" of the Decembrist organization were preparing these military units for any emergency. The Society had also hoped to receive the support of the Moskovsky regiment, though it was less certain about the Izmailovsky, Finliandsky, Jegersky, and Semenovsky regiments, in which there were only a few members, though in these regiments a strong anti-Nicholas sentiment prevailed.[57] The Decembrists thought these regiments might be won over by spreading rumors that Constantine had never renounced his right to the throne and was being kept under arrest while Nicholas was usurping the crown. Thus the form of loyalty would be preserved in the eyes of the soldiers, and their officers would be enabled to exert pressure upon the government and wrest from it political concessions.[58] In order to enhance the prestige of the revolt, Trubetskoi thought of inviting influential men to participate in the government to be established later. On December 13, Ippolit Muraviev-Apostol, who shortly before had received an appointment in the Second Army in the South, left the capital, and Trubetskoi took advantage of this opportunity to dispatch a personal message to Moscow inviting Count Orlov and Fonvizin to St.

[54] *Vospominaniia Bestuzhevykh*, 138.

[55] *Materialy*, I, 70.

[56] *Ibid.*, I, 187, 452; Kotliarevsky, *Dekabristy: Odoevsky i Bestuzhev*, 17.

[57] *Materialy*, I, 36, 64–65; Korf, *op. cit.*, 124.

[58] *Materialy*, I, 65, 185.

Petersburg; he also gave a second message to the Southern Society informing it that the rebellion had been decided upon.[59] The dispatch was received in Moscow after most of the members were already in prison, and in the south Ippolit Muraviev-Apostol arrived in the midst of the revolt, which soon ended in defeat and was followed by his suicide.

The session at Obolensky's home on December 12 had given indications of lack of unity and illusory hopes. The number of military units to support the rebellion appeared to be much smaller than originally estimated. Frankly, the assembled officers stated that, though willing to assist the cause undertaken by the Society, they were not positive of the likelihood of winning many men to their side. Ryleev, to avoid complete discouragement, asked the members to pledge their presence on the Square the next day and to bring with them as many men as they were able to persuade. But the conspirators soon found that it was easier to make pledges than to keep them.

One of the greatest losses which the Society suffered at the very start was the desertion of Sergei Shipov, commander of the newly formed Semenovsky regiment. Shipov had been a close friend of Pestel and at one time a very active member of the organization, and the Society had always considered him one who would assist their cause when the time arrived.[60] But when Trubetskoi cautiously approached him on the eve of the revolt, hinting that he bring his regiment, from which he enjoyed the utmost respect, out on the Square, Shipov refused at once on the ground that the revolt was certain to fail; besides, he was in favor of Nicholas, who was "an enlightened European, while Constantine was a malicious barbarian."[61] This was most disheartening for Trubetskoi.

Other news, still more discouraging, followed. Colonel Alexander Moller and Colonel Alexander Tulubiev, of the Finliandsky regiment, also refused to join the insurgents. Colonel Moller, when approached by N. Bestuzhev, made it clear outright that he did not wish "to serve as a tool and toy of others in an enterprise where the head was not firmly held on the shoulders"; that he had always stood by his word, but this time, he said, he foresaw nothing but failure and did not wish to be quartered.[62] Colonel Tulubiev ad-

---

[59] *Ibid.*, I, 19, 21, 41, 58–59, 164.
[60] *Ibid.*, I, 23, 24.
[61] Trubetskoi, *op. cit.*, 61–62; *Russky Arkhiv*, II (1878), 181–183.
[62] *Vospominaniia Bestuzhevykh*, 84.

hered to the opinion of his colleague.[63] Thus the Finliandsky and Semenovsky regiments were lost, and the Society could only hope for the support of the Grenadiers, the Marine Guards, and the Moskovsky regiment.[64] Even the Marine Guards, who were to play an important part in the seizure of the capital, could not be altogether relied upon. When Arbuzov, the representative of the Society, appeared before the Marine officers, announcing that next day they were to lead their men to the Square in order to force the Senate to confirm the constitution, the response was by no means unanimous. One of the officers, Bodisco, declared that he could neither promise to be on the Square himself, nor, still worse, force his subordinates to be there.[65] The uncertainty of winning in the capital gave rise to the temporary idea of retreating to the Novgorod military colonies where the mobilized masses would undoubtedly give their aid. Trubetskoi even thought for a moment of shifting the center of activities south, to join the uprising in Kiev, but such radical changes demanded time, and there was none too much to spare.[66] Also, since Nicholas was aware of the plans of the Society, any postponement would be equivalent to disaster. All this only emphasizes how immature was the whole uprising, and how little the leaders knew of the actual support they would have at their command on December 14. This also explains in large part why the events of that day proved to be more of a dress rehearsal than an actual revolution. In full haste Trubetskoi drafted a Manifesto to be proclaimed by the Senate; with equal speed he made plans for the seizure of the palace and the arrest of the royal family. The Manifesto declared the end of the old régime, the establishment of a Provisional Government, freedom of speech, religious tolerance, equality before the law, abolition of the military colonies, introduction of a jury system, and various other reforms in the army and navy.[67] But all these schemes were only on paper, for the leaders were compelled to operate with much smaller forces than they had originally expected. Moreover, Ryleev and other members gave so much attention to political programs that they overlooked the simplest and most practical issue of the whole plan, namely, how to win the battle and create a situation whereby all these programs could be executed. Naturally, when the hour struck and every measure had to be undertaken at a minute's

---

[63] Rozen, *op. cit.*, 71.
[64] *Materialy*, I, 19.
[65] *Ibid.*, II, 19.
[66] *Ibid.*, I, 443; Rozen, *op. cit.*, 63.
[67] *Materialy*, I, 107–108. See Appendix.

THE SENATE SQUARE ON DECEMBER 14, 1825.

notice, many of the paper schemes had to be thrown overboard; and still more disheartening disappointments were to follow. To climax the confusion, at the very last hour several of the important members, including the "dictator" himself, deserted the battle-ground: they failed in audacity, the alpha and the omega of revo-lutionary strategy. Lack of a definite strategic plan to secure power, together with absence of leadership, sealed the fate of the uprising.

December Fourteenth.—On December 14, 1825, early in the morning, Mikhail and Alexander Bestuzhev succeeded in inciting a battalion of the Moskovsky regiment to rebel. After informing them of the request to take the oath to Nicholas they added: "All this is a lie; we are compelled to take the oath by force: Emperor Constantine Pavlovich has not abdicated the throne, but is in chains," and they therefore advised the soldiers not to take the oath until Constantine in person requested them to do so. Alex-ander Bestuzhev told the soldiers that Constantine intended to lower the term of military service and raise their pay. The soldiers unanimously shouted "We want no Nicholas—Hurrah! Constan-tine!" and agreed to join the rebellion, and some of the officers who showed resistance were beaten and several of them seriously wounded.[68] The battalion proceeded to the empty Senate Square where the troops refusing to take the oath were to assemble.[69] It was about nine o'clock in the morning. Soon they were joined by some of the Grenadiers and the Marine Guards, who came under the leadership of Nicholas Bestuzhev.

On the same morning Nicholas Bestuzhev came to Ryleev to get the latest information. He learned that Kakhovsky had prom-ised to assassinate Nicholas and that he had been instructed not to reveal his association with the Society. Ryleev was planning to dress in peasant's costume with a knapsack on his back and a rifle in his hand, to symbolize the union between the soldier and the peasant "in the first act of their mutual liberty." Bestuzhev ob-jected to this masquerade; he considered it dangerous because the Russian soldier did not understand "these delicacies of patriotism," and besides, he felt that the time for the National Guard had not yet arrived in Russia. Ryleev agreed that it was too "romantic" and determined to proceed with his plans without putting on any kind of "make-up."[70]

---

[68] *Vospominaniia Bestuzhevykh*, 142.
[69] *Materialy*, I, 232, 248; *Krasnyi Arkhiv*, XIII, 288–292.

There followed a heartbreaking scene. As they started to leave, Ryleev's wife seized Bestuzhev by the arm and commenced imploring him with tears in her eyes to leave her husband alone for she felt he was going to his doom. Both men endeavored to persuade her that there was no danger involved in the undertaking, but she refused to listen. The tragic moment was heightened by the appearance of Ryleev's six-year-old daughter, Nastenka. In despair Madame Ryleev shouted to her daughter at the top of her voice: "Nastenka, beg your father for yourself and my own sake." The little girl embraced her father's knees, pleading with him not to go, and the mother completely collapsed. Ryleev placed her on the divan, tore himself away from his daughter, and ran out toward the Square. Here Nicholas Bestuzhev soon appeared leading the Marine Guard, and Ryleev joined the rebels. He greeted his colleagues and in a dramatic tone proclaimed the beginning of freedom for which he was willing to give his life.[71]

On the Square, so the leaders told the soldiers, the authorities would be requested to show and to read publicly the will of Alexander, which was in the keeping of the Senate.[72] The Senate, which had assembled at seven o'clock that morning, had already taken the oath and departed.[73] The Square was empty and neither Yakubovich, nor Colonel Bulatov, who had been appointed assistant commander, nor the "dictator," Prince Trubetskoi, had appeared.[74] Yakubovich, "the daring Caucasian," who had formerly amazed everyone by his audacity and whom the Society had often feared to have "unleashed," seemed to have lost his revolutionary ardor.[75] Evidently, as M. Bestuzhev said, the audacity of a soldier and that of a conspirator are far from being the same. Only a few days before, Yakubovich had declared to the Society that he could see no success unless Nicholas was assassinated; on the very eve of the fateful day he shocked the Society by suggesting that it "smash the public houses, allow the soldiers and the mob to pillage, then carry out the banners from some church, and march to the palace." His conduct is inexplicable. On the day when the issue was at stake, that same posing Marat marched to the Square carrying his hat on

[70] *Vospominaniia Bestuzhevykh*, 85.
[71] *Ibid.*, 86.
[72] *Materialy*, I, 62.
[73] *Russkaia Starina*, LXXXIX (1897), 464.
[74] *Materialy*, I, 160–161.
[75] *Ibid*, I, 180, 181, 436; II, 285–286.

the tip of his uplifted sword, shouting "Hurrah for Constantine!"
Here he stood for only a moment, then, under the pretense of a
frightful headache, left the place just as the order was given to
load the rifles. "Noticing the criminal intentions of the rebels," he
went to Nicholas and declared that his presence on the Square "was
a result of exclusive zeal and sincere attachment to the young
Emperor."[76] Praised by Nicholas for his loyalty, Yakubovich returned to the rebels and advised them to hold on firmly, for Nicholas was afraid of them. After that he turned around, went home,
loaded his pistol, ordered that no one be allowed to see him, and
sat down contemplating, as Bestuzhev says, "how to betray more
heroically." He remained at home until he was arrested there by
a government official. Yakubovich's later fate was as tragic as that
of the other rebels.[77]

No less inexplicable was the conduct of Colonel Bulatov, the
supposed right-hand man of the "dictator." Noticing the half-
empty Square, he turned back and went to the military headquarters, where he took the oath of allegiance to Nicholas. Then
voluntarily, apparently with no reason whatever, he surrendered
himself to the authorities, confessing that he had had terrible plans
to kill the Emperor.[78] On January 18, 1826, after being arrested
and questioned a few times, he committed suicide by smashing his
head on the cold walls of the fortress.[79]

"Dictator" Trubetskoi.—Strangest of all was the conduct of the
so-called dictator, Prince Sergei Trubetskoi, who was supposed to
take command of all the troops assembled on the Square in revolt
against the government.[80] It may be suspected that with Bulatov
it was a purely psychopathic phenomenon, but the behavior of
Trubetskoi requires the analysis of a psychologist rather than
a psychiatrist. His conduct on December 14 was a mixture of
cowardliness and treason. Yet Trubetskoi was scarcely a coward,
for he had proved himself a brave soldier during the war of 1812–
14, displaying on many occasions excellent self-control and courage, and returning home with honors.[81] Nor can he be accused of

---

[76] *Ibid.*, I, 99, 188, 270; II, 31; *Vospominaniia Bestuzhevykh*, 143, 144;
Mezhdutsarstvie, 96, 113–114.

[77] *Materialy*, II, 280, 283–284; *Krasnyi Arkhiv*, XIII, 286; "Zapiski Nikolaia
I." *Dekabristy. Sbornik otryvkov iz istochnikov*, 327.

[78] Dovnar-Zapolsky, *Memuary dekabristov*, 241–244.

[79] *Russkaia Starina*, I (1887), 218.

[80] *Materialy*, I, 452.   [81] *Bunt Dekabristov*, 134; *Materialy*, I, 4–5.

deliberate betrayal, though he was one of the first of those arrested to present to Nicholas a list of names of all the members of the Society. From his childhood he had "always striven to be an honest man and a true Christian."[82] Later, in exile, his life justified this statement. Nevertheless, in spite of his distinguished record, the blunder he committed stands against Trubetskoi as a serious indictment. Pokrovsky has well characterized his conduct as indeed an example of a brave soldier becoming a cowardly general.[83]

While Bestuzhev was on the Square with the companies of the Moskovsky regiment, Trubetskoi, immediately after promising to come there, too, took a cab and went to the main office of the chief of staff to inquire where he might take the oath to the new Emperor. After receiving the information, he began to wander aimlessly from place to place. Soon he discovered that the Moskovsky regiment had gone to the Senate Square and was shoutng in favor of Constantine. Under the pretense that he felt unwell, Trubetskoi retired to one of the offices, where he remained "despondent and in fear." After several hours of brooding the "dictator" inquired of one of the officials whether it would be possible for him to pass through the Square unnoticed. Being assured that he could, Trubetskoi left and he was found that night in the Austrian Embassy, where he had sought protection.[84]

One of the latest writers has endeavored to justify the behavior of Trubetskoi on the ground that he had given orders to seize the palace and, as commander, was therefore only waiting for results; that, early in the morning, there had been an opportunity to carry out this order when the first companies had arrived on the Square, but the moment had been missed, and therefore the whole plan had to fail. In such circumstances the presence of Trubetskoi had become entirely superfluous, for it could not have changed the situation. The same writer places the blame upon Bestuzhev and the other leaders, not upon Trubetskoi, though he admits that the absence of the "dictator" was an act of treason, but treason to his colleagues only, not to the cause of the Society.[85] Even though it might be admitted, for the moment, that betrayal of his colleagues

---

[82] *Materialy*, I, 34.

[83] *Ibid.*, I, ix.

[84] *Ibid.*, I, 43–44, 71-72. Count Ludwig Lebzeltern, Austrian ambassador in St. Petersburg, was brother-in-law by marriage of Trubetskoi. See *Russky Viestnik*, III (1893), 163.

[85] *Bunt Dekabristov*, 206–207.

PRINCE SERGEI TRUBETSKOI.

was not a violation of party etiquette though betrayal of the Society was, yet the argument cannot stand criticism. In the evening of December 13 Trubetskoi had already realized, so he declared, the futility of the uprising and therefore he did not wish to give any orders at all.[86] How, then, can responsibility be placed upon Bestuzhev, who bravely came to the Square and brought with him the companies, while his superior, Trubetskoi, was inquiring where he could take the oath to Nicholas?

Another apologist for Trubetskoi attempts to justify his conduct by the fact that, since he had realized from the very beginning the hopelessness of the whole enterprise, he could do nothing else.[87] But, even if it had been his right to retire, Trubetskoi should at least have informed his colleagues of so important a decision, involving as it did the lives of others. Yet, on the very morning of December 14 he promised Ryleev and Pushchin to come to the Square.[88] "His absence," states Alexander Bestuzhev, "had a decisive influence upon us and the soldiers, for with few epaulets and without military titles no one dared to take command."[89] Aside from the favorable effect that the presence of Trubetskoi might have had upon the soldiers, as "dictator" he had no moral right to expect that his "plan," known to him alone, could be carried out while he was waiting for impossible reports. As one of the most responsible leaders of the uprising, he was supposed to be on the Square to the last moment; he should not have established headquarters of the existence of which the insurgents knew nothing. The failure of Trubetskoi to lead the revolutionary forces at the most critical moment, no matter how weak they were, together with his taking refuge in the Austrian Embassy, places the heaviest responsibility upon him, a responsibility which in moments of remorse he fully realized.[90]

The "Standing Revolution."—But to return to the Senate Square. Left without leadership, the soldiers on the Square did not know what to do, and there began what became known as the "Standing Revolution." The rebels, "brought to the Square like sheep while the leaders had hidden themselves," as Kakhovsky bitterly complained, stood aimlessly, pierced by the raw north wind, occasionally shouting "Hurrah for Constantine!" and pa-

[86] *Materialy*, I, 19–20.
[87] *Sbornik statei, posviashchennykh Miliukovu*, 456–457, 473, 478; *Materialy*, I, 6.
[88] *Materialy*, I, 38.   [89] *Ibid.*, I, 443.   [90] *Ibid.*, I, 38–39, 152.

tiently wondering what it was all about.[91] Realizing that Trubetskoi was not coming, Prince Obolensky suggested that Nicholas
Bestuzhev take command, but he refused because, as a naval officer, he knew too little of military tactics on land. He therefore
suggested that Obolensky take charge of the rebellion, and Obolensky agreed.[92] Unfortunately, Obolensky lacked initiative as much
as Bestuzhev lacked knowledge, and the confusion continued.[93]

At noon the rebels could count but three thousand men, exactly
one-half the number which Trubetskoi had considered necessary to
win. The government had not less than nine thousand soldiers.[94]
Yet even at that moment there was a possibility of victory had the
leaders of the rebellion shown greater resourcefulness, for they
could have won to their side, if not all, at least a large number of
the government troops.[95] Not only was this opportunity missed,
but another was also overlooked, namely, the possibility of rallying
to the cause civilians who were sympathetic with the purposes of
the Society and who had begun to gather around the Square.[96] The
hours dragged slowly and the government, through the indecision
of its foe, was gaining ground and consolidating its forces. Both
sides stood facing each other: on the Senate Square the rebels;
not far off, on the Admiralty Boulevard, facing the Senate stood
Nicholas, surrounded by his royal staff, among whom was Karamzin. The Emperor was pale, weary, and eager to settle the whole
affair as soon as possible. The rebels believed that in the evening
they would succeed in winning over the loyal troops; the government hoped that at dark the rebels would peacefully return to
their barracks.[97] Whereas the Society leaders hoped for more assistance and did nothing but wait, the government did not passively
watch developments; it began to gather the loyal troops around the
Senate Square, and held them in complete readiness.

Peaceful efforts to end the uprising.—For a while the government hesitated to use force and tried to end the situation by per-

---

[91] *Ibid.*, I, 437.

[92] Rozen, *op. cit.*, 65–67.

[93] *Materialy*, I, 242–243.

[94] *Ibid.*, I, 98.

[95] Gabaev, *Gvardiia v dekabrskie dni 1825 goda*, 203–204; *Katorga i Ssylka*,
VIII (1925), 82–83.

[96] Rozen, *op. cit.*, 68–69; *Krasnyi Arkhiv*, XIII, 286–287; *Vospominaniia
Bestuzhevykh*, 147.

[97] *Russkaia Starina*, XXX (1881), 499.

suasion, but this attempt failed. When Miloradovich, the Governor-General of St. Petersburg, approached the rebels, in an endeavor to persuade them to return to their headquarters, Obolensky requested him to leave the soldiers alone or his life would be in danger.[98] Miloradovich had scarcely turned back when Kakhovsky shot and killed him.[99] This brave general, who had participated in numerous battles without ever having been injured, died of a Russian bullet. Commander Stürler, who also attempted to open negotiations, was warned to depart, but he disregarded the warning and was fatally shot by the same Kakhovsky.[100] Next, the government decided to try spiritual influence and sent the Metropolitan Serafim, who came out in episcopal robes, to pacify those who refused to bow to the new Crown, but this mission met with no greater success. The Father of the Church was advised not to meddle in political affairs but to go back and pray for the souls of the rebels, and he returned empty-handed.[101]

Following these failures, the Grand Duke Mikhail Pavlovich made an attempt to bring the disobedient to their senses, but to no avail. The leaders shouted with one voice that they could not betray their oath and requested him to leave, since he was only endangering his life. After being nearly shot by Wilhelm Küchelbecker, the Grand Duke was forced to return.[102]

Rebellion crushed by force.—Since all efforts to settle the question peacefully were exhausted and the day was nearing its close, Nicholas began to fear that, should the rebels remain on the Square, they might gain the support of the loyal troops, grow stronger, and cause serious complications. As certain evidence shows, this fear was justified; some of the loyal troops had secretly promised to desert the government and to join the rebels as soon as night should come.[103] Nicholas therefore began to think of more effective persuasion. At first, the cavalry attempted a sudden attack in order to clear the Square of the stubborn rebels, but this failed completely, for the horses were not shod and the men were unable to ride them on the icy streets. The endeavor ended in a

---

[98] *Materialy*, I, 225; *Russky Viestnik*, III (1893), 159.

[99] *Materialy*, I, 188, 232–233; *Istorichesky Viestnik*, I (1908), 132ff.

[100] *Materialy*, I, 369–370, 377.

[101] *Ibid.*, I, 355; II, 144, 152; *Krasnyi Arkhiv*, XIII, 287–288; *Istorichesky Viestnik*, I (1905), 166ff.

[102] *Russkaia Starina*, XXX (1881), 498–499.

[103] *Ibid.*, XXX (1881), 499.

shameful retreat amid amused laughter from the other side.[104] Nicholas made one more effort, sending General Sukhozanet to inform the insurgents that they would be pardoned if they would submit and return to their headquarters. Ironically the rebels asked the messenger whether the honorable General had brought with him a constitution. Sukhozanet sharply replied that he had not been sent for negotiations and immediately turned back. Shots followed him, but he managed to return unhurt.[105]

Meanwhile, large crowds began to gather and delay would only have prolonged the tension. Nicholas, who himself was on the Square, saw that the increasing hostility was likely to become serious. The growing crowds were openly against him, and many people asked the officers to hold on for an hour or so and everything would go well.[106] Some even dared to throw firewood which the mob had found piled near by. Bullets were showered, though none hurt the Emperor.[107] Later, in recalling to Prince Eugene, of Württemberg, the sad experience of that day, he said: "What seems to be most inconceivable in this story is the fact that both of us were not shot down."[108]

In justice to Nicholas it must be said that to the last he avoided using force, even when the higher command urged him to do so. General Toll came up to the Emperor with a frank request: "Your Majesty," he said, "either let us clear the Square with gunfire or abdicate." General Sukhozanet, who had returned after failing to obtain the consent of the rebels to clear the Square, suggested that the government open fire, but Nicholas hesitated. "Your Majesty," another member of the royal suite advised him, "it is impossible to lose a minute; there is nothing to be done: canister shot is necessary." "You wish me to shed the blood of my subjects on the first day of my reign?" asked Nicholas. "To save the Empire," was the reply.[109] Nicholas took the fatal step, and three cannon were brought forward. "Violà un joli commencement de règne!" remarked Nicholas.[110]

[104] *Zapiski Nikolaia*, 329.

[105] *Russkaia Starina*, VII (1873), 368.

[106] *Rozen, op. cit.*, 65, 66.

[107] *Krasnyi Arkhiv*, XIII, 286–287; *Zapiski Nikolaia*, 329–330; *Russkaia Starina*, VII (1873), 369–370; *XIX Viek*, I, 204–205; *Shilder, op. cit.*, I, 288.

[108] *Russky Arkhiv*, III (1878), 351; *Zapiski Nikolaia*, 328–329; *Krasnyi Arkhiv*, XIII, 314.

[109] *Mezhdutsarstvie*, 27.

[110] Presniakov, *op. cit.*, 129; *Russky Viestnik*, III (1893), 162.

When the rebels saw the mouths of the cannon pointed toward them, one of the officers, Kornilovich, suggested that an attack be made to seize the guns, but some of the men did not believe their brethren would fire upon them, and others dared not move. The cause of the insurrection was doomed. A warning was given, so that the government might later place the responsibility for the consequences wholly upon the other party. The rebels ignored the warning, and Nicholas gave the order to open fire.

The canister shot had immediate results. Driven back in disorder, the rebels left behind them numerous dead and wounded, among whom were many innocent civilians. No one knows the exact number of victims, many of whom feared to make their wounds known to officials, but the toll must have been heavy.[111] "The Lord be the judge of the officers who led us to this," muttered a wounded soldier, expressing unwittingly the whole tragedy of the lower ranks. Particularly disastrous were the effects of the canister shot along the narrow Galërnaia street and on the Neva River, where the retreating soldiers had hoped to gather their scattered forces. The two cannon balls that dispersed them also broke the ice, and many were drowned.[112] "The firing lasted for an hour," writes a contemporary. "There was no distinction between participants in the rebellion and mere spectators, all being shot down. Many were trodden to death by the panic-stricken masses, assisted by cannon balls and canister shot.[113] Many soldiers sought shelter in private homes, but the gates being locked it was not so easy to gain access or to persuade the inhabitants to let them in, since the latter feared government persecution for harboring rebels. Those who succeeded in escaping were pursued and most of them captured. The "revolution" came to an end. The throne had been saved and the reign of Nicholas I commenced.[114]

After the firing had ceased, the appearance of the Square must have been most unpleasant, for the government took immediate precautions to erase every indication of the tragic occurrence. It

---

[111] A list of killed and wounded, far from complete, may be found in *Byloe*, III (1907), 194–199. See also Gabaev, G., *op. cit.*, 190–192.

[112] *Vospominaniia Bestuzhevykh*, 147–148; *Russkaia Starina*, XXI (1878), 228, 229.

[113] *O Minuvshem*, 110–111.

[114] *Lettres et Papiers du Chancelier Comte de Nesselrode, 1760–1850*, VI, 266–268. On the night of December 14, Nicholas wrote to his brother: "Cher, cher Constantin! Votre volonté est faite, je suis empereur, mais à quel prix grand Dieu, au prix du sang de mes sujets!"—*Mezhdutsarstvie*, 145.

hastily sent workers to the scene to remove the dead and to scrub off the bloodstains.[115] Wishing to dispose of all the bodies as quickly as possible, Alexander Shulgin, the St. Petersburg Chief of Police, hit upon an ingenuous idea : he ordered them thrown into the Neva River, under the ice. It was feared that, among the many dead, there were also thrown in a number of wounded victims.[116] This inhuman act aroused Nicholas. "I am very much dissatisfied with the police here, which do nothing, know nothing and understand nothing," wrote Nicholas to his brother Constantine on December 28, 1825. "Shulgin begins to drink, and I don't think that he can remain useful at his post ; I don't know whom to put in his place."[117]

In the spring, with the coming of the warm weather and the breaking of the ice, an occasional corpse would appear on the bank to betray the ruthlessness of the police and serve as a grim reminder of the events of December 14, 1825.

---

[115] *Vospominaniia Bestuzhevykh,* 149–150; Shishkov, *Zapiski,* II, 275.

[116] *Pamiati Dekabristov,* I, 243–244; *O Minuvshem,* 110–111.

[117] *Mezhdutsarstvie,* 170.

Chapter VIII

THE REVOLT IN THE SOUTH

EVENTS PRECEDING THE UPRISING

BETRAYAL

NEARLY TWO WEEKS elapsed before news of the call to arms in the North reached the Southern Society, but the general plans contemplated by its members had become known to the authorities shortly before the death of Alexander I.

Betrayal.—Activities of the Southern Society were disclosed by several traitors. One of them was the unscrupulous Count Ivan Witt, who, with the assistance of his friend, Alexander Boshniak, warned the Emperor of the conspiracy.[1]

Two other traitors working among the members of the Society were Ivan Sherwood and Arkady Maiboroda. Sherwood was born in Kent, England, in 1798. At the age of two he was brought by his parents to Russia, his father being a skilled mechanic whom Paul I had invited to the country. In 1819 Sherwood joined the Russian army in the South, where he learned of the existence of the Southern Society and reported it to the Emperor, though he had nothing to reveal to the government except superficial knowledge obtained from the vaguest rumors.[2] The case of Maiboroda, a Russian, the other traitor was entirely different. He had been closely associated with the Society, knew many of its secrets, and had been trusted for a long time by Pestel, whom he coolly betrayed. At first, Alexander paid little attention to the reports of Maiboroda, and on one occasion threw a document into the fireplace with the remark: "Rascal, wishes promotion!"[3] But when Count Witt brought information confirming the reports of Maiboroda, Alexander became apprehensive and ordered an investigation which led to the discovery of the entire Southern Society and the arrest of its leaders.[4]

---

[1] *Krasnyi Arkhiv*, IX, 195ff.; Volkonsky, *Zapiski dekabrista*, 423–426; Shilder, *Imp. Nikolai I*, I, 178.

[2] Shilder, *Imp. Aleksandr I.*, IV, 337ff.

[3] Lorer, *Zapiski dekabrista*, 437–438.

[4] *Materialy*, IV, 8ff.; Trotsky, *Zhizn' Shervuda-Vernogo*, 44ff.; *Byloe*, V (1925), 47; *Istorichesky Viestnik*, LXIII (1896), 66.

Arrest of Pestel.—The first victim of the betrayal was Pestel, who was arrested on December 13, 1825, a day before the uprising in the North. His papers and the famous *Russian Justice* he succeeded in concealing, though they were revealed later, in February, 1826. Pestel was probably little aware of the actual situation, believing that his was only an individual instance and that if he denied any knowledge of a society, he would gain freedom. While under arrest he succeeded in having a short interview with Volkonsky, in which Pestel declared that he would reveal nothing of the Society even if forced to undergo horrible torture.[5] He remained true to his promise, and at first declared that he knew nothing of any society and had no connection with a secret organization.[6] It was only after he learned that the government had arrested nearly every member and had obtained sufficient information that he confessed, hoping to win freedom by stating the truth.

Muraviev-Apostol prepares for revolt.—The arrest of Pestel, the heart and mind of the Southern Society, placed a serious problem before the members. Some thought the best policy would be to wait "until the storm passed over," but others considered immediate revolt as the solution. On December 23, while the members were debating what course to pursue, they learned vaguely of the tragic events in the capital, and the question of revolution in order to help their northern colleagues became even more urgent. At that time Sergei Muraviev-Apostol, who seemed to be the logical substitute for Pestel, had gone to Zhitomir to plead before Commander Login Rot a leave of absence for Bestuzhev-Riumin, whose mother had died in Moscow. As a former officer of the Semenovsky regiment during the revolt, Bestuzhev-Riumin had been deprived of the right to leave his regiment, to retire, or be promoted, and Muraviev-Apostol, as his close friend, had gone to obtain permission for him to go to Moscow.[7] At the same time Muraviev-Apostol expected to perform certain duties for the Society and to get into touch with the Polish Society through Count Moszyński, who lived at Zhitomir.[8]

In his absence an order came from St. Petersburg to arrest Muraviev-Apostol and to deliver all his papers, sealed, to the capi-

[5] Volkonsky, *op. cit.*, 437–438.

[6] *Materialy*, IV, 45ff.

[7] *Ibid.*, IV, 241.

[8] *Krasnyi Arkhiv*, XIII, 3; *Materialy*, IV, 261–263, 283; *Vospominaniia i rasskazy*, I, 199; *Dekabristy. Sbornik otryvkov iz istochnikov*, 357.

tal.[9] After a vain search for the leader, the gendarmes seized his papers and continued to look for the man. Immediately the Society took precautions to prevent his arrest, sending Bestuzhev-Riumin to warn him. Meanwhile, at the home of Commander Rot, where he dined on December 25, Muraviev-Apostol had heard of the uprising in the North. The next day, he visited his brother, Alexander, in Troianov, and was informed in greater detail of developments in St. Petersburg.[10]

Realizing that the situation had made an uprising in the South imminent, Muraviev-Apostol went to Liubar, where he stopped at the home of his brother Artamon, commander of the Akhtyrsky regiment and also a member of the Society. The two men were discussing the situation, when Bestuzhev-Riumin arrived post haste with the news that the police were searching the house of Muraviev-Apostol and were on his trail to arrest and deliver him to the authorities in the capital.[11] Now that the situation had reached this stage, there was indeed but one alternative, to submit or to rebel.

At first both Muraviev-Apostol and Bestuzhev-Riumin thought of hiding somewhere, but immediately they abandoned the plan, concluding that revolt was preferable.[12] Muraviev-Apostol then asked his brother, Artamon, to rebel with his regiment, but Artamon decidedly refused, considering such a course futile. Moreover, he began to implore the men to leave his home, begging them: "For God's sake don't ruin me as the father of a family."[13] This was the same Artamon Muraviev-Apostol who only shortly before had urged the Society to act without delay and had even declared that, if revolt were postponed, he would go to Taganrog himself to assassinate Alexander I.[14]

Denied any assistance, Sergei Muraviev-Apostol asked Artamon at least to deliver a message to the United Slavs requesting them to revolt. After some hesitation, Artamon promised to do so, but upon the departure of his brother he destroyed the note.[15] His refusal even to aid in establishing communication with the Slavs inflicted a serious blow upon the plans of the Society. Besides the

[9] *Materialy*, VI, 3.
[10] *Krasnyi Arkhiv*, XIII, 14, 15–16.
[11] *Materialy*, VI, 51–52.
[12] *Krasnyi Arkhiv*, XIII, 23, 24, footnote ii, 49.
[13] *Materialy*, VIII, 131–132, 355–356; *Krasnyi Arkhiv*, XIII, 28–29, 43; *Istorik Marksist*, I (1926), 169–170.
[14] *Krasnyi Arkhiv*, XIII, 3; *Materialy*, IV, 358.
[15] Gorbachevsky, *Zapiski i pisma*, 124–125.

physical support which Artamon Muraviev-Apostol could have given, he deprived the Society of the excellent strategic position that Liubar presented.

The refusal of assistance in Liubar compelled Sergei Muraviev-Apostol to abandon all hope of using the Akhtyrsky regiment, and he set out to find other resources. He went to the headquarters of the Chernigovsky regiment in an endeavor to obtain assistance there, planning thereafter to force his way to Zhitomir and to coördinate activities with the United Slavs, who had been eagerly awaiting an opportunity.[16] When in Trilesy on December 29, where Muraviev-Apostol had felt that he was under suspicion, he dispatched Bestuzhev-Riumin to Brusilov and Zhitomir to reconnoiter and to return at once, should he fail to get into communication with the Slavs. Muraviev-Apostol remained in Trilesy to await results, meanwhile inviting for counsel some of the officers who were members of the United Slavs.[17] But Bestuzhev-Riumin soon discovered that the police were searching for him also, and he therefore returned in disguise to Trilesy.[18]

Defiance of the law.—All further attempts to plan a revolution were suddenly checked, for on the night of December 29, after having searched continuously, the police discovered Sergei Muraviev-Apostol. Early in the morning, however, four members of the Slavs, who had learned of the place where he was quartered, came to Trilesy and found him detained in the house. They asked him what to do next, and Muraviev-Apostol advised them to free him and his brother Matvei, who had also been detained.[19] Without much thought the Slavs released the prisoners by force. Lieutenant-Colonel Goebel, who had made the arrest, was horribly beaten and barely escaped with his life.[20]

REBELLION

Strategy of Muraviev-Apostol.—Now that the initiative had been taken by the United Slavs, the prisoners released, and the law openly defied, there was no recourse but to act at once. With the assistance of a few officers Muraviev-Apostol assembled several companies of the Chernigovsky regiment, declaring to them that they were to perform a great deed: to deliver the people from

---

[16] *Krasnyi Arkhiv*, XIII, 49–50, 54, 55–56.
[17] *Ibid.*, XIII, 7–8.
[18] *Ibid.*, XIII, 24, footnote iii.
[19] *Materialy*, IV, 242.
[20] *Ibid.*, VI, 5–6, 8–9, 14–15, 38; *Russky Arkhiv* (1871), 1728.

slavery, lessen army service, and enforce other beneficial acts, all of which depended entirely upon the soldiers themselves.[21] The soldiers consented, and under the command of Muraviev-Apostol they marched on December 30 to the city of Vasilkov, a small provincial town not far from Kiev. On their way they met Bestuzhev-Riumin, who, after some unsuccessful scouting, joined the rebels.

Vasilkov.—When the inhabitants of Vasilkov learned of the aproaching troops, there was a panic, for the people feared civil war. At three o'clock in the afternoon Muraviev-Apostol captured the city without the least resistance; the soldiers in that city readily joined the rebels.[22] They were all peacefully quartered and order was strictly maintained, since the army was to have nothing in mind but "to emancipate the people."[23] In this connection the name of Lieutenant Ivan Sukhinov must be mentioned, for he displayed remarkable courage and self-control, was constantly on the watch, and helped to preserve military discipline and order.[24] The city was vigilantly guarded from possible spies and all gendarmes were detained.[25]

In Vasilkov, Sergei Muraviev-Apostol seized the military banners and the army treasury and released all prisoners from the military detention house.[26] He also took every precaution to provide the rebels, numbering about eight hundred men, with sufficient food and other necessities. After having given all orders, he began to consider further plans. From Vasilkov there were three strategic possibilities: one to move on Kiev, another on Belaia Tserkov, and a third on Zhitomir, where he could unite with the Slavs. (See map, p. 192.) Decision on what move to make was important, for upon it depended, in large measure, the outcome of the whole matter.

Plans for advancement.—To assist him Muraviev-Apostol had selected four officers, all of them energetic members of the United Slavs. These were Lieutenants Kuzmin, Sukhinov, and Shchepillo,

---

[21] *Krasnyi Arkhiv*, XIII, 35.

[22] *Dekabristi na Ukraini*, 61–62.

[23] *Materialy*, VI, 37.

[24] It may be added that Sukhinov's energy and initiative did not fail him even during his Siberian exile. There he organized a rebellion to free the prisoners, but it was crushed and Sukhinov sentenced to death. He committed suicide on the evening before the sentence was to be executed. See *Krasnyi Arkhiv*, XIII, 258.

[25] *Vospominaniia i rasskazy*, I, 195–196; *Russkaia Starina*, CXXII (1905), 379–380; *Materialy*, IV, 247–248.

[26] *Krasnyi Arkhiv*, XIII, 4, 8–9, 34; *Materialy*, IV, 247–248; VI, 6–7, 24.

and Baron Soloviev.[27] They offered advice on the strategy to be employed, but Muraviev-Apostol did not always accept it readily. He believed in moving slowly and in gaining other regiments step by step; he also hoped that the forces sent against him, instead of fighting, would fraternize with the rebellious regiments. His strategy has recently been interpreted as a move to eliminate the possibility of the domination of the uprising by the United Slavs, but this view cannot be justified by the available evidence.[28]

The United Slavs insisted upon a policy of quick movement and surprise raids, so that the enemy might be caught unawares and unprepared. The first attack, they thought, should be made upon no other place than Kiev. Besides its strategic value, the capture of this city, the heart of southern Russia, would strengthen the morale of the cause. Muraviev-Apostol, however, hesitated to attempt such rash action; though he saw the advantage of occupying Kiev, he feared to risk his small force in attacking that city, where loyal government troops outnumbered the rebels ten times over. Muraviev-Apostol spent the night at Vasilkov over these plans and waited impatiently for replies to messages which he had dispatched with three couriers. Of these messages one was to a member of the Polish Secret Society and two others were to sympathizers of the movement, upon whose support Muraviev-Apostol was counting. With the letters he had also sent several copies of the "Catechism," about which more will be said presently.

Propaganda.—On the same night Muraviev-Apostol was also occupied with another task. He secluded himself at his headquarters and began to labor over a document entitled "An Orthodox Catechism," which he had sketched in French some time before. Now, he thought of a use for it and undertook to revise and translate it, dictating in Russian to several secretaries.[29]

---

[27] *Materialy*, IV, 288.

[28] *Katorga i Ssylka*, VIII (1925), 96. In another work the same author contradicts herself, calling Muraviev-Apostol the first "constitutionalist" and the Decembrists the first "bourgeois revolutionaries who carried out the *coup d'état* from the tsarist palace to the city square; the first revolutionaries who made an attempt to establish contacts with the masses, the first agitators among the soldiers...." See Nechkina and Skazin, *Seminary po dekabrizmu*, 20–21.

[29] The "Orthodox Catechism" was kept secret for a long time. As late as 1903, Shilder, in his life of Nicholas I, wrote: "The contents of this Catechism are such that it cannot be reproduced in the press even now." The text appeared for the first time in 1906 in a collection of documents relating to the Decembrist movement, compiled by A. Borozdin. See *Iz pisem i pokazanii dekabristov*, 85–88.

The next day, December 31, at noon, Muraviev-Apostol ordered all the soldiers to assemble on the City Square. Meanwhile, he called to his headquarters a young local priest, Father Daniel Keizer, to whom he explained the aims of the insurrection, and asked his spiritual assistance. The clergy, he said, had always been on the side of the people; therefore the representative of the Church must aid in the cause he had undertaken. At first confused, the priest did not know what to do. He consented to help the leader, but, in event of failure, he wondered what would happen to his wife and children. Muraviev-Apostol took out two hundred rubles, saying that they were to be given to the priest's family and that Russia would never forget his servce. The priest accepted the offer and followed the leader to the Square.[30]

On the Square Muraviev-Apostol made a speech before the assembled troops, explaining to them the ideal for which they were fighting and declaring that nothing could be nobler than to sacrifice one's life for liberty. The soldiers enthusiastically pledged to follow their leader to fight for the cause of the people. Muraviev-Apostol then took the "Orthodox Catechism," over which he had labored the night before, and asked the priest to read it aloud to the soldiers.[31] The curious document, which proclaimed only one Universal Tsar,—Jesus Christ,—reads in part as follows:[32]

IN THE NAME OF THE FATHER, THE SON, AND THE HOLY GHOST.

Q.: What did the Lord create man for?

A.: So that he would have faith in Him and be free and happy.

Q.: What does it mean to be free and happy?

A.: Without freedom there is no happiness. St. Paul said: Ye were redeemed at the price of blood; be ye not slaves of others.

Q.: Why are the Russian people and the Russian army unhappy?

A.: Because their freedom has been usurped by the Tsars.

Q.: Then the Tsars act against the will of God?

A.: Precisely. The Lord has said: And whosoever will be chief among you, let him be your servant. But the Tsars only tyrannize over their people.

Q.: Must the Tsars be obeyed when they act against the will of God?

A.: No! Christ said: Ye cannot serve God and mammon. That is why the Russian people and the Russian army suffer, because they obey the Tsars.

---

[30] Gorbachevsky, *op. cit.*, 151–152; *Dekabristi na Ukraini*, 63–64.

[31] *Materialy*, VI, 78; Shchegolev, *Istoricheskie etiudy*, 346.

[32] A special study of the "Catechism" was made by Professor P. Shchegolev in 1908. See *Istoricheskie etiudy*, 317. Valuable criticism of this study may be found in *Materialy*, VI, Introduction, pp. l–lii; *Katorga i Ssylka*, V (1926), 278–282; *Dekabristy. Sbornik otryvkov iz istochnikov*, 389–391; *Materialy*, IV, 254–255.

Q. : What then must the Christian Russian army do?

A. : For the emancipation of its suffering families, its country, and the fulfillment of the sacred Christian law, it must, after sincerely and hope-
fully praying to the Lord, the Protector of Truth, and those who firmly
trust in Him, together take up arms against tyranny and restore faith
and liberty in Russia.

AND WHO SHALL DESIST, LIKE JUDAS THE TRAITOR, MAY HE BE CURSED. AMEN.

After the priest had finished the reading of the seditious Catechism, Muraviev-Apostol again asked the soldiers whether they
were willing to join him in pursuing the noble course they had
begun, and they consented. He ended with the words: "Fellows,
be loyal and serve only the Tsar in Heaven—Jesus Christ; and the
one who will betray or desert, he, anathema, will be cursed."[33] The
priest then performed the *Te Deum,* which was concluded with the
blessing of the troops and the hearty "Hurrah!" of the soldiers.
After this the spectacle ended, and the rebels left the city, heading
toward Brusilov.[34]

Daniel Keizer.—At this point may be noted the later fate of the
priest who read the "Orthodox Catechism." Daniel Keizer, the "in-
voluntary Decembrist," as one writer has named him, at first was
asked to follow the rebels, but he refused. After the rebellion was
crushed, Nicholas did everything possible to prosecute him.[35] On
March 22, 1826, Keizer was unfrocked by the Synod, handed over
to the civil authorities, and the government placed its heavy hand
upon him. He was court-martialled, disenfranchised, disinherited,
and sentenced to hard labor. After many years of suffering, the
loss of his wife and children, and his health, he was granted an
amnesty on July 21, 1858, but neither his title (he had been a
noble) nor his property was restored to him, except an annual
pension of 57 rubles and 14–2/7 kopecks![36]

Arrival of Ippolit Muraviev-Apostol.—Before the rebels de-
departed from Vasilkov, Ippolit Muraviev-Apostol arrived from
the capital. He was only nineteen, recently graduated with distinction from military school, appointed member of the general staff
of the Second Army, and had before him the expectation of a
brilliant career.[37] As previously stated, he had left St. Petersburg

---

[33] *Materialy,* VI, 296.

[34] *Ibid.,* VI, 28–30, 61.

[35] *Ibid.,* VI, 181.

[36] Shchegolev, *op. cit.,* 361–363.

[37] Muraviev-Apostol, M. I., *Vospominaniia i pisma,* 54.

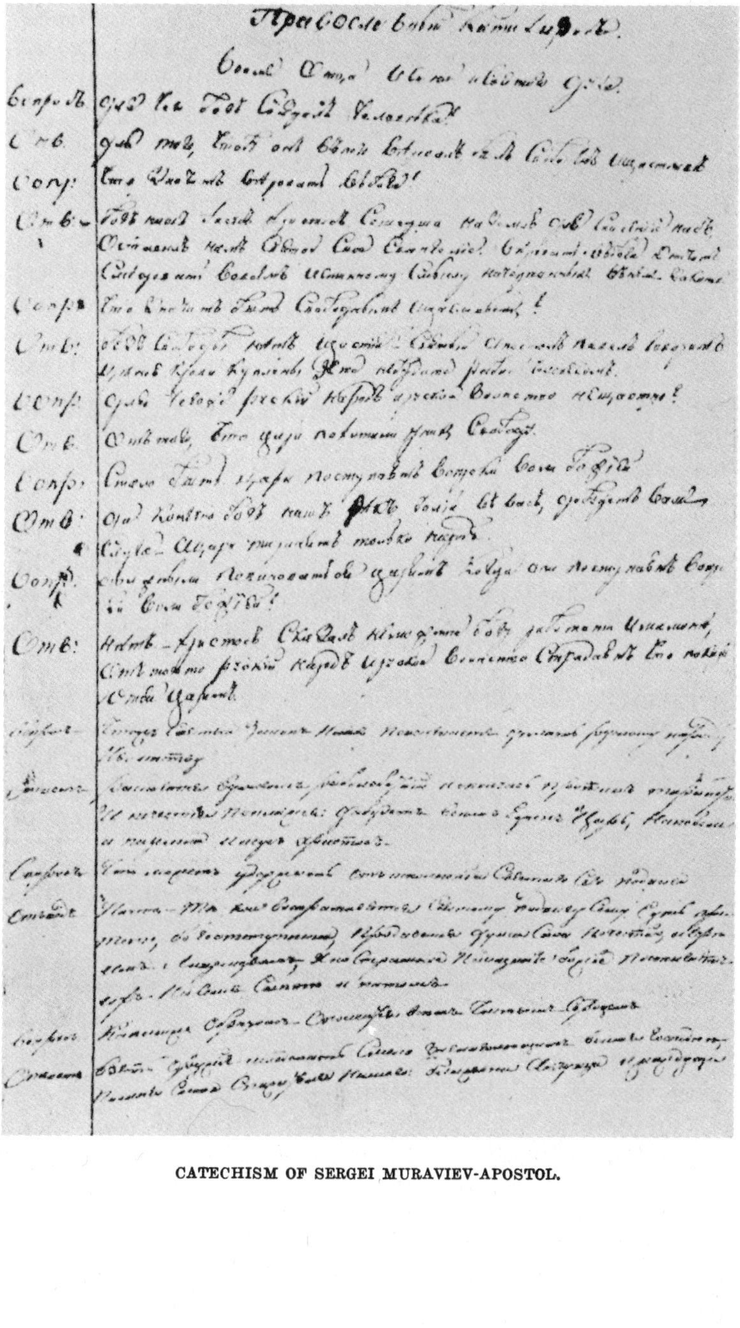

CATECHISM OF SERGEI MURAVIEV-APOSTOL.

on December 13, with a message from Trubetskoi to Tulchin, but to his great surprise he met his brother in Vasilkov. The message from Trubetskoi was to inform the Southern Society that the North planned to revolt and that it hoped to be assisted by the members at Tulchin. While on his way Ippolit Muraviev-Apostol learned of the disastrous end of the uprising in the capital. His friend, Svistunov, with whom he had started for the South, had been detained in Moscow, and fearing that the message, the exact contents of which he did not know, would be intercepted, Ippolit had destroyed it. Nevertheless, the news did not dishearten him, and he proceeded south with the conviction that the whole attempt might yet succeed. Still retaining his faith in the revolutionary cause, he insisted that the Society should continue the task which it had undertaken, for there was but one choice: to win or to die honorably on the battlefield. When implored by his brother, Sergei, to leave the rebels, Ippolit did not wish even to listen to him and declared that he would follow Sergei wherever he went. His courage renewed the hope and inspiration of the rebels and the troops started out.

Motovilovka.—The couriers whom Muraviev-Apostol had sent to Kiev did not return. One of them, Alexander Mozalevsky, was arrested by the authorities, but he succeeded in swallowing the letter with which he had been entrusted. The communication to Major Krupnikov (or Krupennikov) was not delivered because the messenger was unable to find such a person. The fate of the third courier is obscure.[38] In such circumstances the United Slavs as well as Muraviev-Apostol began to doubt whether it was wise to move toward Kiev. Their attention was therefore directed to Brusilov, a strategic point from which an attack could be conducted in two directions, toward Zhitomir or toward Kiev. On the evening of December 31, the rebels reached Motovilovka, where they won over the First Musketeer Company that was stationed there but failed to persuade the Grenadiers. They now numbered a little over a thousand men. The next morning, New Year's Day, Muraviev-Apostol, fearing protests from the soldiers, decided to remain in Motovilovka so as to give them a rest. Unfortunately, this decision was a grave mistake, for while the rebels took a whole day in Motovilovka for rest, the enemy at the same time was preparing to meet the situation. Less reliable troops stationed near the scene of

---

[38] *Materialy,* IV, 248; VI, 18–19.

MOVEMENTS OF THE REBELLIOUS CHERNIGOVSKY REGIMENT.

From Kotova. Syilka, VIII, 1825. Copied by A. M. Regel.

activities were replaced by more dependable ones. The government
declared to its loyal troops that they were to trail soldier-bandits
who pillaged the population. The commander-in-chief ordered that
none of the rebels be spared; wherever possible they were to be
exterminated by canister shot. Officers captured were to be taken
in irons and sent for the time being to the Kiev fortress.[39]

In Motovilovka the rebels attracted the attention of the local
peasants, who belonged to the wealthy but penurious Countess
Branitzka. Evil rumors had been spread that Sergei Muraviev-
Apostol planned to rob the coffers of the Countess for the benefit
of his revolutionary activities, but such tales must be rejected as
deliberate calumny.[40] The soldiers were orderly and all the town's
inhabitants watched the scene without being in the slightest degree molested.[41]

As the peasants came out of the church, they paused to stare
curiously, little aware that the soldiers were risking their lives for
their welfare. Some were troubled about the outcome of the revolt;
others wished the rebels good luck in the struggle they were undertaking. These moments Muraviev-Apostol later considered the
happiest in his life and well worth the sacrifice.[42]

Early on the morning of January 2, 1826, having received no
news from Kiev, the rebels left Motovilovka with the intention of
capturing Belaia Tserkov. Once this town was occupied and se-
cured in the rear, they thought that Kiev would easily fall into
their hands. At Belaia Tserkov Muraviev-Apostol hoped to win
over the Seventeenth Jegersky regiment, in which the Society had
several members, among them Vadkovsky, with whose assistance a
drive against Kiev would be feasible.[43] Greatly to his disappointment, Muraviev-Apostol learned in the night, when camped at
Pologi, a neighboring town, that the Jegersky regiment had been
transferred, no one knew where.[44] Apprehensive of entering Belaia

---

[39] *Ibid.*, VI, 16–18, 34, 35, 36, 71–72.

[40] *Russky Arkhiv* (1871), 1724; VI (1902), 276; *Istorichesky Viestnik*,
LXXIX (1900), 197–198; *Arkhiv kn. Vorontsova*, XVII, 574–575; *Ostafievsky
Arkhiv*, V, Second Issue, 159.

[41] The various rumors spread during this period may be found in a secret
report to the government, not published until 1871. See *Russky Arkhiv* (1871),
279.

[42] Interesting material relating to the time spent by the rebels in Motovilovka may be found in the *Memoirs* of the Polish landlord, Joseph Kazimierz
Rulikowski. See *Dekabristi na Ukraini*, 51ff.

[43] *Krasnyi Arkhiv*, XIII, 15, 20–21.   [44] *Materialy*, VI, 12.

Tserkov and finding himself surrounded by the enemy, he recon-
sidered his original plan. Instead of proceeding to Belaia Tserkov
and then to Kiev, he turned toward Pavoloch, through Kovalevka
and Trilesy, hoping from there to reach Zhitomir, where he could
join the United Slavs and perhaps the Polish Secret Society. (See
map, p. 192.) Pavoloch also attracted the rebels because stationed
there was the Fifth Artillery Company, whose assistance would
greatly facilitate the drive on Kiev. But all these ambitions remained unfulfilled. In abandoning the attack on Kiev, the rebels
assured their own defeat, as subsequent developments show.

Pologi.—At Pologi in the night several officers deserted their
soldiers, and, though all the privates remained loyal to the cause,
the morale was little by little undermined.[45] Rumors began to spread
that they were fighting a lost cause and that it would be ridiculous,
with their small number, unaided by artillery or cavalry, to challenge the much superior forces of the government. Time and again
Sergei Muraviev-Apostol had emphasized the fact that he forced
no one and that a handful of unworthy rascals must not cause the
ideals for which they were fighting to be abandoned. The soldiers
seemingly agreed with the argument, but underneath was a streak
of that doubt which always precedes failure.[46]

Trilesy.—On January 3 at sunrise the rebels left Pologi. In the
afternoon of the same day they met a detachment of government
hussars and artillery which had been sent to reconnoiter.[47] From
a soldier's point of view the place of meeting was most unfavorable
to the rebels: it was a bare space with no means of entrenchment
and no natural facilities for self-defense. Furthermore, all that
Muraviev-Apostol could count upon was about a thousand infan-
trymen, and the enemy was in possession of cavalry and artillery.
The result of the encounter can easily be imagined. For a moment
the rebels were encouraged, believing that it was the artillery unit
commanded by Captain Matvei Pykhachev, a member of the Southern Society. They were ignorant of the fact that only the night
before Pykhachev had been arrested and that the detachment sent
against them was being led by General Geismar.[48]

Scarcely had the rebels appeared on the horizon when they were

[45] *Vospominaniia i Rasskazy,* I, 198.

[46] Gorbachevsky, *op. cit.,* 169–170, 172-173.   [47] *Materialy,* VI, 38–39.

[48] *Krasnyi Arkhiv,* XIII, 22; Muraviev-Apostol, M. I., *op. cit.,* 54; *Materialy,*
VI, 144.

met by canister shot, the first of which killed several men in front. Muraviev-Apostol was attempting to bring his forces together to resist the enemy when a second shot wounded him in the head, at the same time killing his gallant assistant, Shchepillo, one of the Slavs who had released the leader in Trilesy and who had not left him since that time.[49] Deprived of their commander, the soldiers did not know what to do. The courage of many officers in this unequal combat was truly remarkable, but they were helpless against the destructive canister shot of the enemy.[50] If in St. Petersburg the battle was lost because the revolutionaries lacked initiative in seizing the enemy's cannon by a bold attack at the very beginning, here such tactics was unthinkable; in the open fields for infantry to move against cannon fire would have been sheer madness.[51]

Defeat.—Bleeding terribly but disregarding the excruciating pain, Muraviev-Apostol still made an effort to lead his troops. He began with difficulty to climb his horse, but at that moment a dashing assault of the enemy's cavalry inflicted the last blow, dispersing the rebels hither and thither. Ippolit Muraviev-Apostol, himself wounded in the arm, saw his brother lying in a pool of blood and thought him killed. There being no hope whatever of success, with the cavalry upon them, Ippolit, preferring death to disgrace, shot himself in the head. Embittered against the officers and in the rage of despair, the soldiers attacked Muraviev-Apostol and would have killed him had not Baron Soloviev saved him from the mob.[52] The cavalry began to gather the scattered rebels and to deliver them, under strong guard, to Trilesy.[53] Muraviev-Apostol, having been brought inside, finally collapsed from loss of blood. His close assistant, Kuzmin, who had succeeded in hiding a pistol in his sleeve, shot himself in the presence of them all at the first opportunity.[54] Very few succeeded in escaping from the scene; most of the rebels were arrested, put in irons, and taken to Mogilev.[55] Afterwards the leaders were sent to St. Petersburg, where they joined all the members implicated in the northern revolt.

---

[49] *Krasnyi Arkhiv*, XIII, 13–14.

[50] *Materialy*, VI, 69–70.

[51] *Ibid.*, VI, 58–59, 63.

[52] Gorbachevsky, *op. cit.*, 176–177.

[53] A list of those implicated in the uprising may be found in *Materialy*, VI, 80ff.

[54] *Krasnyi Arkhiv*, XIII, 21.

[55] *Russkaia Starina*, VI (1899), 586; *Katorga i Ssylka*, VI (1926), 115–116.

The uprising, which had had an opportunity to become a wide revolutionary movement, was destroyed in embryo. The avenging hand of the government spared no one. Every person under the least suspicion of being even remotely related to the movement was brought to the capital, where investigations were conducted on a large scale. The savageness with which the authorities eradicated the movement, indicting many of the oldest Russian nobles, for example, the Muravievs (eight members of that family were involved), gave rise to the popular belief that it was the deliberate policy of the Germans, like Generals Geismar, Saken, Rot, or Benckendorff, to eliminate from the state their rivals, the purely Slav nobility.[56] Whatever the cause of the relentless suppression, for their ambition and their venture to win a better social order, all the Decembrists, northern and southern, paid a heavy penalty.[57] In the meantime the authorities celebrated their victory over the revolt, while General Geismar and Commander Rot quarreled over who should receive the laurels for crushing the uprising.[58]

The government had the situation well in hand and felt certain that the revolution was ended, though for a long time it feared other outbursts. Sparks of the abortive revolt still appeared here and there, but quick measures prevented them from turning into a social conflagration. Of these, one incident may be mentioned, which occurred at the fortress of Bobruisk. Here two daring young officers, members of the United Slavs, attempted early in February, 1826, to start a rebellion. One of them, Trusov, during a parade came out in front shouting for the soldiers to rise against the tyrant, Nicholas I, and win freedom from Russia. According to the official report of the occurrence, the offender used such language in the presence of the entire battalion that it could not be repeated to the Sovereign. The two officers implicated in the affair were both seized and speedily tried. Trusov was sentenced to hard labor for life; the other, Emelian Trotsky, was given one year in prison. The Commandant of Bobruisk, General Berg, received a reprimand and a warning that he had better take care "to eliminate disorders in the future."[59]

---

[56] *Russkaia Starina*, XII (1895), 161.

[57] *P.S.Z.*, No. 514, Series 2.

[58] *Materialy*, VI, 73–74; *Russky Arkhiv*, VI (1902), 278–279.

[59] Nechkina, *Obshchestvo Soedinënnykh Slavian*, 186–187; Gorbachevsky, *op. cit.*, 200–201; *Dekabristi na Ukraini*, 172.

SERGEI MURAVIEV-APOSTOL.

Causes of the defeat.—A word should be said concerning the failure of the revolt in the South. No one could accuse Sergei Muraviev-Apostol of lack of courage, an accusation that was made against the northern "dictator." He led the rebels to the scene of battle and stood with them to the last, facing the enemy without fear.[60] Brought down with a serious wound, he still attempted to command the troops, but was crushed by a much superior force, captured, taken to St. Petersburg, and hanged a few months later. Such gallantry and martyrdom make it difficult to speak disparagingly of Muraviev-Apostol. Yet it is necessary to indicate certain errors which seem to have caused the failure of his adventure.

One of the greatest mistakes of Muraviev-Apostol was his slowness in strategy, dangerous at any time but fatal in civil war. It is clear that he should have acted as speedily as possible, always seizing the government forces unaware. True, he had a small number of men with which to operate, but swift action would have won him other regiments. A quick attack on Kiev, then on Zhitomir, when neither city was prepared to resist, would have changed the situation in his favor; and who knows what it might have meant to Russia?[61] Had the rebels seized Kiev, they would have had an opportunity to capture the arsenal and might very probably have been joined by the artillery, among whom the members of the United Slavs had been working incessantly and not without success.[62] The rebels would have found similar support in Zhitomir, where the Slavs had their stronghold, and from there communication with the Poles might have been established. The rebels might have attracted many to them. Even in the detachment of General Geismar the artillerymen hesitated to fire on the rebels. Only after the General had warned the soldier at the gun that if he did not shoot he would lose his head, did he open fire on his brethren.[63]

Instead of a strategy of swift action, Muraviev-Apostol went about cautiously, trying to secure a base, advocating ideas of liberty, composing semireligious, semipolitical leaflets, and arranging a theatrical performance led by a priest, which had no effect whatever upon the soldiers. His semireligious concept of revolution can of course be understood only by appreciating the spirit of the

[60] *Krasnyi Arkhiv*, XIII, 18.

[61] Gorbachevsky, *op. cit.*, 189–190.

[62] *Krasnyi Arkhiv*, XIII, 43–44; *Materialy*, VI, 35; *Vospominaniia i rasskazy*, I, 193.

[63] *Russkaia Starina*, XXXII (1881), 732–733.

time and the general attitude of the younger generation. Muraviev-Apostol saw religious faith and civil liberty as one and inseparable, never as in conflict. In his view, faith was not interpreted in a strictly orthodox sense, but, as professed by most young men at the turn of the century, it was a deistic, rational conception of religion, a pure Christian ideal free of spurious theological speculation. Could such a religion oppose political freedom? Did not the Spanish clergy assist the rebels in freeing their country from the aggression of Napoleon?[64]

Muraviev-Apostol was convinced that the church, by virtue of its very nature, would have to take the side of the common people and he therefore saw in that institution an active ally rather than an enemy or even an indifferent observer. He believed that the common man was subconsciously inclined toward religion and that one had only to awaken that dormant sentiment to induce him to fight for it. It was for this and for no other reason that he maintained during debates, long preceding the uprising, that the army would defend liberty only when awakened by religious motives fused with political aims, rather than by purely materialistic ideals; it was only by reading the Bible and its simple interpretation that the people would inevitably be roused to political opposition.[65] Alas, experience proved the unsoundness of this theory: the whole ceremony performed by Muraviev-Apostol and the priest, Daniel Keizer, completely passed over the heads of the soldiers and the inhabitants of Vasilkov, to whom the document was nothing but "some kind of Catechism." Immediately after the "Catechism" was read and the *Te Deum* performed, one of the soldiers turned to an officer standing near by and politely asked whether the officer could tell him to what Tsar the oath of allegiance had just been given![66] Later Muraviev-Apostol admitted that he had realized, soon after the reading, that the soldiers had not understood what it was all about and therefore he had been forced to resort to a different policy, namely to insist that they remain loyal to the oath taken to Constantine.

Muraviev-Apostol is accused, and with reason, of insisting too often that the soldiers had a free choice to stay with him or to

---

[64] A penetrating analysis of the Catechism and the influence of the Spanish revolution upon its author may be found in Shchegolev, *Dekabristy*. See particularly pp. 242–246. Cf. *Materialy*, VI, li-lii.

[65] Gorbachevsky, *op. cit.*, 83–84.

[66] *Materialy*, VI, 295.

depart. Naturally, espionage gained advantage by such liberty; those who opposed the movement went over to the other side and informed officials of the situation, and those unable to understand what was going on remained indifferent.[67] Slow movement and long encampments, like the day spent in Motovilovka, only aided the enemy. In justice to Muraviev-Apostol it must be mentioned that the weather during some of his marches was most unfavorable and probably was, in part, the cause of the slow movement.[68] His march to Kovalevka on December 29, for example, was made through a terrible blizzard. A much worse blunder which Muraviev-Apostol committed was his choice of following the highway rather than side roads, like that from Kovalevka to Trilesy (see map, p. 192) or roads passing through many settlements, where fighting would have been difficult for the enemy and would have facilitated self-defense. Instead, he took the main road through the open steppes, making his troops vulnerable to any force that possessed artillery or cavalry.

Another mistake was the poor organization of communication with the United Slavs and the Polish Secret Society, a condition inevitable, perhaps, because of the sudden development of events. The lack of adequate intercourse with the Slavs, who longed for action and preferred "to die fighting rather than to rot in chains for the rest of their lives," and their consequent isolation from events, prevented the aid that they would have given.[69]

In criticizing Muraviev-Apostol the historian must not be too severe. The possibilities which lay before the southern leader may, in retrospect, differ radically from conditions as they could be seen at the time. It is not always easy to estimate a complex situation in the midst of its development, save perhaps for a military genius, which Muraviev-Apostol was not. The uprising was sadly premature and everything concerning it had to be decided under desperate pressure.[70]

The daring adventure of the Decembrists in the North as well as in the South can be truly considered the prelude to the long struggle between Autocracy and Democracy in Russia. The democratic ideas of those who opened the struggle may seem but feeble to later generations, the contribution of the Decembrists but small; but the shot was fired, Old Russia was challenged, and faith in

---

[67] *Dekabristi na Ukraini*, 67–68.
[68] *Ibid.*, 60.

[69] *Krasnyi Arkhiv*, XIII, 59.
[70] *Materialy*, IV, 358.

future success deepened as time went on. As for Muraviev-Apostol, his genuine heroism and later his magnanimous assumption of the entire blame for the uprising place him among the foremost of the early nineteenth-century political martyrs.[71]

[71] *Ibid.*, IV, 244, 288. In this respect, how differently Muraviev-Apostol acted from Trubetskoi, who immediately presented a list of all the names of the Society, Northern as well as Southern.

Chapter IX

THE TRIAL

Lasciate ogni speranza voi ch'entrate!—DANTE.

ON JANUARY 10, 1826, Prince Metternich wrote to Count Lebzeltern, Austrian Ambassador to St. Petersburg :[1] "The revolt of December 14 (26) had the advantage of allowing the character of the young monarch to be seen by the public, and of showing him that Russia is, unhappily, as easy to agitate as all other countries in our time. I hope a thorough inquiry will be made as to those who seduced the soldiery, for they were certainly in this case only tools in wicked hands." Prince Metternich need not have been concerned about the young Russian Emperor, for Nicholas I at once showed the skill of a prosecutor and displayed even greater zeal in maintaining "order" in Europe than did the famous Austrian statesman.

Investigations.—Immediately after the revolt was suppressed a committee headed by Nicholas himself, with headquarters at the Winter Palace, began to conduct a thorough investigation, determined "to get to the very bottom, whatever it might be !" Questioning of all detained rebels continued throughout the night. As arrests increased, material constantly accumulated which led to more arrests; there were not enough cells, and adjacent barracks had to be turned into prisons.[2] The cells were mostly dark and extremely damp because of the heaviest flood, in 1824, that St. Petersburg had ever experienced.[3] Yet the hand of justice continued to reach out for all those who were still hidden whether at home or elsewhere, and the numbers of the prisoners continued to increase. In this respect General Benckendorff distinguished himself as a servant worthy of his master; he thoroughly searched the capital and sent detachments outside the city to prevent escapes. On December 17 Nicholas could write to Constantine : "Our arrests pass successfully and in our hands are all the main heroes of the day except one." Troops were kept in full readiness, and the palace

---

[1] *Memoirs of Prince Metternich*, IV, 315.
[2] Muraviev, A. M., *Zapiski*, 19–20.
[3] Zavalishin, *Zapiski dekabrista*, I, 364.

was especially guarded lest new outbreaks should occur.[4] The apprehensions of the government were groundless, however : the rebellion had been thoroughly crushed and the leaders one by one were seized and delivered to headquarters. Among them was Ryleev, who, only the night before, having predicted the end, had left his wife and daughter ; Prince Trubetskoi, who was just ready to go to bed, was brought from the Austrian Embassy ; soon Yakubovich, Prince Obolensky, and all the others who were chiefly responsible for the short-lived uprising were delivered up. A few weeks later there began to arrive all those arrested in the South, and the stage was set for the first great political trial in Russia.

Nicholas as prosecutor.—Nearly every person arrested was presented to the new Emperor, who, after a few questions, attached an order indicating to the Commandant of the Fortress, Alexander Sukin, the treatment each prisoner was to receive : whether he was to be kept in chains, placed under special surveillance, or allowed more liberty. These orders, one hundred and fifty of them, often written on small pieces of paper, are preserved and they constitute a remarkable record.[5] They show the keen interest that Nicholas took in the whole affair and his determined effort to obtain at any price maximum evidence from every person detained ; they display the bestial vengeance of this gifted gendarme in the purple robe. "Ryleev," reads the note accompanying him, "to be placed in the Peter and Paul fortress, but his hands not tied ; no communication with others, give him writing paper and whatever he writes daily deliver to me personally." "Upon receiving Bestuzhev, as well as Obolensky and Shchepin," reads another, "order them to be manacled." A third reads : "Yakushkin to be treated severely and not otherwise than a villain."

Treatment of the prisoners changed as they became more willing to confess. Those who showed any stubbornness were not only rigorously handled but often deprived of food, left on bread and water, as was the Decembrist, Semënov. The harsh prison régime, the scanty diet, the heavy chains, and the damp cell often achieved the purpose sought and even more : few of the members could endure the dreadful trials and many began to break down, to confess, and to involve others. Even today some of the confessions represent heartbreaking documents, manifestly written by men on

---

[4] *Russkaia Starina*, LXXXIX (1897), 468.
[5] Shchegolev, *Dekabristy*, 267.

the verge of total mental or physical collapse. Only characters like
Yakushkin's were able to stand firm and resist the strain, but men
like him were few.

Physical discomfort as a means of extracting evidence did not
suffice for Nicholas; he was an artist who assumed a pose befitting
the character of each defendant. His talent enabled him to deceive
even La Ferronnays, the French Ambassador, before whom he shed
tears, pretending to be an innocent and inexperienced Sovereign
forced by conditions to occupy a throne to which he had never
aspired, and one whom evil plotters wished to betray. However,
he assured the Ambassador that, notwithstanding his lack of experience in political affairs, he had the most honest intention to
rule justly and was determined upon the extermination of all sedition in the country. So well did he dramatize the scene that La
Ferronnays hastened to inform his government that Russia had an
enlightened Peter the Great on its throne.[6]

If Nicholas could deceive such a skilled diplomat as La Ferronnays, there is little wonder at his still greater success with the
Decembrists, who took his pretended sympathy at its face value.
Before all the defendants Nicholas put on a show rarely equaled
by any prosecuting attorney. Writes Shchegolev:[7]

From all corners of Russia, one after another, there were brought to Petersburg, to the Winter Palace, those implicated in the affair. Tensely, the Tsar
waited in his cabinet, selecting masks, every time a new one for a new person.
For one he was a severe monarch offended by a loyal subject; for another—a
citizen of the Fatherland equal to the one who was arrested and stood before
him; for a third—an old soldier, who had suffered for the honor of the uniform; for a fourth—a monarch ready to proclaim constitutional covenants;
for a fifth—the Russian lamenting over the evils of the Fatherland and
passionately striving for their correction. But in reality he was not the first,
nor the second, nor the third: he simply feared for his existence and inde-
fatigably sought all threads of the plot with the purpose of unraveling these
threads and gaining his peace of mind.

Violently hating every member, no matter how remotely he had
been associated with the events, even years afterward Nicholas
could not speak of the Decembrists without evident irritation.
Orlov belonged to that type of men whose "stupid pride over-
shadows their minds," and who consider themselves born to reform
Russia; he was "impudent and a great talker." Obolensky had a
"black soul," which Nicholas long had sensed. "His face had a

---

[6] *Russky Viestnik*, IV (1893), 16.   [7] Shchegolev, *op. cit.*, 200–201.

bestial and mean expression and common scorn toward him was
strongly felt. . . . Nikita Muraviev was an example of an obdurate
villain. . . . Pestel was a villain in the full sense of the word, without
the least shade of remorse, with a beastly expression and the most
impertinent audacity in his denials; I think that there is rarely
to be found an equal monster. . . . Artamon Muraviev was nothing
else but a murderer, an outcast without any qualities. . . . Sergei
Volkonsky was a stuffed fool . . . liar and scoundrel in the full sense
. . . most repellent example of an ungrateful villain and most fool-
ish man. . . ."[8] Such are a few of the opinions Nicholas held concerning the Decembrists whose lives were at his mercy. But whatever his opinions, they had to be concealed for the time being, for
above all else he considered it necessary to win the confidence of
those arrested and to obtain all possible evidence. Hence all the
dramatization, the appearance before each man in a different mask.

Presented first of all to the Emperor, each member of the Decembrists faced a royal chameleon. Lorer, he threatened with
capital punishment; before Kakhovsky he posed as a believer in
reforms, as a "genuine Russian," considering himself a "first citizen of the Fatherland." Kakhovsky, who only shortly before had
intended to rid the country of the tyrant, was easily won by this.
"Sovereign," he wrote to Nicholas, "I can not, am unable and wish
not to flatter: but since last night I have become fond of you as a
man, and with my whole heart wish to love in you my Monarch and
the Sire of my Fatherland."[9] Before the Decembrist, Steingel,
Nicholas posed as the kindly monarch, compelled by his official
position to be severe; in a fatherly tone he reproached the offender
for concealing the existence of the secret society and hinted to him
in a rather crude manner that the Emperor would care for his large
family if Steingel would only reveal the testimony sought. Toward
Madame Ryleev, Nicholas showed special kindness, granting her
a generous pension, which immediately softened the heart of Ryleev and made him advise his wife to pray for the royal house and
not to complain against the Lord nor the Sovereign.[10] But that did
not prevent Nicholas from sending off Steingel, the father of a
large family, to Siberia, and Ryleev, the gracious husband and
tender father, to the gallows.

---

[8] *Mezhdutsarstvie*, 32, 33, 34.
[9] *Iz pisem i pokazanii dekabristov*, 19, 21.
[10] Ryleev, *Sochineniia*, 501, 518.

Before Yakushkin Nicholas posed as the merciless ruler who would not stop before any measure which the interest of the state would demand; he would crush all enemies regardless of who they were, though he seemed somewhat perturbed about what would happen to them in the other world. But with Yakushkin his artifice utterly failed, for here Nicholas struck flint. The brief examination of Yakushkin deserves quotation.[11]

Nicholas: You have violated your oath?

Yakushkin: I am guilty, Sovereign.

Nicholas: What is waiting for you in the other world? Damnation. The opinion of the people you can scorn, but what is confronting you in the other world should terrify you. However, I do not wish to ruin you completely; I will send you a priest. Why, then, do you answer me nothing?

Yakushkin: What do you wish of me, Sovereign?

Nicholas: I think I speak to you plainly enough; if you do not wish to ruin your family and to be treated as a swine you must confess everything.

Yakushkin: I gave my word of honor to name no one. Still, whatever I knew about myself, I have said to His Excellency. [Pointing to General Levashev, who sat at a distance in a dignified pose.]

Nicholas: What has "His Excellency" and your contemptible "word of honor" to do with it?!

Yakushkin: Sovereign, I can name no one.

Nicholas: [Leaping three steps back and pointing his hand toward Yakushkin.] Put him in chains so that he cannot move.

But even in chains in which "he could not move" Yakushkin revealed little that was new to the authorities.[12]

But what delight Nicholas must have had at the interview with Trubetskoi, who on his knees, kissing the Sovereign's hands, begged that his life be spared.[13] From "dictatorship" to such humility a more tragic personal degradation can scarcely be imagined! Here Nicholas triumphed completely.

The investigation committee.—One of the first measures taken by Nicholas was the creation of a special committee for the investigation of all secret societies. With the assistance of General A. Tatishchev, Minister of War, and his associate, A. Borovkov, a plan was worked out which on December 17 received the royal

---

[11] Yakushkin, I., *Zapiski*, 77–78. The only other member who remained firm was I. I. Pushchin. See Pushchin, I., *Zapiski o Pushkine* (M., 1934), 163–164.

[12] *Materially*, III, 60. [13] *Mezhdutsarstvie*, 62.

approval. It designated the purpose, function, and method of the
Committee in conducting the investigation. Appointed by Nicholas
I, the members of the Committee were State-Secretary D. Bludov,
Prince A. Golitsyn, Minister of Education, P. Golenishchev-Kutu-
zov,[14] Grand Duke Mikhail Pavlovich, the recently appointed Gov-
ernor-General of St. Petersburg, A. Benckendorff, Generals V.
Levashev, A. Potapov, and A. Chernyshev. Grand Duke Nikolai
Mikhailovich, in a much later description, characterized these so-
called judges as follows :[15]

> The chairman of the Committee for Investigations was Minister of War
> Tatishchev, an entirely obscure figure, of the members of the Committee
> Chernyshev, Levashev, Golenishchev-Kutuzov and Potapov were known for
> their heartlessness and servility; Prince A. Golitsyn—for his hypocrisy, D. N.
> Bludov—for his liberalism in theory and cowardliness in reality; only one,
> Benckendorff, was considered more independent and constantly tried to miti-
> gate the Emperor.

This Committee, or "Inquisitorial Tribunal," supposed to be secret,
was instructed to begin an immediate and most exhaustive investigation of all conspiratory societies in Russia, their purposes, and
means of eradicating them. Information which the Committee
gathered was to be presented with recommendations to the Emperor. The Committee was warned that its judgment must be based
on the principle long held by the royal house, namely, "Better to
free ten guilty than to punish one innocent." Unfortunately, this
principle was forgotten from the first day the Committee began to
function, for vengeance and fear dominated sane judgment.[16]

Every person implicated in the movement was asked countless
questions and usually examined at nighttime. The Committee did
not hesitate to use any means of extracting the desired information,
even exploiting the clergy. It sent for priests, nominally for "spiritual consolation," actually to obtain confessions.[17] Kept in dreadful conditions, in heavy chains, often under the threat of physical
and—still worse—moral torture, many Decembrists collapsed.[18]
The situation is vividly described by Fonvizin, as follows.[19]

---

[14] This is the same Golenishchev-Kutuzov who participated in the assassination of Paul I. See *Obshchestvennye Dvizheniia v Rossii*, I, 448.

[15] *Istorichesky Viestnik*, VII (1916), 108. Cf. Zavalishin, *op cit.*, I, 363.

[16] Yakushkin, I., *op. cit.*, 75–78.

[17] Muraviev, A. M., *op. cit.*, 20–21; Zavalishin, *op. cit.*, I, 363.

[18] *Materialy*, III, 60; Luppol, I. K., *Istoriko-filosofskie etiudy* (M., 1935),
253.

[19] *Obshchestvennye Dvizheniia v Rossii*, I, 197–198.

Against the prisoners were used means which struck their imagination and destroyed their spirit, irritating them either by deceitful hopes or by fear of torture, with only one purpose—of extorting confessions. At night the door of a cell would suddenly be opened; over the prisoner's head a blanket would be thrown; then he would be conducted through the corridors and passages of the fortress to a brightly lighted courtroom. Here, after the blanket was removed, members of the Committee would suddenly give the prisoner questions and, without allowing him any time to think, would rudely demand instant and affirmative replies. In the name of the Tsar they promised the defendant pardon in case of straightforward confession, accepted no justification, invented nonexisting testimonies by other defendants and often refused even to call them to testify to it. The one who did not give the desired replies, because of ignorance of the events concerning which he was asked, or because he hesitated to ruin by some careless word an innocent person, was transferred to a dark and damp cell, given only bread and water, and burdened with heavy arm and leg fetters. The fortress doctor was ordered to see whether the prisoner could endure the most severe physical pain.

Little wonder that many prisoners, whose nerves were unable to endure such a test, broke down and began to reveal everything they knew, sometimes adding fantastic exaggerations, implicating their friends and often people who were only remotely connected with the Decembrist movement. Such was the case of Peter Falenberg, who, in mental torment, gave distorted facts and most innocently went to Siberia, or of Alexander Bulatov, who ended his life in prison, or of Kakhovsky, who frequently begged the Committee, "For God's sake, do whatever you wish with me, but do not ask me about anything."[20]

The Committee made no endeavor to analyze the underlying social forces of the movement nor the psychological aspect of the testimonies. It took bare facts, or, as Obolensky says, it accepted "for truth that which was said or done in moments when imagination was guided by feverish outbursts," and used this evidence against the Decembrists. It overemphasized the terroristic plans of the Society and disregarded constructive projects which the members had suggested. Since this sort of testimony served as a basis for the prosecution of the Decembrists, it is surprising indeed that only five members were forced to mount the scaffold.

Final report of the committee.—For several months the Committee was occupied with investigations before it could present the final report to the Emperor. Constant fear that some detail might be omitted was the reason for the long period that elapsed. Also,

---

[20] See *Materialy*, I, 348, 356; *Vospominaniia i rasskazy*, I, 223; *Memuary dekabristov*, pp. iiiff.; Shilder, *Imp. Nikolai I*, I, 517, footnote 345.

several delicate matters were involved requiring considerable time
for investigation : there was strong suspicion that certain foreign
diplomats were implicated with the Decembrists. For example,
there was Count Lebzeltern, under whose roof Prince Trubetskoi
had sought protection, and Lord Canning, who was sympathetic
with the Polish movement for independence.[21] Several important
statesmen and military men in the country, including Speransky,
Admiral Mordvinov, Generals Kiselev and Ermolov in the South,
and outstanding literary figures like Pushkin and Griboedov, were
mentioned as being implicated in the conspiracy. But the Committee lacked conclusive evidence, though the shadow of suspicion
hovered over these men for some time, and over Pushkin till his
death.[22] So panic-stricken were many that even Nicholas thought
he had good reasons for believing that the whole conspiracy could
be traced to the State Council, though he did not wish to commence
the prosecution until he was in possession of more convincing evidence.[23] After long and tedious investigation and still in fear that
roots of the conspiracy yet remained to be found, the Committee
finally presented on May 30, 1826, a detailed report, followed by
a list of alleged leaders of the rebellion.[24]

Special Supreme Court.—On June 1, 1826, Nicholas I appointed
a Special Supreme Court consisting of representatives of the State
Council, the Senate, the Ministry, and the Synod, with the addition of a number of military and civil service men.[25] Prince Peter
Lopukhin, a man totally deaf, was appointed Chief Justice, and
Prince Dimitry Lobanov-Rostovsky, Minister of Justice, of whose
mental capacities even Nicholas had great doubts, was made Attorney-General.[26] The Supreme Court opened its session on June 3,
and adjourned June 11, 1826. From the beginning it was clear that
the Court would merely confirm the recommendations submitted
by the Committee of Investigation. The prisoners were never called

---

[21] Lord Canning's journey through Poland and his visit to Warsaw in 1825
aroused suspicion in St. Petersburg. See Lane-Poole, S., *The Life of Stratford
Canning*, I, 355ff. Also *Pechat' i Revoliutsiia*, VIII (1925), 31; *Bunt Dekabristov*, 284; *Russkaia Starina*, IX (1907), 529; *Materialy*, IV, 272, 289–290,
457; *Russky Viestnik*, IV (1893), 21.

[22] See Lemke, M., *Nikolaevskie zhandarmy i literatura 1825–1855* (St. P.,
1908), 465; Shchegolev, *Istoricheskie etiudy*, 302–303, 315.

[23] *Mezhdutsarstvie*, 168.

[24] *Gosudarstvennye prestupleniia*, I, 24.

[25] Shishkov, *Zapiski*, II, 281.

[26] *Mezhdutsarstvie*, 207. See also Vigel, *Zapiski*, V, 66.

before the Court but were visited in their cells by members of a
Special Committee who simply asked each man whether the testimony given to the Committee on Investigation was correct and
whether the signature under it was authentic. If the defendant refused to acknowledge his signature he was unceremoniously told
that it would not make much difference.[27] After the testimonies
were confirmed—although most of the defendants were unaware
for what purpose they had been questioned—the Special Committee presented the testimonies to the Court as final. This so-called
evidence was then handed over to another committee, which was
supposed to determine the degree of individual guilt. Strangely
enough, among the members of this committee was Speransky, who
only a decade or so before had himself suffered because of his political views.[28] His appointment was in accord with the deliberate
policy of his political enemies, including Nicholas, who wished to
test Speransky's loyalty to the Crown. "Among the individuals
against whom evidence was given," writes Nicholas, "though insufficient for commencing investigation, were such men as N. S.
Mordvinov, Senator Sumarokov, and even against M. M. Speransky. Such testimony gave rise to exceedingly painful doubts and
distrust, which for a long time could not be dispelled."[29]

The invitation to Speransky to participate in the prosecution of
the Decembrists was not only a test to the veteran statesman now
under the shadow of suspicion, but also a harsh political humiliation on the part of the young Sovereign over the former champion
constitutionalist, brought to the feet of His Majesty. It was placing
the thief to guard the property: Nicholas knew that any leniency
shown by Speransky would justify that suspicion, and to rid himself of it he would have to be harsh. Speransky was no less aware
of this. It was not an easy task to swallow such a bitter pill; his
daughter, in her recollections, tells how she often witnessed her
father in tears during those days, and showing signs of painful
inner struggle. It must have been distressing indeed to serve on a
committee to pass judgment upon the Decembrists, many of whom
had even been his friends and frequent visitors at his home. During
the reading of the sentence to the Decembrists, Basargin recollects,
Speransky sat at the table. "He was acquainted with my father and

[27] Zavalishin, *op. cit.*, I, 365.

[28] Korf, M. A., *Zhizn grafa Speranskogo*, II, 308–309.

[29] *Mezhdutsarstvie*, 30.

with our entire family," he writes. "I myself had been at his home a couple of times when I was in St. Petersburg. I thought that he glanced sadly at me, then lowered his head, and it seemed as if a tear dropped from his eye."[30]

But in spite of his sympathetic sentiment this was no longer the Speransky of a decade and a half ago: his political ordeals had changed him deeply. To avoid suspicion of complicity in the plot he went so far as to consent to the humiliating appointment and to approval of the sentence. How explain such extraordinary submission and criminal desertion of one's ideals? A recent writer seems to think the underlying motive was sheer physical fear, which was quite possible at that time, amidst the prevalent social hysteria and stifling "psychological atmosphere."[31] Yet, one can but wonder at this rarely curious incident in history: a man who conspirators had hoped would head their Provisional Government, their fellow Mason since 1810, was sitting on the bench to deliver royal justice and recommend severe penalties for those who had shortly before sought his political aid! This is the darkest page in the life of Speransky—a page which his biographer, Baron M. A. Korf, cautiously avoids mentioning. The only fact that slightly lightens his moral responsibility for the injustice dealt the Decembrists was that he did faintly endeavor to prove that there was no legal justification for applying capital punishment to the defendants.[32] But how pale this effort stands against the background of the savage verdict!

On July 9, 1826, the Court passed the sentence and forwarded it to the Emperor. Altogether there were brought to trial five hundred and seventy-nine persons, of whom two hundred and ninety were acquitted; of the remaining two hundred and eighty-nine men, one hundred and twenty-one were selected as the most responsible conspirators, one hundred and thirty-four were found guilty of minor offenses and, after military degradation, were scattered through various military units, or left under the surveillance of local police authorities; four were expelled from the country, twenty died before or during the trial; the fate of the other nine defendants is obscure. Of the hundred and twenty-one

[30] Basargin, *Zapiski*, 71.

[31] Aldanov, "Speransky i Dekabristy." *Sovremennye Zapiski*, XXVI (1925), 234, 235.

[32] *Russky Arkhiv*, 1871, 1220–1221.

leaders, sixty-one were members of the Northern Society, thirty-seven of the Southern, and twenty-three of the United Slavs. One of the members, Nicholas Turgenev, was at that time abroad; all diplomatic efforts to obtain his return, all personal letters of Nicholas to Metternich and to the "old King of Saxony," as well as arguments before the British Foreign Office, proved futile.[33]

The sentence in respect to the hundred and twenty-one leaders recommended that five, namely, Pestel, Sergei Muraviev-Apostol, Ryleev, Kakhovsky, and Bestuzhev-Riumin, be quartered. The other hundred and sixteen were to be divided into eleven degrees: first-degree convicts, thirty-one persons, were sentenced to death by decapitation; the remainder were to suffer exile to Siberia, some with hard labor, for various terms, according to the degree of their offense. This was the last word which the highest dignitaries of the Empire could present to Nicholas I, and even this Draconian sentence seemed too mild to some of them. Among the members of this Areopagus were men like Senator Lavrov, who demanded that not fewer than sixty-three of the hundred and twenty-one be quartered, three "to die shamefully and one honorably."[34] Only one person had the courage to vote against capital punishment, namely, Admiral Mordvinov, whose signature was not attached to the final sentence.[35]

The sentence passed by the Supreme Court was modified by Nicholas. The five leaders, "to be delivered from bloodshed," were to be hanged; thirty-one were exiled with hard labor to Siberia for life, and the remaining eighty-five for various terms. This altered verdict was in no sense an act of clemency: the fate of the Decembrists was sealed long before the Court even commenced its procedure, but it was in keeping with the characteristic posing of Nicholas to present to the world with due formality a political trial. In reality the court was a mere tool in the hands of the Emperor, as the verdict shows; in presenting to His Majesty the final sentence, it indicated that "to the kindness emanating from the autocratic power the law could place no limitations whatever." The defendants were assembled in the fortress to hear the final decision,

---

[33] *Na Chuzhoi Storone*, XIII (1925), 172–173; *Mezhdutsarstvie*, 169, 181; *Tainye obshchestva v Rossii* (M., 1926), 91.

[34] Shilder, *op. cit.*, I, 544.

[35] Ikonnikov, *Graf N. S. Mordvinov*, 382–383, 443–444. See also Shishkov, *op. cit.*, II, 281–284.

which was no small surprise to them, for they did not even know
that they had been put on trial, much less that the trial which had
been held without them was over.[36]

The sentences were not only harsh, but in most instances appall-
ingly unjust. In a country where the "death penalty *de jure* did
not exist," the verdict was bound to produce a shocking impression
upon many people, and the belief that the Emperor would com-
mute the sentence was prevalent to the last moment. "How horrible! And with what precipitance!" were the general comments
overheard by government agents.[37] In his *Memoirs* Herzen recollects, from his boyhood :[38]

Every one expected some mitigation of the sentence on the condemned men—
the coronation was about to take place. Even my father, in spite of his caution
and his skepticism, said that the death penalty would not be carried out, and
that all this was done merely to impress people. But, like every one else, he
knew little of the youthful monarch. . . . The citizens of Moscow could scarcely
believe their eyes when they read in the *Moscow News* of the terrible event of
the fourteenth of July.

The procedure itself stands as a crying example of the prejudiced
methods used by the government which sought the incrimination
of the defendants. If, on the one hand, many innocents found themselves among the guilty, on the other hand, a number of guilty
were acquitted. Men like Koloshin, who was among the authors of
the constitution of the early Society, and Glinka, at whose home
the Union of Welfare was founded and who was an active participant, escaped punishment. Others, only remotely related to the
organization, suffered imprisonment and exile ; for example, Basargin, who was among the least active and the most moderate, and
who seldom attended the meetings of the Society ; and Shchepin,
who was not even a member but happened on the eve of December
14 to be drawn into the fateful whirlpool of events. As his colleague states, "too much steam was driven into that machine," with
the result that many feared lest Shchepin should burst with
ecstasy on the Senate Square.[39] Alexander Bestuzhev, who led the
soldiers to the Square, though exiled to Siberia, was soon allowed
to join the Caucasian army as a private; but Batenkov, who was
not on the Square, spent twenty years of solitary confinement in

[36] *Obshchestvennye Dvizheniia v Rossii*, I, 456.

[37] *Dekabristy. Neizdannye materialy*, 38.

[38] Herzen, *My Past and Thoughts*, I, 62.

[39] *Vospominaniia Bestuzhevykh*, 140.

PETER FALENBERG.

the dreadful Peter and Paul fortress.[40] Lunin and Yakushkin had kept aloof from the Society since 1820, the former serving in Warsaw, the latter residing in his village, yet both men were sent to Siberia. Artamon Muraviev, who had deserted the Society on the eve of the uprising by refusing to incite the Akhtyrsky regiment to rebel, thereby inflicting a decisive blow on the uprising in the South, received life exile; but General Orlov, who was morally at least equally responsible for the conspiracy, was freed entirely.[41] Sergei Trubetskoi, as "dictator" and active leader to the very last moment, suffered exile; and Pestel, who was arrested on the eve of the uprising, who was unaware of developments in the North, and who had no direct relation whatever to the rebellion in the South, who had only theorized about the future revolution, was hanged.[42] Not a single conspirator of those who assassinated the father of Nicholas was brought to trial; but those who had only schemed to kill his deceased brother, "the angel Emperor," had to pay with their lives.

That the trial was indiscriminate, unjust, and revengeful is strikingly illustrated by the story of Falenberg. This story will be told in detail, for it demonstrates the callous fashion in which the whole affair was handled, how panic-stricken the officials were, and how hasty the judgment that was passed. Peter Falenberg was initiated into the Southern Society in 1822 or 1823. He represents those obscure laymen-members who displayed much idealism but little energy. Shortly after joining the Society he obtained a leave of absence, in the course of which he became engaged to Evdokiia Raevskaia, a relative of the eminent General Raevsky. As his engagement absorbed all his time, he participated little in the affairs of the Society and knew still less of its activities. In May, 1825, Falenberg returned with his recently wedded wife to Tulchin. They had scarcely settled down in that place when Madame

---

[40] See Modzalevsky, B. L., "Dekabrist Batenkov." *Russky Istorichesky Zhurnal*, V (1918). There exist various versions explaining the particularly cruel fate of Batenkov. Some believe that it was Batenkov's own wish to remain in solitude. Others place the entire blame upon Speransky, who, fearing that Batenkov might involve him as his former protégé, sought special isolation of the defendant. The exact reason is difficult to state, though the latter suggests plausible deduction. *Pisma G. S. Batenkova, I. I. Pushchina i E. G. Tollia* (M., 1936), 44–47.

[41] "One thing that puzzles me . . . is the conduct of Orlov, how he came out of the water dry and left without being brought to trial," wrote Constantine to Nicholas.—*Mezhdutsarstvie*, 196.

[42] Zavalishin, *op. cit.*, I, 356–357.

Falenberg fell ill, and her grief-stricken husband remained constantly at her bedside.

On January 15, 1826, Falenberg was arrested and sent to St. Petersburg. He was in despair lest his detention might prove fatal to his sick wife, so he told her that he had been ordered on an urgent mission to Bessarabia, that he would be absent not more than three weeks, and promised to write to her daily. Foreseeing possible complications, he wrote a number of letters and left them with her physician, who was to have them mailed to her from time to time. On January 24 Falenberg was brought before General Levashev for examination. Here he testified that he knew nothing of the Society nor of Bariatinsky, who had initiated him, and after signing his testimony he was returned to his cell. In prison he met another member, who told him that all those who testified only the truth were immediately released. Tormented by the thought of his sick wife, he decided, in order to gain his freedom, to reveal all he knew of the Society, and perhaps a little more; should he not do that, thought Falenberg, his position might still be endangered through the testimony of others.

With little further thought he sat down and wrote a letter begging the authorities for another hearing, which was accorded him on February 2. At this time he amended his previous statement, by admitting that he did belong to the Southern Society, that he had been initiated by Bariatinsky, and that the purpose of the organization was to obtain a constitution from the Emperor, all of which was true. "And what if the Emperor would not consent to grant it?" General Levashev cunningly asked. Suspecting nothing and without thinking, Falenberg replied that in that event it was considered necessary to stop at no measure even to the sacrificing of the Emperor—an extremity, true enough, to which the Society had been ready to go, but a part of its policy which had never been revealed to Falenberg. By this reply his fate was sealed: instead of the royal grace which he had expected for stating the truth, the prisoner was ordered again to his cell. His further revelation had only increased the suspicion of the authorities that he was concealing something.

To complicate matters still further, Falenberg, torn by his desire for reunion with his wife and his worry concerning her condition, wrote another letter, this time denying all his former testimony. Blinded by his passionate urge to win freedom, he thought that self-accusation would aid his cause. His wife's belief that he had deserted her, his inability to explain his position—he had been commanded to write only that he was alive and in good health, but that his whereabouts was a state secret—all this nearly drove the man insane. Add the responsibility for involving his colleague, Bariatinsky, who had never told him of any plans to assassinate the Emperor, and the condition of this unfortunate victim needs no description. On July 12 Falenberg received his sentence. He was deprived of all his titles and was to be exiled to Siberia for fifteen years at hard labor, to be followed by permanent residence in that part of the Empire. Nicholas, in revising the verdict of the Decembrists, left the sentence of Falenberg unaltered except for reducing the term of hard labor from fifteen to twelve years.[43] Falenberg's sentence is typical of the treatment which the Decembrists received from the government of Nicholas. But what justice could have been expected from a verdict motivated by sheer servility on the part of all the judicial sages and vengeance on the part of Nicholas. "We, his subjects, his brothers," writes Nicholas to Constantine, after having revealed that Yakushkin wished to assassinate Alexander in 1817, "must revenge Russia and our national pride. For such offenders there is no mercy!"[44]

Governments always have crushed and doubtless always will crush any force that tends to impair their existence. But rarely has there been a judicial case in which defendants suffered more savage and inequitable punishment than that of the Decembrists. A descendant of the Decembrist Volkonsky writes:[45]

... Here the difference is only in the degree of severity and in the scale of application. That difference is, so to speak, quantitative. But there is also a qualitative difference, revealing itself in how the law is applied. Here the observance of humanitarian demands is more or less of significance. After all, capital punishment will always remain capital punishment, and its harshness cannot be softened by anything, but its cruelty could always be increased. And in that is expressed the level of humaneness of that government which applies it: all that derision and humiliation which accompanies the sentenced victim to that terrible threshold, beyond which begins the equality of all men. For a long time it seemed to us, the cruelty of the punishment of the Decembrists could not be exceeded. ...

[43] The story of Falenberg is related in his brief but graphic *Memoirs*. See *Vospominaniia i rasskazy*, I, 205ff.; also *Dekabristy. Sbornik materialov*, 39–40.

[44] *Mezhdutsarstvie*, 181.

[45] Volkonsky, *O dekabristakh po semeinym vospominaniiam*, 47.

Execution of sentences.—On July 13, 1826, at three o'clock in the morning, the sentence was administered. All the prisoners were called for the ceremony of military degradation: insignias were stripped, uniforms were taken off, and the men were given special robes; each man's sword was broken over his head and thrown into a bonfire built for that purpose. Afterward, the execution of the five men began. The hanging was accompanied by a horrifying episode. During the night it had rained and the ropes were wet; the executioner did not tighten the noose enough, and three of the five men, namely, Muraviev-Apostol, Ryleev, and Kakhovsky fell down when the stools were pulled from under their feet. Muraviev-Apostol, whose legs were broken, remarked bitterly: "Poor Russia, she cannot even hang decently!" Kakhovsky swore. General Chernyshev, in charge of the execution, immediately ordered that the men be taken back to the scaffolds.[46] Shortly afterward the five bodies were taken down and buried in a secret place, which still remains unknown.[47]

It should be noted that not even the dead Decembrists were spared: Ippolit Muraviev-Apostol, Shchepillo, and Kuzmin, who perished in the uprising in the South, could not escape the all-reaching hand of the official Nemesis. The verdict demanded that on their graves be placed, not crosses, but scaffolds with inscriptions indicating "the eternal disgrace" of their names.[48]

On July 13, 1826, General Golenishchev-Kutuzov reported to Nicholas:[49]

The execution was carried out with due tranquillity and order on the part of the troops participating as well as the spectators, of whom there were a few. Because of the inexperience of our executioners and their lack of knowledge in constructing scaffolds, at the first attempt, three, namely, Ryleev, Kakhovsky and Muraviev[-Apostol] dropped, but were soon again hanged and thus received deserved death. About which I most devotedly report to Your Royal Majesty.

Replying to the report of the execution, Nicholas thanked God that everything had ended happily and ordered that vigilance be redoubled in the country.[50] That same day the Emperor went to

---

[46] Lorer, *Zapiski dekabrista,* 113–114; Yakushkin, I., *op. cit.,* 99–100. Cf. *Russky Arkhiv,* II (1881), 342.

[47] *Russky Arkhiv,* II (1881), 342, 345–346.

[48] *P.S.Z.,* Series II, Vol. I, No. 514; *Dekabristy. Tainye Obshchestva,* 153.

[49] *Byloe,* III (1906), 226.

[50] Shilder, *op. cit.,* I, 455; *Byloe,* III (1906), 232.

church to pray and was mostly alone. In the evening he had tea with the Empress. He was pale, in a melancholic mood, and silent. . . .[51]

The exile of all the privates of the Moskovsky and Chernigovsky regiments began in February, 1826. About fifteen hundred soldiers were sent to the Caucasus, where war with Persia was imminent; a few, after undergoing severe corporal punishment, were sent to the East.[52] On July 13, 1826, there began the exodus to Siberia of the first party of convicts. Among them were Prince Trubetskoi, Prince Obolensky, Yakubovich, Peter and Andrei Borisov, Prince Volkonsky, and Artamon Muraviev, all of whom were chained and sent to the Nerchinsk mines. The party was soon followed by others. Some of the wives of the prisoners, determined to drink the bitter cup with their husbands, trod the long road to Siberia, setting an example of heroic devotion and leaving a monument to Russian womanhood.[53]

Thus ended the first act in the drama of the struggle for liberty in Russia. It revealed the medieval state of the country and the archaic system which was responsible for depriving Russia of the flower of her youth.[54] In the words of Shilder, the court biographer of Nicholas I, "That which has been said is sufficient: let the curtain down to cover these sad pages of our past."[55]

---

[51] *Istorichesky Viestnik,* VII (1916), 103–107.

[52] The war with Persia began on September 16 (28), 1826. *Dekabristi na Ukraini,* 120–121; *Russkaia Starina,* XI (1890), 488–499.

[53] *Istorichesky Viestnik,* XII (1884), 650ff.

[54] *Materialy,* VIII, *passim.* It may be of interest to note the ages of the hundred and twenty-one "most dangerous state criminals." They are:

From: 20 to 25	37 men	From: 36 to 40	10 men
26 to 30	45 men	41 to 45	2 men
31 to 35	26 men	46 and up	1 man

[55] Shilder, *op. cit.,* I, 339.

Chapter X

THE DECEMBRISTS IN SIBERIA

Deep in the Siberian mine,
Keep your patience proud;
The bitter toil shall not be lost,
The rebel thought unbowed.

. . . .

The heavy-hanging chains will fall,
The walls will crumble at a word;
And Freedom greet you in the light,
And brothers give you back the sword.

—A. PUSHKIN. Translated by MAX EASTMAN.

SIBERIA, THE UNKNOWN, in the earlier half of the nineteenth
century seemed to many people a land of eternal cold and
wilderness. The thought of spending the rest of a lifetime in
that part of the Empire must have been very depressing indeed. "I
am going from here to Turukhansk," wrote Krivtsov, one of the
Decembrists, to his sister from Krasnoiarsk, "almost at the frontier
of an uninhabited realm, where ice and cold like Herculean col-
umns draw the line for man, saying: *'ne plus ultra.'* "[1] Basargin,
another Decembrist, upon learning that he was sentenced to settlement in Siberia, considered himself no longer an inhabitant of this
world.[2] Though the hearts of many who were sent from European
Russia to Siberia were filled with grief and a feeling of hopelessness, yet some of the exiles did not abandon their expectation of
returning some day to the West.[3] Others, at the thought of being
imprisoned for life or during the best part of it, looked to the future with despair. Still others were driven to the point of insanity.[4]
Artamon Muraviev cursed Yermak for ever conquering Siberia,
"the source of anguish and graves for exiles."[5]

But not all the exiles gave way to despair. Among the Decembrists who bore their lot with heroic determination were men

[1] Gershenzon, *Dekabrist Krivtsov*, 244–245.

[2] Basargin, *Zapiski*, 74.

[3] *Sibir i Dekabristy*, 56ff., 63.

[4] *Sbornik statei, posviashchennykh Platonovu*, 405–408; Rozen, *Zapiski
dekabrista*, 135, 190; Shchegolev, *Istoricheskie etiudy*, 392–393; Yakushkin, I.,
Zapiski, 124.

[5] Rozen, *op. cit.*, 185.

like Yakushkin, Sukhinov, Küchelbecker, and Obolensky. Nothing could break their faith, or their will to live and to struggle for the ideal they had once conceived. All the prisoners passed through periods of despair, but their fortitude was sustained by the conviction that their suffering was for a noble cause. From Olonki, a village about forty miles from Irkutsk, Raevsky wrote :[6]

> Nay, nay, I will not exchange my cruel fate
> For a gilded yoke . . .
> In my hands is the lamp of pure faith,—
> Which will light my thorny road.

Nor did thirty-six years of exile destroy the faith of Gorbachevsky in his ideal. From Siberia, where he remained to the last day of his life, he wrote :[7]

. . . I have always regretted the past and never was I able to forget it. Neither a woman nor a family could ever compel me to abandon my ideal, which I had hoped to achieve and for which I sacrificed myself. Indeed, now I see myself that the life of an old bachelor is terrible: lonely, sad and without a future. But one thing still supports me—that is faith in some better future, in the ideal which I shall abandon only when I cease to breathe. Truly, in spite of my frequent illness, in spite of my failing enterprises, in spite of the exorbitant prices here, and in addition all kinds of deprivations which I experience and tolerate,—I still stand firmly, hope for something, still love people, share with them the last I have, wish them good and all kindness. And all that derives from the ideal which you well know I live by, and which thus far has not permitted me to reach the state of despair.

One of the strongest characters, M. Lunin, "citizen of the world," as he called himself, went to Siberia with the conviction that here the political martyrs were obliged "to serve by word and deed" the ideals to which they had originally devoted themselves.[8] To his last day he maintained this confident belief. As an aged man he used to say that, though he had only one tooth left in his mouth, even that one was directed against Nicholas.[9] There were others, like Sukhinov and Lutsky, who did not capitulate easily to their fate but gallantly, though vainly, began to contemplate means of wresting freedom from their hard lot by force or through escape.[10] On

---

[6] *Russkaia Starina*, IX (1903), 579, 582.

[7] Gorbachevsky, *Zapiski i pisma*, 281–282.

[8] Lunin, *Sochineniia i pisma*, 26; Golovachev, *Dekabristy. 86 portretov*, 131.

[9] Popov, I. I., *Minuvshee i perezhitoe. Sibir i emigratsiia*, 35.

[10] *Krasnyi Arkhiv*, XIII, 258; *Byloe*, V (33) (1925), 109; *Russky Arkhiv*, 1870, 919–920; Rozen, *op. cit.*, 160; *Russkoe Proshloe*, V (1923), 54–55; *Vospominaniia i rasskazy*, II, 28–31; Gorbachevsky, *op. cit.*, 218ff.

the whole, despite the depressing circumstances in which many of the Decembrists found themselves, a goodly number determined to face the future boldly even in distant Siberia.

Adolph Erman, a notable scholar and traveler, who met Alexander Bestuzhev in Siberia, describes his impressions as follows:[11]

> Hardheartedness and stoical indifference are all that could be expected of a man who had awakened all at once from dreams of liberty to chains and a dungeon. . . . Such a man, nevertheless, had here preserved, in features, language, and demeanor, all the freshness of youth and the brilliance of great talent. He confessed to me that the cheerfulness of his disposition constantly revived in him against his will; the burden of the past and the hopeless future were enough to weigh him down, yet he was attached to the present, and had spirit to enjoy it.

To a few of the Decembrists Siberia was not entirely alien. Batenkov was born in Tobolsk; Baron Steingel spent his childhood in Eastern Siberia, in Kamchatka, and received his early education in Irkutsk; Zavalishin had visited Siberia on previous occasions. Still others had shown interest in Siberian administration and had suggested reforms in this direction.[12]

Impressions of Siberia.—As the Decembrists came into closer contact with the country and the people, the fears they had felt in western Russia were gradually dispelled and opinions previously held began to change. While on the way to their destined places, some began to consider Siberia more favorably. One of them, Basargin, writes as follows:[13]

> The farther we moved on in Siberia, the more that country won in my eyes. The common people seemed to me much more free, more clever, even more educated than our Russian peasants and in particular more so than the peasants of the landlords. Here they better appreciate human dignity, value more highly man's rights. Later, on more than one occasion, I heard from those who visited the United States or who lived there that Siberians have much in common with Americans in their manners, customs, and even in their mode of life.

In his *Memoirs* Baron Rozen compares Siberia, as did Basargin, with the United States and predicts that the former, like the United States in the past, will become in future a haven for all refugees from political and religious persecutions, and that, as in America,

---

[11] Erman, A., *Reise um die Erde*, Erste Abteilung, Zweiter Band, 269 (*Travels in Siberia* [London, 1848], II, 388).

[12] *Vospominaniia i rasskazy*, II, 145ff.; *Materialy*, V, 126–127; *Russky Arkhiv*, II (1881), 276.

[13] Basargin, *op. cit.*, 94.

THE PRISON AT PETROVSKY ZAVOD.

a new, great and prosperous state will arise in that vast and distant region because of this circumstance.[14]

Places of exile.—The exiled were sent chained and in small groups, each group of four being accompanied by a guard.[15] The guard, to make his personal profits as great as possible, transported the prisoners to Siberia with such speed that at times their lives were in actual danger.[16] M. Bestuzhev was almost killed by being thrown out of the coach as it was rolling madly down hill. He was caught by his chains in the wheel and was dragged like "Hector behind the chariot of Achilles." Even the guard became alarmed and shouted to the coachman to hold the horses, to which the coachman could only reply: "Well, your Highness, now hold them yourself!"[17]

The places to which the men were exiled were scattered and long distances apart so as to prevent any close association. The largest group of prisoners was the one sent to Chita and three years afterward transferred to Petrovsky Zavod, near Nerchinsk. This group included the outstanding leaders of the Decembrist movement and later also a number of Polish revolutionaries. These prisoners were concentrated in a large group because of the argument of the Siberian Governor-General, Lavinsky, that it would be easier to guard one large unit than several small ones.[18] This may have facilitated the guarding of the prisoners, but the large group, according to M. Bestuzhev, enabled the Decembrists "to exist politically beyond political death."[19] The places to which the other men were sent were Berezov, Narym, Surgut, Pelym, Irkutsk, Yakutsk, Viliuisk, and some others.

Most of these settlements were inhabited by very few Russians, the greater part of the population being Siberian aborigines, Tunguses, Yakuts, Tartars, Ostiaks, Mongols, or Buriats. Some of these places had already been used by the government for purposes of exile;[20] for example, Ilimsk, Yakutsk, Berezov, and Nerchinsk.

---

[14] Rozen, *op. cit.*, 213. See also Pushchin, I., *Zapiski o Pushkine* (M., 1934), 178–179.

[15] Zavalishin, *Zapiski dekabrista*, II, 58.

[16] *Byloe*, IV (1906), 220–221; Rozen, *op. cit.*, 141–142.

[17] *Vospominaniia Bestuzhevykh*, 205–206.

[18] Rozen, *op. cit.*, 159.

[19] *Vospominaniia Bestuzhevykh*, 209.

[20] *Sibirskaia Sovietskaia Entsiklopediia*, II, 575.

In Ilimsk there lived in exile the outstanding political prisoner
of the eighteenth century, Alexander Radishchev. There are no
data concerning the size and nature of the settlements to which the
Decembrists were sent, but as one writer states : "If the main administrative center, the town of Yakutsk, counted only 2458 inhabitants, what could be said about the number of inhabitants of
the circuit towns of Olekminsk, Viliuisk, Verkhoyansk, or Sredne-
Kolymsk ?"[21]

Attitude of the population.—The Siberian population met the
Decembrists very hospitably. In many places they were received
in a friendly manner and given encouragement. In Kostroma, a
man came up to the exiles saying : "Gentlemen, be brave, you are
suffering for the most beautiful, the most noble cause! Even in
Siberia you will find sympathy."[22] The Decembrists were assisted
by the inhabitants, especially the numerous sectarians, such as the
Dukhobors, who aided them in communicating with their friends
and relatives and among whom some of them, Raevsky for example, established their residence.[23] A sympathetic attitude was also
shown during their long years of exile by other classes of Siberian
society, by the merchants and state employees, among whom was
a considerable number of liberal-minded persons.[24] "I am unable
to praise Zhdanov and Arbuzov sufficiently," writes Gorbachevsky
to Obolensky concerning two local merchants. "They took such an
interest in me, as if I were their kin or some kind of former benefactor."[25] To the masses the exiled Decembrists were "generals who
had refused to take the oath to Nicholas I."[26] In the village communities the scattered Decembrists were novelties at first, but the
natives seemed intuitively to realize that they had suffered political persecution and that they were on the side of the people. With
the exception of very few, on the whole, the attitude toward them
was more favorable than otherwise.[27] A number of the Decembrists
in distress received the friendliest attention from local peasants.

---

[21] *Sbornik Trudov Irkutskogo Universiteta,* Otdiel I, Vypusk 2 (Irkutsk,
1921), 111.

[22] *Vospominaniia i rasskazy,* I, 133 ; Zavalishin, *op. cit.,* II, 71–72.

[23] *Obshchestvennye dvizheniia v Rossii,* I, 262–263 ; Erman, *op. cit.,* English
translation, II, 182–183.

[24] *Russkaia Starina,* VII (1881), 329 ; Muraviev-Apostol, M. I., *Vospominaniia i pisma,* 57–58 ; Rozen, *op. cit.,* 143.

[25] Gorbachevsky, *op. cit.,* 239.

[26] *Sibir i Dekabristy,* 16.

[27] Maksimov, *Sibir i katorga,* 390–392, 434.

A COMMON CELL AT THE CHITA PRISON.

This can be seen from the last testaments of different members, in which they bequeathed everything to those whose hospitality they had enjoyed or from whom they had received excellent care during illness.[28]

Settlement régime.—Upon the delivery of the exiles to the assigned places they were obliged to comply with many regulations, and the government continued to enforce a régime often unnecessarily strict; it regulated every move and watched every step the exiles attempted to make. For example, they were forbidden to have their pictures taken to send to their relatives or friends, since this might arouse sympathy with the Decembrists or awaken interest in their situation.[29] It is owing to Nicholas Bestuzhev's talent as a painter that the historian is in possession of many remarkable portraits and sketches of the Decembrists in Siberia.[30]

The activities of the Decembrists were noted by the local police and in the absence of the police the duties of surveillance were imposed upon the natives.[31] The régime established by the local authorities can be judged from the following incident. As late as 1842, when less restriction might have been expected, Zavalishin was put in chains and thrown into prison for refusing to take off his hat before a lieutenant of Petrovsky Zavod. After a short investigation the offender was sentenced to a month of hard labor, "as an example to other exiles."[32] Another episode may complete the picture of the type of officials with which the Decembrists had occasion to cope. When the head of the Nerchinsk mines received the prisoners and read the instructions he became indignant, exclaiming:[33]

So that is the way instructions are written! .... All is well, all is well, but then comes at the end a little hitch: "to watch their health!" What is that? Without that hitch I would get rid of them within two months, but now, pray, how can I act with tied hands?!

Close surveillance.—Not only political and social activities were carefully watched or prevented and a semimilitary rule enforced, but there was also interference even in respect to religious convictions. Shakhovskoi's interest in natural sciences aroused suspicion in the eyes of the local clergy. This resulted in his being accused of

[28] *Sibir i Dekabristy*, 30–31.
[29] *C.I.O.I.D.R.*, IV (1895), 23–24.
[30] Lorer, *Zapiski dekabrista*, 148.
[31] Yakushkin, I., *op. cit.*, 124.
[32] *Dekabristy v Zabaikalie*, 37–38.
[33] *Vospominaniia Bestuzhevykh*, 256.

lack of religious faith and of "heresy."[34] A similar accusation was made against some other members. In one of the monthly reports of 1844 the local authorities wrote that the two Decembrists, Gorbachevsky and Mozalevsky, were not only absent from confession, according to the archbishop, but they had not even attended church for the last five years. Also, rumors reached the officials that the same persons revealed atheistic tendencies. The report therefore advised that the offenders be "restrained and instructed and that with the assistance of the local priest they be persuaded to attend church and perform the Christian duty of penitence."[35] Furthermore, should an investigation establish that Gorbachevsky had uttered certain sacrilegious words, as had been rumored, he was to be prosecuted, together with those who heard and had not reported his remarks to the government. An investigation immediately proceeded, but the final decision is obscure, since all the documents are not available. However, the whole matter evidently left a bad impression upon the authorities, as the following document clearly indicates.[36]

CHIEF ADMINISTRATION
OF EASTERN SIBERIA

Division I
Table 3
December 3, 1846
No. 154

IRKUTSK

DIRECTOR OF THE PETROVSK
MINING REGION, CAPTAIN TASKIN

The state criminal Ivan Gorbachevsky asks me to increase his subsidy paid by the Treasury. I order you, Dear Sir, to inform the state criminal, Gorbachevsky, that he does not conduct himself so as to permit anything [to be] done in his favor. Therefore his present petition I [have] left without favorable consideration. At the same time see to it that ninety kopecks in silver be collected from him, Gorbachevsky, for not using properly stamped paper.

Governor-General, Lieutenant-General,

(Signed) Ruport.

From time to time special visiting inspectors were sent from the capital. Often such visits resulted in greater and still more annoying restrictions upon the freedom of the exiles. A more rigid censorship would be enforced over their correspondence with relatives;

---

[34] *Sbornik statei, posviashchennykh Platonovu*, 406–407.

[35] *Dekabristy v Zabaikalie*, 41.

[36] *Ibid.*, 43.

or they would be deprived of such privileges as the possession of
hunting rifles, which in Siberia signified great hardship and sometimes even danger from wandering criminals exiled there.[37]

Correspondence was carried on chiefly by the wives of the Decembrists, who naturally enjoyed more freedom and who considered it their sacred duty to act as secretaries for the men.[38] All
letters, even those of the wives, had to be written clearly, mailed
open, and passed through the hands of the proper authorities in
Siberia and again in St. Petersburg.[39] Bestuzhev writes:[40]

> Even the correspondence with our close relatives was brief and careful;
> every phrase was thought over ten times before it was written down, in order
> that, when it passed the first censorship, that of Leparsky, it did not compel
> (which often happened) our kind women to rewrite our letters once more; in
> order that neither our relatives nor the commandant be responsible (which
> also frequently occurred). This correspondence was so colorless, so lifeless,
> bore such a vulgar imprint of officiality, that madness would seize me every
> time I wrote letters.

If this was true of letters addressed to relatives, what could be said
about those exchanged among the Decembrists in Siberia?

General Leparsky, in charge of the Decembrists in Chita, had
to go over every message very carefully before it reached the Third
Division of the political intelligence service at St. Petersburg. He
was in constant fear lest the higher authorities should find something that might throw a bad light upon his administration or show
him as too lenient. On one occasion a message of Madame Annenkova was forwarded directly to the capital without passing the
censorship of Leparsky. This caused much excitement and Leparsky feared complications might result. He called Madame Annenkova to inquire personally concerning the contents of the letter,
which was known to Nicholas himself. "I wrote only one thing,
that the General is an honest man," replied Madame Annenkova.
Poor Leparsky, seizing his head in both hands, began to pace the
floor, muttering: "I am lost."[41]

Government aid.—The right to receive financial aid and other
forms of assistance was also strictly regulated and limited to a
certain amount. The law allowed the exile to receive not more than

---

[37] *Sibir i Dekabristy*, 142, 144, 151.

[38] Basargin, *op. cit.*, 108; Yakushkin, I., *op. cit.*, 137–138.

[39] *Dekabristy v Zabaikalie*, 40, 44.

[40] *Vospominaniia Bestuzhevykh*, 254.

[41] Annenkova, *Vospominaniia*, 162–163.

two thousand rubles for settlement purposes and not more than one thousand rubles annually.[42] This sum, however, would have to be sent to the governor-general, who in turn would pay it in monthly installments or otherwise, as he deemed it convenient. Those of the Decembrists who were unable to receive financial aid from their relatives were granted a government subsidy equal to that paid to a private soldier (one hundred and fourteen rubles and twenty-three and one half kopecks), and in addition summer and winter clothes.[43] The allowance was too meager, and the hardships these men had to undergo and their struggle for existence can be judged from some of the appeals frequently presented to the government.[44] To make matters still worse, the authorities in 1832 issued an "advice" to all local merchants of Petrovsky Zavod that no credit be extended to exiled persons.[45]

Those of the exiles who received a fair allowance from home often assisted their colleagues.[46] Still, even this proved insufficient, and the wretched existence of some of the Decembrists very shortly drew the attention of the government. Nicholas I therefore ordered that each man be given fifteen *desiatins* of land (about forty-two acres) in order to gain a livelihood. For various reasons this provision did not always prove a satisfactory solution. In some instances the soil was so poor that a ten-year investment of labor failed to return any results.[47] In others, the men were totally unfamiliar with the tilling of land or they lacked capital and implements with which to begin anything. Ygelstrom, one of the Decembrists, writes:[48]

Thus I am requested to plow the soil. I spent ten years in the military school, ten in military service and seven in various prisons; the question is, where could I have learned agriculture?

Finally, for some, the amount of land assigned was not sufficient, especially for those who had families to support. When Rozen asked permission to buy additional land, the government refused it; to

---

[42] *Sibir i Dekabristy*, 141.

[43] *C.I.O.I.D.R.*, IV (1895), 13.

[44] *Sibir i Dekabristy*, 131–132, 134–135, 146–147.

[45] *Dekabristy v Zabaikalie*, 35–36.

[46] *Istorik Marksist*, I (1926), 192; Yakushkin, I., *op. cit.*, 134–135; Sibir i Dekabristy, 143.

[47] *Vospominaniia Bestuzhevykh*, 246.

[48] *Sibir i Dekabristy*, 142. Concerning Ygelstrom, see *Diela i Dni*, I (1920), 240.

M. S. LUNIN.

this request Nicholas I sardonically remarked that Rozen seemed to wish to live in Siberia as a landlord.[49] Though the government seems to have taken an interest in the welfare of the Decembrists, their predicament was most difficult indeed, as the following illustration shows. Since quite a number of the Decembrists lived in towns, the land was allotted to them outside of the town limits. The law regulating the status of the exiles, however, provided that no offender could leave the town limits in which he was settled unless special permission was given him each time he wished or needed to do so. It is easy to imagine the awkwardness of such a situation.[50]

Political surrender.—Under the stress of these difficulties some of the Decembrists, shortly after their arrival and at the price of humiliating concessions, began to appeal for pardon. They expressed political remorse and their willingness to redeem their prestige by enlisting as private soldiers in the war being waged at that time in the Caucasus. On February 10, 1829, Alexander Bestuzhev wrote:[51]

> To the noble soul trained in battles are understandable the sufferings of a military man destined to rot in idleness, when the glory of the Russian arms thunders over the cradle of the ancient world, over the grave of Mohammed. Asking you this grace, I do not seek advantages nor distinction: I only seek an opportunity to shed my blood for the glory of the Sovereign and honorably end the life granted to me, in order that after it the name criminal shall not be known.

Only a few appealed and still fewer succeeded in winning royal pardon. The events of December 14, 1825, were too fresh in the memory of Nicholas. Strangely enough, even those who succeeded in winning pardon did not accept it enthusiastically and, as one observer remarked, they left Siberia with an uneasy conscience.[52] Most of the Decembrists considered an appeal to the government too humiliating. Writes Küchelbecker to Obolensky:[53]

> Little by little I am getting used to it. Man, I think, can become used even to Hell, and therefore I think that there is no eternal torment for sinners. . . . Looking closer at the people and locality, I find that life is still possible here. To go as a private soldier I did not wish because of my view: I consider it

---

[49] Rozen, *op. cit.*, 203.

[50] *Sibir i Dekabristy*, 122–124, 142, 155; *Vospominaniia Bestuzhevykh*, 257.

[51] *Russkaia Starina*, XII (1881), 886; *Sibir i Dekabristy*, 56.

[52] Erman, *op. cit.*, English translation, II, 184. See also *Istorik Marksist*, I (1926), 185; Küchelbecker, *Dnevnik*, 302.

[53] *Dekabristy. Neizdannye materialy i stat'i*, 162.

shameful to appeal, especially to be a soldier. If I were drafted, I would hardly refuse at the beginning, but to beg is a different matter.

Among those who remained in bitter opposition to the government and allowed no compromise with it was M. S. Lunin. Upon his learning that some of the members had asked for pardon from the government, he wrote with biting sarcasm :[54]

I hear that some of our political exiles have expressed their desire to serve as privates in the Caucasian army, hoping to make peace with the government. In my opinion it is unwise for them to do so before subjecting themselves to some slight scrutiny. The first day one should request that he be flogged fifty times, the second day a hundred, and the third day two hundred times, so that altogether it would make three hundred and fifty times. After such a scrutiny one could proclaim: *dignus, dignus est intrare in isto docto corpore.*

To his last day Lunin remained loyal to the cause of liberty and believed that the Decembrists must carry on a course of intensive propaganda wherever they were.[55] The letters which Lunin succeeded in dispatching to his sister, Countess Uvarova, were in reality political pamphlets designed for propaganda purposes, or, as he said, "to tease the white bear." "The publicity," states Lunin in one letter, "which my letters enjoy through numerous copies transforms them into a political weapon which I must use for the defense of freedom."[56] His sister implored him to cease challenging the government, but without avail. The letters were copied and widely read by many people in various towns in Siberia and elsewhere. The force with which Lunin expressed his convictions and his strong opposition to autocratic government had great influence upon many of his readers and associates. "Lunin is bold," writes Vadkovsky to Obolensky, "amusing, and cheerful. By his courage and iron will he has gained a kind of moral predominance over all the inhabitants of Urik."[57]

Finally the attention of the government was directed to Lunin's writings, particularly to an essay in which he expressed his views concerning secret societies in Russia. As a result, on August 5, 1838, Lunin was forbidden to correspond with anyone. Permission was granted to him again about a year later, on October 28, 1839, but Lunin did not surrender and continued to pursue his policy.[58]

[54] Lunin, *op. cit.,* 32.

[55] *Ibid.,* 26, 29, 60.

[56] *Ibid., op. cit.,* 60.

[57] *Dekabristy. Neizdannye materialy i stat'i,* 214.

[58] *Pamiati Dekabristov,* I, 207; *Materialy,* VIII, 346–347.

"From the sighs of those living under thatched roofs storms are born which destroy palaces," he writes.[59] Again, in respect to the recent restrictions upon his correspondence, he states: "Let them show me the law which forbids one to express political ideals in letters to relatives."[60]

Lunin's curiosity to see the law forbidding him to write to his sister on political problems proved costly. When some of his writings designed for the foreign press were seized, Nicholas ordered the prisoner removed to a more isolated place.[61] On the night of March 27, 1841, he was suddenly arrested and transferred to Akatui, a desolated strip of territory on the Chinese border, which was known as the "notorious and dreadful place even in Siberia," "gloomier than any to be found in the entire Transbaikal."[62] Though the régime here was worse than in any previous prison, yet he managed to write, and to study Greek, and sought to discover Homer's religious conceptions.[63] "In England," writes Lunin, "they would say: 'Lunin is a member of the opposition.' . . . My only weapon is thought, at times in harmony, at times in opposition with the course of the government . . . opposition is characteristic of every political order."[64] In Russia, however, this political doctrine was not at all popular in the days of Lunin, and the "member of the opposition" instead of being sent to Parliament was sent to Akatui, where, according to the wife of one of the Decembrists, Madame Annenkova, "because of the silver mines the air was so heavy that no bird could live within a radius of a hundred and fifty miles."[65] The terrible loneliness must have been unbearable even to such a remarkably strong character as Lunin. He became still more reserved and led the existence of a hermit, spending his entire time over books. On December 3, 1845, while resting after lunch, he suddenly died. The autopsy, performed by the local doctor, was as terrible as the life of Lunin. Having no proper instruments, he opened the head with an ax. . . . The funeral was attended only by a Polish priest and a few Polish exiles who resided in Akatui.[66]

---

[59] Lunin, *op. cit.*, 53.

[60] *Ibid.*, 47.

[61] Zavalishin, *op. cit.*, II, 277–278; *Katorga i Ssylka*, I (1930).

[62] Maksimov, *op. cit.*, 92.

[63] *Atenei*, III (1926), 19. Lunin was a mystic and while in Warsaw became a devout Catholic. See *Russky Arkhiv*, III (1885), 360–362; Zavalishin, "Dekabrist Lunin." *Istoririchesky Viestnik*, I (1888), 140, 146.

[64] Lunin, *op. cit.*, 40.

[65] Annenkova, *op. cit.*, 166.   [66] Golovachev, *op. cit.*, 138.

Social amalgamation.—Nearly all the Decembrists were of the aristocracy, but in Siberia, where there was no traditional nobility, all social barriers were dissolved. As "state criminals" they were stripped of all titles and deprived of all political and social privileges. Thrown in the midst of the peasant masses, many of the exiles found themselves placed on a level with that class. They did not shrink before the situation, and even abandoned lightheartedly their former social status, amalgamating with the "lower classes" with which they were forced to labor side by side. Many who were single married peasant girls and established their families in the distant Siberian towns and villages. Among these were Frolov, Bechasnyi, Falenberg, Chernyshev, the Kriukov brothers, Lutsky, Küchelbecker, Raevsky, Mikhail Bestuzhev, and Obolensky, who married his servant girl.[67] "My wife," wrote Obolensky to one of his friends, "is not from the higher circles, but a simple, illiterate girl; honestly and unselfishly did I seek her hand, and she has given herself to me as honestly and unselfishly."[68] And Wilhelm Küchelbecker remarks in his Diary : "Though my wife did not always understand me, still I have always valued her excellent character."[69] In their wives the Decembrists found friends who alleviated their material burdens and brought color into the gray monotony of their existence. These women endured hardships stoically.[70] They voluntarily took upon themselves the heavy responsibility of family life and bore it heroically, in the manner characteristic of Russian womanhood. The heroism of these women inspired the well-known Russian poet, N. Nekrasov, to write his poem "Russian Women."[71]

The stupidity of the regulations enforced upon the women and the humiliations to which they were often subjected were at times intolerable. Some of the wives became pregnant and began to ask their relatives to send them necessities. General Leparsky, who

---

[67] *Dekabristy. Neizdannye materialy i stat'i*, 162–163 ; Struve, V., *Vospominaniia o Sibiri*, 26–27 ; *Russkaia Starina*, VII (1881), 368 ; *Vospominaniia Bestuzhevykh*, 248 ; *Sibir i Dekabristy*, 163 ; *Istorichesky Viestnik*, XXXIV (1888), 755.

[68] *Sibir i Dekabristy*, 28.

[69] *Russkaia Starina*, VII (1875), 353.

[70] On the judicial status of the wives of the Decembrists see Shchegolev, *op. cit.*, 409ff.

[71] Nekrasov's "Russian Women" has been translated into English by Mrs. Juliet M. Soskice. See *Poems by N. Nekrasov*, Series of "World's Classics," No. CCCXL (London, Oxford Press, 1929) ; *Zvenia*, VI, 701ff.

MME M. N. VOLKONSKAIA.

read the letters, became a little perturbed and refused to forward them, informing the women that he was unable to do so. "Allow me to say, mesdames," he endeavored to explain in great confusion to the expectant mothers, whom he had summoned to his office, "that you have no right to become pregnant. When the babies are born, well, then it is a different matter."[72]

In the dreary days of their banishment the Decembrists owed much to the sympathetic friendship of their wives, whether they were Siberian peasant girls or women from European Russia who had cast aside all social privileges and comfort to follow their husbands to Siberia.[73] During the first years in Petrovsky Zavod, some of the wives spent the daytime with their husbands in the dim prison. The light was terrible, scarcely reaching the prisoners through the minute holes in the walls, but the men did not care. "For what do we need windows when we have with us four suns," Trubetskoi used to say, referring to the four women, Naryshkina, Trubetskaia, Rozen, and Volkonskaia.[74]

Activities of the Decembrists.—Living under the constant watchfulness and petty restrictions of the police, compelled to struggle with poverty, far removed from civilization and the pulse of national life, the Decembrists found political activity very difficult if not impossible.[75] What political activity, indeed, could be expected in such places as Viliuisk, which is "neither a city, nor a village, nor is it a hamlet," and where "in the winter the day is so short and the icy windows let through such a dim light, that it is necessary to sit the entire day with a candle?"[76] Nor were the Siberian "metropolises," such as Yakutsk, intellectual stimuli. "Those who've been to London or to Rome, who Venice, Paris may have seen," undoubtedly must have felt it a too restricted field for their ambitions.

---

[72] Annenkova, *op. cit.*, 161.

[73] *Russkie Propilei*, I, 4. Those who joined their husbands in Siberia were Mesdames Trubetskaia, Volkonskaia, Davydova, Rozen, Entaltseva, Naryshkina, Muravieva, and Annenkova. The last-named came as a fiancée (Pauline Gueuble) and married Annenkov in prison.

[74] Rozen, *op. cit.*, 170.

[75] It was only in 1848, with the appointment of N. N. Muraviev-Amursky as Governor-General of Eastern Siberia, that the restrictions were lessened. See Barsukov, *Graf Nikolai N. Muraviev-Amursky*, I, 185; *Istorichesky Viestnik* XXXII (1888), 407.

[76] *Russkaia Starina*, IX (1886), 530; Muraviev-Apostol, M. I., *Vospominaniia i pisma*, 61.

Notwithstanding the difficulties which the Decembrists had to encounter, the years they spent in Siberia were not without fruit. Their influence during the three or four decades of their exile entered Siberian life through numerous visible and invisible channels, leaving traces in various fields, though neither the inhabitants nor the Decembrists were clearly aware of it. Political influence, to be sure, was negligible, especially during the first decade or so of their exile, and none could be expected, considering the standing of the "state criminal." Their presence was more definitely felt culturally and economically. In their daily intercourse with the peasants, especially with the younger generation, the Decembrists accomplished much and their work was later keenly appreciated by the Siberians.[77]

Educational activities.—Soon after settling down, many of the Decembrists began to devote themselves to cultural work among the natives. For a while the officials refused even to consider granting the exiles permission to teach. But the exiles found a way to carry out their plans so that "the wolves would not be hungry and the sheep would remain unhurt." They asked permission to organize a class to which they might teach church music and the request was granted. But in order to learn to read music, one had to be literate, hence those who joined the group were compelled to learn first to read and write.[78]

The Bestuzhevs and Obolensky were the first exiles to open a school, at Nerchinsk, which was later continued by Gorbachevsky. Similar schools for natives were opened by Zavalishin in Chita, Raevsky in Olonki, the Beliaev brothers in Minusinsk, Yakushkin in Yalutorovsk, M. I. Muraviev-Apostol in Viliuisk, and the Borisov brothers at Malaia Razvodnaia. The school organized by Yakushkin graduated in all about sixteen hundred pupils.[79] The Decembrists were familiar with and favored the Lancasterian system of education and tried to carry out its principles in Siberia.[80] Raevsky, that "first Decembrist," it will be remembered, was exiled for his liberal activities and his organization of Lancasterian schools in the southern army. Among the most active teachers were

[77] Maksimov, *op. cit.*, 440–441; *Istorichesky Viestnik*, XI (1908), 537–538.

[78] *Vospominaniia Bestuzhevykh*, 220, 232; Zavalishin, *op. cit.*, II, 97–98.

[79] *Sibirskie Ogni*, III (1924), 179; Muraviev-Apostol, *op. cit.*, 63–64; *Russkaia Starina*, VII (1881), 345–346; Maksimov, *op. cit.*, 434.

[80] Erman, *op. cit.*, English translation, I, 386–387.

the Bestuzhev brothers, whose work in the field of vocational education proved of lasting effect. The wives of the Decembrists must not be overlooked, for they, too, worked most devotedly and gave generously for the cause of public education in the communities in which they happened to live.[81] In 1925 there were still a few survivors who had been former pupils of the Decembrists, and in Olonki the school established by Raevsky and the garden planted by him still exist and bear his name.[82]

Much was done by the exiles in the field of women's education. P. Svistunov and A. Muraviev were the exiles chiefly responsible for the founding of schools for girls in Siberia.[83] In this respect Yakushkin's educational activities in Yalutorovsk are most noteworthy. Being unable, as an exile, to develop pedagogical activities as he wished, he commenced to work through his colleague and sympathizer, the local priest, Znamensky, though even here not without the opposition of the local police. After a long struggle, however, "the illegal child," as Yakushkin jovially called the school, made its appearance. It was soon making rapid progress, and served as a model for others.[84] Later Yakushkin determined, in memory of his recently deceased wife, to found a second school, this time for girls. Soon the school expanded to such a degree that the problem of housing became acute. In less than four years the number of attendants reached fifty, and lack of sufficient housing equipment and other supplies seriously handicapped its further progress.[85] But in spite of these hindrances, the foundation was laid and its later progress was in large measure the result of Yakushkin's early efforts in the first school founded by him.

Agricultural activities.—Another field in which the Decembrists were keenly interested and to which they contributed much was agriculture. As the result of experimental work by means of hotbeds and artificial heating, many previously unknown crops were introduced and the area under cultivation was expanded.[86] Almost from the first the attention of the exiles was attracted by the lack of vegetables in northern and eastern Siberia, an ancient problem

[81] *Russky Arkhiv*, XII (1885), 653.
[82] *Sibir i Dekabristy*, 70; *Sibirskie Ogni*, III (1924), 178; *Sibirsky Arkhiv*, I, No. 5 (March, 1912), 376–377.
[83] Golovachev, *op. cit.*, 224.
[84] *Sibirsky Sbornik*, III, 1886, 89–90.
[85] *Ibid.*, III, 1886, 94–95, 97.
[86] *Sibir i Dekabristy*, 154; *Russkaia Starina*, VII, 1881, 330, 353–354.

which had borne serious political consequences.[87] This fact compelled many of them to specialize in vegetable gardening. In the distant settlement of Viliuisk, M. Muraviev began to cultivate potatoes and millet. He succeeded with the first product but, mainly because of early frosts, failed with the second. Nevertheless, he proved to the natives that, by persistent labor and experimenting, success was possible.[88] A. Poggio, in Chita, introduced the cultivation of a number of vegetables including asparagus, melons, cucumbers, and cauliflowers.[89] Other Decembrists ordered seed from European Russia or exchanged among themselves whatever crop they enjoyed; they taught the natives the art of hothouse cultivation and other advanced methods in agriculture.[90] Through their instructions the natives learned how to cultivate tobacco, rye, buckwheat, barley, and how to produce hemp oil.[91]

Organization of medical aid.—Great service was performed by the Decembrists in the field of medicine. Here some of them, indeed, proved indispensable, since in many settlements in Siberia there were no physicians. According to Rozen, Siberia had one doctor to each forty thousand inhabitants at distances of about two hundred and fifty miles apart.[92] Among the Decembrists were several trained doctors, including Dr. Wolf. Others possessing some knowledge of medicine were Mikhail Küchelbecker, Zavalishin, Madame Trubetskaia, Artamon Muraviev, M. Muraviev-Apostol, Naryshkin, and Madame Yushnevskaia.[93] These persons did much to promote or organize medical aid among the natives, the Tunguses and Buriats. Küchelbecker organized a small hospital in his home at Barguzin. The work of these men was highly appreciated not only by the inhabitants of the settlements in which they happened to live, but also by people from neighboring villages. The fame of Doctor Wolf, who saved many lives, was widespread.[94]

[87] Kerner, Robert J., "Russian Expansion to America." *The Papers of the Bibliographical Society of America*, XXV (1931), 114–115; Vernadsky, G., "Protiv Solntsa." *Russkaia Mysl'*, I (1914), 65, 75–76.

[88] Muraviev-Apostol, *op. cit.*, 63.

[89] Rozen, *op. cit.*, 149; Annenkova, *op. cit.*, 151–152; Maksimov, *op. cit.*, 435.

[90] *Dekabristy v Zabaikalie*, 26.

[91] *Russkaia Starina*, VII (1881), 347; *Tainye obshchestva v Rossii* (M., 1926), 173–174.

[92] Rozen, A., *op. cit.*, 200; Basargin, *op. cit.*, 100–101; Muraviev-Apostol, *op. cit.*, 64; *Sibir i Dekabristy*, 128–129.

[93] Muraviev-Apostol, *op. cit.*, 76–77; Rozen, *op. cit.*, 174; *Istorichesky Viestnik*, XII (1888), 754; Lorer, *op. cit.*, 145–146.

[94] *Istorik-Marksist*, I, 1926, 180; Basargin, *op. cit.*, 157–158, 173; *Russkaia Starina*, VI (1882), 713.

Activities of the Decembrists in urban districts.—The influence
of the Decembrists upon the peasants, wherever they happened
to meet them, was exercised either through educational work or
through the introduction of advanced methods in agriculture. In
the towns, where the cultural level was usually higher than that
of the villages, their influence was quite as marked, if not more so.
In whatever town circumstances forced them to reside, social circles
soon appeared. There were circles in Olekminsk, Tobolsk, Berezov,
Yalutorovsk, Krasnoyarsk, and Kiakhta. The homes of exiles like
Trubetskoi and Volkonsky became the centers of social life and
represented the cream of local society.[95] Their influence was soon
felt, also, in those obscure towns where previously the population
had been living within narrow provincial realms, little troubled
by the outside world. In them an intellectual awakening was undoubtedly stimulated by the Decembrists: literary writings began
to appear, sometimes of an unlawful character, such as the *Polar
Star* or the *Bell*, famous Russian papers published in London by
Herzen.[96] Some local citizens ordered books from Moscow and St.
Petersburg; others began subscribing to periodical literature. M.
Bestuzhev succeeded in publishing a local newspaper in Kiakhta,
one of the earliest in Siberia. Sometimes, too, current problems
were discussed in the circles and the policy of the government
condemned.[97]

In Chita, where the largest group of Decembrists was concentrated, they gave a good part of their time to self-education. They
obtained permission to receive books, magazines, and newspapers
and succeeded in building up a fair-sized library.[98] These books
served not only the narrow circle of the exiled but also many other
people in Chita.[99] A school, or an "academy" as they called it, was
organized, in which each member lectured in the field with which
he was most familiar. Nikita Muraviev taught military science.
Doctor Wolf, physics, chemistry, and anatomy, Kornilovich, Russian history, and Obolensky, literature. Zavalishin devoted him-

---

[95] Struve, *op. cit.*, 25–26; *Vospominaniia Bestuzhevykh*, 261; *Istorichesky
Viestnik*, XXXIV (1888), 757.

[96] Popov, *op. cit.*, II, 40–42, 44; *Dekabristy v Zabaikalie*, 20–21; *Istorichesky
Viestnik*, CXIV (1908), 539; *Byloe*, IV (1906), 187–188.

[97] *Sibirskie Ogni*, III (1925), 161–162; *Katorga i Ssylka*, VIII (21) (1925),
161–162.

[98] *Vospominaniia Bestuzhevykh*, 231.

[99] Erman, *op. cit.*, English translation, II, 184.

self to the study of languages and after a number of years had mastered thirteen.[100] Political developments in Western Europe were watched with keen interest by most of the exiles. When word reached the prisoners that revolution had broken out in France and that Charles X had fled to England, they received the news with joy and the singing of the Marseillaise.[101]

Even in their isolated settlements many of the Decembrists continued, so far as conditions permitted, to read and to follow important events, and political and literary developments, or else they lived in cultural memories of their proud past. It may be of interest, in connection with this statement, to tell of the acquaintance of Erman, the eminent traveler, with Raevsky in Siberia. Erman writes :[102]

> He wore a caftan very little better than that of an ordinary peasant, and came up to his friend to show him a bank note for five roubles which he had just earned. . . . Mr. Raevsky spoke with admiration of Zacharias Werner, whom he had known in early youth in Warsaw, and from whose compositions he still drew no less consolation than intellectual refinement.

When Erman inquired concerning Raevsky's fate and how he happened to be in Siberia, Raevsky, in a half-humorous, half-significant manner, confined his reply to a quotation from Werner in German :[103]

> In einer Nacht, wo Sturm und Wetter rasen,
> Entglänzt' ein Licht von einer Grabesflur,
> Der Stürme Wuth versucht' es auszublasen,
> Es lischt—jedoch auf Augenblicke nur!

Influence in Siberian administration.—The Decembrists had a certain influence on Siberian administration, which was still in a lamentable condition in spite of the recent inspection of Speransky and the recommendation for its improvement. Because of their personal intercourse with members of the local government and their gradually increasing prestige in the community, they were able to introduce greater efficiency, and they endeavored also to combat the unparalleled corruption. Small wonder that some of the officials disliked the Decembrists and at every opportunity sought

---

[100] Rozen, *op. cit.*, 156; Yakushkin, *op. cit.*, 130; Lorer, *op. cit.*, 145.

[101] Lorer, *op. cit.*, 154.

[102] Erman, *op. cit.*, English translation, II, 184.

[103] Erman, A., *op. cit.*, German edition, II, 81. Werner, Zacharias (1768–1823), German dramatist of the romantic school.

to undermine their influence! A few of the exiled men received
the right to hold minor offices and in that capacity gained popularity with the masses.[104] In these modest positions in the local
government, some proved more capable, possessed more initiative,
and displayed more intelligence than their superiors. This was
true, for example, of Baron Steingel's valuable service in Tobolsk
and Basargin's in Turinsk.[105]

The most notable illustration of the interest of the Decembrists
in Siberia and of their competence in political affairs was given by
Zavalishin. Dimitry Zavalishin, residing in Chita until 1863, became one of the most influential counselors of the local administration as well as an authority on Pacific and Far Eastern affairs.[106]
His disagreements with Muraviev-Amursky in this respect are
noteworthy, because they reveal Zavalishin's definite views in regard to the foreign policy of Russia in the Far East and his rare
competence, which even his enemies had to acknowledge. "This
morning I was with Zavalishin," writes Kropotkin in his diary for
October 28, 1862. "One of the extraordinary personalities, has
much initiative. He is a terrible enemy of Muraviev, of the despotism in his administration, as he himself says; of his personality,
as others say. He is terribly ambitious, but it is interesting to con-
verse with him."[107] Zavalishin's open disapproval of the policy of
Muraviev-Amursky ended with his enforced departure from Chita
to Kazan, whence he moved to Moscow.[108] The duel between Zavalishin and Muraviev-Amursky is of much interest, for it represents
a certain view, evidently held by a good many people in Siberia,
and, since the issue remains vital even in the twentieth century,
it merits greater attention.

Zavalishin and Muraviev-Amursky.—Zavalishin came to Chita
when that city was becoming an important center of the Russian
possessions in the Far East. In 1851 Chita was made the capital
city of the recently organized Transbaikal Province, and it became
necessary to obtain competent persons to handle the numerous
problems with respect both to foreign affairs and to local administration. The presence of Zavalishin with his unquestioned ability

---

[104] *C.I.O.I.D.R.*, IV (1895), 34.

[105] Yadrintsev, N., *Sibir kak koloniia*, 628–629; Muraviev-Apostol, *op. cit.*,
72.

[106] *Russkaia Starina*, VI (1883), 634; IV (1905), 123.

[107] Kropotkin, *Dnevnik*, 61.

[108] *Byloe, V* (33) (1925), 148–149.

was therefore most timely. His activities in connection with the political development of Chita were important, though it is not quite true that "if Chita will ever be known, it will be only because Zavalishin lived and worked there."[109] Zavalishin was conceited to the point of obsession, especially when the discussion concerned eastern affairs, but that was because he considered the matter as too vital. Whatever others might think of Zavalishin, the importance of his rôle in the development of Chita was recognized even by his bitter opponents, and even by Muraviev-Amursky himself.[110] Naturally, however, when Muraviev-Amursky came to Eastern Siberia as Governor-General he brought with him his own policy, which was quite different from that of Zavalishin, and a conflict immediately arose.

Muraviev-Amursky had come to Siberia with a policy much broader than that of any of his predecessors. He was not the kind of man who could be satisfied with merely routine administrative work, unless it was a part of his *Weltpolitik*. The plan Muraviev-Amursky conceived was that of Russian territorial expansion, involving the annexation of the Amur region, which Russia had lost in 1689 at the conclusion of the Nerchinsk treaty with China.[111] Fearing that the aggressive policy of England in China after the "Opium War" of 1842 might lead to the absorption of Eastern Siberia by "perfidious Albion," Muraviev-Amursky insisted upon prompt action.[112] This became his life's ambition and anyone standing in the way of the execution of this plan he sought mercilessly to remove.[113] "Muraviev," Nicholas said to him on one occasion, "some day you will lose your head over the Amur question!"[114]

Being a man of action, Muraviev-Amursky began to work at once. Every administrative measure was subordinated to this plan. It was his opinion that Russia, in order to consolidate her power in the Far East, must sacrifice her possessions on the American continent to the United States.[115] This idea particularly aroused Zavalishin's vigorous opposition, for he considered the American

---

[109] Zavalishin, *op. cit.*, II, 255–256, 265–266ff., 274–275. Cf. *Russkaia Starina*, VI (1882), 710–712.

[110] *Russkaia Starina*, X (1881), 390–391; Zavalishin, *op. cit.*, II, 331–332.

[111] China. *Treaties, Conventions, etc. between China and Foreign States* (Shanghai, 1917), I, 4–13.

[112] Barsukov, *op. cit.*, I, 206–207, 288.

[113] *Russkaia Starina*, IV (1905), 123.

[114] Barsukov, *op. cit.*, I, 325.   [115] *Ibid.*, I, 322–324.

possessions of vital importance to Siberia.[116] Not only did he consider the policy of Muraviev-Amursky too arbitrary, but the idea of forced colonization of the Amur region as believed in and carried out by him, Zavalishin regarded as a grave blunder. Finally, thought Zavalishin, the overemphasis of the Amur problem would result in retarding prosperity for the entire Transbaikal Province.[117] In a number of articles in leading periodicals, Zavalishin outlined his views, pointing out the dangers of the deceptive notions which some people held with respect to the Amur Province.[118] The appearance of these articles in the press made a profound impression in Siberia as well as in Western Russia.[119] The author began to receive numerous congratulations, and the periodicals in which the articles appeared were instantly sold out.[120] But to Muraviev-Amursky this success was like a red flag waved before a bull. It intensified the antagonism to a point where one side would be forced to give in, and, since Zavalishin was only a "former state criminal," the outcome of the conflict could be easily foreseen.

Meanwhile Muraviev-Amursky was recalled to St. Petersburg. M. S. Korsakov, who succeeded him as acting Governor-General, had even less patience with Zavalishin than his predecessor had had, and opportunity for ridding himself of the annoying "authority on Eastern Siberia" was finally found. By a royal order, in February, 1863, Zavalishin was forced to leave Chita and go to a place "with a milder climate." After strong protests and some delay, Zavalishin, on August 14, 1863, had to comply with the order.[121] The local officials, long angered by Zavalishin's active opposition to abuses and corruption, naturally sought to execute this order as speedily as possible.[122] Zavalishin had fought for a lost cause and

[116] See Mazour, A. G., "Dimitry Zavalishin: Dreamer of a Russian-American Empire." *Pacific Historical Review*, March, 1936, 26–34.

[117] *Morskoi Sbornik*, VII (1859), 51–52; *Russkaia Starina*, IX (1881), 89–90, 93–94, 95–96, 97; Letter of Zavalishin to the newspaper *Vladivostok*, cited in *Izvestiia Primorskogo Gubernskogo Arkhivnogo Biuro*, I, Vypusk 2 (1923), 17–21; Zavalishin, *op. cit.*, II, 345–346.

[118] *Morskoi Sbornik*, XI (1858); V, VI, VII (1859); *Viestnik Promyshlennosti*, XII (1859). For an exhaustive bibliography of Zavalishin's writings, see Chentsov, *Vosstanie Dekabristov. Bibliografiia*, 367–378.

[119] Zavalishin, *op. cit.*, II, 387–388, 395–396.

[120] *Russkaia Starina*, X (1881), 401–404, 406–418 *passim;* Barsukov, *op. cit.*, I, 562.

[121]*Dekabristy v Zabaikalie*, 60, 63–66; *Byloe*, V (33) (1925), 149–154.

[122] Gorbachevsky, *op. cit.*, 272. Cf. Bakunin, M., *Sobranie sochinenii* (M., 1935), IV, 303ff.

against inevitable odds, but the circumstances show that his influence must have been considerable if two governor-generals were obliged to wage such a prolonged fight against him.

Scholarly activities. — The Decembrists were interested not merely in local problems but also in broader ones that concerned Siberia at large. Some of the men spent much time in the study of Siberian economic problems, including population and administration. M. Muraviev-Apostol made a statistical investigation of the Yalutorovsk region.[123] Baron Steingel conducted a similar research in the Ishimsk region, a territory within the Gubernia of Tobolsk. The results of his work later appeared, in 1843, under an assumed name in the *Publications* of the Ministry of the Interior.[124] A general survey of Siberian problems, administrative, economic, social, and educational was made by Basargin, a man of keen, analytical judgment.[125] Zavalishin made a study of the Amur region, gathered all possible information about it, and produced one of the best maps of the Transbaikal Province.[126] Gorbachevsky gathered material pertaining to shamanism in Eastern Siberia, and Küchelbecker was interested in local folklore and native customs. The Borisov brothers undertook botanical research; they also gathered a notable collection of insects, and developed a system of entomological classification that was later adopted by the French Academy of Sciences.[127] Alexander Bestuzhev, better known in literature as Marlinsky, wrote a number of stories in which Siberian life and character are admirably described. He also made a study of the various dialects of the aborigines. His brother, Nicholas Bestuzhev, busied himself with ethnographical studies; he compiled a Buriat dictionary and collected native legends and also made seismological observations.[128] Nicholas Bestuzhev was also a talented painter and he has left many interesting sketches of Siberian landscapes as well as portraits of the Decembrists.[129]

---

[123] *Istorichesky Viestnik*, XXXIV (1888), 758.

[124] [Steingel, Baron V. I.,] "Statisticheskoe opisanie Ishimskogo okruga Tobolskoi gubernii." *Zhurnal Ministerstva Vnutrennikh Diel*, II (1843), 3–48, 200–255.

[125] Basargin, *op. cit.*, 178ff.

[126] Zavalishin, *op. cit.*, 274.

[127] *Obshchestvennye Dvizheniia v Rossii*, I, 276.

[128] *Atenei*, III (1926), 23–24; *Vospominaniia Bestuzhevykh*, 317–318; Kotliarevsky, *Dekabristy: Odoevsky i Bestuzhev*, 234–235.

[129] *Vospominaniia Bestuzhevykh*, 316.

1

2

3

HOMES OF THE BESTUZHEVS (1 AND 3) AND TORSON (2).

Yakushkin made meteorological observations, some of which were later reported to the Berlin Academy of Sciences. Falenberg occupied himself with a topographical survey of the country, and Doctor Wolf studied the mineral waters in Siberia.[130]

Several Decembrists contributed to the study of Siberia by generously aiding distinguished scholars who conducted scientific expeditions to the East. Among these were the well-known expeditions of the nineteenth century conducted by Erman, Lessing, Humboldt, Middendorff, Hanstee, Due, and others.[131] Strange as it may seem, the willingness of the Decembrists to assist these scholars was opposed by the government and often involved such complications that all good intentions had to be abandoned. When Yakubovich wished to give valuable statistical data to the academician, Middendorff, a whole setup of bureaucratic machinery was brought into motion to obtain permission to comply with his innocent request. After a great deal of commotion and waste of paper, permission was granted; but it came a little too late: in Yeniseisk, on September 3, 1845, Yakubovich died.[132]

In 1828–29 Erman visited Siberia with an expedition which was a part of the one conducted by Humboldt. The members met many of the Decembrists, M. I. Muraviev-Apostol, Bestuzhev, Nazimov, Andreev, and others. These did their best to assist the scholars in securing the information they sought, even enriching the collections of the expedition by sacrificing some of their own accumulated articles and curiosities. Zaikin, who was a mathematician, lent his talent to the scientific magnetical observations.[133] Even the wives of the Decembrists were not indifferent to the interests of the scientists. Through their assistance Erman learned much about the artistic life of the natives. He writes:[134]

From none did I ever hear a more just appreciation of Siberian character. Their representation of the pantomimic dances, with which the natives accompany their songs, was given with such impressive grace as to surpass every performance that I had hitherto witnessed in Russia.

The assistance given by the Decembrists to the visiting scholars did not always end happily. Upon the return of Humboldt from

---

[130] *Ibid.*, 222–224; Zavalishin, *op. cit.*, II, 95ff.; Maksimov, *op. cit.*, 418.

[131] *Russkaia Starina*, VI (1881), 353–354.

[132] *Sibir i Dekabristy*, 111–112.

[133] Muraviev-Apostol, *op. cit.*, 66, 68.

[134] Erman, *op. cit.*, English translation, II, 180–181.

Siberia to St. Petersburg, he had a personal interview with Nicholas. The Emperor wished to know the impression that Humboldt had received in Siberia. As a compliment to the Emperor, Humboldt remarked that he was struck by the intelligence and courtesy of the Siberian officials. To his great annoyance Nicholas learned that the eminent scholar was referring to Semënov, a Decembrist who had been attached to Humboldt's company during his travels in the Province of Omsk. Extremely disappointed, Nicholas ordered Semënov transferred to Tobolsk, where stricter surveillance could be enforced, and the authorities responsible for allowing a "state criminal" to go on such a mission received a stern reprimand.[135]

The exile of the Decembrists resulted in the permanent implantation in Siberia of an intelligentsia. The fact is noteworthy for the reason that, previously, whatever there was of a Siberian intelligentsia strove always to move westward, but the Decembrists, the flower of the national youth, were forced eastward. Previously, all those who came to Siberia looked upon that country merely as a source of enrichment, and came with the ultimate intention to return to Western Russia as soon as the material gains were achieved. The greater part of the Decembrists, on the contrary, knew they were coming as permanent residents, and so they made themselves a part of Siberian society and participated in the development of the country. Zavalishin writes:[136]

We were the first to appear in Siberia as people of the higher class, entirely approachable and in addition with rules totally opposite to those which the inhabitants were accustomed to see displayed by their superiors and officials: they saw sympathy and the performance of good instead of oppression and extortion. For this reason no one ever kept a secret from us, be it a Russian, Siberian native, old inhabitant, or colonist, Cossack or sectarian—all of them revealed to us that which they would never have revealed to the government. Therefore we could study the country in its true light.

When on August 26, 1856, with the ascent of Alexander II to the throne, the Decembrists received an amnesty, their rights and privileges as well as titles being restored to them, not all of those who still survived availed themselves of the opportunity to return

[135] Muraviev-Apostol, M. I., *op. cit.*, 74–75; Lorer, *op. cit.*, 180–181.
[136] *Sibir i Dekabristy*, 96.

GRAVES OF THE BESTUZHEVS AND TORSON.

to the West.[137] Some of the Decembrists, though willing to return, were unable to do so on account of financial difficulties; others did not know where to go, being in total ignorance of the whereabouts of their relatives. Still others were unable to make the long journey because of old age. Bashmakov declined his amnesty, reasoning that the grave would be no warmer in Western Russia than in Siberia.[138] Those who returned to Russia entered with enthusiasm upon the enforcement of the Emancipation Reforms of 1861.[139] A few, like Raevsky, after long vacillation, returned two years after the amnesty had been granted. "The majority will not make use of the late grace," wrote Raevsky concerning the amnesty. "But that grace will be for their children. Of the hundred and twenty men, there remained alive, it seems, about twenty-five or twenty; they could be pardoned,—most of them are half-corpses."[140] Many of these "half-corpses" indeed preferred to continue their lives and to die in the country to which they had been exiled some three decades before. After a short sojourn in Western Russia, Raevsky, realizing that Siberia was more truly his home than was his birthplace, returned to Olonki, where he had lived in exile.[141] Among those who died in Siberia after the granting of the amnesty were Lutsky, M. Küchelbecker, Nicholas Bestuzhev, Gorbachevsky, and Raevsky.[142]

Those few Decembrists who survived to look back upon the years they had spent in Siberia, realized with a certain satisfaction that the years of exile had not been entirely wasted. Their presence in that country had left definite traces and had proved beneficial not only in a material sense, but in a cultural and moral one as well.[143] Despite extreme want, numerous unfavorable conditions, administrative tyranny, and other hardships, the Decembrists could show,

[137] *P.S.Z.*, No. 30883, Art. xv. The amnesty did not grant the surviving Decembrists complete liberty. First, it forbade them to reside in the two capitals, Moscow and St. Petersburg. Secondly, a secret police surveillance was continued throughout the rest of their days, a fact which some of them vigorously protested.—*Sibirskie Ogni*, V (1924), 152–154; *Diela i Dni*, I (1920), 410–413.

[138] *Sibirskie Ogni*, V (1925), 157.

[139] *Velikaia Reforma*, V, 229; Gorbachevsky, *op. cit.*, 260–298 *passim*.

[140] Altogether there were thirty-four Decembrists in Siberia at the time the amnesty was granted: thirteen in Western Siberia, and twenty-one in Eastern Siberia.

[141] Shchegolev, *Dekabristy*, 75.

[142] *Sibirskie Ogni*, V (1924), 155; Kubalov, *Dekabristy v Vostochnoi Sibiri*, 167; Golovachev, *op. cit.*, 172–176.

[143] Rozen, *op. cit.*, 212–213; Basargin, *op. cit.*, 215.

as a trophy of their Odyssey to Siberia, a generation that had been
educated by them or that had been, indirectly, influenced by them.
Pupils of the Decembrists remembered their teachers and followed
their instructions as they pursued the various walks of life. A few
of these pupils survived to witness the centennial jubilee of December 14, 1925.[144]

[144] Gorbachevsky, *op. cit.*, 264; Maksimov, *op. cit.*, 440; *Sibir i dekabristy*, 67–68; Kubalov, *op. cit.*, 190–191.

CONCLUSION

*I have long divided Russian history into two periods:
the first—Feudalism, since Rurik; the second—Despotism,
since Ivan III; as for the third the seed was sown on De-
December 14.*—M. POGODIN.

THE DECEMBRIST MOVEMENT represents a complex phenomenon in which deeply rooted economic, political, and social
factors were closely interwoven. To dissociate these from the
movement would be to lose its entire meaning; to limit the history
of the movement to the actual existence of the Decembrist Society,
1816–1825, would be to oversimplify its significance; and to attribute its origin solely to French influence is to be naïve. The
Decembrist movement was the outgrowth of a national condition
which can be traced far back into the eighteenth century. "Decembrism" itself was not merely a short-lived revolutionary idea; it
was an attitude held by at least two generations, a philosophy of
political rebellion which came to a climax on December 14, 1825.

The history of the eighteenth century, particularly of its second
half, distinctly pointed out the road which Russia was forced to
follow. It was during this period that the monarchy established
its centralized apparatus, enslaved the peasant masses, and refused
to recognize the disastrous consequences to which such a policy
would lead. The line of demarcation between Old and New Russia
was clearly drawn in the reign of Catherine II, and, strangely
enough, indirectly with her assistance. Beginning her reign with
ambitious projects for reforms, she inspired the hope that the
situation might be remedied by the government. The Legislative
Assembly soon proved the inefficacy of this noble gesture, and the
further enslavement of peasants convinced many of the futility
of expecting relief from above. The breach between the government
and the masses widened, or, in the words of one of the Decembrists,
the throne and the people drew apart.

In reply to the failure of the government to relieve the peasant
situation, the rebellion of Pugachev broke out and it was crushed
at the expense of an enormous loss of lives and property. But the
victory of the government did not eliminate the ills of Russia: the
peasant remained enslaved; the increasing urban population expected reforms which would grant it political recognition in this

[261]

medieval structure of society; developing industry desired an emancipated peasantry which it could exploit in the form of free labor. In the face of growing demands for reform, Prince Mikhail Shcherbatov, with the blind selfishness of his class, declared his amazement that anyone should think of depriving the nobility of some of its rights.[1]

With the accession to the throne of Alexander I, the hope that reform would be brought about by the government was again revived, not only because of economic necessity but also because of the more definite liberal tradition that the new generation had inherited from its predecessor. The names of Novikov, Radishchev, Pnin, and later of Ryleev and Pestel stand as symbols of two generations in two different centuries, each maintaining the same political idea. The fate of these men and the disillusion that followed the "constitutional Saturnalia" of the early reign of Alexander intensified the growing restlessness out of which arose the Decembrist movement.

On more than one occasion the government was given an opportunity to meet the demands of the time. Any one of the numerous constitutional projects of Radishchev, Mordvinov, Speransky, or Novosiltsov might have been taken as a pattern for beginning the great political task, but none of them was accepted sufficiently to pacify the grumbling of the masses. The peasant remained in his wretched condition, the institution of serfdom was preserved, and the monarchy continued as despotic as ever. All the attempts of statesmen like Speransky and economists like Mordvinov were disregarded. The crisis deepened. The lamentable financial condition handed over to Alexander went from bad to worse. The wars of 1805–6, the Continental Blockade, and, finally, the war of 1812–14 seriously undermined the economic structure of the state. The government tried to alleviate the situation by establishing military colonies, by giving a free hand to Arakcheev, and by assisting Metternich to maintain "peace and order" in Europe.

This unwillingness on the part of the government to make any appreciable attempt to institute reforms stimulated the formation of the Decembrist Society, a group which constituted the earliest political party, with a constructive program, to seek the overthrow, by force if necessary, of the existing government. The Decembrists strove chiefly for two aims: the abolition of serfdom, that gangrene

---

[1] *S.I.R.I.O.*, VIII, 59.

in the national body, and the limitation of autocratic power by some kind of representative government. In the program of the Decembrists these were the vital issues around which centered all reforms and from the solution of which derived other liberal legislation.

Conservative though the program of the Decembrists seems today, in the eyes of their contemporaries it was too radical. Thirty-six years later the son of the Emperor who had sent to the gallows the five leading Decembrists was compelled to embrace a part of that program, namely, emancipation of the serfs. Lack of statesmanship on the part of Nicholas I prevented the enforcement of a plan which would have spared much of the later unrest in the state. Instead, he created a popular martyrology, a beacon for succeeding generations, which shone ever brighter as time made it more distant. On the eve of his death Nicholas may have realized his mistaken policy when, in the Crimea, backward Russia was shattered by the blows of more advanced nations. It is said that, after witnessing the frightful corruption of the administration during that war, he sadly remarked: "Pestel and Bestuzhev would never have treated me in this fashion."

On December 14, 1825, Russian constitutionalism met a decisive defeat in its combat with autocracy, from which it did not recover for nearly two decades. Yet the Decembrists had their opportunity to wrest power from the old government. There were potentialities which only a few Decembrists duly appreciated and which nearly all of them were fearful of awakening. The main cause ascribed for their defeat was the dread, on the part of the leaders, of bringing about a social revolution and prolonged civil strife. "Of the 250,000 inhabitants of Moscow," warned a contemporary of the Society, "90,000 are serfs, ready to take up arms and go to all kinds of extremes."[3] The leaders of the Northern Society had planned the establishment of a government for the people but not by the people. Did not Riego restore the Spanish constitution with a handful of soldiers?

Leading members of the movement, especially those of the North, hoped, with the support of the army or at least a good proportion of it, that they could bring about a "peaceful revolution." "From now on Russia is free," reads a proclamation produced by Mu-

[2] Zavalishin, *Zapiski dekabrista*, I, 347–348.

[3] *Obshchestvennye Dvizheniia v Rossii*, I, 436.

raviev-Apostol and Bestuzhev-Riumin at the time of the revolt in
the South, "but, as true sons of the Church, let us not attempt any
crime, but without civil strife [let us] establish a government
of the people, based on the law of God which proclaims that 'whosoever will be chief among you, let him be your servant'." The
participation of the army or a part of it, so thought "dictator" Trubetskoi, would not necessarily mean an "armed revolution," but
only some form of demonstration or "armed pressure" which would
force the Monarchy to comply with the constitutional demands of
Russia.[4] The army was to have been kept in an orderly way at a
convenient place while negotiations were in process, and the change
was to have ended without serious social and economic upheaval.
The revolution was to preserve a lawful nature; otherwise, if
violence began and the army took part in it, "not even the devil
would be able to stop it."[5] The only violence that Trubetskoi would
admit of, was the possible necessity of assassinating the Emperor,
and this policy was a typical heritage of the political philosophy
of the old Guard.[6]

Thinking in terms of eighteenth-century palace revolutions
which were chiefly maneuvered by the Guard, the Decembrists,
as products of their time, endeavored to transform the Senate
Square into a *Place de la Révolution,* and their attempt was sadly
inadequate. Experience proved to the leaders the fallacy of such
idealistic plans when they came face to face with the grim reality
of the Russian monarchy. Even the more gallant stand taken by
the Southern Society had to fail, partly for the same reasons. Instead of a general social uprising, it proved to be merely the revolutionary outburst of an insignificant minority of young apostates
of their class who were scorned by the nobility and misunderstood
by the masses. If Countess Branitzka was willing to donate three
tons of iron for fetters for the rebels, ordinary folk regretted that
the sons of nobles were not all whipped or hanged in order to equalize them with the common people.[7] A true example of a tragedy of
political loneliness!

---

[4] *Materialy,* I, 18, 36–38, 65–66.

[5] Trubetskoi always dreaded social revolution. Some twenty years later he
wrote, "The present form of government cannot exist for ever, and woe if it
is changed by an uprising of the people!"—*Zapiski:* 85. See also *Materialy,* I,
18, 37–38.

[6] *Materialy,* I, 62–63.

[7] *Dekabristy. Neizdannye materialy,* 40. See also Gorbachevsky, *Zapiski i
pisma,* 359ff.

The opinion has occasionally been expressed that the attempt at violence drove the government to reaction and prevented the more evolutionary process of liberal reforms which Alexander I began. Such a belief is not justified by the evidence. It might be recalled that reaction began long before Nicholas came to the throne and that it was the despotic régime of Arakcheev which gave an impulse to the Decembrist movement. The subsequent reign of Nicholas was the concluding note of a chord originally struck by Arakcheev under the baton of Alexander. The spirit of the Holy Alliance had hovered over Russia long before December 14. Developments following that date, with all their absurdities, led to their logical conclusion, building up a political structure which had to collapse with the death of Nicholas in 1855. Scarcely had the bloodstains been washed off the Square when Nicholas pledged the assembled diplomatic corps to continue an unwavering policy of eradicating all sedition in his country in order "to give a lesson to Russia and to do a favor to Europe."[8] Like Alexander in the later years of his life, Nicholas was inclined to consider every liberal expression merely as a pernicious influence emanating from the plague-stricken West. Had not almost every Decembrist indicated that his ideas were derived from foreign books and magazines, from travels in Western Europe or from foreign tutors? The December uprising therefore convinced Nicholas of the importance of consolidating the Holy Alliance in order to check further revolutionary outbreaks elsewhere and thus eliminate possible repercussions at home; it proved also the necessity of isolating Russia from the West, where there was constant political fermentation. That this policy was introduced almost from the first day Nicholas came to the throne is indicated by the following quotation from his letter of December 28, 1825, to Constantine:[9]

According to news which reached me today there is proof that in yesterday's mail there is a notice about the arrival of eighty-four foreigners—French, Swiss and Germans. Since there is enough of our own rabble, I think it would be profitable and consistent with conditions of the present moment to forbid such facility of entrance into the country.

The Decembrists, or "mes amis de quatorze" as Nicholas used to refer to them, left an indelible impression upon him. Throughout his whole reign, no matter what happened, he always considered

---

[8] *Russkaia Starina,* IX (1907), 534; *Russky Viestnik,* IV (1893), 9.

[9] *Mezhdutsarstvie,* 170.

developments from a viewpoint determined by his sad memories of December 14; the least opposition he interpreted as an attempt to curb his monarchical power, and a limited monarchy Nicholas could not conceive of. In his political vocabulary there were but two terms, autocracy and republic, the former, of course, being the superior; to him a limited monarchy simply did not exist. The defeat of the rebels he was prone to consider a great victory, since he was inclined to magnify all opposition. And in defeating the hydra of revolution at home, insignificant as it was,—for it represented a trifling force as compared to that at the disposal of the state,—Nicholas carried away the impression that it was his duty to continue the battle further, into the very heart of all the trouble, Western Europe. Hence his boundless hatred for anything and anybody who threatened to upset the *status quo* and his unquestioned conviction that it was his sacred obligation, a divine mission, to maintain peace on the Continent and safeguard the ideals pronounced at the Congress of Vienna.

The Decembrists represented the liberal nobility, the Guard, and the younger army officers. This fact made Nicholas distrust these classes and build up his state on a more trustworthy basis, namely, on a rigid bureaucratic class subordinated to the Crown. Not counselors but soldiers who would faithfully execute his will Nicholas sought in the state. Every sign of localism, particularism, or striving for national autonomy was suspected as political heresy and quickly suppressed; everything was brought into submission, leveled, made subject to the cold northern capital, seat of Imperial Russia, where bureaucratic routine dominated human nature. Public opinion and free thought were declared taboo, and the newly instituted and much dreaded Third Division sought quite effectively to keep under its thumb every expression of social life. Never in the history of Russia did the government assist so much in widening the gap between society and the Crown. The two led an independent life, the first living on hope, the second on harsh reality. It was a dark time in the life of the nation—the "empty days"—which impelled Herzen to proclaim from his exile: "May the rule of Nicholas be damned for ever and ever! Amen!"

There is, however, a brighter light in the scene, which escaped the eye of the contemporary. In spite of the fact that it failed to achieve immediate positive results, the revolt of December 14, 1825, bore healthy seed. The testimonies of the Decembrists directed the government's attention to the gravity of the general condition in the state, to the increasing discontent, and the necessity for economic improvements. The government, to be sure, undertook no definite measures to relieve the situation, but there are sufficient indications that it began to realize the urgency of reform. The old state pilots of the time of Alexander were soon removed by Nicholas. On December 20, 1825, the mighty Arakcheev was dismissed from his duties as Director of the Imperial and Ministerial Chancellery, and five months later he retired of his own volition from the administration of the military colonies. The dismissal of Arakcheev was soon followed by that of other notorious figures of the preceding reign: Admiral Shishkov, the ill-famed Magnitsky, and Runich, and the none too saintly Father Fotius, all were compelled to retire. Mordvinov, General Ermolov, and Speransky had been for some time under the shadow of suspicion as tacit sympathizers with the Decembrist cause, but Speransky regained monarchical confidence and was thereby enabled to perform valuable service for the country in the improvement of conditions in respect to Russian law.

As a direct result of the trial Nicholas turned his attention to internal problems. On February 6, 1827, Borovkov, one of the chief secretaries of the Committee of Investigation, presented to Nicholas at his request a detailed Memorandum pertaining to the general national situation as based on the testimonies of the Decembrists. This document the Emperor kept on his desk during his whole reign and frequently referred to it. Borovkov himself had once been not immune to "dangerous ideas," but he quickly recovered under the blows of Nicholas, fully rehabilitated his political physique, and became a loyal subject of his master-sovereign. Attempting to reconcile his past idealism with present reality, he had cleverly composed a document in which he endeavored to show chiefly the constructive aspects of the efforts of the Decembrists, realized by officials, alas, only after the authors had been scattered through Siberia or had paid for them with their lives. He showed how the preceding reign of Alexander had unwittingly "fed youth with the milk of free thought," and how the whole administration had been shattered because of the lack of an efficient bureaucracy and clearly prescribed laws. He recommended codification of the body of national law, the enforcement of justice, a higher level of moral discipline among the clergy, the consolidation of the noble class, upon which the state might depend, a revival of commerce and industry through favorable legislation and liberal credits, improvements in the field of agriculture, abolition of the sale of serfs, encouragement of naval construction, and eradication of all political corruption and administrative sluggishness.[10] The recommendations of the Memorandum, which represented in reality a plagiarized Decembrist program, though honestly pursued were far from being fulfilled: the peasant problem remained practically unsolved; in the field of education the ruinous policy of Uvarov intensified the need for school reforms; and the outlawing of sects aided little toward an amicable solution of religious problems. Yet in certain fields Nicholas succeeded; and this, be it remembered, indirectly under the pressure of his hated "amis de quatorze."

One of Borovkov's recommendations, the necessity of compiling and codifying all Russian law, dates back to the early part of the eighteenth century. It was only natural that Nicholas, the ardent believer in strong government, who was convinced that happiness and prosperity depend upon well-specified laws, should undertake this task which his predecessors had failed to accomplish. Its importance was supported by frequent comments of the Decembrists indicating the legal chaos which prevailed in the country, to which, it may be added, they themselves fell victims. Kakhovsky, Alexander Bestuzhev, Steingel, Yakubovich, all those who were imprisoned, from their cells raised a common cry against "the total absence of law and justice in legal procedure," against the "evident sale of justice," and the lack of its enforcement, and against a system where bribery ruled decision, "where not life, honor and property of the citizen are protected, but biased verdicts are sold for gold and other advantages."[11]

Shortly after Nicholas came to the throne, Speransky, also, had directed the Emperor's attention to the necessity of reviving the work of codification. On April 25, 1826, a special commission headed by Speransky set to work, with the result that on April 1, 1830, there appeared the First Series of the *Complete Code of Russian Law*, in forty-five volumes, and two years later the Second Series in six volumes, an achievement which can scarcely be overlooked even by the antagonists of Nicholas I. This systematization and compilation continued during nearly all his reign.

---

[10] *Russkaia Starina*, XI (1898), 353ff.

[11] *Iz pisem i pokazanii dekabristov*, 25, 40, 57, 77.

ПОЛЯРНАЯ ЗВѢЗДА

25 Іюля 1826 года.

"THE FIVE CRUCIFIXIONS."

In addition to the influence which the Decembrists exercised in governmental matters, there might be added another sort of influence that was more important though less tangible, namely, the martyrdom of the Decembrists and the legend thus bequeathed to succeeding generations. During all Nicholas' reign, the press was forbidden to make any reference to the Decembrists or their whereabouts, and this fact alone was sufficient to create a "Decembrist myth." "The historical value of revolutions," stated a speaker at the hundredth anniversary of the Decembrist uprising, "depends upon three conditions: upon what they destroy, upon what they create, and upon the legends which they leave behind. . . . The Decembrists have not destroyed anything nor created anything. The value of their accomplishment consists entirely in their legend. But that is sufficient."[12] The revolutionaries of Russia soon hallowed the Decembrists as victims of autocratic injustice. Alexander Herzen, champion of the liberal cause and editor of the noteworthy *emigré* paper, *The Bell*, was mainly responsible for this glorification of the martyrs and for a constant emphasis upon the "five crucifixions." "I swore," he wrote in 1855, "to avenge the murdered men, and dedicated myself to the struggle with that throne, with that altar, with those cannons. I have not avenged them, the Guards and the throne, the altar and the cannon all remain, but for thirty years I have stood under that flag and have never once deserted it."[13] The legend of the Decembrists was no small contribution indeed: in awakening Herzen, it stimulated political agitation and opened the way for the revolutionary activities of the nineteenth century.[14] Herzen writes:[15]

The heritage we received from the Decembrists was the awakened feeling of human dignity, the striving for independence, the hatred for slavery, the respect for Western Europe and for the Revolution, the faith in the possibility of an upheaval in Russia, the passionate desire to take part in it, the youth and freshness of our energies.

The canister shot on the Senate Square awakened many of the youth in the country, including not only army officers, but also students and literary men who belonged to the Russian "Third

---

[12] Aldanov, "Pamiati dekabristov." *Golos Minuvshego na Chuzhoi Storone,* 2 (XV) (1926), 44.

[13] Herzen, *My Past and Thoughts,* I, 63.

[14] See Plekhanov, "14 dekabria 1825 goda." *Ocherki po istorii russkoi obshchestvennoi mysli XIX vieka. Sbornik statei,* 5.

[15] Herzen, *op. cit.,* VI, 204.

Estate."[16] Herzen, Ogarev, Chernyshevsky, Pisarev, Belinsky, and Petrashevsky, were all typical representatives of the generation that raised the banner of the Decembrists still higher and carried it to larger masses of the people during the dark reign of Nicholas, a reign truly characterized by Herzen as the "curious time of outer slavery and inner emancipation." Ryleev's dimly conceived notions of civil liberty, the broad federalist schemes of Nikita Muraviev, the revolutionary agrarian and political program of Pestel, the Pan-Slavic conception of the Borisov brothers, and the terroristic designs of Kakhovsky became the flesh and blood of the nineteenth-century social movement in Russia. The kinship between Pestel and Petrashevsky, between Ryleev and Herzen, between Kakhovsky, the would-be assassin of Alexander I, and Grinevetsky, the assassin of Alexander II, between the philosophical concepts of Zavalishin and those of Count Leo Tolstoi, is much closer than might appear to a superficial observer.[17] The "twenties," the "forties," the "sixties," the "eighties," all stand as distinct landmarks along the road of a struggle between Autocracy and Democracy that lasted through almost two decades of the twentieth century. The struggle ended with the downfall of Autocracy; it ended, also, with the emergence of a Democracy wearing a face so strange that a distrustful world refused it recognition.

---

[16] *Sbornik statei, posviashchennykh Lamanskomu,* II, 708–710.

[17] See *Dekabristy. Neizdannye materialy,* 194–195, footnote 1; *Pamiati Dekabristov,* III, 126.

APPENDIX

EXTRACTS FROM PESTEL'S TESTIMONY[1]

QUESTION 6 : How did the revolutionary ideas gradually develop and become implanted in men's minds? Who first conceived these ideas and continued to preach and spread them throughout the State?

ANSWER 6 : This question is very difficult to answer, for it must go beyond the realm of discussion about the secret Society. However, in order to fulfill the demand of the Committee I shall try so far as I can to explain it.

Political books are in the hands of everyone; political science is taught and political news spread everywhere. These teach all to discuss the activities and conduct of the Government, to praise one thing and assail another. A survey of the events of 1812, 1813, 1814, and 1815, likewise of the preceding and following periods, will show how many thrones were toppled over, how many others were established, how many kingdoms were destroyed, and how many new ones were created ; how many Sovereigns were expelled, how many returned or were invited to return and were then again driven out ; how many revolutions were accomplished ; how many *coup d'états* carried out—all these events familiarized the minds of men with the idea of revolutions, with their possibilities, and with the favorable occasions on which to execute them. Besides that, every century has its peculiar characteristic : ours is marked by revolutionary ideas. From one end of Europe to the other the same thing is observed, from Portugal to Russia, without the exception of a single state, not even England or Turkey, those two opposites. The same spectacle is presented also in the whole of America. The spirit of reform causes mental fermentation (*faire bouillir les esprits*). Here are the causes, I think, which gave rise to revolutionary ideas and which have implanted them in the minds of people. As to the cause of the spread of the spirit of reform through the country, it could not be ascribed to the Society, for the organization was still too small to have any popular influence.

---

[1] *Materialy,* IV, 94, 105.

EXTRACT FROM A LETTER OF KAKHOVSKY TO GENERAL LEVASHEV[2]

Your Excellency,

　　Dear Sir!

The uprising of December 14 is a result of causes related above. I see, Your Excellency, that the Committee established by His Majesty is making a great effort to discover all the members of the secret Society. But the government will not derive any notable benefit from that. We were not trained within the Society but were already ready to work when we joined it. The origin and the root of the Society one must seek in the spirit of the time and in our state of mind. I know a few belonging to the secret Society but am inclined to think the membership is not very large. Among my many acquaintances who do not adhere to secret societies very few are opposed to my opinions. Frankly I state that among thousands of young men there are hardly a hundred who do not passionately long for freedom. These youths, striving with pure and strong love for the welfare of their Fatherland, toward true enlightenment, are growing mature.

The people have conceived a sacred truth—that they do not exist for governments, but that governments must be organized for them. This is the cause of struggle in all countries; peoples, after tasting the sweetness of enlightenment and freedom, strive toward them; and governments, surrounded by millions of bayonets, make efforts to repel these peoples back into the darkness of ignorance. But all these efforts will prove in vain; impressions once received can never be erased. Liberty, that torch of intellect and warmth of life, was always and everywhere the attribute of peoples emerged from primitive ignorance. We are unable to live like our ancestors, like barbarians or slaves.

But even our ancestors, though less educated, enjoyed civil liberty. During the time of Tsar Aleksei Mikhailovich the National Assembly, including representatives of various classes of the people, still functioned and participated in important affairs of the State. In his reign five such Assemblies were summoned. Peter I, who killed everything national in the State, also stamped out our feeble liberty. This liberty disappeared outwardly but lived within the hearts of true citizens; its advancement was slow in our country. Wise Catherine II expanded it a little; Her Majesty inquired

---

[2] *Iz pisem i pokazanii dekabristov*, 3–18.

from the Petersburg Free Economic Society concerning the value
and consequences of the emancipation of peasants in Russia. This
great beneficial thought lived in the heart of the Empress, whom
the people loved. Who among Russians of her day and time could
have read her Instruction without emotion? The Instruction
alone redeems all the shortcoming of that time, characteristic of
that century.

Emperor Alexander promised us much; he, it could be said,
enormously stirred the minds of the people toward the sacred rights
of humanity. Later he changed his principles and intentions. The
people became frightened, but the seed had sprouted and the roots
grew deep. So rich with various revolutions are the latter half of
the past century and the events of our own time that we have no
need to refer to distant ones. We are witnesses of great events. The
discovery of the New World and the United States, by virtue of its
form of government, have forced Europe into rivalry with her. The
United States will shine as an example even to distant generations.
The name of Washington, the friend and benefactor of the people,
will pass from generation to generation; the memory of his devotion to the welfare of the Fatherland will stir the hearts of citizens.
In France the revolution which began so auspiciously turned, alas,
at the end from a lawful into a criminal one. However, not the
people but court intrigues and politics were responsible for that.
The revolution in France shook all the thrones of Europe and had
a greater influence upon the governments and peoples than the
establishment of the United States.

The dominance of Napoleon and the war of 1813 and 1814 united
all the European nations, summoned by their monarchs and fired
by the call to freedom and citizenship. By what means were countless sums collected among citizens? What guided the armies? They
preached freedom to us in Manifestoes, Appeals, and in Orders!
We were lured and, kindly by nature, we believed, sparing neither
blood nor property. Napoleon was overthrown! The Bourbons were
called back to the throne of France and, submitting to circumstances, gave that brave, magnanimous nation a constitution, pledg-
ing themselves to forget the past. The Monarchs united into a Holy
Alliance; congresses sprang into existence, informing the nations
that they were assembled to reconcile all classes and introduce
political freedom. But the aim of these congresses was soon revealed; the nations learned how greatly they had been deceived.

The Monarchs thought only of how to retain their unlimited power, to support their shattered thrones, and to extinguish the last spark of freedom and enlightenment.

Offended nations began to demand what belonged to them and had been promised to them—chains and prisons became their lot! Crowns transgressed their pledges, the constitution of France was violated at its very base. Manuel, the representative of the people, was dragged from the Chamber of Deputies by gendarmes! Freedom of the press was restricted, the army of France, against its own will, was sent to destroy the lawful liberty of Spain. Forgetting the oath given by Louis XVIII, Charles X compensates *émigrés* and for that purpose burdens the people with new taxes. The government interferes with the election of deputies, and in the last elections, among the deputies only thirty-three persons were not in the service and payment of the King, the rest being sold to the Ministers. The firm, courageous Spanish people at the cost of blood rose for the liberty of their country, saved the King, the Monarchy, and the honor of the Fatherland; of their own volition the people themselves received Ferdinand as King. The King took the oath to safeguard the rights of the people. As early as the year 1812, Alexander I recognized the constitution of Spain.

Then the Alliance itself assisted France by sending her troops, and thus aided in dishonoring her army in the invasion of Spain. Ferdinand, arrested in Cadiz, was sentenced to death. He summoned Riego, swore to be once more loyal to the constitution and to expel the French troops from his territory, and begged Riego to spare his life. Honest men are apt to be trustful. Riego gave guaranty to the Cortes for the King, and he was freed. And what was the first step of Ferdinand? By his order Riego was seized, arrested, poisoned and, half-alive, that saint-martyr hero who renounced the throne offered to him, friend of the people, savior of the King's life, by the King's order is now taken through the streets of Madrid in the shameful wagon pulled by a donkey, and is hanged like a criminal. What an act! Whose heart would not shudder at it? Instead of the promised liberty the nations of Europe found themselves oppressed and their educational facilities curtailed. The prisons of Piedmont, Sardinia, Naples, and, in general, of the whole of Italy and Germany were filled with chained citizens. The lot of the people became so oppressive that they began to regret the past and to bless the memory of Napoleon the conqueror! These are the incidents which enlightened their minds and made them realize that it was impossible to make agreements with Sovereigns. . . . .

The story told to Your Excellency that, in the uprising of December 14 the rebels were shouting "Long live the Constitution!" and that the people were asking "What is Constitution, the wife of His Highness the Grand Duke?" is not true. It is an amusing invention. We knew too well the meaning of a constitution and we had a word that would equally stir the hearts of all classes— LIBERTY!

* * *

The events of December are calamitous for us and, of course, must be distressing to the Emperor. Yet the events of this date should be fortunate for His Imperial Highness. After all, it was necessary sometime for the Society to begin its activities, but hardly could it have been so precipitate as in this instance. I swear to God, I wish the kind Sovereign prosperity! May God aid him in healing the wounds of our Fatherland and to become a friend and benefactor of the people. . . .

Most obedient and devoted servant of Your Excellency,

1826   PETER KAKHOVSKY.

February, 24th day

EXTRACT FROM A LETTER OF A. BESTUZHEV TO NICHOLAS I[3]

Your Imperial Highness!

Convinced that You, Sovereign, love the truth, I dare to lay before You the historical development of free thinking in Russia and in general of many ideas which constitute the moral and political basis of the events of December 14. I shall speak in full frankness, without concealing evil, without even softening expressions, for the duty of a loyal subject is to tell his Monarch the truth without any embellishment. I commence.

The beginning of the reign of Emperor Alexander was marked with bright hopes for Russia's prosperity. The gentry had recuperated, the merchant class did not object to giving credit, the army served without making trouble, scholars studied what they wished, all spoke what they thought, and everyone expected better days. Unfortunately, circumstances prevented the realization of these hopes, which aged without their fulfillment. The unsuccessful, ex-

---

[3] *Iz pisem i pokazanii dekabristov,* 33–44.

pensive war of 1807 and others disorganized our finances, though we had not yet realized it when preparing for the national war of 1812. Finally, Napoleon invaded Russia and then only, for the first time, did the Russian people become aware of their power; only then awakened in all our hearts a feeling of independence, at first political and finally national. That is the beginning of free thinking in Russia. The government itself spoke such words as "Liberty, Emancipation!" It had itself sown the idea of abuses resulting from the unlimited power of Napoleon, and the appeal of the Russian Monarch resounded on the banks of the Rhine and the Seine. The war was still on when the soldiers, upon their return home, for the first time disseminated grumbling among the masses. "We shed blood," they would say, "and then we are again forced to sweat under feudal obligations. We freed the Fatherland from the tyrant, and now we ourselves are tyrannized over by the ruling class." The army, from generals to privates, upon its return, did nothing but discuss how good it is in foreign lands. A comparison with their own country naturally brought up the question, Why should it not be so in our own land?

At first, as long as they talked without being hindered, it was lost in the air, for thinking is like gunpowder, only dangerous when pressed. Many cherished the hope that the Emperor would grant a constitution, as he himself had stated at the opening of the Legislative Assembly in Warsaw, and the attempt of some generals to free their serfs encouraged that sentiment. But after 1817 everything changed. Those who saw evil or who wished improvement, thanks to the mass of spies were forced to whisper about it, and this was the beginning of the secret societies. Oppression by the government of deserving officers irritated men's minds. Then the military men began to talk: "Did we free Europe in order to be ourselves placed in chains? Did we grant a constitution to France in order that we dare not talk about it, and did we buy at the price of blood priority among nations in order that we might be humiliated at home?" The destructive policy toward schools and the persecution of education forced us in utter despair to begin considering some important measures. And since the grumbling of the people, caused by exhaustion and the abuses of national and civil administrations, threatened bloody revolution, the Societies intended to prevent a greater evil by a lesser one and began their activities at the first opportunity. . . .

You, Sovereign, probably already know how we, inspired by such a situation in Russia and seeing the elements ready for change, decided to bring about a *coup d'état*. . . . . Here are the plans we had for the future. We thought of creating a Senate of the oldest and wisest Russian men of the present administration, for we thought that power and ambition would always have their attraction. Then we thought of having a Chamber of Deputies composed of national representatives. . . . . For enlightenment of the lower classes we wished everywhere to establish Lancasterian schools. And in order to bring about moral improvement we thought of raising the standard of the clergy by granting to them a means of livelihood. Elimination of nearly all duties, freedom from distillation and road improvement for the state, encouragement of agriculture and general protection of industry would result in satisfying the peasants. Assurance and stability would attract to Russia many resourceful foreigners. Factories would increase with the demand for commodities, while competition would stimulate improvement, which rises along with the prosperity of the people, for the need of commodities for life and luxury is constant. . . .

Most devoted servant of
Your Imperial Highness,
ALEXANDER BESTUZHEV.

[No date]

EXTRACT FROM A LETTER OF V. STEINGEL TO NICHOLAS I[4]

. . . No matter how many members there may be found of the secret Society or those who had only known of it; no matter how many may be deprived of freedom on account of it, there still remain a great many people who share those ideas and sentiments. Russia is already so educated that even shopkeepers read newspapers and newspapers report what is said in the Chamber of Deputies in Paris. Is not the first thought to occur in everyone's mind, "Why cannot we discuss our rights?" The greater number of professors, literary men, and journalists have to adhere wholeheartedly to those who wish a constitutional government, for freedom of the press is to their personal advantage. So do booksellers and merchants. Finally, all those who were in foreign countries, and some who were educated there, and all those who served or serve now in the Guard hold the same opinions. Who of the young

---

[4] *Iz pisem i pokazanii dekabristov*, 69–70.

men, even somewhat educated, have not read and have not been fascinated with the works of Pushkin, which breathe freedom? Who has not cited the fables of Denis Davydov, such as his "Head and Feet"? Perhaps among those who have the fortune to surround Your Honor, there are such. Sovereign! In order to eradicate free thinking, there is no other means than to destroy an entire generation, born and educated in the last reign. But if this is impossible, there remains one thing—to win hearts by kindness and attract minds by decisive and evident means toward the future prosperity of the state.

Most devoted,

January 11th day   Baron Vladimir Ivanov Steingel.
1826

Extract from a Letter of A. Yakubovich to Nicholas I[5]

Your Highness!

... In describing the condition of Russia I did not reproach the authorities, but pointed out the source of present-day evils and those which threaten us in the distant future. Sovereign! The antiquated structure of the state administration demands important changes. The Empire, in the little over a hundred years since it emerged from the darkness of crude ignorance, has undergone every quarter of a century complete changes in the formation of ideas and in moral demands. Grant equal advantages to Your soldiers by lowering the term of military service; by decisive legislative measures and strict execution make everyone fulfill his duties, spread the light of science and education, give liberty to commercial activities, and the restless or the *Carbonari* will vanish like darkness in the face of the sun. You will be the benefactor and savior of the Fatherland from many calamities, and the love of Your grateful fifty-two million subjects will only be the beginning of Your immortal glory.

Devoted subject of Your
Imperial Highness,

1825, December 28
Peter and Paul Fortress   Alexander Yakubovich.
Cell No. 3

---

[5] *Iz pisem i pokazanii dekabristov*, 81.

RELATIONS BETWEEN THE SOUTHERN AND POLISH SECRET SOCIETIES[6]

(From the Testimony of M. Bestuzhev-Riumin)

At the Kiev fair in 1824 I learned from Chodkiewicz that there existed a Society, which, upon finding that we had a similar organization, wished to enter into negotiations. I reported this to the Directory, which gave me instructions to conclude an agreement. This agreement consisted:

ON OUR PART:

(1) Russia, preferring to have noble allies instead of secret enemies, upon completing her reforms would grant Poland independence.

(2) There would be a new delimitation, and for the sake of retaining friendly and beneficial relationships the provinces which have not been sufficiently Russified would be restored to Poland.

(3) At the same time the interests of those who would be compelled to remain on Russian soil on account of strategic demarcation would be respected.

(4) The Poles could, however, hope to receive back the Provinces of Grodna, part of Vilna, Minsk, and Volynsk.

(5) With the confirmation of the agreement, the Russian Society would give protection to Poles who happened to carry on their work in Russia, provided that that work was not in conflict with national interests.

(6) The Russian Society would use all means to eradicate the antagonism which exists between the two peoples, realizing that in the age of enlightenment in which we live the interests of all peoples are identical, and imbedded hatred is the attribute only of barbaric ages.

(7) For further relations each party appoints deputies who will be instructed:

(*a*) That they communicate to their respective directories everything designated for them or present information requested by the other party.

(*b*) Polish deputies will inform the Russian Society concerning developments in Western Europe.

(*c*) It is strictly forbidden to deputies to name or request them to name any members of either society.

---

[6] *Dekabristy. Otryvki iz istochnikov*, 203–204.

(*d*) If a Russian deputy meets members of the Polish Society, or a Polish deputy meets members of the Russian Society, they must not reveal that the two organizations have entered into any relationships.

(*e*) All intercourse between the two directories is to be carried out through deputies only.

(*f*) The deputies cannot agree to nor promise anything without the consent of their respective directories.

ON THE PART OF THE POLES:

The Poles are obligated to:

(1) use all means, regardless of what kind, to prevent Grand Duke Constantine Pavlovich from returning to Russia;

(2) rebel simultaneously with us;

(3) attack the Lithuanian Corps, should it move against us;

(4) give us all possible assistance at their disposal;

(5) arrange relations between us and political societies which function in Western Europe;

(6) inform us about all important matters as soon as they know of them;

(7) act during the revolution according to the instructions of our Society, and recognize themselves as our subordinates;

(8) adopt a republican form of government.

The Oath for Members Who Enter the United Slavs[7]

Upon joining the United Slavs for the liberation of myself from tyranny and for the restoration of freedom, which is so precious to the human race, I solemnly pledge on these arms brotherly love, which is to me divine and from which I expect the fulfillment of all my desires. I swear to be always virtuous, always loyal to our aim, and to observe the deepest secrecy. Hell itself with all its horrors will not be able to compel me to reveal to the tyrants my friends and their aims. I swear that only when a man proves undoubted desire to become a participant, will my tongue reveal the Society; I swear, to the last drop of my blood, to my last breath, to assist you, my friends, from this sacred moment. Special activity will be my first virtue, and mutual love and aid my sacred duty. I swear that nothing in the world will be able to move me. With sword in hand I shall attain the aim designated by us. I will pass

---

[7] *Materialy*, V, 17.

through a thousand deaths, a thousand obstacles — I will pass through, and dedicate my last breath to freedom and the fraternal union of the noble Slavs. Should I violate this oath, then let remorse be the first vengeance for my hideous offense, let the point of this sword turn against my heart and fill it with hellish torment; let the moment of my life that is injurious to my friends, be the last one; let my existence be transformed into a chain of unheard misery from the fatal moment that I forget my pledge. May I see all that is dear to my heart perish by this weapon and in horrible suffering, and this weapon, reaching me, the criminal, cover my body with wounds and cast infamy upon me; and the accumulated burden of physical and moral evil shall impress on my forehead the sign of a monstrous son of Nature.

A MANIFESTO, DRAWN BY "DICTATOR" TRUBETSKOI[8]
ON THE EVE OF DECEMBER 14, 1825

The Manifesto of the Senate should proclaim:

(1) abolition of the former government;

(2) establishment of a Provisional Government until a permanent one is decided upon by representatives;

(3) freedom of the press, hence abolition of censorship;

(4) religious tolerance to all faiths;

(5) abolition of the right to own men;

(6) equality of all classes before the law and therefore abolition of military courts and all sorts of judicial commissions from which all cases proceed to civil courts;

(7) announcement of rights for every citizen to occupy himself with whatever he wishes and therefore—nobleman, merchant, middle-class man, peasant—all to have equal right to enter military, civil, or clerical service, trade wholesale or retail, paying established taxes for such trade; to acquire all kinds of property such as land, or houses in villages and cities; make all kinds of contracts among themselves, or summon each other for trial;

(8) cancellation of poll tax and arrears;

(9) abolition of monopolies on salt and alcohol; permission for free distillation and for the procuring of salt with payment of tax according to the respective amounts of salt and alcohol produced;

(10) abolition of recruiting and military colonies;

[8] *Materialy*, I, No. 43, pp. 107–108.

(11) reduction of the term of military service for privates to be followed by equalization of military service of all classes;

(12) retirement without exception of all privates who have served fifteen years;

(13) the creation of Community, County, Gubernia, and Regional administrations, which are to be substituted for all civil service men appointed formerly by the government;

(14) public trials;

(15) introduction of a jury system in criminal and civil courts. There shall be created an administration of two or three persons to which all the highest officers of the government shall be subordinated, such as the Ministry, the Council, the Ministerial Committee, the Army and Navy: in a word, the entire Supreme Executive government, but not the legislative nor judicial. For the latter there remains the Ministry subordinated to the Provisional Government, but for decision of cases not passed upon by the lower courts there will remain a department of the Senate which shall handle civil and criminal cases; its members shall remain in service until a permanent administration is established.

The Provisional Government is instructed to:

(1) equalize all classes;

(2) form all local, Community, County, Gubernia, and Regional administrations;

(3) form a National Guard;

(4) form a judicial branch with a jury;

(5) equalize recruiting obligations among all classes;

(6) abolish a permanent army;

(7) establish a form of election of representatives to the Lower Chamber which will have to ratify the future form of Government.

AN APPEAL[9]

The Lord took pity on Russia and sent death to our tyrant. Christ said: you shall not be slaves of men, for you were redeemed by my blood. The world did not listen to this sacred command and fell into misery. But our suffering moved the Lord, and today He is sending us freedom and salvation. Brethren! Let us repent of our long servility and swear: let there be a sole Tsar in Heaven and on Earth, Jesus Christ.

[9] *Materialy*, IV, 256.

All misfortunes of the Russian people derived from autocratic government. It broke down. By the death of the tyrant the Lord signifies His will—that we throw off from ourselves the chains of slavery, which are repugnant to Christian law. From now on Russia is free. But as true sons of the Church, let us not attempt any crime, but, without civil strife, establish a government of the people, based on the law of God which proclaims: "And whosoever will be chief among you, let him be your servant."

The Russian army hopes to establish a government of the people, based upon sacred law. And so, let this pious people of ours remain in peace and tranquillity and pray the Lord for the most speedy accomplishment of our sacred undertaking. The servants of the altar who have been forsaken in poverty and scorned to this day by the impious tyrant now pray the Lord for us in restoring in all glory the Temples of God.

[Written by S. Muraviev-Apostol and M. Bestuzhev-Riumin.]

THE MEMORY OF PESTEL IN THE VIATSKY REGIMENT[10]

Report of Yaretsky, Secretary of the Zaslavsky Lower Court, November 22, 1826

Since my appointment I have had nothing worth while to report to you, but, at the moment the Viatsky Infantry Regiment was quartered in the town of Zinkov, I tried to investigate what rumors were popular among the military men, and I have found as follows.

(1) All privates and officers are sorry for Pestel, their former commander, saying that they were well off under him, and that they had been expecting something even better. Should any one among the military men happen to recall Pestel, suddenly everyone with a heavy sigh and in tears replies that such a commander there never was nor ever will be. I have heard this myself from many; and Jews, almost all of them, who also heard it from military men, have reported the same to me.

(3) The head musician who is quartered at the home of the Jewess Dreizee, while drunk in the presence of many Jews, scolded Maiboroda for having reported Pestel, praised the latter, and expressed sorrow for him. At the same time, he said that Pestel before his death made a statement to the effect that what he, Pestel, had sown, would come up, nay, it would necessarily have to come

---

[10] *Russky Arkhiv*, VI (1905), 309–310.

up. Filatov repeated this before Volee Zeilikovich and other privates as well as many Jews.

(4) On the whole, all officers and privates hate the new commander terribly, revile him behind his back, and call him stupid, a fool, a boor, and other epithets.

EMPEROR NICHOLAS TO GRAND DUKE CONSTANTINE[11]

December 23, 1825

St. Petersburg

Cher Constantin! Je commence par Vous assurer, qu'avec l'aide de Dieu, tout est rentré ici dans l'ordre habituel; l'esprit est très bon et le deviendra encore plus, quand on Vous verra ici.

Depuis ma dernière, Komarovsky, que j'avais envoyé à Moscou, est revenue porteur ou plutôt pour confirmer toutes les excellentes nouvelles que j'avais déjà. Un semblable rapport m'est déjà parvenu de Finlande et de Mohilew; j'en attends de la 2de armée.

Nos enquêtes vont parfaitement, ainsi que les arrestations de tous les individus apportés, membres de cet horrible et extraordinaire complot; un extrait de ce qui se passe sous ce rapport Vous est envoyé par ce courrier; Vous y verrez des noms bien connus, et j'ai les soupçons les plus fondés pour être persuadé que cela remonte jusqu'au Conseil d'État, nommément jusqu'à Mordvinoff; mais comme j'ai pour règle de ne mettre la main que sur ceux qui sont dévoilés ou trop fortement soupçonnés pour pouvoir les laisser libres je ne presse rien.

Lounine est positivement de la bande, et quant à moi, j'y vois l'énigme de sa rentrée au service chez Vous et de tout le zèle qu'il a fait voir; il est de fait, qu'il est chargé de se faire un parti là-bas; mon opinion, si j'ose en avoir, serait de ne pas l'arrêter, mais de tâcher de le prendre sur le fait, ce qui ne peut ni tarder, ni manquer. Ici l'on est tout zèle pour m'aider à cette affreuse besogne; *des pères m'amènent leurs fils;* tous désirent des exemples et surtout voir leur famille purgée de pareils êtres et même de soupçons de ce genre.

J'attends *Michel Orloff* et *Lopouchin* qui doivent déjà être arretés; ceux de la 2de armée sont les plus importants, ce que Vadkofsky, amené hier, ainsi que tous les autres confirment. C'est surtout Pestel et Serge Volkonsky, qu'il m'importe d'avoir; j'attends aussi Mouravieff et Tchernischeff; violà, où nous en sommes.

[11] *S.I.R.I.O.*, CXXXI, 12–13.

Je suis abîmé de besogne, Vous le comprendrez, me plaindrez et ne m'en voudrez pas du désordre de ce lignes; mais la tête me tourne, et l'essentiel est que Vous sachiez tout. J'ai écrit au prince-lieutenant; j'ai cru bien faire. Grabowsky, que j'ai chargé au sujet de l'armée : sur cela dictez ce que Vous voulez. Michel m'a parlé de l'événement du corps de Lithuanie, j'attends Vos ordres et la forme pour cela que Vous désirez. Adieu, adieu, à Vous pour la vie de toute mon âme et de tout mon cœur.

NICOLAS.

Je baise les pieds à ma sœur, que Dieu nous la conserve; j'embrasse Paul et Kourouta.

NICHOLAS TO CONSTANTINE[12]

January 5, 1826
St. Petersburg

La nouvelle, que je reçois à l'instant de la révolte du régiment de Tchernigoff, par Mouravieff-Apostol, au moment même, où il devait être arrêté, m'engage sans délai de Vous faire part, cher Constantin, que je mets le 3 corps sous Vos ordres, ce dont j'ai écrit à Sacken, et je Vous autorise de prendre toutes les mesures que Vous jugerez nécessaires pour empêcher les progrès de ce germe de révolte; Vous pouvez en conséquence faire marcher toutes les troupes de *Vos deux corps,* que Vous trouverez nécessaire d'employer, en informant le général en chef, pour qu'il puisse, de son côté, régler les démarches de son armée. Je désirerai éviter de faire entrer en Russie les troupes de l'armée Polonaise, à moins que la chose ne devienne indispensable.

Le général en chef a pris les mesures qu'il fallait; je ne puis en dire autant de Tscherbatoff, qui a laissé passer un temps précieux, ce qui me fait craindre, vu la direction qu'a prise Muravieff, que le régiment de Poltava, commandé par Tisenhausen, n'aura pas été arrêté, ainsi que celui des hussards d'Achtir et une batterie à cheval, dont les commandants devaient aussi être arrêtés, ne se joignent. Le prince Volkonsky, qui est dans le voisinage, s'il n'est pas déjà arrêté, probablement se joindra à eux; ainsi voilà à peu près 6.000 à 7.000 hommes de probables, à moins qu'il ne se trouve des honnêtes gens qui sauront maintenir l'ordre.

J'attends des nouvelles ultérieures et me réglerai là-dessus pour donner la publicité nécessaire à la chose, pour prévenir les faux bruits.

---

[12] *S.I.R.I.O.*, CXXXI, 25–26.

Je ne puis Vous en dire davantage, ni Vous répondre sur Votre chère et excellente lettre, reçue ce matin du 31, et pour celle par Guillaume ; je n'en puis plus. Que Dieu nous préserve de nouveaux malheurs. Je Vous embrasse de cœur et d'âme, pour la vie, avec le plus sincère et inaltérable dévouement. Mettez-moi aux pieds de ma belle-sœur et embrassez Paul.

Votre tout dévoué et fidèle frère et ami

NICOLAS.

Mille tendresses à Kourouta.

CONSTANTINE TO NICHOLAS[13]

June 14, 1826
Warsaw

C'est Opotchinine que je charge de cette lettre, cher et excellent frère, et que je commence par Vous remercier pour celle que Vous m'avez écrite en date du 16/28 de ce mois et que j'ai reçu par un *feldjäger*. Je ne saurais assez Vous témoigner toute ma reconnaissance pour tout ce que Vous m'y dites, ainsi que pour la confiance, que Vous voulez bien avoir en moi ; soyez persuadé, cher frère, que je n'en abuserai pas et que je m'efforcerai de la mériter par tous mes moyens ; je Vous remercie, de même, pour tous les papiers que Vous m'avez envoyés au sujet des enquêtes et de la mise en jugement des coupables ; il faut convenir que le rapport est un tissu d'horreurs, dont rien n'approche et, si jamais exemple était nécessaire, c'est bien la cas ; toutes Vos dispositions et tout ce que Vous voulez bien me marquer à ce sujet est parfaitement conforme à mon opinion. Il est inouï, pourtant, comment est-ce que chose semblable a pu se couver si longtemps sans être découverte ; une chose qui m'étonne et que je Vous soumets, en toute confiance, c'est la conduite d'Orloff et comment est-ce qu'il a fait pour tirer son épingle du jeu et rester sans mise au jugement. La *Rousskaya Pravda* de Pestel est une véritable bouffonade, si la chose ne serait pas si sérieuse ; je lui croyais plus de bon sens et d'esprit et il ne dénote qu'un fou et un brouhaha d'idées mal conçues et mal digérées,—c'est à hausser les épaules ! Que le bon Dieu Vous assiste, cher frère, dans ces moments de sévérité, si nécessaire malheureusement.

Chez nous, grâce à Dieu, tout est parfaitement tranquille jusqu'à

---

[13] *Ibid.*, CXXXI, 79–80.

ce moment et tout marche d'après les principes donnés et comme par le passé. J'espère de Sa toute clémence, qu'il daignera nous maintenir dans cet état de choses au futur. . . .

CONSTANTIN.

NICHOLAS TO CONSTANTINE[14]

July 14, 1826
Elagin Ostrov

Le bon Dieu a permis, cher et excellent Constantin, que nous voyons la fin du terrible procès; hier l'exécution a eu lieu; cinq des plus coupables d'après la décision du tribunal suprême ont été pendus; les reste dégradé, cassé et condamné, à vie ou à des termes plus ou moins longs, au travaux forcés et à perpétuité. Que Dieu soit mille fois béni de nous avoir sauvés et qu'Il daigne faire en sorte que ni nous, ni nos petits enfants n'ayons plus de scènes pareilles. Tout s'est passé avec le plus grand calme, ordre et indignation.

Aujourd'hui à la même place, où le 14 le pauvre Miloradowitsch est tombé, nous avons servi un Te Deum et des prières funèbres pour lui et ceux qui ont péri ce jour; la garnison était sous les armes et il n'y a pas eu un spectateur, qui n'ait été vivement ému, en commençant par Votre serviteur. Que Dieu en soit encore mille et mille fois béni. N'allez pas croire cependant que je croie que l'on puisse s'endormir à cette heure; bien au contraire, je prêche à chacun de redoubler d'attention, pour éviter des esclandres ou des contre-coups, et il faut constamment avoir l'œil au guet. . . .

NICOLAS.

MADAME VOLKONSKAIA TO HER MOTHER FROM SIBERIA[15]

Blagodatsky rudnik
Nerchinsk
Ce 12 février 1827

Chère et bonne Maman, je suis enfin établie dans le même village que mon adoré Serge, c'est beaucoup, mais cependant mon cœur n'est point satisfait. D'abord je ne saurai vous donner une idée de la maigreur et de l'air malade de mon pauvre Mari. Sa santé m'inquiète il a besoin de tous mes soins et je ne puis les lui donner. Non, je ne le quitterai point tant que son sort n'ait éprouvé un

---

[14] *S.I.R.I.O.*, CXXXI, 85–86.

[15] *Russkie Propilei*, I, 4–5.

grand soulagement, je ne donnerai point un regret à mon fils, je ne reviendrai à lui qu'avec l'âme parfaitement tranquille, dusse-je attendre les quatorze ans.—Quelque pénibles que soient les conditions que l'on impose à mon cœur pour prix de mon séjour ici je m'y soumets avec une fidélité religieuse, je ne ferai aucune tentative pour voir mon Mari hors les jours désignés, je dois être reconnaissante pour ce que l'on m'accorde déja pour atteindre le but de mon existence. Oui, chère Maman, plus mon Mari est malheureux et plus il doit compter sur mon attachement et ma persévérance. Je n'en veux pas à mes parens de ce qu'ils m'aient privé jusqu'ici de la seule consolation que je puis avoir celle de partager le sort de Serge; je sais qu'il est bien plus difficile de souffrir pour son enfant que pour soi-même, et c'est pourquoi je ne me permets pas un murmure; bien au contraire je suis heureuse de leur avoir prouvé que je sais remplir mes devoirs envers eux, j'ai patienté et aussi chacune de mes actions a été accompagnée des bénédictions de mon vénérable Père.—Il me reste maintenant à leur donner les consolations qu'il est dans mon pouvoir de leur procurer encore et c'est pourquoi je désire que mon fils retourne dans ma famille; d'ailleurs climat de Petersbourg lui est fort nuisible, je n'oublierai jamais tout ce que j'y ai souffert lorsque mon pauvre enfant y a gagné le croupe.

Adieu ma chère Maman, ne communiquez point ma lettre à ma bonne sœur Sophie, l'ange consolateur de Serge, elle pourait l'attrister et nuire à sa faible santé. Je compte lui écrire, sous peu, et la tranquilliserai de mon mieux. Chargez-vous chère Maman de mes respects pour mon frère Répnine, dites lui que je ne cesserai jamais de voir mon second Père en lui, mille tendresses de ma part à sa respectable femme ainsi qu'à mes chères Neveux et Nièces surtout Varette Répnine.

Votre obéissante fille,
Marie Wolkonsky.

Reflections Upon the Fate of the Decembrists[16]

(From the Archives of Count N. S. Mordvinov)

Les criminels de la dernière conjuration sont morts pour la Russie Européenne et ne doivent à jamais y jouir des droits civils. Mais ils ont tous reçu, à l'exception d'un très petit nombre, l'édu-

---

[16] *Arkhiv grafov Mordvinovykh*, VIII, 41–42.

cation cultivée; ils possèdent tous les éléments nécessaires pour redevenir des hommes utiles à l'état, et les connaissances acquises peuvent servir pour acquérir d'autres d'une utilité plus majeure que celles qu'ils possèdent.

La plupart d'eux s'occupaient de la poésie, de la politique abstraite, des sciences métaphysiques, qui exercent l'imagination, égarent et souvent corrompent la raison. La Sibérie n'a pas besoin de ces sciences. Mais la méchanique, la physique, la chimie, la minéralogie, la métallurgie, la géologie et l'agriculture, sciences positives, peuvent faire prospérer la Sibérie, le pays que la nature a enrichi de ses dons. Ces mêmes criminels peuvent devenir des professeurs de ces sciences, se régénérer à l'utilité publique.

Le but est grand et puissant pour reformer même le moral vicieux, qui les a rendus criminels. On pourrait former d'eux une académie, dont le principe serait celui que les membres ne s'occupent que des sciences ci-dessus mentionnées et qu'il n'y ait dans la bibliothèque de l'académie que des livres dont l'objet est purement de celles qui sont positives.

Ayant perdu la noblesse en Russie, il serait de leur réserver le droit d'acquérir celle de la Sibérie. Leur avancement à cette dignité pourrait être institué sur les règles académiques. Et puisque les épouses de ces malheureux veulent généreusement suivre leurs maris et partager leurs sort, il serait de la magnanimité de notre auguste souverain d'accorder à leurs enfants futurs les droits de la noblesse sibérienne, circonscrite dans les limites de cette partie de la Russie. Les enfants et ceux qui ne sont pas mariés et qui pourraient le devenir, jouiront des droits accordés à l'éducation académique.

1826.

BIBLIOGRAPHY

THE ENORMOUS AMOUNT of material with which the student of the Decembrist movement must deal makes the task of bibliographical selection difficult. An attempt will be made to classify and to discuss the materials in the following order: (1) bibliographical guides, (2) sources, (3) memoirs, (4) secondary accounts, and (5) periodical literature. These will be discussed only so far as they pertain strictly to the Decembrist movement.

BIBLIOGRAPHICAL GUIDES

1. General Bibliographies.—For a general bibliography on Russian history, V. I. Mezhov, *Russkaia Istoricheskaia Bibliografiia* ("Russian Historical Bibliography"), and V. S. Ikonnikov, *Opyt Russkoi Istoriografii* ("A Treatise of Russian Historiography"), are the standard works. Though published more than three decades ago, these books contain numerous references bearing directly upon the Decembrist movement. Of particular value is the work of Ikonnikov, which gives a superb evaluation of all Russian archival material, without which much would remain terra incognita. The only adequate bibliography in English is that of Robert J. Kerner, *Slavic Europe*. In searching for material the student will also find it helpful to consult two comparatively smaller bibliographies, which constitute a convenient supplement to the bibliographies of Mezhov and Ikonnikov. These are: *Dva Vieka Russkoi Literatury* ("Two Centuries of Russian Literature") by N. K. Piksanov, and *Ukazatel' Zhurnal'noi Literatury* ("A Guide to Periodical Literature") by N. A. Ulianov and V. N. Ulianova. For current publications the best bibliographies are: *Knizhnaia Lietopis'* ("Annals of Book Publications") and *Zhurnal'naia Lietopis'* ("Annals of Periodical Literature"). The first is a weekly publication, listing all books, the second a bimonthly, giving an exhaustive list of articles, conveniently classified by subject, which appear in current Russian periodicals.

2. Topical Bibliographies.—Among the topical bibliographies there is the monumental work of N. Chentsov, *Vosstanie Dekabristov. Bibliografiia* ("The Uprising of the Decembrists. A Bibliography"), representing the result of long and scholarly labor, and including material published to 1929 that concerns the Decembrist

movement. It is to be hoped that in the near future Mr. Chentsov
will be able to supplement his bibliography with an additional
publication of material now rapidly accumulating. This bibliography includes 4451 titles, classified by subject with many sub-
divisions and numerous cross-references, citing verbatim tables of
contents, thus making it possible to judge the exact nature of the
works listed. The only regrettable comment on the work is that it
lacks a convenient index.

Of the other topical bibliographies there might be mentioned
the one by Militsa V. Nechkina and E. V. Skazin, *Seminary po
Dekabrizmu* ("A Seminar on Decembrism"), and another by
A. Shilov, *Chto Chitat' po Istorii Russkogo Revoliutsionnogo
Dvizheniia* ("What to Read on the History of the Russian Revolutionary Movement"). Both bibliographies, particularly the first,
are compiled for graduate students, and sources are arranged according to the various subjects which a study of the Decembrist
movement might suggest.

3. Bibliographical Reviews.—In addition to the aforementioned
bibliographies, there are the excellent bibliographical reviews
which recently appeared in *Istorik Marksist,* by Nechkina, and in
Le Monde Slave. The first is valuable for its bibliographical suggestions in respect to recent historical writings of Ukrainian
scholars. Finally, there is a thorough review by IU. G. Oksman of
the sources pertaining to the uprising in the South, in the form
of a Preface to the sixth volume of documents of the Decembrist
movement, *Vosstanie Dekabristov. Materialy* ("The Uprising of
the Decembrists. Sources"), Vol. VI, pp. ix-lxvii.

Sources

Most of the sources published prior to 1925 are too fragmentary.
Among those worthy of notice are *Memuary Dekabristov* ("Memoirs
of the Decembrists"), edited by M. Dovnar-Zapolsky⟨ *Iz Pisem i
Pokazanii Dekabristov* ("Extracts from Letters and Testimonies
of the Decembrists"), compiled by A. K. Borozdin; and the collection of documents edited by Bazilevsky (Bogucharsky), *Gosudarstvennye Prestupleniia v Rossii v XIX Vieke* ("State Offenses
in Russia in the Nineteenth Century"). The first two consist of
extracts from memoirs, the testimonies of various Decembrists, and
their letters to Nicholas I. The collection of Borozdin, it should be
noted, is a careless one, containing many errors, and is therefore

recommended with some hesitance. The compilation of Bazilevsky is significant as it contains reprints from many government papers and journals, most of which are today unavailable outside of Russia. Such, for example, is the official paper, *Russky Invalid* ("Russian Invalid"), or *Senatskie Viedomosti* ("Senate Journal"), or *Viedomosti St. Peterburgskoi Gorodskoi Politsii* ("St. Petersburg Police Gazette"). Other sources can be found in the *Sbornik Imperatorskogo Russkogo Istoricheskogo Obshchestva* ("Publications of the Royal Russian Historical Society"). Volumes CXXXI and CXXXII are of special significance, for they contain the correspondence of Nicholas I and Constantine in which the events of 1825–26 are well reflected.

Source material has been greatly enriched in the last few years, thanks to the interest displayed in the Decembrist movement by the Soviet authorities. The hundredth anniversary of the Decembrist uprising, which was celebrated in 1925, marked an increased publication of various documents pertaining to the subject. Of these there must be mentioned first the monumental publication of the *Proceedings* of the trial, under the title *Vosstanie Dekabristov. Materialy* ("The Uprising of the Decembrists. Sources"). It is to comprise eight volumes (the seventh has not yet appeared) and represents the basic source for a study of the rise and development of Decembrist secret societies. The testimonies of the chief defendants, numerous official documents, and correspondence are fully cited, with the original form of spelling, and supplemented by many facsimiles. Of this set the first, fourth, and sixth volumes are the most important: the first two because they contain the testimonies of the leaders of the Northern and Southern Societies; the last because it throws a new flood of light upon an insufficiently explored field of the Decembrist movement, the Society of the United Slavs and the uprising of the Chernigovsky regiment.

Among the publications which have lately appeared and which have greatly enriched the sources is the *Krasny Arkhiv* ("Red Archive"). Volume XIII, a jubilee issue, is of special interest, containing important material, for example, the Memoranda of Nicholas Turgenev and Mikhail Orlov to Nicholas I concerning their relation to the Decembrist movement; the recently discovered economic treatise of Pestel, which appears in print for the first time; the official correspondence concerning the uprising in the Zerentuisk mines, led by I. Sukhinov in an attempt to free the

prisoners, and a number of other equally significant documents.
For those who are handicapped because of poor library facilities,
the special collection of abridged documents, entitled *Dekabristy.
Sbornik Otryvkov iz Istochnikov* ("Decembrists. A Collection of
Extracts from Sources"), will prove of great assistance. The editor
of this publication, IU. G. Oksman, has succeeded in compiling
a unique source book, including extracts from official papers,
memoirs, and testimonies, texts of the various constitutional projects of the Decembrists, the text of the *Green Book,* extracts from
Russian Justice, and other documents not easily available outside
of Russia.

MEMOIRS

There is no lack of *Memoirs* of the Decembrists themselves nor
of their contemporaries. Particularly deserving of attention are
those of Turgenev, Yakushkin, Zavalishin, Trubetskoi, Obolensky,
Lorer, Rozen, Gorbachevsky, and Beliaev. Additional light may
be obtained in the somewhat lesser known *Memoirs* of Poggio,
Gangeblov, and M. I. Muraviev-Apostol. Reminiscences of various
laymen-Decembrists have recently appeared in a series of publications entitled: *Vospominaniia i Rasskazy Deiatelei Tainykh
Obshchestv 1820-kh godov* ("Reminiscences and Narratives of Participants of Secret Societies of the 1820's").

The abundance of autobiographic literature does not necessarily
assist in clarifying various episodes; in fact, it often adds confusion. Many of these "Memoirs" and "Reminiscences" contradict
each other or interpret certain facts variously; others, like those
of Turgenev, were written to rehabilitate the authors; finally, there
are the *Memoirs* of the type "I told you so," like those of Zavalishin. These sources, therefore, cannot be accepted indiscriminately. They were nearly all written years later, in the form of
apologies, some with a distinct bias, others unwittingly partial,
when the long time that had passed had obscured many details.

Yet the student may find in the *Memoirs* many sidelights which
can scarcely be obtained elsewhere. The characteristics of individuals or of certain important events, as frequently revealed in
these personal recollections, assist in presenting a fuller picture of
the period. Such are the invaluable descriptions of the Bestuzhev
brothers, where a narration of the northern uprising is to be
found in interesting and fairly authentic detail; of Gorbachevsky,

which similarly describe the southern uprising and the Society of United Slavs; of Trubetskoi and Yakushkin, whose accounts of Nicholas during the trial are illuminating; or those of Zavalishin, Basargin, Rozen, and Steingel in respect to exile life in Siberia. The recent publication of documents relating to the trial of the Decembrists revealed that the *Memoirs* of Gorbachevsky represent a remarkably reliable source; in spite of certain minor errors, on the whole the book gives a fairly accurate picture of the developments in the South. Strangely enough, Gorbachevsky's *Memoirs* and personal letters to his close friend, Prince Obolensky, have been overlooked by many students and only recently have begun to receive a more appropriate appreciation.

Finally, the student of early nineteenth-century Russian history should not overlook the valuable *Memoirs* of N. Grech and F. F. Vigel, which contain a wealth of material pertaining to the political and literary aspects of the time. The postwar period, the growing liberal movement, and the new generation affected by these events are admirably described in both these sources.

Secondary Authorities

Distinguished among the secondary works on the Decembrist movement is the study of that eminent scholar V. I. Semevsky, *Politicheskie i Obshchestvennye Idei Dekabristov* ("The Political and Social Ideas of the Decembrists"), which, though outstanding in its field, is limited to a study of the origin of liberal ideas among the Decembrists. The author deals neither with the formation of the Society nor its activities. In this connection two other studies must be mentioned. They are: *Idealy Dekabristov* ("The Ideas of the Decembrists") and *Tainoe Obshchestvo Dekabristov* ("The Secret Society of the Decembrists"), by M. Dovnar-Zapolsky. These works deal with the general political situation during the second half of the reign of Alexander I and the formation of secret societies. Economic aspects are barely touched upon and the uprising itself is completely omitted.

On the revolt in the North there has recently been published an admirable study by A. E. Presniakov, *14 Dekabria 1825 Goda* ("December 14, 1825"), based on the latest evidence, but it has no footnotes and lacks a bibliography. The book is supplemented by an equally admirable analysis, written by G. Gabaev, of the military aspects of the northern uprising, a subject barely dealt with in historical literature. This work may be recommended to persons interested in the art of civil warfare.

The Southern Society has received less attention among writers, though in many respects it played a more important rôle. The Slavs, especially, have scarcely been considered at all. Lately a study of the history of the Society of United Slavs has been made by M. V. Nechkina. This is the best work to date, but the subject is by no means exhausted and demands further investigation. Valuable contributions in this field have been made in collected studies of Ukrainian scholars, by the Ukrainian Academy of Sciences, in publications entitled *Dekabristi na Ukraini* ("The Decembrists in the Ukraine") and *Rukh Dekabristiv na Ukraini* ("The Decembrist Movement in the Ukraine"). The movement is presented mainly as related to the national aspirations of the Ukrainian people, a subject of considerable interest to contemporary writers.

Among the general histories of Russia containing important chapters devoted to the Decembrist movement may be mentioned those by A. Pypin, by the late M. N. Pokrovsky, and by N. Rozhkov respectively. The first represents the school of the second half of the nineteenth century which was inclined to overidealize the whole subject, and the latter two give the Marxian interpretation of the movement. The more conservative views are set forth in the works of M. A. Bogdanovich and of the court historian, N. K. Shilder. In spite of Shilder's definite conservatism his work is of significance since the author in his well-known biographies of Alexander I and Nicholas I cites a large number of documents, some of which are of utmost importance.

PERIODICAL LITERATURE

The periodical literature is rich in all sorts of publications, beginning with official sources, memoirs, secondary works, and monographs. Of the two periodicals of particular value must be mentioned *Russkaia Starina* ("Russian Antiquity") and *Russky Arkhiv* ("Russian Archive"). Both contain a wealth of material which no student can afford to overlook. Numerous personal accounts, official documents, important scholarly contributions, and extracts from private family archives in these two publications make them indispensable for the study of modern Russian history. The student will also be rewarded for his consultation of the archives of various eminent Russian families, for example, those of the Raevskys, Mordvinovs, Vorontsovs, and Viazemskys. Many articles and monographs by outstanding Russian scholars may be found in the prerevolutionary periodicals, *Viestnik Evropy* ("The Messenger of Europe"), *Istorichesky Viestnik* ("Historical Messenger"), *Russkaia Mysl'* ("Russian Thought"), *Russky Viestnik* ("Russian Messenger"), and *Zhurnal Ministerstva Narodnogo Prosvieshcheniia* ("Journal of the Ministry of Public Education"). Of the later publications *Krasny Arkhiv* ("Red Archive"), previously referred to, must be remembered. It is an irregular periodical dealing mainly with nineteenth-century Russian history, the bulk of its matter consisting chiefly of documents of various kinds. Finally, the *Istorik Marksist* ("The Marxist Historian"), representing the Marxian point of view and published by the Institute of the Communist Academy, is of great value. In this periodical are the contributions of contemporary Russian scholars, together with a bibliography, frequently critical, which makes it possible to follow the current historical publications in Soviet Russia.

Those interested in the lives of the Decembrists in Siberia will find the recent publications of official documents indispensable. These are: *Sibir i Dekabristy* ("Siberia and the Decembrists") and *Dekabristy v Zabaikalie* ("The Decembrists in the Transbaikal"). Valuable contributions have been made in this field by individual scholars, particularly by A. I. Dmitriev-Mamonov, who gathered important data concerning the Decembrists in western Siberia, and by B. Kubalov, whose interest in the exiles was much more extensive. In a series of penetrating monographs Professor Kubalov gives a description of how the Decembrists, in spite of the most adverse circumstances, succeeded in becoming useful members of Siberian society. Scattered articles dealing with the lives of the Decembrists in their exile may be found in the various Siberian periodicals such as *Sibirskie Ogni* ("Siberian Lights"), *Zhizn' Buriatii* ("Life of Buriatia"), *Sovetskaia Sibir* ("Soviet Siberia"), and *Severnaia Aziia* ("Northern Asia").

Materials other than those mentioned above are also listed in the following bibliography. In addition, it may be stated that, because of the unexpected length which this bibliography had already attained, many titles cited in the text had to be omitted. To facilitate the finding of sources mentioned in the footnotes only, special care was taken to indicate all necessary information concerning place and date of publication.

BIBLIOGRAPHICAL GUIDES

I. GENERAL BIBLIOGRAPHIES

IKONNIKOV, V. S. *Opyt russkoi istoriografii* (A treatise of Russian historiography). Kiev, 1891–1908. Four parts in 2 vols.

KERNER, ROBERT J. *Slavic Europe. A selected bibliography in the western European languages.* Cambridge, Harvard University Press, 1918.

Knizhnaia Lietopis' (Annals of book publications). Rossiiskaia tsentral'naia palata pri gosudarstvennom izdatel'stve. M., I, 1907–.

MEZHOV, V. I., *Russkaia istoricheskaia bibliografiia za 1865–1876 gg.* (Russian historical bibliography, 1865–1876). St.P., 1882–90. 8 vols.

Supplement: *Bibliographie des livres et articles russes d'histoire et sciences auxiliaires de 1800–1854.* St.P., 1892–93. 3 vols.

PIKSANOV, N. K., *Dva vieka russkoi literatury* (Two centuries of Russian literature). M., 1923.

ULIANOV, N. A., AND ULIANOVA, V. N. *Ukazatel' zhurnal'noi literatury, alfavitnyi, predmetnyi, sistematichesky, 1896–1905 gg.* (A guide to periodical literature, alphabetic, topical, systematic, 1896–1905). Ed. 2. M., 1913.

Zhurnal'naia Lietopis' (Annals of periodical literature). Tsentral'naia knizhnaia palata. M., I, 1926–.

2. TOPICAL BIBLIOGRAPHIES

Bibliografiia revoliutsionnogo rukhu v Odesi, 1820–1920 (A bibliography of the revolutionary movement in Odessa, 1820–1920), I, new series. Odessa, Pratsi Odes'koi derzhavnoi Naukovoi Biblioteki, 1933.

CHENTSOV, N. M. *Vosstanie dekabristov. Bibliografiia* (The uprising of the Decembrists. Bibliography). M.-L., Tsentrarkhiv, 1929.

NECHKINA, M. V., AND SKAZIN, E. V., *Seminary po dekabrizmu* (A seminar on Decembrism). Ed. by V. NEVSKY. M., "Prometei," 1925.

SHILOV, A. *Chto chitat' po istorii russkogo revoliutsionnogo dvizheniia. Ukazatel' vazhneishikh knig, broshiur i zhurnal'nykh statei* (What to read on the history of the Russian revolutionary movement. A guide to the most important books, pamphlets and articles). L., 1922.

3. BIBLIOGRAPHICAL REVIEWS

A. P. "Bibliographie décabriste." *Le Monde Slave*, XII (1925), 473–480.

A. P. "La littérature russe sur le Décabrisme." *Ibid.*, I (1926), 124–139.

NECHKINA, M. V. "Novye materialy o vosstanii dekabristov (New sources pertaining to the uprising of the Decembrists)." *Istorik Marksist, V* (1927), 217–220.

NECHKINA, M. V. "Stoletie vosstaniia dekabristov v iubileinoi literature, 1825–1925 gg. (The hundredth anniversary of the Decembrist uprising in the jubilee literature, 1825–1925)." *Istorik Marksist*, II (1926), 238–250.

NECHKINA, M. V. "Ukrainskaia iubileinaia literatura o dekabristakh (Ukrainian jubilee literature on the Decembrists)." *Ibid.*, III (1927), 187–195.

OKSMAN, IU. G. "Vosstanie Chernigovskogo polka. Obzor istochnikov i printsipy ikh publikatsii (The uprising of the Chernigovsky regiment. A review of the sources and the methods of their publication)." *Vosstanie Dekabristov. Materialy,* VI, pp. ix–lxvii.

SOURCES

ANDERSON, JAMES. *The constitutions of Free-Masons.* London, 1723.

Arkhiv brat'ev Turgenevykh (The archive of the brothers Turgenev). Petrograd, 1911–1921. 6 vols.

Arkhiv dekabrista S. G. Volkonskogo (The archive of the Decembrist S. G. Volkonsky). Edited by Prince S. M. VOLKONSKY and B. MODZALEVSKY. Petrograd, 1918.

Arkhiv grafov Mordvinovykh (The archive of the Mordvinov family). Foreword and notes by V. A. BILBASOV. St.P., 1901–3. 10 vols.

Arkhiv kniazei Viazemskikh. See *Ostafievsky Arkhiv.*

Arkiv kn. Vorontsova (The archive of Prince Vorontsov). M., 1870–95. 40 vols.

BAGALY, OLGA. "Materialy do istorii dekabriskogo rukhu na Ukraini (Sources pertaining to the history of the Decembrist movement in the Ukraine)." *Narisi z Sotsial'no-Ekonomichnoi Istorii Ukraini,* I, 295–324. Kiev, 1932.

BAZILEVSKY, V. (ED.) See *Gosudarstvennye prestupleniia. . . .*

BOROZDIN, A. K. (COMP.). See *Iz pisem i pokazanii dekabristov.*

Dekabrist N. I. Turgenev. Pis'ma k bratu S. I. Turgenevu. M., Akademiia Nauk SSSR., 1936.

Dekabristi na Ukraini. Zbirnik (The Decembrists in the Ukraine. A collection). Zbirnik prats komisii dlia doslidi v gromads'kikh techii na Ukraini. Za red. akad. S. Efremova ta V. Miiakovskogo. Kiev, Ukrainska Akademiia Nauk. Zbirnik istorichno-filologichnogo viddilu, No. 37 (1926).

Dekabristy. Neizdannye materialy i stat'i (The Decembrists. Unpublished sources and articles). Edited by B. L. MODZALEVSKY and IU. G. OKSMAN. M., 1925.

Dekabristy. Sbornik materialov (The Decembrists. A collection of sources). L., "Priboi," 1926.

Dekabristy. Sbornik otryvkov iz istochnikov (The Decembrists. A collection of extracts from sources). Compiled by IU. G. OKSMAN, N. F. LAVROV, and B. L. MODZALEVSKY. M., Tsentrarkhiv, 1926.

Dekabristy i tainye obshchestva v Rossii (The Decembrists and secret societies in Russia). M., Izd. V. M. Sablina, 1906.

Dekabristy na poselenii. Iz arkhiva Yakushkinykh (The Decembrists in exile. From the archive of the Yakushkin family). M., 1926.

Dekabristy v Buriatii (The Decembrists in Buriatiia). Verkhneudinsk, 1927.

Dekabristy v Minusinskom okruge (The Decembrists in the Minusinsk region). Minusinsk, 1925.

Dekabristy v Zabaikalie (The Decembrists in the Transbaikal). Neizdannye materialy pod red. A. V. Kharchevnikova. Chita, 1925.

DOVNAR-ZAPOLSKY, M. *Memuary dekabristov.* See *Memuary dekabristov.*

DUBROVIN, N. "K istorii russkoi tsenzury 1814–1820 gg. (Concerning the history of Russian censorship, 1814–1820)." *Russkaia Starina,* XII (1900), 643–664.

Gosudarstvennye prestupleniia v Rossii v XIX vieke. Sbornik iz ofitsialnykh izdanii pravitelstvennykh soobshchenii (State offenses in Russia in the XIX century. A collection of official editions of government information). Compiled by BAZILEVSKY (BOGUCHARSKY), V. Stuttgart, 1903–4. 2 vols.

Graf Arakcheev i voennye poseleniia 1809–1831 gg. Materialy dlia noveishei russkoi istorii (Count Arakcheev and the military colonies, 1809–1831. Sources pertaining to recent Russian history). St.P., Izd. Russkaia Starina, 1870.

"Imushchestvennoe polozhenie dekabristov (Property status of the Decembrists)." *Krasnyi Arkhiv,* XV, 164–213.

Istoricheskie dokumenty iz vremeni tsarstvovaniia Aleksandra I (Historical documents pertaining to the time of the reign of Alexander I). Ed. 3. Leipzig, 1880.

"Iz arkhiva dekabrista V. L. Davydova. Neizdannye pis'ma (From the archive of the Decembrist V. L. Davydov. Unpublished letters)." With commentaries by N. K. PIKSANOV. *Istorik Marksist,* I (1926), 175–200.

"Iz arkhiva K. F. Ryleeva (From the archive of K. F. Ryleev)." *Byloe,* V (1925), 28–46.

Iz pisem i pokazanii dekabristov (Extracts from letters and testimonies of the Decembrists). Compiled by A. K. BOROZDIN. St.P., 1906.

KARAMZIN, N. M. *Zapiska o drevnei i novoi Rossii* (Memorandum of an old and new Russia). St.P., 1914.

Krasnyi Arkhiv (Red Archive). Vol. XIII is of special importance.

KROPOTKIN, P. A., *Dnevnik* (Diary). M., 1923.

LEHMANN, A. (ED.) *Der Tugendbund.* Aus den hinterlassenen Papieren des Ministers Professor Dr. Hans Friedrich Gottlieb Lehmann. Berlin, 1867.

Lettres et Papiers du Chancelier Comte de Nesselrode, 1760–1850; extraits des ses archives. Paris, 1904–12. 11 vols.

MARTENS, F. *Recueil des traités et conventions, conclus par la Russie avec les puissances étrangères.* St.P., 1874–1909. 15 parts in eight volumes.

"Materialy po istorii buntov v voennykh poseleniiakh pri Aleksandre I (Sources pertaining to the history of the uprisings in the military colonies during [the reign of] Alexander I)." *Diela i Dni,* III (1922), 148–165.

Memuary dekabristov (Memoirs of the Decembrists). Comp. by M. DOVNAR-ZAPOLSKY. Kiev, 1906.

Mezhdutsarstvie 1825 goda i vosstanie dekabristov v memuarakh i perepiske chlenov tsarskoi sem'i (The interregnum of 1825 and the uprising of the Decembrists as reflected in memoirs and correspondence of the members of the royal family). Compiled by B. E. SYROECHKOVSKY. M., Tsentrarkhiv, 1926.

Ostafievsky Arkhiv kniazei Viazemskikh (The Ostafievsk archive of the Viazemsky family). St.P., 1899–1913. 5 vols.

Pamiati Dekabristov. Sbornik materialov (In memory of the Decembrists. A collection of sources). Leningrad, Akademiia Nauk, 1926. 3 vols.

PAVLOV-SILVANSKY, N. *Dekabrist Pestel pered verkhovnym ugolovnym sudom* (The Decembrist Pestel before the supreme criminal court). Rostov n/D., 1907.

PESTEL, P., "Prakticheskie nachala politicheskoi ekonomii (Practical beginnings of political economy)." *Krasnyi Arkhiv*, XIII, 1925, 174–249.

PESTEL, P., *Russkaia Pravda. Nakaz Verkhovnomu Vremennomu Pravleniiu* (Russian Justice. Instruction to the Supreme Provisionary Government). Edited by P. SHCHEGOLEV. St.P., 1906.

Polnoe Sobranie Zakonov Rossiiskoi Imperii s 1649 po 1825 god (Complete code of laws of the Russian Empire from 1649 to 1825). First Series. St.P., 1830. 45 vols.

"Les rapports de l'ambassade d'Autriche à Saint-Pétersbourg sur la conjuration des Décabristes." *Le Monde Slave*, XII (1925), 447–473; I (1926), 89–124; II, 293–315; III, 448–470.

"Raskhody gosudarstvennogo kaznacheistva na dekabristov (Expenditures of the state treasury on the Decembrists)." *Byloe*, V (1925), 79–108.

REDDAWAY, W. F. (ED.) *Documents of Catherine the Great; the Correspondence with Voltaire and the Instruction of 1767, in the English text of 1768.* Cambridge, England, University Press, 1931.

REMIZOV, ALEXIS (ED.) "Lettres de la famille Pestel." *Le Monde Slave*, XII (1925), 400–413.

Rukh dekabristiv na Ukraini (The Decembrist movement in the Ukraine). IUvileine vidaniia Ukrtsentrarkhiva, Kharkiv, 1926.

RYLEEV, K. F. *Polnoe Sobranie Sochineniia* (Complete works). M., "Academia," 1934.

Sbornik Imperatorskogo Russkogo Istoricheskogo Obshchestva (Publications of the Royal Russian Historical Society). St.P., 1867–1916. (Cited as S.I.R.I.O.) 148 vols.

Sibir i Dekabristy (Siberia and the Decembrists). Pod red. M. K. AZADOVSKOGO, M. E. ZOLOTAREVA, and B. G. KUBALOVA. Irkutsk, 1925.

"Tri pis'ma dekabrista Petra Borisova (Three letters of the Decembrist Borisov)." *Katorga i Ssylka*, VI (1926), 57–65.

VERNADSKY, G. *La charte constitutionelle de l'empire russe de l'an 1820.* Paris, 1933.

Vosstanie dekabristov. Materialy po istorii vosstaniia dekabristov. Diela verkhovnogo ugolovnogo suda i sledstvennoi komissii, kasaiushchiesia gosudarstvennykh prestupnikov (The uprising of the Decembrists. Sources pertaining to the history of the Decembrist uprising. Proceedings of the supreme criminal court and the committee for investigation, concerning the state criminals). Editor, M. N. POKROVSKY. M., Tsentrarkhiv, 1925–29. 8 vols. (The seventh volume has not yet appeared. The source is cited as *Materialy*.)

YAKUSHKIN, V. E. (ED.) *Gosudarstvennaia vlast' i proekty gosudarstvennoi reformy v Rossii* (The power of the state and projects for state reforms in Russia). St.P., 1906.

MEMOIRS

ANNENKOVA, POLINA. *Vospominaniia* (Reminiscences). M., 1929.

ARSEN'EV, I. A. "Vospominaniia (Reminiscences)." *Istorichesky Viestnik*, XXVII (1887), 69–81ff.

BASARGIN, N. V. *Zapiski* (Memoirs). Petrograd, 1917.

BELIAEV, A. P. "Vospominaniia (Reminiscences)." *Russkaia Starina,* XXIX, 1–42ff. Separate edition, St.P., 1882.

BOLOTOV, A. *Zhizn' i prikliucheniia* (Life and adventures). M., 1931. 3 vols.

BOROVKOV, A. D. "Avtobiograficheskie zapiski (Autobiographic notes)." *Russkaia Starina,* IX (1898), 533–564ff.

CHAIKOVSKY, M. "Zapiski (Memoirs)." *Russkaia Starina,* XI (1895), 155–184ff.

CZARTORYSKI, A. *Memoirs and correspondence with Alexander I.* Edited by ADAM GIELGUD. London, 1888. 2 vols.

DIVOV, P. G. "Dnevnik (Diary)." *Russkaia Starina,* LXXXIX (1897), 459–494.

ERMAN, G.-A. *Reise um die Erde.* Berlin, 1838. English translation, *Travels in Siberia.* London, 1848. 2 vols.

FONVIZIN. See VonVisin.

FROLOV, A. F. "Vospominaniia (Reminiscences)." *Russkaia Starina,* V (1882), 465–482ff.

GANGEBLOV, A. S. "Vospominaniia (Reminiscences)." *Russky Arkhiv,* VI (1886), 181–268.

GEBEL, A. G. "Iz zapisok (From notes)." *Russky Arkhiv,* 1871, 1717–1728.

GOLOVINA, V. N. *Memoirs of Countess Golovine, a lady at the court of Catherine II.* London, 1910.

GORBACHEVSKY, I. I. *Zapiski i pisma* (Memoirs and letters). M., 1925.

GRECH, N. *Zapiski o moei zhizni* (Memoirs of my life). M., 1930.

HERZEN, A. *Byloe i dumy* (My past and thoughts). M., 1931–32. 3 vols. English translation, London, 1924–27.

KÜCHELBECKER, V. K. *Dnevnik* (Diary). Leningrad, 1929.

LORER, N. I. *Zapiski dekabrista* (Memoirs of a Decembrist). M., 1931.

LUBIANOVSKY, F. P. "Vospominaniia (Reminiscences)." *Russky Arkhiv,* 1872, 98–185, 449–533.

LUNIN, M. S. *Sochineniia i pisma* (Works and letters). Edited and annotated by S. SHTRAIKH. Petersburg, 1923.

MEDOKS, ROMAN. *Pokhozhdeniia russkogo avantiurista XIX vieka* (Life of a Russian adventurer of the XIXth century). M., "Federalist," 1929.

METTERNICH, PRINCE. *Memoirs.* New York, 1881–82. 5 vols.

MIKHAILOVSKY-DANILEVSKY, A. I. "Vospominaniia (Reminiscences)." *Russky Viestnik,* 1890. Continued in *Russkaia Starina,* XC, 453–482ff.

MURAVIEV-APOSTOL, M. I. *Vospominaniia i pisma* (Reminiscences and letters). Petrograd, "Byloe," 1922.

NICHOLAS I. "Zapiski (Memoirs)." *Krasnyi Arkhiv,* VI, 222–234. See also *Dekabristy. Sbornik otryvkov iz istochnikov,* 323–331; *Mezhdutsarstvie,* 9–36.

OBOLENSKY, E. P. "Vospominaniia (Reminiscences)." *Obshchestvennye Dvizheniia v Rossii,* I, 231–281.

ORLOV, M. F. "Kapituliatsiia Parizha v 1814 godu (Capitulation of Paris in 1814)." *Russkaia Starina,* XII (1877), 633–662.

POPOV, I. I. *Minuvshee i perezhitoe* (Past and experience). *Sibir i emigratsiia.* Leningrad, 1924.

POTOCKA, ANNA. (Tyszkiewiz). *Memoirs.* New York, 1901.

PRZHETSLAVSKY, O. "Vospominaniia (Reminiscences)." *Russkaia Starina,* XI (1874), 450–477ff.

ROSTOPCHIN, F. V. "Zapiski (Memoirs)." *Russkaia Starina,* XII (1889), 643–725.

ROZEN, A. E. *Zapiski dekabrista* (Memoirs of a Decembrist). St.P., 1907.

RULIKOWSKI, JOSEPH KAZIMIERZ IGNACY. "Rokosz pulku Czernihowskiego." *Nasza Przyslose,* VI (1908), 217–236; VII, 341–382. For a translation from the Polish see *Vospominaniia i Rasskazy,* II, 373–429.

RUNICH, D. P. "Zapiski (Memoirs)." *Russkaia Starina,* CV (1901), 47–77ff.

SHERWOOD, I. V. "Ispoved' Shervuda-Vernogo (The confession of Sherwood the Loyal)." *Istorichesky Viestnik,* LXIII (1896), 66–85.

SHISHKOV, A. S. *Zapiski, mneniia i perepiska* (Memoirs, opinions and correspondence). Berlin, 1870. 2 vols.

STAËL, MME DE. *Considérations sur les principaux événemens de la révolution françoise.* Londres, 1818. 3 vols.

STEINGEL, V. I. "Zapiski (Memoirs)." *Obshchestvennye Dvizheniia v Rossii,* I, 321–475.

STURDZA, A. S. "O sud'be pravoslavnoi tserkvi russkoi (Concerning the fate of the Russian Orthodox Church)." *Russkaia Starina,* II (1876), 266–288.

SUKHOZANET, I. "Vospominaniia. 14 dekabria 1825 goda. (Reminiscences. December 14, 1825)." *Russkaia Starina,* VII (1873), 361–370.

TARASOV, D. K. "Vospominaniia moei zhizni (Reminiscences of my life)." *Russkaia Starina,* IV (1871), 223–261ff.

TRUBETSKOI, S. P. *Zapiski* (Memoirs). Edited by his daughters. St.P., 1907.

TURGENEV (TOURGENEFF), N. I. *La Russie et les russes. Mémoires d'un poscrit.* Paris, 1847. 3 volumes. Vol. I has been translated into Russian and edited by A. A. KIZEVETTER. *Rossiia i russkie.* M., 1915.

VARNHAGEN VON ENSE, K. A. *Denkwürdigkeiten des eignen Lebens.* Ed. 2. Leipzig, 1843. 3 parts in one volume.

VIGEL, F. F. *Zapiski* (Memoirs). M., 1891–93. 7 vols.

VOLKONSKY, S. G. *Zapiski dekabrista* (Memoirs of a Decembrist). St.P., 1902. Ed. 2. See review by M. Dovnar-Zapolsky, in *Zhurnal Ministerstva Narodnogo Prosvieshcheniia,* IV (1902), 467–482.

VON-BRADKE, E. F. "Zapiski (Memoirs)." *Russky Arkhiv,* I, 1875, 1–53ff.

VONVISIN (FONVIZIN), M. A. "Obozrenie proiavlenii politicheskoi zhizni v Rossii (A survey of the manifestation of political life in Russia)." *Obshchestvennye Dvizheniia v Rossii,* I, 97–203.

Vospominaniia Bestuzhevykh (Reminiscences of the Bestuzhevs). Edited and annotated by M. K. AZADOVSKY and I. M. TROTSKY. M., 1931.

Vospominaniia i rasskazy deiatelei tainykh obshchestv 1820-kh godov (Reminiscences and narratives of participants of secret societies of the 1820's). Edited by IU. G. OKSMAN and S. N. CHERNOV. M., 1931–.

WÜRTTEMBERG, E., PRINCE OF. "Vospominaniia (Reminiscences)." *Russky Arkhiv,* I (1878), 42–75; III, 330–359.

YAKUSHKIN, I. *Zapiski* (Memoirs). M., 1925.

"Zapiska kniazia Grabbe-Gorskogo (Memorandum of Prince Grabbe-Gorsky)." *XIX Viek,* I, 201–212.

"Zapiski de-Sanglena (Memoirs of de-Sanglen)." *Russkaia Starina*, XXXVI, 443–498ff.

Zapiski Ksenofonta Alekseevicha Polevogo (Memoirs of K. A. Polevoi). St.P., 1888.

"Zapiski kvakera o prebyvanii v Rossii (Memoirs of a Quaker concerning his sojourn in Russia)." *Russkaia Starina*, I (1874), 1–36.

"Zapiski Maevskogo (Memoirs of Maevsky)." *Russkaia Starina*, VIII (1873), 125–168ff.

"Zapiski Martosa (Memoirs of Martos)." *Russky Arkhiv*, VII (1893), 305–368; VIII, 449–468.

"Zapiski polkovnika Vadkovskogo (Memoirs of Colonel Vadkovsky)." *Russkaia Starina*, V (1873), 635–650.

ZAVALISHIN, D. I. *Zapiski dekabrista* (Memoirs of a Decembrist). München, 1904. 2 vols.

ZOTOV, R. M. "Zapiski (Memoirs)." *Istorichesky Viestnik*, LXIV (1896), 762–797ff.

SECONDARY ACCOUNTS

AFANAS'EV, A. N. *Russkie satiricheskie zhurnaly 1769–74 gg.* (Russian satirical magazines 1769–74). M., 1859. Ed. 2. Kazan, 1871.

ANICHKOV, E., BOROZDIN, A. K., AND OVSIANIKO-KULIKOVSKY, D., (EDITOR). *Istoriia russkoi literatury XIX vieka* (History of Russian literature of the XIXth century). M., 1911. 2 vols.

ASKENAZY, SZYMON. *Rosya-Polska, 1815–1830.* Lwow, 1907. (Tr. *Tsarstvo Polskoe, 1815–1830*). M., 1915.

AULARD, A. *The French Revolution, a political history, 1789–1804.* Tr. from the French by B. MIALL. London, 1910. 4 vols.

BAGALEI, D. I. *Ocherki po russkoi istorii* (Sketches from Russian history). Kharkov, 1913.

BARSKOV, L. *Perepiska moskovskikh masonov XVIII vieka* (Correspondence of the Moscow Masons of the XVIIIth century). Petrograd, 1915.

BARSUKOV, I. *Graf Nikolai Nikolaevich Muraviev-Amursky* (Count N. N. Muraviev-Amursky). Po ego pismam, offitsialnym dokumentam, rasskazam sovremennikov i pechatnym istochnikam. M., 1891. 2 vols.

BAZILEVICH, V. M. *Dekabristi na Kiivshchini* (Decembrists in the Province of Kiev). Kiev, 1926. (In Ukrainian.)

BELIAEV, I. D. *Krestiane nà Rusi; issledovanie o postepennom izmenenii znacheniia krestian v russkom obshchestve* (The peasants in Russia; a study of the gradual modification of the significance of the peasants in Russian society). M., 1879.

BERNHARDI, T. VON. *Geschichte Rußlands und der Europäischen Politik in den Jahren 1814 bis 1831.* Leipzig, 1863–77. 3 vols.

BLUM, KARL L. *Ein russischer Staatsmann; (des Grafen Jakob Johan Sievers Dekwürdigkeiten zur Geschichte Rußlands).* Leipzig, 1857–58. 4 vols.

BOGDANOVICH, M. A. *Istoriia tsarstvovaniia imperatora Aleksandra I* (History of the reign of Emperor Alexander I). St.P., 1869–71. 6 vols.

BOGOLIUBOV, V. A. *Nikolai Ivanovich Novikov i ego vremia* (N. I. Novikov and his time). M., 1916.

BORSUK, N. *Rostopchinskie afishi* (Rostopchin's proclamations). St.P., n.d.

BRODSKY, N. L. (ED.) See *Literaturnye salony.*

BRZHESKY, N. N. *Gosudarstvennye dolgi Rossii* (State debts of Russia). St.P., 1884.

BULICH, N. N. *Ocherki po istorii russkoi literatury i prosvieshcheniia s nachala XIX vieka* (Sketches of the history of Russian literature and education from the beginning of the XIXth century). St.P., 1912.

DESTUTT-DE-TRACY, A. *Commentaire sur "l'Esprit de lois" de Montesquieu.* Paris, 1819. German translation, *Kritischer Commentar über Montesquieu's "Geist der Gesetze."* Heidelberg, 1820.

DMITRIEV-MAMONOV, A. I. *Dekabristy v Zapadnoi Sibiri* (The Decembrists in western Siberia). St.P.,1905. Also in *Chteniia v Imperatorskom Obshchestvie Istorii i Drevnostei Rossiiskikh*, IV (1895). (Cited as *C.I.O.I.D.R.*)

DOVNAR-ZAPOLSKY, M. *Idealy dekabristov* (The ideals of the Decembrists). M., 1907.

DOVNAR-ZAPOLSKY, M. *Obzor noveishei russkoi istorii* (A survey of recent Russian history). Kiev, 1912.

DOVNAR-ZAPOLSKY, M., *Tainoe obshchestvo dekabristov* (The secret Decembrist society). M., 1906.

DUBROVIN, N. *Pugachev i ego soobshchniki* (Pugachev and his associates). St.P., 1884. 3 vols.

ENGELMANN, JOHANNES. *Die Leibeigenschaft in Rußland; eine rechtshistorische Studie.* Leipzig, 1884.

Entsiklopedichesky Slovar' Brokhausa i Efrona (Encyclopedic dictionary). St.P., 1890–1904. 41 vols.

ESHEVSKY, S. *Sochineniia po russkoi istorii* (Works on Russian history). M., 1900.

EVSTAF'EV, P. P. *Vosstanie novgorodskikh voennykh poselian* (The uprising of the Novgorod military colonists). M., 1934.

FEOKTISTOV, E. M. *Magnitsky; materialy dlia istorii prosvieshcheniia v Rossii* (Magnitsky; sources pertaining to the history of education in Russia). St.P., 1865.

FINDEL, G. J. *Geschichte der Freimaurerei.* Ed. 4. Leipzig, 1878.

FROST, THOMAS. *The Secret societies of the European Revolution, 1776–1876.* London, 1876. 2 vols.

GERSHENZON, M. O. *Dekabrist Krivtsov.* Ed. 2. Berlin, 1923.

GERSHENZON, M. O. *Istoriia molodoi Rossii* (History of young Russia). M., 1923.

GESSEN, SERGEI. *Dekabristy pered sudom istorii, 1825–1925* (The Decembrists before the bar of history, 1825–1925). M., 1926.

GOLOVACHEV, P. M. *Dekabristy. Vosem'desiat shest' portretov* (The Decembrists. Eighty-six portraits). M., 1906.

GOLOVINE, IVAN G. *Histoire d'Alexandre Ier, empereur de Russie.* Paris, 1859.

GOLOVINE, IVAN G. *La Russie sous Nicolas Ier.* Paris, 1845. Tr., *Russia under the autocrat, Nicholas the First.* London, 1846.

GULISHAMBAROV, S. O. *Vsemirnaia torgovlia v XIX vieke i uchastie v nei Rossii* (World trade in the XIXth century and Russia's participation in it). St.P., 1898.

HAXTHAUSEN-ABBENBURG, A. *Studien über die innere Zustände, das Volks-leben und insbesondere die ländlichen Einrichtungen Rußlands.* Hannover-Berlin, 1847–52. 3 vols.

HERZEN (ISKANDER), A. *Du développement des idées révolutionnaires en Russie.* Ed. 2. London, 1863.

HILDT, J. C. *Early diplomatic negotiations of the United States with Russia.* Baltimore, The Johns Hopkins Press, 1906.

IKONNIKOV, V. S. *Graf N. S. Mordvinov* (Count N. S. Mordvinov). *Istori-cheskaia monografiia.* St.P., 1873.

IKONNIKOV, V. S. *Krestianskoe dvizhenie v Kievskoi gubernii v 1826–27 gg. v sviazi s sobytiiami togo vremeni* (Peasant movement in Kiev gubernia in 1826–27, in relation to the events of that time). St.P., 1905. Also in *Sbornik statei, posviashchennykh Lamanskomu.* See under latter title.

KIZEVETTER, A. A. *Istoricheskie ocherki* (Historical sketches). M., 1912.

KLIUCHEVSKY, V. O. *Kurs russkoi istorii* (A course in Russian history). M., 1904–23. 5 vols. Tr. by C. T. HOGARTH. London, 1911–31.

KORF, M. A. *Vosshestvie na prestol imperatora Nikolaia I* (The accession of Nicholas I). Ed. 3. St.P., 1857. Tr., London, 1857.

KORF, M. A. *Zhizn' grafa Speranskogo* (The life of Count Speransky). St.P., 1861. 2 vols.

KORF, S. A. *Dvorianstvo i ego soslovnoe upravlenie za stoletie 1762–1855 godov* (The nobility and their class administration during the century from 1762 to 1855). St.P., 1906.

KORNILOV, A. *Kurs russkoi istorii XIX vieka* (A course in Russian history of the XIXth century). M., 1918. 3 vols. English translation, New York, 1917.

KOTLIAREVSKY, N. *Dekabristy: kniaz' A. Odoevsky i A. Bestuzhev* (The De-cembrists: Prince A. Odoevsky and A. Bestuzhev). St.P., 1909.

KOTLIAREVSKY, N. *Ryleev.* St.P., 1908.

KUBALOV, B. *Dekabristy v vostochnoi Sibiri* (The Decembrists in Eastern Siberia). Irkutsk, Arkhivbiuro, 1925.

KULISHER, I. *Istoriia russkogo narodnogo khoziaistva* (History of Russian national economy). M., 1925. 2 vols.

LEE, ROBERT. *The last days of Alexander and the first days of Nicholas, emperor of Russia.* Ed. 2. London, 1854.

LIAKHOV, A. *Osnovnye cherty sotsial'nykh i ekonomicheskikh otnoshenii v Rossii v epokhu Aleksandra I* (Basic features of the social and economic relations in Russia in the reign of Alexander I). M., 1912.

LIASHCHENKO, P. *Istoriia russkogo narodnogo khoziaistva* (History of Russian national economy). M., 1927.

Literaturnye salony i kruzhki (Literary salons and circles). Leningrad, "Akademia," 1930.

LODYZHENSKY, N. *Istoriia russkogo tamozhennogo tarifa* (History of the Rus-sian tariff). St.P., 1886.

LONGINOV, M. *Novikov i moskovskie martinisty* (Novikov and the Moscow Martinists). M., 1867.

LONGINOV, M. *Novikov i Schwarz.* (Novikov and Schwarz). M., 1857.

MAKSIMOV, S. *Sibir i katorga* (Siberia and convict labor). St.P., 1900.

MASARYK, T. G. *The Spirit of Russia*. London, 1919. 2 vols.

MAVOR, JAMES. *An Economic History of Russia*. Ed. 2. London-New York, 1925.

MIGULIN, P. P. *Russky gosudarstvennyi kredit* (Russian state credit). Kharkov, 1899–1907. 3 vols.

MILIUKOV, P. *Le mouvement intellectuel russe*. Paris, 1918.

MILIUKOV, P. *Ocherki po istorii russkoi kul'tury* (Outlines of the history of Russian culture). St.P., 1896–1909. 3 vols. Jubilee edition, Paris, 1931.

MILIUKOV, P., SIEGNOBOS, C., AND EISENMANN, L. *Histoire de Russie*. Paris, 1932–33. 3 vols.

NADLER, V. K. *Imperator Aleksandr i idea sviashchennogo soiuza* (Emperor Alexander and the idea of the Holy Alliance). Kharkov, 1886–88. 4 vols.

NECHKINA, M. V. *Dekabristy* (The Decembrists). M., 1930.

NECHKINA, M. V. *Obshchestvo soedinënnykh slavian* (The Society of United Slavs). M., 1927.

NEZELENOV, A. I. *Nikolai Ivanovich Novikov, izdatel' zhurnalov, 1769–85* (N. I. Novikov, publisher of magazines, 1769–85). St.P., 1875.

Obshchestvennye dvizheniia v Rossii v pervuiu polovinu XIX vieka (Social movements in Russia in the first half of the XIXth century). Vol. I. Dekabristy: M. Fonvizin, Prince E. P. Obolensky and Baron V. I. Steingel. Compiled by V. SEMEVSKY AND P. E. SHCHEGOLEV. St.P., 1905.

PARADIZOV, P. *Dekabristy* (The Decembrists). Kharkov, 1930.

PARADIZOV, P. *Ocherki po istoriografii dekabristov* (Outlines of the historiography of the Decembrists). M., 1929.

PAVLOV-SILVANSKY, N. *Ocherki po russkoi istorii XVIII-XIX v.* (Outlines of Russian history of the XVIIIth-XIXth centuries). St.P., 1910.

PAZHITNOV, K. A. *Razvitie sotsialisticheskikh idei v Rossii ot Pestelia do grupy "Osvobozhdeniia Truda"* (Development of socialistic ideas in Russia from Pestel to the group "Emancipation of Labor"). Petrograd, 1924.

PETROV, D. K. *Ocherki po istorii politicheskoi poezii XIX vieka. Rossiia i Nikolai I v stikhotvoreniiakh Espronsedy i Rossetti* (Outlines of the history of political poetry of the XIXth century. Russia and Nicholas I in the poetry of Espronceda and Rossetti). St.P., 1909.

PLEKHANOV, G. V. *Sochineniia* (Works). Edited by D. RIAZANOV. M., 1923–27. 24 vols.

POKROVSKY, M. N. *Dekabristy. Sbornik statei* (The Decembrists. A collection of articles). M., 1927.

POKROVSKY, M. N. *Istoriia Rossii s drevneishikh vremën* (A history of Russia from the earliest times). M., Gosudarstvennoe sotsialnoe-ekonomicheskoe izdatelstvo, 1933–34. 4 vols.

POKROVSKY, V. I. *Sbornik svedenii po istorii i statistike vneshnei torgovli Rossii. Izdanie Departamenta Tamozhennykh Sborov* (Collection of historical and statistical data on Russian foreign commerce. Published by the Department for the Collection of Custom Duties). St.P., 1902.

POKROVSKY, V. I. *Zheny dekabristov* (Wives of the Decembrists). M., 1906.

POLIEVKTOV, M. *Nikolai I. Biografiia i obzor tsarstvovaniia* (Nicholas I. Biography and survey of his reign). M., 1918.

PRESNIAKOV, A. E. *Aleksandr I* (Alexander I). Petrograd, 1924.

PRESNIAKOV, A. E. *14 dekabria 1825 goda* (December 14, 1825). S prilozheniem voenno-istoricheskoi spravki G. S. Gabaeva, "Gvardiia v dekabrskie dni 1825 goda." M., 1926.

PYPIN, A. *Obshchestvennoe dvizhenie v Rossii pri Aleksandre I* (Social movements in Russia under Alexander I). St.P., 1885. Ed. 4 1908.

PYPIN, A. *Religioznye dvizheniia pri Aleksandre I* (Religious movements in the reign of Alexander I). *Petrograd*, 1916.

PYPIN, A. *Russkoe Masonstvo* (Russian Masonry). Petrograd, 1916.

RADISHCHEV, A. N. *Polnoe sobranie sochinenii* (Complete collection of works). Ed. by V. KALLASH. M., 1907.

ROBINSON, G. T. *Rural Russia under the old régime*. New York, 1932.

ROMANOVICH-SLAVATINSKY, A. *Dvorianstvo v Rossii ot nachala XVIII vieka do otmeny krepostnogo prava* (The nobility in Russia from the beginning of the XVIIIth century to the abolition of serfdom). Kiev, 1912.

ROZHKOV, N. *Russkaia istoriia* (History of Russia). M., 1924. 10 vols.

SCHIEMANN, T. *Die Ermordung Pauls und die Thronbesteigung Nicolaus I.* Berlin, 1902.

SCHIEMANN, T. *Geschichte Rußlands unter Kaiser Nicolaus I.* Berlin, 1904–19. 4 vols.

SEMENNIKOV, V. P. *Radishchev. Ocherki i issledovaniia* (Radishchev. Sketches and investigations). M., 1923.

SEMËNOV, A. *Izuchenie istoricheskikh svedenii o rossiiskoi vneshnei torgovle i promyshlennosti s poloviny XVII stoletiia po 1858 god* (A study of historical data concerning Russian foreign trade and industry from the middle of the XVIIth century to 1858). St.P., 1859.

SEMEVSKY, V. *Krestiane v tsarstvovanie imperatritsy Ekateriny II* (Peasants during the reign of Empress Catherine II). St. P., 1888. Ed. 2, revised and enlarged. 1903. 2 vols.

SEMEVSKY, V. *Krestiansky vopros v Rossii v XVIII i pervoi poloviny XIX vieka* (The peasant question in Russia in the XVIIIth and first half of the XIXth century). St.P., 1888. 2 vols.

SEMEVSKY, V. *Politicheskie i obshchestvennye idei dekabristov* (Political and social ideas of the Decembrists). St.P., 1909.

SHCHEGOLEV, P. E., *Dekabristy. Sbornik statei* (The Decembrists. A collection of articles). Leningrad, 1926.

SHCHEGOLEV, P. E. *Istoricheskie etiudy* (Historical studies). M., 1913.

SHCHEGOLEV, P. E. *Pëtr Grigorevich Kakhovsky.* M., 1919.

SHEBUNIN, A. N. *Nikolai Ivanovich Turgenev.* M., 1925.

SHILDER, N. K. *Imperator Aleksandr I, ego zhizn' i tsarstvovanie* (Emperor Alexander I, his life and reign). St.P., 1898. 4 vols.

SHILDER, N. K. *Imperator Nikolai I, ego zhizn' i tsarstvovanie* (Emperor Nicholas I, his life and reign). St. P., 1903. 2 vols.

SHTRAIKH, S. IA. *Brozhenie v armii pri Aleksandre I* (Unrest in the army under Alexander I). Petrograd, 1922.

SIPOVSKY, V. *Novikov, Schwarz i moskovskoe masonstvo* (Novikov, Schwarz and Moscow Masonry). Supplement to his book *N. M. Karamzin*. St.P., 1899.

Skabichevsky, A. *Ocherki istorii russkoi tsenzury, 1700–1836 gg.* (Outlines of the history of Russian censorship, 1700–1836). St.P., 1892.

Sokolovskaia, T. *Russkoe Masonstvo i ego znachenie v istorii obshchestven- nogo dvizheniia* (Russian Masonry and its importance in the history of social movements). St.P., n.d.

Storch, H. *Rußland unter Alexander dem Ersten.* St.P., 1804.

Svatikov, S. *Obshchestvennoe dvizhenie v Rossii, 1700–1895* (Social move- ments in Russia, 1700–1895). Rostov n/D., 1905.

Tarasov, E. I. *Dekabrist N. I. Turgenev* (The Decembrist N. I. Turgenev). Samara, 1923.

Trifil'ev, E. P. *Ocherki iz istorii krepostnogo prava v Rossii. Tsarstvovanie Pavla I.* (Outlines from the history of serfdom in Russia. The reign of Paul I). Kharkov, 1904.

Trotsky, I. M. *Zhizn' Shervuda-Vernogo* (The life of Sherwood the Loyal). M., 1931.

Tugan-Baranovsky, M. *Russkaia fabrika* (The Russian factory). M., 1922.

Vasilich, G. *Vosshestvie na prestol imperatora Nikolaia I* (The accession of Emperor Nicholas I). M., n.d.

Vernadsky, G. *Russkoe Masonstvo v tsarstvovanie Ekateriny II* (Russian Masonry under Catherine II). Petrograd, 1917.

Voronitsyn, I. P. *Dekabristy i religiia* (The Decembrists and religion). M., 1928.

Voznesensky, S. *Razlozhenie krepostnogo khoziaistva i klassovaia bor'ba v Rossii, 1800–1866 gg.* (The decadence of serfdom and class struggle in Russia, 1800–1866). M., 1932.

Waliszewski, K. *La Russie il y a cent ans. Le règne d'Alexandre Ier.* Paris, 1923–25. 3 vols.

Wischnitzer, Markus. *Die Universität Göttingen und die Entwicklung der liberalen Ideen in Rußland in ersten Viertel des XIX Jahrhunderts.* Ber- lin, 1907.

Zablotsky-Desiatovsky, A. P. *Graf P. D. Kiselëv i ego vremia'* (Count P. D. Kiselev and his time). St. P., 1882. 4 vols.

PERIODICALS, ALMANACS, AND JUBILEE PUBLICATIONS

Arkhiv Istorii Truda v Rossii (Archive of the History of Labor in Russia). Petrograd, 1921–23. 10 vols.

Bunt Dekabristov. IUbileinyi Sbornik 1825–1925 (Uprising of the Decem- brists. A Jubilee collection, 1825–1925). Edited by IU. G. Oksman and P. E. Shchegolev. *Leningrad*, 1926.

Byloe. Istorichesky Zhurnal (The Past. Historical Magazine). I–XXII, 1906–7; I–XXXV, 1917–26.

Chteniia v Imperatorskom Obshchestve Istorii i Drevnostei Rossiiskikh pri Mos- kovskom Universitete (Publications of the Royal Society of Russian His- tory and Antiquity at the University of Moscow). I–CXXXV, 1861–1916. (Cited as *C.I.O.I.D.R.*)

Dekabristi na Ukraini. Zbirnik (The Decembrists in the Ukraine. Publications). Zbirnik prats komisii dlia doslidi v gromads'kikh techii na Ukraini. Za red. akad. S. Efremova ta V. Miiakovskogo. Kiev, Ukrainska Akademiia Nauk; Zbirnik istorichno-filologichnogo viddilu, No. 37, 1926.

Dekabristy v Zabaikalie (The Decembrists in the Transbaikal). Neizdannye materialy pod red. A. V. Kharchevnikova. Chita, 1925.

Deviatnadtsatyi Viek (The Nineteenth Century). M., I–II, 1872. (Cited as *XIX Viek.*)

Diela i Dni. Istorichesky zhurnal (Events and Days. Historical magazine). Petrograd, I–III, 1920–22.

Golos Minuvshego (Voice of the Past). M., 1913–26(?).

Istorik Marksist (The Marxist Historian). M., I, 1926–.

Istorichesky Viestnik; Istoriko-Literaturnyi Zhurnal (Historical Messenger; an historical-literary magazine). Petrograd, I–CL, 1880–1917.

Izvestiia Akademii Nauk (Publications of the Academy of Sciences). Petrograd, I, 1779–. (Titles vary.)

Katorga i Ssylka (Convict Labor and Exile). M., I, 1923–.

Krasnyi Arkhiv (Red Archive). M., I, 1922–.

Krestiansky Stroi (The Peasant Organization). Sbornik statei A. Kornilova, A. Lappo-Danilevskogo, V. Semevskogo i M. Strakhovskogo. St.P., 1905.

Masonstvo v ego Proshlom i Nastoiashchem (Masonry in its Past and Present). Ed. by S. P. MELGUNOV and N. P. SIDOROV. M., 1914–15. 2 vols.

Minuvshie Gody (Past Years). St.P., I–XII, 1908.

Le Monde Slave. Paris, I, 1924–.

Rukh Dekabristiv na Ukraini (The Decembrist Movement in the Ukraine). IUvileine vidaniia, Ukrtsentrarkhiva. Kharkiv, 1926. (In Ukranian.)

Russkaia Mysl' (Russian Thought). M., 1880–1924.

Russkaia Starina (Russian Antiquity). St.P., I–CLXXII, 1870–1918.

Russkie Propilei (Russian Propylaea). M., I–VI, 1915–19.

Russkoe Bogatstvo (Russian Wealth). M., I–LXII, 1896–1914.

Russkoe Proshloe (Russian Past). Petrograd, I–V, 1923.

Russky Arkhiv (Russian Archive). M., 1863–1916.

Russky Viestnik (Russian Messenger). M.-St.P., I–CCCVI, 1856–1906.

Sbornik statei, posviashchennykh P. N. Miliukovu (A Collection of articles dedicated to P. N. Miliukov). Praha, 1929.

Sbornik statei, posviashchennykh S. F. Platonovu (A Collection of articles dedicated to S. F. Platónov). Petrograd, 1922.

Sbornik statei, posviashchennykh V. I. Lamanskomu (A Collection of articles dedicated to V. I. Làmansky). St.P., 1908.

Sbornik statei, posviashchennykh V. O. Kliuchevskomu (A Collection of articles dedicated to V. O. Kliuchevsky). M., 1909.

Sibirskie Ogni (Siberian Lights). Khudozhestvenno-literaturnyi i nauchno-publistichesky zhurnal. Novo-Nikolaevsk, I, 1922–.

Velikaia Reforma. Russkoe Obshchestvo i Krestiansky Vopros v Proshlom i Nastoiashchem (The Great Reform. Russian Society and the Peasant Question in the Past and Present). Jubilee edition. M., I–VI, 1911.

Viestnik Evropy (The Messenger of Europe). St.P., I–CCCXCVI, 1866–1917.

XIX Viek. See *Deviatnadtsatyi Viek.*

Zhurnal Ministerstva Narodnogo Prosvieshcheniia (Journal of the Ministry of Public Education). St.P., 1834–1917. (*Z.M.N.P.*)

Zvenia (Links). Sbornik materialov i dokumentov po istorii literatury, iskusstva i obshchestvennoi mysli XIX vieka. M., I, 1932–.

PERIODICAL LITERATURE

ALDANOV, M. "Speransky i dekabristy (Speransky and the Decembrists)." *Sovremennye Zapiski* (Paris), XXVI (1925), 224–240.

"ALEKSANDR MIKHAILOVICH BULATOV." *Russkaia Starina*, LIII (1887), 203–222.

ALEKSANDRENKO, V. "Iz zhizni russkikh studentov v Oksforde v tsarstvovanie Ekateriny II (The life of Russian students in Oxford during the reign of Catherine II)." *Zhurnal Ministerstva Narodnogo Prosvieshcheniia*, I–II (1893), 1–14.

ALEKSANDROV, G. "Zametki o byvshikh voennykh poseleniiakh (Notes concerning former military colonies)." *Russky Arkhiv*, VII (1873), 1716–1722.

ASKENAZY, SZYMON. "Russia. Poland and the Polish Revolution." *The Cambridge Modern History*. X, 413–474.

BAGALII, OLGA. "Materialy do istorii dekabristskogo rukhu na Ukraini (Sources pertaining to the history of the Decembrist movement in the Ukraine)." *Narisi z Sotsial'no-Ekonomichnoi Istorii Ukraini*. Kiev, Vseukrainska Akademii Nauk U.S.S.R., I (1932), 295–324.

BALABANOV, M. "Narodnye massy i dvizhenie dekabristov (The masses and the Decembrist movement)." *Krasnaia Nov'*, III (1926), 140–159.

"BARON F. K. GEISMAR." *Russkaia Starina*, XXXII (1881), 721–762.

"BIBLEISKIE OBSHCHESTVA V ROSSII (BIBLE SOCIETIES IN RUSSIA)." *Entsiklopedichesky Slovar' Brockhausa i Efrona*, III (A), 696–708.

BIRIUKOVICH, V. "Sud'ba Ukaza o svobodnykh khlebopashtsakh v tsarstvovanie Aleksandra I (The fate of the Decree concerning the free farmers in the reign of Alexander I)." *Arkhiv Istorii Truda v Rossii*, I (1921), 63–79.

BOGDANOVICH, M. "Bezporiadki v Semenovskom polku (Disorders in the Semenovsky regiment)." *Viestnik Evropy*, XI (1870), 55–84.

BOGUCHARSKY (Bazilevsky) V. "Zapiski dekabrista D. I. Zavalishina (Memoirs of the Decembrist D. I. Zavalishin)." *Byloe*, I (1906), 304–310. (Review.)

BRAILOVSKY, S. "V. I. Tumansky. Iz ego bumag (V. I. Tumansky. From his papers)." *Russkaia Starina*, LXVII (1890), 378–386.

"Bunt Chernigovskogo polka (The uprising of the Chernigovsky regiment)." *Russky Arkhiv*, I (1871), 257–287.

CHECHULIN, N. D. "Ocherki po istorii russkikh finansov v tsarstvovanie Ekateriny II (Outlines on the history of Russian finances during the reign of Catherine II.") *Zhurnal Ministerstva Narodnogo Prosvieshcheniia*, I (1904), 1–91ff.

CHECHULIN, N. D. "Russkoe provintsialnoe obshchestvo vo vtoroi polovine XVIII vieka (Russian provincial society in the second half of the XVIIIth century)." *Zhurnal Ministerstva Narodnogo Prosvieshcheniia*, III–IV (1889), 45–71ff.

CHERNOV, S. N. "K istorii politicheskikh stolknovenii na Moskovskom 's'ezde 1821 goda (Concerning the political conflicts at the Moscow conference of 1821)." *Uchenye Zapiski Saratovskogo Universiteta*, IV (1925), 103–140.

CHERNOV, S. N. "Neskol'ko spravok o 'Soiuze Blagodenstviia' pered Moskovskim s'ezdom 1821 goda (A few inquiries concerning the 'Union of Welfare' before the Moscow conference of 1821)." *Uchenye Zapiski Saratovskogo Universiteta*, II (1925), 34–67.

DE-PULE, M. "Krestianskoe dvizhenie pri imperatore Pavle Petroviche (Peasant movement in the reign of Paul I)." *Russky Arkhiv*, 1869, 525–577.

DUBROVIN, N. "Nashi mistiki-sektanty (Our mystic-sectarians)." *Russkaia Starina*, X (1895), 33–64ff.

DUBROVIN, N. "Posle otechestvennoi voiny (After the national war)." *Russkaia Starina*, CXVI, 241–271ff.

DURYLIN, S. "Liudi 14 dekabria i Goethe (The men of December 14 and Goethe)." *Literaturnoe Nasledstvo*, IV–VI (1932), 374–421.

EVREINOV, B. "Reforma vysshikh gosudarstvennykh uchrezhdenii v Rossii v tsarstvovanie imperatora Aleksandra I (The reform of the supreme state institutions in Russia in the reign of Alexander I)." *Conférence des historiens des états de l'Europe orientale et du Monde slave*, IIme Partie (Varsovie, 1928), 63–84.

EVROPEUS. "O voennykh poseleniiakh (Concerning the military colonies)." *Istorichesky Viestnik*, XXIX (1887), 640–649.

FILIPPOV, A. N. "Znachenie Speranskogo v istorii russkogo zakonodatel'stva (The importance of Speransky in the history of Russian legislation)." *Russkaia Mysl'*, IV (1889), 1–21.

GALAKHOV, I. A. "Obzor misticheskoi literatury v tsarstvovanie Aleksandra I (A survey of the mystical literature in the reign of Emperor Alexander I)." *Zhurnal Ministerstva Narodnogo Prosvieshcheniia*, XI–XII (1875), 87–175.

GEORGIEVSKY, A. P. "Slaviansky vopros v mirovozzrenii dekabristov (The Decembrists' conception of the Slav question)." *Uchenye Zapiski Istoriko-Filologicheskogo Fakulteta Gosudarstvennogo Dalnevostochnogo Universiteta* (Vladivostok), I, 2 (1921), 103–123.

GOLOVINSKY, M. "Dekabrist kniaz' E. P. Obolensky (The Decembrist Prince E. P. Obolensky)." *Istorichesky Viestnik*, I (1890), 115–145. Note also III (1890?), p. 736.

GRIBBE, A. K. "Graf A. A. Arakcheev (Count A. A. Arakcheev)." *Russkaia Starina*, I (1875), 84–123.

IKONNIKOV, V. S. "Krestianskoe dvizhenie v Kievskoi gubernii v 1826–27 gg. v sviazi s sobytiiami togo vremeni (The peasant movement in the Kiev gubernia in 1826–27 in relation to the events of that period)." *Sbornik statei, posviashchennykh V. I. Lamanskomu*, Part II, 657–742.

KARNOVICH, E. P. "Tsarevich Konstantin Pavlovich, 1779–1831 gg. (Crown Prince Constantine Pavlovich, 1779–1831)." *Russkaia Starina*, XIX (1877), 217–254ff.

KHIN, M. M. "Zheny dekabristov (The wives of the Decembrists)." *Istorichesky Viestnik*, XII (1884), 650–683.

KIZEVETTER, A. "Graf F. V. Rostopchin (Count F. V. Rostopchin)." *Russkaia Mysl'*, XII (1912), 1–54.

KLIUCHEVSKY, V. O. "Vospominaniia o Novikove i ego vremeni (Recollection of Novikov and his time)." *Russkaia Mysl'*, I (1895), 38–61.

KORNILOV, A. "The Napoleonic wars and later Russian history." *The Russian Review* (London), I, No. 4 (1912), 55–75.

KOROBKA, N. "Dekabristy bratia Borisovy i Obshchestvo Soedinënnykh Slavian (The Decembrist brothers Borisov and the Society of United Slavs)." *Sovremennik*, V (1911), 11–35.

KOROBKA, N. "Pol'skie obshchestva 20-kh godov i dekabristy (Polish societies of the 20's and the Decembrists)." *O Minuvshem; Istorichesky Sbornik*, 189–234.

KOROL'KOV, M. "Poruchik Feodor Krechetov (Lieutenant Feodor Krechetov)." *Byloe*, IV (1906), 42–59.

KOTLIAREVSKY, N. "Literaturnaia deiatelnost dekabristov. Ryleev (Literary activities of the Decembrists. Ryleev)." *Russkoe Bogatstvo*, VII (1905), 44–82.

KOVALEVSKY, M. "Russkaia Pravda Pestelia (Pestel's 'Russian Justice')." *Minuvshie Gody*, I (1908), 1–20.

KOZLOVSKY, V. M. "Imperator Aleksandr I i Jefferson (Emperor Alexander I and Jefferson)." *Russkaia Mysl'*, X (1910), 79–95.

KRAUSHAR, ALEXANDER. "Z tajnego archiwum Senatora Nowosilcowa. Uwagi nad Konstitucya Krolestwa z roku 1815." *Przęglad Historyczny*, II (1906), 108–115.

KUBALOV, B. "Dekabristy i amnistiia (The Decembrists and the amnesty)." *Sibirskie Ogni*, V (1924), 143–159.

KUBALOV, B. "Sibirskoe obshchestvo i dekabristy (Siberian society and the Decembrists)." *Katorga i Ssylka*, VIII (1925), 139–172.

KUBALOV, B. "Zabytyi dekabrist A. N. Lutsky (A forgotten Decembrist A. N. Lutsky)." *Russkoe Proshloe*, V, 50–60.

KULISHER, I. "La grande industrie aux XVIIᵉ et XVIIIᵉ siècles: France, Allemagne, Russie." *Annales d'Histoire Économique et Sociale*, January, 1931, 11–46.

LANGERON, GRAF. "Russkaia armiia v god smerti Ekateriny II (The Russian army in the year of the death of Catherine II)." *Russkaia Starina*, III (1895), 147–166ff.

LAVROVSKY, N. A. "Vospominaniia o Vasilii Nazaroviche Karazine, 1773–1873 (Recollections of V. N. Karazin)." *Zhurnal Ministerstva Narodnogo Prosvieshcheniia*, I–II (1873), 294–311.

LEGRAS, JULES. "Autour de Décabristes." *Le Monde Slave*, XII (1925), 350–374.

LYKOSHIN, A. S. "Poseleniia voennye (Military colonies)." *Entsiklopedichesky Slovar'*, XXIV (48), 663–672.

MAKSIMOVICH, E. "Kniaz' S. P. Trubetskoi v podgotovke k 14-mu dekabria 1825 goda (The rôle of Prince S. P. Trubetskoi in the preparation of the uprising of December 14 1825)." *Sbornik statei, posviashchennykh P. N. Miliukovu*, 451–478.

MILIUKOV, P. "La place de Décabrisme dans l'évolution de l'intelligencija russe." *Le Monde Slave*, XII (1925), 333–349.

MIRKIN-GUETZEVITCH, B. "Les idées politiques des Décabristes et l'influence française." *Le Monde Slave*, XII (1925), 374–385.

"Mitropolit Serafim na Senatskoi ploshchadi 14 dekabria 1825 goda (The Metropolitan Serafim on the Senate Square on December 14, 1825)." *Istorichesky Viestnik*, I (1905), 166–172.

MODZALEVSKY, B. L. "Dekabrist Shakhovskoi (The Decembrist Shakhovsky)." *Sbornik statei, posviashchennykh S. F. Platonovu*, 396–408.

MOZHAISKY, I. P. "Vremena voennykh poselenii (The period of the military colonies)." *Istorichesky Viestnik*, XXV (1886), 350–364.

NECHKINA, M. V. "Obshchestvo Soedinënnykh Slavian (The Society of United Slavs)." *Istorik Marksist*, I (1926), 154–174.

NECHKINA, M. V. "Vosstanie Chernigovskogo polka (The uprising of the Chernigovsky regiment)." *Katorga i Ssylka*, VIII (1925), 87–113.

NIKOLAI MIKHAILOVICH, GRAND DUKE. "Kazn' piati dekabristov 13 iulia 1826 goda i imperator Nikolai I (The execution of the five Decembrists on July 13, 1826 and Emperor Nicholas I)." *Istorichesky Viestnik*, VII (1916), 98–110. Cf. Shchegolev, P. *Dekabristy*, 277–292.

OBOLENSKY, E. "Iz vospominanii o K. F. Ryleeve (From recollections of K. F. Ryleev)." *Deviatnadtsatyi Viek*, I, 312–332.

P. "Tsarevich Konstantin Pavlovich (The Crown Prince Constantine Pavlovich)." *Russkaia Starina*, CI, 619–641ff.

PAVLOV, P. "Vospominaniia ochevidtsa o bunte voennykh poselian v 1831 godu (Recollections of an eyewitness of the rebellion of the military colonists in 1831)." *Istorichesky Viestnik*, LV (1894), 738–788.

PAVLOV-SILVANSKY, N. "Pestel pered Verkhovnym Sudom (Pestel before the Supreme Court)." *Byloe*, II (1906), 124–158ff.

POPOV, M. M. "Konets i posledstviia bunta 14 dekabria 1825 goda (The end and the consequences of the rebellion of December 14, 1825)." *O Minuvshem*, 110–132.

PREDTECHENSKY, A. V. "K voprosu o vliianii kontinental'noi blokady na sostoianie torgovli i promyshlennosti v Rossii (Concerning the question of influence of the continental blockade upon the state of trade and industry in Russia)." *Izvestiia Akademii Nauk SSSR*. Seriia VII, Otdelenie Obshchestvennykh Nauk (Leningrad, 1931), No. 8, 893–920.

PRESNIAKOV, A. E. "Samoderzhavie Nikolaia I (The autocracy of Nicholas I)." *Russkoe Proshloe*, II (1923), 3–21.

PRUGAVIN, A. S. "Dekabrist kniaz' F. P. Shakhovsky (The Decembrist Prince F. P. Shakhovsky)." *Russkoe Bogatstvo*, I (1911), 55–83.

PYPIN, A. "Nachatki novogo dvizheniia (The beginning of the new movement)." *Viestnik Evropy*, XII (1894), 732–780.

"Radishchev, A. N." *C.I.O.I.D.R.*, Book III (July-September, 1865), 67–108.

ROZHKOV, N. "Dekabristy (The Decembrists)." *Russkoe Proshloe*, I (1923), 13–42.

Rozhkov, N. "Dvenadtsatyi god v ego vliianii na sovremennoe emu russkoe obshchestvo (The year 1812 in its influence upon the contemporary Russian society)." *Sovremennyi Mir*, VII (1912), 203–234.

Rubinstein, N. L. "Ekonomicheskoe razvitie Rossii v nachale XIX vieka, kak osnova dvizheniia dekabristov (The economic development of Russia at the beginning of the XIX century as a basis of the Decembrist movement)." *Katorga i Ssylka*, VIII (1925), 9–35.

Rusanov, N. S. "Vlianie evropeiskogo sotsializma na dekabristov i molodogo Gertsena (The influence of European socialism upon the Decembrists and young Herzen)." *Minuvshie Gody*, XII (1908), 170–190.

Semevsky, V. I. "Dekabristy-masony (Decembrists-Masons)." *Minuvshie Gody*, II (1908), 1–51ff.

Semevsky, V. I. "Krestiansky vopros v obshchestvakh dekabristov (The peasant question in the Decembrist societies)." *Krestiansky Stroi*, I (1905), 209–242.

Semevsky, V. I. "Nikolai Ivanovich Turgenev o krestianskom voprose v tsarstvovanie Aleksandra I (N. I. Turgenev about the peasant question during the reign of Alexander I)." *Viestnik Evropy*, I (1909), 166–195, 548–580.

Semevsky, V. I. "Pervyi politichesky traktat Speranskogo (The first political treatise of Speransky)." *Russkoe Bogatstvo*, I (1907), 46–85.

Semevsky, V. I. "Volnenie v Semenovskom polku v 1820 g. (Unrest in the Semenovsky regiment in 1820)." *Byloe*, I (1907), 1–35ff.

Semevsky, V. I. "Vopros o preobrazovanii gosudarstvennogo stroia Rossii v XVIII i pervoi chetverti XIX vieka (The question of constitutional reform in Russia in the XVIIIth and first quarter of the XIXth century)." *Byloe*, I (1906), 1–53ff.

Shebunin, A. N. "Dekabristy i voprosy vneshnei politiki (The Decembrists and questions of foreign policy)." *Russkoe Proshloe*, IV (1923), 21–35.

Shebunin, A. N. "Obshchestvennye i politicheskie vzgliady N. I. Turgeneva v Aleksandrovskuiu epokhu (Social and political views of N. I. Turgenev during the reign of Alexander)." *Sovremennik*, V (1913), 187–213; VI, 192–213.

Sirotinin, A. N. "K. F. Ryleev." *Russky Arkhiv*, VI (1890), 113–208.

Skazin, E. V. "14 dekabria 1825 goda (December 14, 1825)." *Katorga i Ssylka*, VIII (1925), 65–87.

Smirnov, V. A. "Dekabristy v Krasnoiarske (Decembrists in Krasnoiarsk)." *Sibirskie Ogni*, III (1925), 149–162.

Sokolovskaia, T. "Lozha Trëkh Dobrodetelei i eia chleny-dekabristy (The Lodge 'Three Virtues' and its member-Decembrists)." *Russky Arkhiv*, X (1908), 218–230.

Sukhomlinov, M. "F.-C. Laharpe, vospitatel' imperatora Aleksandra I (F.-C. Laharpe, tutor of Emperor Alexander I)." *Z.M.N.P.*, CLIII, 47–75, 156–278. Also in the author's collected works, *Issledovaniia i Stat'i* (Investigations and Articles), (St.P., 1889), II, 35–204.

Syromiatnikov, B. I. "Politicheskaia doktrina 'Nakaza' P. I. Pestelia (The political doctrine of Pestel's 'Instruction')." *Sbornik statei, posviashchennykh V. O. Kliuchevskomu*, 679–718.

TARASOV, E. I. "Russkie 'gettingentsy' pervoi chetverti XIX vieka i vliianie ikh na razvitie liberalizma v Rossii (Russian students at Göttingen during the first quarter of the XIXth century and their influence upon the development of liberalism in Russia)." *Golos Minuvshego*, IV (1914), 195–209.

TROTSKY, I. "Likvidatsiia Tul'chinskoi upravy IUzhnogo Obshchestva (The end of the Tulchin group of the Southern Society)." *Byloe* (1925), 47–75.

"Tsenzura v Rossii pri Imperatore Pavle (Censorship in Russia during the reign of Paul)." *Russkaia Starina*, XIV (1875), 454–469.

TUMANOV, M. "A. N. Radishchev." *Viestnik Evropy*, II (1904), 680–703.

"Unichtozhenie masonskikh lozh v Rossii (The abolition of Masonic Lodges in Russia)." *Russkaia Starina*, III (1877), 455–479.

VERNADSKY, G. "Alexandre Ier et le problème slave pendant la première moitié de son règne." *Revue des Études Slaves*, VII (1927), 94–111.

VERNADSKY, G. "Beiträge zur Geschichte der Freimaurerei und des Mystizismus in Rußland." *Zeitschrift für Slavische Philologie*, Band IV, Heft 1/2 (1927), 94–111.

VERNADSKY, G. "Pushkin and the Decembrists." *Centennial Essays for Pushkin*, edited by Samuel H. Cross and Ernest J. Simmons (Cambridge, Mass.: Harvard University Press, 1937), 45–76.

VESHNIAKOV, V. "Russkaia promyshlennost' i eia nuzhdy (Russian industry and its needs)." *Viestnik Evropy*, XI (1870), 85–141.

VOITLOVSKY, L. "Dekabristy (The Decembrists)." *Krasnaia Nov'*, XII (1925), 122–143.

"Vospominaniia o dekabristakh v Sibiri, zapisannye so slov ikh uchenitsy O. I. Balakshinoi. (Recollections of the Decembrists in Siberia, recorded from dictation by their pupil O. I. Balakshina.)" *Sibirskie Ogni*, III (1924), 178–181.

YAKUSHKIN, V. E. "Nikolai Ivanovich Novikov (N. I. Novikov)." *Pochin. Sbornik Obshchestva Liubitelei Rossiiskoi Slovesnosti*, (M., 1895), 152–182.

YAKUSHKIN, V. E. "Radishchev i Pushkin (Radishchev and Pushkin)." *C.I.O.I.D.R.*, I (1886), 1–58.

ZAVALISHIN, D. I. "Dekabristy (The Decembrists)." *Russky Viestnik*, II (1884), 820–861.

ZHIZHKA, M. *Radishchev*. In *Seriia Biografii. Zhizn' Zamechatel'nykh Liudei*, pod red. M. Gorkogo, L. Kameneva, M. Koltsova and A. Tikhonova. M., 1934.

ZHUKOVICH, P. "Senator Novosiltsov i professor Golukhovsky (Senator Novosiltsov and Professor Golukhovsky)." *Istorichesky Viestnik*, XXIX (1887), 602–619.

ZVAVICH, I. "Vosstanie 14 dekabria i angliiskoe obshchestvennoe mnenie (The uprising of December 14 and English public opinion)." *Pechat' i Revoliutsiia*, VIII (1925), 31–52.

BIBLIOGRAPHICAL SUPPLEMENT, 1961

AKSENOV, K. *Severnoye obshchestvo dekabristov* (The northern society of the Decembrists). Leningrad, 1951.

BARANOVSKAYA, M. *Dekabrist Nikolai Bestuzhev* (The Decembrist Nikolai Bestuzhev). M., 1954.

CHENTSOV, N. M. *Dvizhenie dekabristov. Ukazatel' literatury, 1928-1959.* (The Decembrist Movement. Guide to literature, 1928-1959.) Sostaviteli R. G. Eimontova i A. A. Solennikova. Izdanie Gosudarstvennoi istoricheskoi bibliotekoi pod rukovodstvom Akad. M. V. Nechkinoi. Izd-vo Vsesoiuznoi knizhnoi palatoi, Moscow, 1960.

CHUKOVSKAIA, LIDIA. *Dekabristy issledovateli Sibiri* (Decembrists—Explorers of Siberia). M., 1951.

Dekabristy [A Collection of Documents]. Izdanie Gosudarstvennogo Literaturnogo Muzeia. *Letopisi.* Book 3. Moscow, 1938.

Dekabristy i ikh vremia. Materialy (The Decembrists and their time. Sources). M.-L., Academy of Sciences, 1951.

Dekabristy-Literatory (Decembrists—Men of Letters). In *Literaturnoe nasledstvo*, Vol. 59. M., 1954.

GERNET, M. N. *Istoriia tsarskoi tiurmy* (A history of tsarist prisons). M., 1951-56. 5 vols.

KRESTOVA, L. V. "Dvizhenie dekabristov v osveshchenii inostrannoi publitsistiki (The Decembrist movement as presented in the foreign press)." *Istoricheskie Zapiski*, No. 13, 1942, 222-233.

NECHKINA, M. V. *Dvizhenie dekabristov* (The Decembrist movement). M., Academy of Sciences, 1955. 2 vols.

NECHKINA, M. V. *Griboedov i dekabristy* (Griboedov and the Decembrists). M., 1947.

NIKANDROV, P. F. *Mirovozzrenie P. I. Pestelia* (The philosophy of P. I. Pestel). Leningrad, 1955.

OLSHANSKY, P. *Dekabristy i Pol'skoe natsional'no-osvoboditel'noe dvizhenie* (The Decembrists and the Polish national liberation movement). M., 1959.

PIGAREV, K. *Zhizn' Ryleeva* (Life of Ryleev). M., 1947.

SCHWARZ-SOCHOR, JENNY. "P. I. Pestel. The Beginning of Jacobin Thought in Russia." *International Review of Social History*, Volume 3, Part 1, 1958, 71-96.

VENTURI, FRANCO. *Il moto decabrista e i fratelli Poggio.* [Milan], G. Einaudi, 1956. See review in *Voprosy istorii*, No. 3, 1957, 165-68.

ZETLIN, M. *The Decembrists.* New York, International Universities Press, 1958.

In addition the following serial publications mentioned in the preceding Bibliography have now been completed:

LIASHCHENKO, P. *Istoriia narodnogo khoziaistva SSSR.* M., 1927-56. 3 vols. This has been translated as *History of the national economy of Russia to the 1917 Revolution.* N.Y., Macmillan, 1949.

Le Monde Slave. Paris, 1924-38.

Sibirskie Ogni. Novo-Nikolaevsk, 1922-39 (?).

Vosstanie dekabristov. M., Tsentrarkhiv, 1925-58. 11 vols.

Zvenia. M., 1932-36. 6 issues.

INDEX

INDEX

Agrarian: problem, 7, 94, 105–107, 113; class, 14; plans of France, 107; Pestel's, program, 115, 125

Agriculture: in Russia, 14; period of prosperity of, 17; crisis in, 18; danger of stagnation of, 105; Russian prosperity lies in, 106; Pestel's faith in, 113; in Siberia, 245 f.

Akhtyrsky regiment, 183, 184, 217

Alexander I: apprehensions of, 1; attitude of, toward serfdom, 2–5, 6; debt at end of reign of, 15, 262; tariff policy of, 16; "unofficial committee" of, 19, 20; reforms attempted by, 20 ff., and their failure, 28; religious-mystical fervor during reign of, 31; and Mme Krüdener, 32; press censorship during reign of, 36; military colonies created by, 37–38, 41, 43, and their failure, 44; submission of, to Metternich's schemes, 57, 61, 62; demands made of, 57–58; seriously alarmed, 62; Polish policy of, 65; attitude of Decembrists toward, 69; speech of, at Moscow, 71, 87; assassination of, considered, 71, 131, 132, 136, 142, 153, 154, 183, 219, 264; *Green Book* known to, 75; secret military police established by, 79; Orlov's *Memorandum* to, 82; *Curious Conversation* read by, 95; death of, 137, 155, 157, 181; will of, 158, 170; warned of conspiracy, 181; hope for reforms at accession of, 262

Alexander II, amnesty granted to Decembrists by, 256

Arakcheev, Count, 41–42 *passim*, 43, 44, 51, 53, 56, 59, 61, 63, 68, 71, 130, 156, 262, 265, 267

Arbuzov, 88, 128, 166

Bariatinsky, Prince, 118, 218, 219

Basargin, 84, 214, 222, 249, 252

Batenkov, 128, 129, 130, 131, 214, 224

Benckendorff, General, 49, 196, 203, 208

Bestuzhev, Alexander, 6, 7, 16, 28, 130, 136, 157, 158, 164, 169, 175, 214, 224, 233, 237, 244, 245, 252, 255, 268

Bestuzhev, Mikhail, 164, 169, 170, 171, 227, 240, 244, 245, 247

Bestuzhev, Nicholas, 128, 130, 157, 158, 165, 169, 170–172 *passim*, 176, 204, 231, 244, 245, 252 *passim*, 259

Bestuzhev-Riumin, Mikhail, 99, 138, 139, 140, 148–151 *passim*, 152, 153, 154, 182–183 *passim*, 185, 213, 264

Borisov, Andrei, 142, 143, 221, 244, 252, 272

Borisov, Peter, 64, 142, 143, 147, 151 *passim*, 152, 221, 244, 252, 272

Borovkov, A., 207, 267, 268

Boshniak, Alexander, 164, 181

Bulatov, Colonel Alexander, 159, 170, 171, 209

Burtsev, Ivan, 77, 79, 81, 83, 84, 98

Cantonist settlements, 43

Catherine II, 6, 14, 19, 38, 48, 53, 72, 261

Caucasus, 103, 132, 135, 221

Chernigovsky regiment, 148, 154, 184, 221

Chernov, Constantine, 130

Chernyshev, General A., 208, 220, 240

Chodkiewicz, Count, 139, 140

Code of the Union of Welfare. See *Green Book*

Committee for Investigation, 117, 143, 207; purpose and function of, 208; members of, 208; instructions to, 208; examinations by, 208–209; report of, 209–210; Special Supreme Court to confirm recommendations made by, 210–211

Complete Code of Russian Law, 268

Conspiratory society, 65, 66, 75, 80, 83, 122, 143

Constantine, Grand Duke, 49, 61, 138, 141, 142, 203; throne renounced by, 155; oath of allegiance to, 156, 158, 169, 200; refusal of, to return to capital, 157; associated with liberal reforms, 159; conflict between Polish people and, 159–160; rule of, in Poland, 160; shouting in favor of, in Senate Square, 172. *See also* Poland

Davydov, Colonel Vasily, 118, 119, 138

December 14, 1825, catastrophe of, 63, 68, 117, 137, 157, 162, 166, 169, 171, 175–180, 203, 214, 237, 261, 263, 265, 266; slogan of, revolt, 161

Decembrist movement, xv, xvii, 2, 6, 7, 32, 58 *passim*, 64, 66, 79, 87, 95, 119, 142, 209, 227, 261, 262, 265

Decembrist Society, 7, 36, 51, 62, 66, 67, 68–70, 121, 135, 136, 261, 262. *See also* Northern Society; Southern Society

DATE DUE

APR 7 '67	AP 29 '85		
APR 8 '67	JUN 2 '86		
MAR 19 '68	FEB 7 '89		
APR 1 '68	FEB 20 '89		
APR 18 '68			
JUL 1 '68			
MAR 5 '69			
APR 28 '69			
OCT 15 '69			
FEB 11 '70			
APR 20 '70			
MAR 13 '72			
MAR 2 '73			
MR 29 '79			
AP 24 '79			
AP 2 2 '80			
FE 24 '84			
DEC 3 '84			
GAYLORD			PRINTED IN U.S.A.